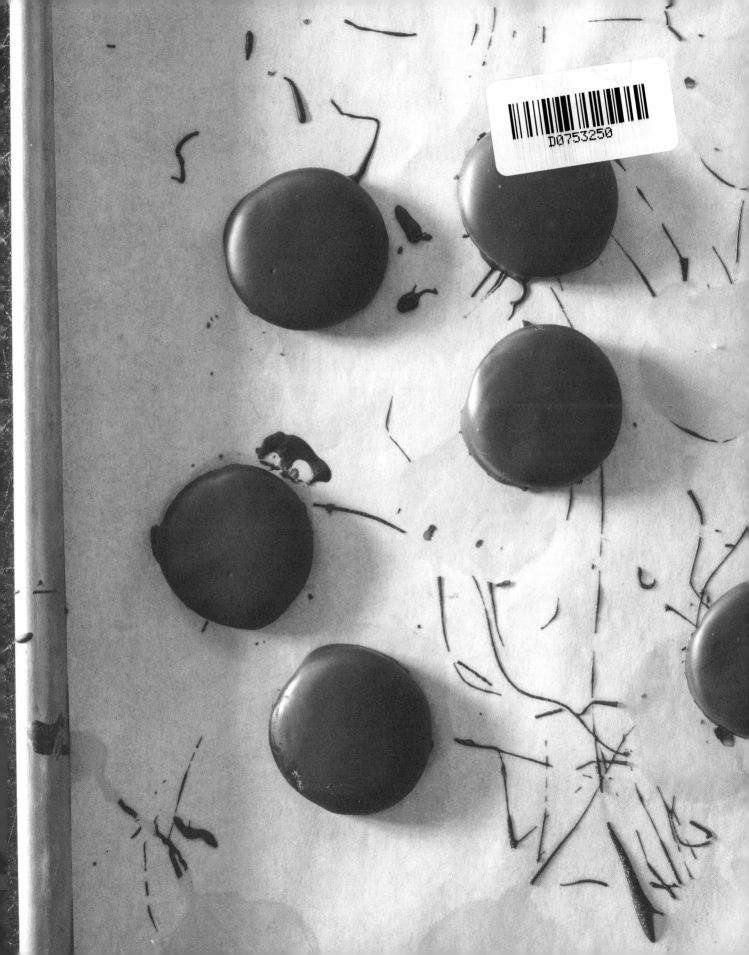

also by the editors at america's test kitchen

The Complete Slow Cooker

The Complete Make-Ahead Cookbook

The Complete Mediterranean Cookbook

The Complete Vegetarian Cookbook

The Complete Cooking for Two Cookbook

What Good Cooks Know

Cook's Science

The Science of Good Cooking

Bread Illustrated

Master of the Grill

Kitchen Smarts

Kitchen Hacks

100 Recipes: The Absolute Best Ways to Make the True Essentials

The New Family Cookbook

The America's Test Kitchen Cooking School Cookbook

The Cook's Illustrated Meat Book

The Cook's Illustrated Baking Book

The Cook's Illustrated Cookbook

The New Best Recipe

Soups, Stews, and Chilis

The America's Test Kitchen Quick Family Cookbook

The America's Test Kitchen Healthy Family Cookbook

The America's Test Kitchen Family Baking Book

The Best of America's Test Kitchen (2007–2018 Editions)

The Complete America's Test Kitchen TV Show Cookbook 2001–2018

Food Processor Perfection

Pressure Cooker Perfection

Vegan for Everybody

Naturally Sweet

Foolproof Preserving

Paleo Perfected

The How Can It Be Gluten-Free Cookbook: Volume 2

The How Can It Be Gluten-Free Cookbook

The Best Mexican Recipes

Slow Cooker Revolution Volume 2: The Easy-Prep Edition

Slow Cooker Revolution

The Six-Ingredient Solution

The America's Test Kitchen D.I.Y. Cookbook

Pasta Revolution

THE COOK'S ILLUSTRATED ALL-TIME BEST SERIES

All-Time Best Sunday Suppers

All-Time Best Holiday Entertaining

All-Time Best Appetizers

All-Time Best Soups

COOK'S COUNTRY TITLES

One-Pan Wonders

Cook It in Cast Iron

Cook's Country Eats Local

The Complete Cook's Country TV Show Cookbook

FOR A FULL LISTING OF ALL OUR BOOKS

CooksCountry.com

AmericasTestKitchen.com

praise for other america's test kitchen titles

"This book is a comprehensive, no-nonsense guide . . . a well-thought-out, clearly explained primer for every aspect of home baking."
THE WALL STREET JOURNAL ON *THE COOK'S ILLUSTRATED BAKING BOOK*

"With 1,000 photos and the expertise of the America's Test Kitchen editors, this title might be the definitive book on bread baking."
PUBLISHERS WEEKLY ON *BREAD ILLUSTRATED*

"Cooks with a powerful sweet tooth should scoop up this well-researched recipe book for healthier takes on classic sweet treats."
BOOKLIST ON *NATURALLY SWEET*

"The 21st-century *Fannie Farmer Cookbook* or *The Joy of Cooking*. If you had to have one cookbook and that's all you could have, this one would do it."
CBS SAN FRANCISCO ON *THE NEW FAMILY COOKBOOK*

"The sum total of exhaustive experimentation . . . anyone interested in gluten-free cookery simply shouldn't be without it."
NIGELLA LAWSON ON *THE HOW CAN IT BE GLUTEN-FREE COOKBOOK*

"A one-volume kitchen seminar, addressing in one smart chapter after another the sometimes surprising whys behind a cook's best practices. . . . You get the myth, the theory, the science, and the proof, all rigorously interrogated as only America's Test Kitchen can do."
NPR ON *THE SCIENCE OF GOOD COOKING*

"The perfect kitchen home companion. . . . The practical side of things is very much on display . . . cook-friendly and kitchen-oriented, illuminating the process of preparing food instead of mystifying it."
THE WALL STREET JOURNAL ON *THE COOK'S ILLUSTRATED COOKBOOK*

"Another winning cookbook from ATK. . . . The folks at America's Test Kitchen apply their rigorous experiments to determine the facts about these pans."
BOOKLIST ON *COOK IT IN CAST IRON*

Selected as one of Amazon's Best Books of 2015 in the Cookbooks and Food Writing Category
AMAZON ON *THE COMPLETE VEGETARIAN COOKBOOK*

"Some 2,500 photos walk readers through 600 painstakingly tested recipes, leaving little room for error."
ASSOCIATED PRESS ON *THE AMERICA'S TEST KITCHEN COOKING SCHOOL COOKBOOK*

"An exceptional resource for novice canners, though preserving veterans will find plenty here to love as well."
LIBRARY JOURNAL (STARRED REVIEW) ON *FOOLPROOF PRESERVING*

"A terrifically accessible and useful guide to grilling in all its forms that sets a new bar for its competitors."
PUBLISHERS WEEKLY (STARRED REVIEW) ON *MASTER OF THE GRILL*

"The go-to gift book for newlyweds, small families, or empty nesters."
ORLANDO SENTINEL ON *THE COMPLETE COOKING FOR TWO COOKBOOK*

"This encyclopedia of meat cookery would feel completely overwhelming if it weren't so meticulously organized and artfully designed. This is Cook's Illustrated at its finest."
THE KITCHN ON *THE COOK'S ILLUSTRATED MEAT BOOK*

"Further proof that practice makes perfect, if not transcendent. . . . If an intermediate cook follows the directions exactly, the results will be better than takeout or Mom's."
THE NEW YORK TIMES ON *THE NEW BEST RECIPE*

"There are pasta books . . . and then there's this pasta book. Flip your carbohydrate dreams upside down and strain them through this sieve of revolutionary, creative, and also traditional recipes."
SAN FRANCISCO BOOK REVIEW ON *PASTA REVOLUTION*

THE
perfect
cookie

YOUR ULTIMATE GUIDE TO FOOLPROOF
cookies, brownies & bars

the editors at
America's Test Kitchen

Library of Congress Cataloging-in-Publication Data

Names: America's Test Kitchen (Firm)
Title: The perfect cookie : your ultimate guide to
    foolproof cookies, brownies & bars / the editors at
    America's Test Kitchen.
Description: Brookline, MA : America's Test Kitchen,
    [2017] | Includes index.
Identifiers: LCCN 2017008692 | ISBN 9781940352954
Subjects: LCSH: Cookies. | Brownies (Cooking) | LCGFT:
    Cookbooks.
Classification: LCC TX772 .P386 2017 |
    DDC 641.86/54--dc23
LC record available at https://lccn.loc.gov/2017008692

AMERICA'S
TEST KITCHEN ®

AMERICA'S TEST KITCHEN
21 Drydock, Suite 210E, Boston, MA 02210
Manufactured in the United States of America
10 9 8 7 6 5 4 3 2 1

Distributed by Penguin Random House
Publisher Services
Tel: 800.733.3000

PICTURED ON FRONT COVER Almond-Raspberry Sandwich
Cookies (page 161)

PICTURED ON BACK COVER Ultimate Turtle Brownies
(page 252), Lemon Bars (page 280), Jam Thumbprints
(page 133), Chocolate-Dipped Potato Chip Cookies
(page 69), Chocolate-Hazelnut Diamonds (page 312),
Lemon Thins (page 117), Spumoni Bars (page 98),
Peppermint Mocha Cookies (page 391)

CHIEF CREATIVE OFFICER Jack Bishop

EDITORIAL DIRECTOR, BOOKS Elizabeth Carduff

EXECUTIVE EDITOR Julia Collin Davison

PROJECT EDITOR Sacha Madadian

EDITORIAL ASSISTANT Alyssa Langer

DESIGN DIRECTOR, BOOKS Carole Goodman

DEPUTY ART DIRECTOR Allison Boales

PHOTOGRAPHY DIRECTOR Julie Bozzo Cote

PHOTOGRAPHY PRODUCER Mary Ball

SENIOR STAFF PHOTOGRAPHER Daniel J. van Ackere

STAFF PHOTOGRAPHER Steve Klise

FEATURE PHOTOGRAPHY Keller + Keller and Carl Tremblay

FOOD STYLING Catrine Kelty, Kendra McKnight, Marie Piraino,
Elle Simone Scott, and Sally Staub

PHOTOSHOOT KITCHEN TEAM

  SENIOR EDITOR Chris O'Connor

  ASSOCIATE EDITOR Daniel Cellucci

  ASSISTANT TEST COOKS Mady Nichas and Jessica Rudolph

PRODUCTION DIRECTOR Guy Rochford

SENIOR PRODUCTION MANAGER Jessica Lindheimer Quirk

PRODUCTION MANAGER Christine Walsh

IMAGING MANAGER Lauren Robbins

PRODUCTION AND IMAGING SPECIALISTS Heather Dube, Dennis Noble,
and Jessica Voas

COPY EDITOR Elizabeth Emery

PROOFREADER Ann-Marie Imbornoni

INDEXER Elizabeth Parson

CONTENTS

Welcome to America's Test Kitchen

This book has been tested, written, and edited by the folks at America's Test Kitchen. Located in Boston's Seaport District in the historic Innovation and Design Building, it features 15,000 square feet of kitchen space including multiple photography and video studios. It is the home of *Cook's Illustrated* magazine and *Cook's Country* magazine and is the workday destination for more than 60 test cooks, editors, and cookware specialists. Our mission is to test recipes over and over again until we understand how and why they work and until we arrive at the best version.

We start the process of testing a recipe with a complete lack of preconceptions, which means that we accept no claim, no technique, and no recipe at face value. We simply assemble as many variations as possible, test a half-dozen of the most promising, and taste the results blind. We then construct our own recipe and continue to test it, varying ingredients, techniques, and cooking times until we reach a consensus. As we like to say in the test kitchen, "We make the mistakes so you don't have to." The result, we hope, is the best version of a particular recipe, but we realize that only you can be the final judge of our success (or failure). We use the same rigorous approach when we test equipment and taste ingredients.

All of this would not be possible without a belief that good cooking, much like good music, is based on a foundation of objective technique. Some people like spicy foods and others don't, but there is a right way to sauté, there is a best way to cook a pot roast, and there are measurable scientific principles involved in producing perfectly beaten, stable egg whites. Our ultimate goal is to investigate the fundamental principles of cooking to give you the techniques, tools, and ingredients you need to become a better cook. It is as simple as that.

To see what goes on behind the scenes at America's Test Kitchen, check out our social media channels for kitchen snapshots, exclusive content, video tips, and much more. You can watch us work (in our actual test kitchen) by tuning in to *America's Test Kitchen* or *Cook's Country from America's Test Kitchen* on public television or on our websites. Listen in to test kitchen experts on public radio (SplendidTable.org) to hear insights that illuminate the truth about real home cooking. Want to hone your cooking skills or finally learn how to bake—with an America's Test Kitchen test cook? Enroll in one of our online cooking classes. If the big questions about the hows and whys of food science are your passion, join our Cook's Science experts for a deep dive. However you choose to visit us, we welcome you into our kitchen, where you can stand by our side as we test our way to the best recipes in America.

facebook.com/AmericasTestKitchen

twitter.com/TestKitchen

youtube.com/AmericasTestKitchen

instagram.com/TestKitchen

pinterest.com/TestKitchen

google.com/+AmericasTestKitchen

AmericasTestKitchen.com

CooksIllustrated.com

CooksCountry.com

CooksScience.com

OnlineCookingSchool.com

GETTING STARTED

Introduction

In the world of baking, the cookie might just be the most beloved treat—and the most versatile. Whether they're an afternoon snack or the sweet ending to a meal, cookies are welcome anywhere and anytime. The test kitchen has almost 25 years of experience baking cookies and bars of all kinds. Our test cooks have worked to make foolproof versions of everything from your standard favorites, such as Classic Chewy Oatmeal Cookies, to a variety of new, creative, and fun options, such as Frosted Red Velvet Cookies and even a Chocolate Chip Skillet Cookie. These recipes and the techniques for executing them have appeared in our books and magazines. We've tinkered with recipes for our annual *Cook's Country* holiday cookie feature and developed unique sweets for *Christmas Cookies* special interest publications. Yes, you could say we know a thing or two about making perfect cookies. We wanted to combine all of that knowledge and build on it in one go-to resource, with recipes for any cookie or bar you could imagine making, as well as techniques for all aspects of cookie baking—from mixing up a batch of Fudgy Brownies to quell a weeknight chocolate craving to methodically rolling out puff pastry to create multilayered Palmiers.

Cookies are a blank canvas: You can include mix-ins such as oats, chocolate chips, dried fruit, and candies; you can frost or fill them; you can coat them in sugar; and you can even fry them (check out our Danish Kleiner). The variations are virtually limitless. We've grouped our recipes into 10 cookie-packed chapters: We start with Drop Cookies, which is a good place to look for simple but superlative recipes for American classics like Chewy Sugar Cookies or cross-hatched Peanut Butter Cookies. We then move on to Slice-and-Bake Cookies; Rolled, Shaped, and Pressed Cookies; and Sublime Sandwich Cookies. In the Let's Get Fancy chapter, we showcase cookies that have

multiple intriguing components like Raspberry-Almond Torte Cookies, which feature a jam filling, billowy frosting, and candied almond topping. We also highlight our versions of cookies from around the world like Greek Honey Cakes. We explore rich, indulgent, layered treats in Brownies and Blondies and Bar Cookies chapters. No-Bake Cookies and Candies is the place to look when you want to create something special—like Chocolate Fluff Cookies or Salted Caramels—without turning on your oven. And of course, it wouldn't be the holidays without cookies, so we devote an entire chapter to our favorites, from Soft and Chewy Gingerbread People to twisted red-and-white Peppermint Candy Canes. We even share gluten-free recipes, so you can bake for just about anyone. In addition to the recipes, we've included detailed photographed steps, ingredient information, and essential tips throughout the book.

Since understanding the whys and hows of baking is important for turning out perfect cookies, you'll find a comprehensive introduction section. We clearly lay out the universal key steps to cookie baking and outline what you need to outfit your kitchen—both equipment and pantry items—for baking the very best cookies whenever the mood strikes. Then we dig a little deeper, discussing the science of cookie baking so you can learn just what makes a cookie crunchy versus chewy or how baking soda impacts the cracks that form on the surface of some cookies. Follow our troubleshooting tips so you know how to handle any dough you work with.

We hope you'll bake your way through the countless foolproof cookie recipes in this definitive guide. Just as important, we hope you'll enjoy learning more about how cookie baking works along the way, so you can turn out perfect cookies every time.

Core Cookie-Baking Techniques

This book covers cookies of all kinds, from those you form into balls and "drop" on a baking sheet and ones that you roll out and cut into shapes, to those you pat in a baking pan to create bars. But while different types of cookies may require different techniques and methods to achieve the desired outcome, all cookie recipes have five key steps in common: measuring, mixing, forming, baking, and cooling. In the photos below, we use our Frosted Walnut Drops (page 208) to illustrate each of those processes. Before these cookies are frosted, this recipe uses the most basic (but also most essential) techniques that apply to most cookies. In the pages that follow, we'll dive deeper into each step of the cookie-making process, so you'll understand why proper execution of each one is important. We'll also break down the variations on these techniques and the ingredients used in them, so you'll be confident that you can tackle any cookie recipe with success.

1 MEASURING

It might sound obvious, but measuring—the first step to creating perfect cookies—takes care: Baking is a science, and inexact measurements will yield inferior results. We provide weights for dry ingredients in our recipes and use a digital scale (see page 6) to weigh them; we strongly recommend you do, too. But if you're dead set on measuring these ingredients by volume, there's a way to increase your accuracy: the dip and sweep method.

Dip the measuring cup (see page 6) into the flour, sugar, or other dry ingredient and sweep away the excess with a straight-edged object, such as the back of a butter knife.

For wet ingredients, we use a liquid measuring cup (see page 6). For an accurate reading, set the cup on a level surface and bend down to read the bottom of the concave arc at the liquid's surface, known as the meniscus line, at eye level. And for sticky ingredients, we recommend using an adjustable measuring cup (see page 6). If you don't own one, spray a dry measuring cup with vegetable oil spray before filling it; when emptied, the liquid should slide right out of the cup.

2 MIXING

Once your ingredients are measured, mixing can begin. Depending on the recipe and the desired outcome, doughs can be mixed by hand, by using a mixer, or in a food processor. The most common and basic mixing method—which we use for the walnut drops—is called creaming, and it's done in a stand mixer. You beat softened butter and the sugar together until the mixture is pale and fluffy; next, you mix in the egg(s) (adding them one at a time to ensure they're combined), followed by the dry ingredients (these are added gradually to avoid overmixing, which yields tough cookies). This approach accomplishes two things: First, it makes the butter malleable, which allows other ingredients to blend in easily. Second, the tiny sugar crystals act like extra beaters, helping to incorporate air into the butter as it's creamed. These tiny air pockets expand during baking, giving the cookie lift and forming its crumb. Occasionally scraping down the bowl with a spatula guarantees that everything is incorporated.

any way you mix it

While creaming may be the most common mixing method, it's not the only one, and some of the doughs in this book use other methods. Each serves a specific purpose, so it's important to use the right technique to ensure that your cookies have the desired texture and shape. These are the two other main mixing methods we use in this book.

Reverse Creaming

We use reverse creaming when we want tender but sturdy cookies, with minimal rise and flat tops. It's perfect for recipes like our Foolproof Holiday Cookies (page 367), which we glaze and decorate, or our striking Vanilla Bean–Apricot Sandwich Cookies (page 166), which we fill with jam. You start by combining all of the dry ingredients and then you incorporate softened butter. Finally, you add any liquid ingredients. During this process, the butter coats the flour particles, therefore minimizing gluten development for a tender, fine crumb. Just as important, since the butter isn't beaten with sugar, less air is incorporated, which translates to less rise and a sturdier cookie.

Creaming
This cookie has a domed top.

Reverse Creaming
This cookie has a flat top.

By Hand
When a cookie recipe calls for melted butter, it makes sense to simply stir together the soft dough by hand. But there's another reason to do this: Typically when melted butter is called for in a cookie recipe, as it is in our Perfect Chocolate Chip Cookies (page 27) and our Brown Sugar Cookies (page 39), the goal is to create a very chewy cookie. Once the butter is melted, the water in it can more freely interact with the flour to develop gluten, the protein that gives baked goods chew. Vigorously mixing the ingredients together in a bowl facilitates this process and doesn't incorporate air the way a stand mixer does. The result is chewy—not cakey—cookies.

CAN YOU USE A HANDHELD MIXER?

We use a stand mixer in many of our cookie recipes. To see if an electric handheld mixer was up to the task and could produce the same results, we conducted side-by-side tests by making oatmeal cookies with the two. Although the stand mixer produced a dough with more volume, the baked cookies were identical in number, texture, and flavor. Neither mixer had trouble mixing oatmeal and nuts into the stiff dough on low speed. That being said, the stand mixer offers greater flexibility and versatility, so we call for it in our recipes; in addition, its freestanding base leaves the cook free to accomplish other tasks. However, with some adjustments for time and technique, a handheld mixer generally yields comparable cookies. Our favorite is the **KitchenAid 5-Speed Ultra Power Hand Mixer** ($69.99).

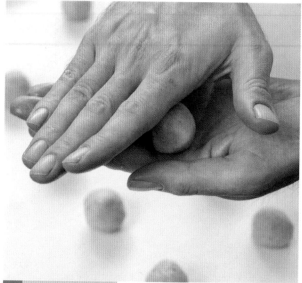

3 FORMING

Once you've created a cohesive dough, the next step is shaping the cookies. For drop cookies like this one, you'll portion off a measurement of dough according to the recipe—anywhere from a tablespoon for these walnut drops to ¼ cup for our big, chewy Chocolate Chunk Oatmeal Cookies with Pecans and Dried Cherries (page 33)—and roll it between your hands to form a ball. Doing this, rather than just dropping mounds of dough on the baking sheet, ensures cookies of equal size that bake evenly. As you form the dough balls, you space them evenly on parchment paper–lined baking sheets; even spacing is particularly important so the cookies don't spread into one another in the oven and so they bake evenly.

the fridge is your friend
Some recipes, often slice-and-bake recipes like Chocolate-Toffee Butter Cookies (page 93) (60 small cookie planks) and rolled and cutout cookies like Cornmeal-Orange Cookies (page 118) (84 thin rounds), yield a large number of cookies. In this case, we like to keep a portion of the dough chilled while we form cookies from another portion. If all of the dough is left out for the entire process, it could become too soft and sticky, making it hard to work with and turning out misshapen cookies—think flat-edged Vanilla Icebox Cookies (page 75) or armless Gingerbread People (page 368).

4 BAKING

Once shaped, the cookies are ready for baking, during which starches gelatinize to set the cookie's crumb and sugars caramelize to brown the cookie. But you can't just set them and forget them: Make sure your oven is at the proper temperature by using an oven thermometer (see page 8) and switch (if using more than one baking sheet) and rotate the position of the baking sheet(s) so that the cookies brown and bake evenly. If you're baking in batches, be sure to let the baking sheets cool and reline them with fresh parchment before reusing.

what pan to use

We bake all cookies on a sturdy rimmed baking sheet. Rimless "cookie sheets" will work; however, cookies baked on a rimless pan brown more quickly and can finish baking several minutes before those on a rimmed pan. Why? Heat rises from the element at the bottom of the oven and circulates in currents to warm the entire chamber. A rimmed baking sheet's raised edges divert hot-air currents from the cookies to the top of the oven. A rimless sheet allows hot air to immediately sweep over the cookies. Flimsy sheets of either type will result in overbaked cookies.

what rack to bake on

We develop cookie recipes with the oven racks set to specific positions, so when you use our recipes, you want to make sure to adjust the racks as directed. When we're baking just one sheet of cookies at a time, we nearly always bake them on the middle rack. When we're baking two sheets at a time, we use the upper-middle and lower-middle positions. The middle of the oven is always a safe bet; the closer to the bottom of the oven, the browner the bottoms of your cookies will be relative to the tops.

avoiding uneven baking

Baking two trays of cookies at a time may be convenient, but the cookies on the top tray are often browner around the edges than the ones on the bottom tray. If you have two sheets in the oven, you should switch their positions halfway through baking. For cookies with an especially finicky texture, we call for baking the cookies one sheet at a time so heat circulates around the baking sheet evenly for the entire baking time. Even the best ovens have hot and cold spots, so rotating the baking sheet (the cookies that were in the front will now be in the back of the oven) is essential.

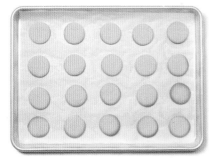

No Rotating = Uneven Baking

5 COOLING

Different cookies require different cooling methods to ensure they set up properly. Many basic drop cookies, such as these walnut drops, require a short rest on the baking sheet—typically about 5 minutes—so they are firm enough to move; after that, they are transferred to a wire rack, where air can circulate around them, to finish cooling. If you're filling a cookie with jam or chocolate or topping it with frosting or glaze, it needs to be completely cool before you apply these ingredients.

Equipment and Tools

There are certain pieces of equipment that make cookie baking easy (and more accurate). These are the basic tools you'll need and the specialty items you'll want.

PREPPING COOKIES

digital scale

We weigh dry ingredients to ensure consistent results. We prefer digital scales for their readability and precision. Look for one that has a large weight range and that can be "zeroed." The **OXO Good Grips 11 lb. Food Scale with Pull Out Display** ($49.95) has clear buttons, and its display can be pulled out from the platform for easy viewing when weighing bulky items.

dry measuring cups

While we much prefer to weigh our dry ingredients for cookie baking, we understand that many will measure by volume. (And you still need a set of measuring cups for small quantities of ingredients.) Look for heavy, well-constructed, evenly weighted stainless-steel models, with easy-to-read measurement markings and long, straight handles. We use the very accurate **OXO Good Grips Stainless Steel Measuring Cups** ($19.99).

liquid measuring cups

Cookies don't always include liquid ingredients such as milk, but when they do, we turn to the industry-standard durable, accurate **Pyrex 2-Cup Measuring Cup** ($5.99).

adjustable measuring cup

Sticky ingredients such as peanut butter, molasses, honey, and shortening can be difficult to measure and scrape out of liquid measuring cups. Enter: the adjustable-bottom liquid measuring cup. This style of measuring cup has a plunger-like bottom that you set to the correct measurement and then push up to extract the ingredient. Our favorite is the **KitchenArt Adjust-A-Cup Professional Series, 2-Cup** ($12.95).

measuring spoons

We prefer heavy, well-constructed steel measuring spoons with long, sturdy, well-designed handles. Choose deep bowls; shallow bowls allow more leavener or extract to spill with the shake of an unsteady hand. The **Cuisipro Stainless Steel Measuring Spoons Set** ($11.95) is our recommended set.

rasp grater

We flavor lots of cookies and bars with citrus zest, so you'll need a rasp grater. We also use a rasp to grate fresh nutmeg or chocolate. Our top rasp is the **Microplane Classic Zester** ($12.35); it handles these ingredients smoothly and almost effortlessly. Plus, the black plastic handle is very comfortable.

MIXING DOUGHS

stand mixer

A stand mixer, with its hands-free operation, numerous attachments, and strong mixing arm, is a worthwhile investment if you plan on baking cookies regularly. Heft matters, as does a strong motor that can mix stiff or chunky dough with ease. Our favorite stand mixer is the **KitchenAid Pro Line Series 7-Qt Bowl Lift Stand Mixer** ($549.95). Our best buy is the KitchenAid Classic Plus Series 4.5-Quart Tilt-Head Stand Mixer ($229.99).

food processor

In addition to chopping nuts or grinding them to a fine flour with ease, we use a food processor to make some cookie doughs as well. Look for a workbowl that has a capacity of at least 11 cups. With a powerful motor, responsive pulsing action, sharp blades, and a simple design, the **Cuisinart Custom 14 Food Processor** ($199.99) aced our tests.

rubber spatula

For scraping down bowls, folding ingredients, mixing caramel, and spreading batters you'll want the practical, no-nonsense **Rubbermaid Professional 13½-Inch High-Heat Scraper** ($14.50) and the **Di Oro Living Seamless Silicone Spatula—Large** (10.97). The Rubbermaid spatula has a large enough head to properly fold ingredients; the Di Oro Living spatula is a good multipurpose tool.

wooden spoon

A wooden spoon is great for hand-mixing stiff cookie doughs when a light touch is required. The **SCI Bamboo Wood Cooking Spoon** ($2.40) has a comfortable rectangular handle and a well-designed head.

bench scraper

This basic tool is handy for transferring dough from one surface to another and for cutting dough into pieces. Our winner is the **Dexter-Russell 6" Dough Cutter/Scraper—Sani Safe Series** ($7.01). It has a comfortable handle and the deeply beveled edge cuts through dough quickly and easily.

bowl scraper

The best way to remove sticky dough from the bowl is with a scraper. This handheld spatula is curved, with enough grip to scrape the bowl clean and enough rigidity to move heavy dough easily. Our favorite models are made of contoured silicone covering a metal insert, like the **iSi Basics Silicone Scraper Spatula** ($5.99).

FORMING COOKIES

portion scoop

A spring-loaded ice cream scoop is helpful for portioning drop cookie dough into even-size mounds. Manufacturers identify scoops in different ways: by volume, by diameter, or, most commonly—and most confusingly—according to a numbered system. In this system, scoops are given numerical "sizes" based on the number of level scoops it would take to empty a quart; for example, it would take twenty level scoops with a #20 scoop (a bit more than 3 tablespoons per scoop). Our favorite, the **OXO Good Grips Large Cookie Scoop** holds about this much, but we also find #60, #30, and #40 sizes useful.

rolling pin

There are many styles of rolling pins, but our preference is for French-style wood pins without handles. These pins come straight and tapered. We tend to reach for straight pins, which make achieving even dough thickness and rolling out large disks easy. The **J.K. Adams Plain Maple Rolling Dowel** ($13.95) has a gentle weight and a slightly textured surface for less sticking.

ruler

A ruler is helpful for measuring the diameter of dough as you roll it or cutting dough into pieces of a certain size. Stainless steel is best because it's easy to clean. An 18-inch ruler will handle all cookie tasks.

cookie cutters

We prefer metal cutters to plastic ones because the former are sharper and more likely to make clean cuts. Look at the cutting edges and make sure they are thin and sharp. Ideally, cutters will be at least 1 inch tall (so they can cut through thicker cookie dough as well). A rounded or rubber top offers nice protection for your hands.

piping sets

Some cookies are piped onto baking sheets. Floppy cloth pastry bags can stain or cling to smells. Canvas bags tend to be stiff. We prefer disposable plastic bags; they're easy to handle and effortless to clean. In addition you'll want 6 key tips: #4 round, #12 round, #70 round, #103 petal, #2D large closed star, and #1M open star, as well as four couplers, plastic nozzles that adhere the tip to the bag. We like **Wilton** supplies.

BAKING COOKIES

baking sheets

Although rimless baking sheets are commonly referred to as "cookie sheets," we prefer using rimmed sheets in our cookie recipes. They're best for baking cookies evenly and can usually fit more cookies per sheet. Buy large (18 by 13 inches is ideal), heavy-duty baking sheets—you'll want more than one. We like the thick, sturdy **Wear-Ever Half Size Heavy Duty Sheet Pan (13 gauge) by Vollrath** ($23.25).

parchment paper

Lining your baking sheets with parchment paper is a simple way to make sure your baking sheets stay clean and your cookies release effortlessly. We prefer parchment to reusable pan liners (such as Silpat baking mats), which can transfer flavors and stain over time. (We do, however, like the baking mats for our thin Tuile Cigars on page 190.) Look for rolls that will fit inside 18 by 13-inch rimmed baking sheets. If you bake a lot of cookies, you might want to mail-order flat sheets that are already cut to fit 18 by 13-inch baking sheets.

baking pans

We prefer metal baking pans to glass baking dishes for brownies and bar cookies; glass baking dishes retain heat longer, which could lead to overbaking. Plus, we like the straight sides and nonstick surface of metal pans. Our favorite: the **Williams-Sonoma Goldtouch Cake Pan**. It's good to own both 8- and 9-inch square metal pans as well as a 13 by 9-inch metal pan for bars of all yields.

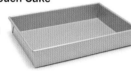

oven thermometer

It's common for ovens to run hot or cold, which can lead to cookies that are either overbaked or underbaked. This can easily be solved by checking your oven temperature. The most reliable way to know the exact temperature of your oven is to use a thermometer. The **CDN Pro Accurate Oven Thermometer** ($8.70) has a clear display and attaches to the oven rack securely. Note that it is manufactured in two factories, so your model may not look exactly like the picture.

instant-read thermometer

A thermometer is essential for some confections, such as the caramel topping of our Ultimate Turtle Brownies (page 252), the lemon curd for Lemon Bars (page 280), and candies like Chocolate-Hazelnut Brittle (page 362). A digital instant-read thermometer (rather than a slow-registering stick candy thermometer) will tell you the temperature of your food almost immediately. Thermometers with long probes easily reach into deep pots. The **ThermoWorks Thermapen Mk4** ($99) has every bell and whistle.

COOLING AND STORING COOKIES

wire cooling rack

Properly cooling cookies is an essential step that shouldn't be overlooked. A good wire rack allows air to circulate all around the cookies as they cool. Be sure to buy a sturdy one that will fit inside a standard 18 by 13-inch rimmed baking sheet so it can accommodate a full batch of cookies and can be used for tasks beyond cooling (we bake slices of our Almond Biscotti (page 206) on a wire rack, for example). The **Libertyware Half Size Sheet Pan Cooling Rack** ($15.99 for a set of two; $7.99 each) is our favorite.

cookie spatula

Reaching between cookies on a crowded baking sheet and removing brownies from a pan are tricky with a full-size spatula. Enter the **OXO Good Grips Cookie Spatula** ($6.99), a remarkably small, maneuverable silicone spatula that's safe for nonstick cookware. The flexible edge of its 2 by 3-inch head, attached to an angled 6.5-inch handle, glides effortlessly beneath sugar, chocolate, and oatmeal cookies as well as brownies.

cookie jars

Novelty jars look nice but you want a cookie jar that actually keeps cookies fresh, intact, and easy to grab. Unlike most cookie jars, **OXO Good Grips Pop Storage Container, Big Square 4 Quart** ($16.99) has an airtight seal (activated by a pop-up button on the lid). And its clear plastic (BPA-free) jar shows off your baking accomplishments.

Flour, Butter, Sugar, Eggs: The Cookie Building Blocks

Part of what makes cookie baking so accessible is that it relies on these four simple ingredients, all of which you probably stock regularly. But while these ingredients may be basic, they can be manipulated in a number of ways to yield widely varying results. Here's how we put The Big Four to work.

FLOUR

Flour is arguably the most important ingredient for just about any cookie; it gives baked goods structure, crumb, and chew. While a majority of cookie recipes call for all-purpose flour, we also employ cake flour from time to time. The main difference between flour varieties is the amount of protein they contain. More protein leads to more gluten development, which, in turn, translates to chewier cookies—or, depending on the proportion of other ingredients, tough, dense cookies. For that reason you won't see us using bread flour, the white flour with the highest protein content, in our cookie recipes. Here are the flours we use in this book.

all-purpose flour

All-purpose flour is the most versatile variety, with a moderate protein content (10 to 11.7 percent, depending on the brand). We develop our recipes with easy-to-find Gold Medal Unbleached All-Purpose Flour (10.5 percent protein). Pillsbury All-Purpose Unbleached Flour (also 10.5 percent protein) offers comparable results. If you use an all-purpose flour with a higher protein content (such as King Arthur Unbleached All-Purpose Flour, with 11.7 percent protein) in our recipes that call for all-purpose flour, the cookies may be a bit drier and denser.

cake flour

Cake flour has a low protein content (6 to 8 percent) and delivers delicate, fine-crumbed cookies. You can approximate cake flour by mixing cornstarch with all-purpose flour. For each cup of cake flour, use 7/8 cup of all-purpose flour mixed with 2 tablespoons cornstarch. We use cake flour in Madeleines (page 187) and Italian Rainbow Cookies (page 204), since those cookies are essentially little cakes.

whole-wheat flour

Whole-wheat flour gives baked goods a distinctive flavor and texture because it's made from the entire wheat berry unlike white flours, which are ground solely from the grain's endosperm. Whole-wheat flour has a high protein content (about 13 percent), but it behaves differently than white flour and can result in dense baked goods. For that reason we usually combine whole-wheat flour with all-purpose flour in our cookies like healthful Trail Mix Cookies (page 61) for the best balance of nutty whole-wheat flavor and good texture. We use King Arthur Premium Whole Wheat Flour in the test kitchen.

storing flour

It's best to store all-purpose and cake flour in the pantry, away from light and heat. Whole-wheat flour contains more fat than refined flours and quickly turns rancid at room temperature, so it should be stored in the freezer. Make sure to bring flour kept in the freezer to room temperature before using. To quickly accomplish this, spread the flour in a thin layer on a baking sheet and let it sit for about 30 minutes.

BUTTER

Most of the recipes in this book use butter—rather than oil or shortening—for its satisfyingly rich flavor. But fat in cookies isn't just for flavor; the amount of fat in a recipe helps determine the texture of the cookies' crumb as well. When you add fat in large amounts, your cookies will be more tender, and sometimes, more crumbly; the fat coats the flour proteins, inhibiting their ability to form a strong gluten network.

use unsalted butter

In the test kitchen, we use only unsalted butter in our recipes. The amount of salt in salted butter varies from brand to brand, which is problematic in cookie recipes for a couple reasons: First, it makes it impossible to know how much salt to call for in a recipe. Second, salted butter often contains more water than unsalted does, and the excess water can affect gluten development.

plain, premium, and cultured butter

We use regular unsalted butter in all the cookies in this book. We usually don't think high-fat butters are worth the extra money; Land O'Lakes Unsalted Sweet Butter has received top ratings in our taste tests for its clean dairy flavor. Regular supermarket butter contains about 82 percent fat or less. (The rest is mostly water, with some milk solids, too.) Premium butters, many of which are imported from Europe, have a slightly higher fat level—up to 86 percent. But in baking tests, we've had trouble telling the difference between cookies made with premium butter and those made with regular butter. Our favorite premium butter, Plugrá European-Style Unsalted Butter, is better saved for spreading on toast or for making croissants. Similarly, we leave cultured butter on the supermarket shelves when baking. Culturing, or fermenting, cream before churning it into butter builds tangy, complex flavors—which are lost when baked into cookies.

storing butter

Butter can pick up off-flavors and turn rancid when kept in the refrigerator for longer than a month, as its fatty acids oxidize. For longer storage (up to 4 months), move it to the freezer. And because butter quickly picks up odors and flavors, we like to slip the sticks into a zipper-lock bag, whether it's stored in the refrigerator or in the freezer.

butter temperature

The temperature of butter affects the texture of finished cookies. We soften butter for creaming so it's malleable enough to be whipped but firm enough to retain air—vital to providing structure and leavening for drop cookies like Lemon Sour Cream Cookies (page 64). In reverse creaming, softened butter coats the flour particles for a tender texture in our Foolproof Holiday Cookies (page 367). We chill small cubes of butter when we need to cut the butter into the flour to create flaky layers like in Russian Cheese Cookies (page 127). When we melt butter, whether to create chew in cookies like Chewy Sugar Cookies (page 36) or to encourage spread like in Thin and Crispy Chocolate Chip Cookies (page 29), it should be cooled so you don't warm up the other ingredients. Here are our techniques for achieving the right butter temperature for the recipe at hand.

Chilled Butter (about 35 degrees)
- *Method:* Cut butter into small pieces; freeze until very firm, 10 to 15 minutes.
- *How to Test It:* Press with a finger—it should be cold and unyielding.

WHAT ABOUT OTHER FATS?

We prefer the flavor of butter, but other fats serve a specific purpose in some of our recipes.

Shortening

Shortening has a bland flavor, but it's OK to use in strongly flavored cookies such as our cinnamon-rolled Snickerdoodles (page 53). We sometimes use it when we want a crispy-edged cookie, as we do for Biscochitos (page 128), or one that is tall and tender like Italian Anise Cookies (page 221). Shortening is 100 percent fat, so it adds no extra moisture to dough. It also has a higher melting point than butter; the structure of cookies made with shortening sets before the shortening fully melts, resulting in a taller cookie.

Vegetable Oil

Sometimes we add oil (a largely unsaturated fat) in addition to butter (a largely saturated fat) to cookie doughs for a 3:1 ratio of unsaturated to saturated fat that makes cookies like our Classic Chewy Oatmeal Cookies (page 30), well, chewy. This combination of fats forms a sturdier crystalline structure than butter does alone, and it requires more force to bite through. (For more information, see page 30.) But we rarely use oil as the sole fat in a cookie; cookies made with only oil tend to be greasy and stodgy since oil doesn't aerate. Also, cookies made with an abundance of oil can develop an almost fried exterior after baking.

Made with Butter
This cookie is moderately chewy with a rich flavor.

Made with Shortening
This cookie is taller and more cakey.

Made with Oil
This cookie is greasy and has fried edges.

Softened Butter (65 to 67 degrees)

- *Method:* Let refrigerated butter sit at room temperature for about 30 minutes; cut the butter into pieces for faster softening. (Or, if you are in a hurry, you can place the cold butter in a zipper-lock bag and pound it with a rolling pin to the desired temperature and consistency.)
- *How to Test It:* The stick will easily bend without breaking and will give slightly when pressed.

Melted and Cooled Butter (85 to 90 degrees)

- *Method:* Melt butter in a small saucepan or microwave-safe bowl; let cool for about 5 minutes.
- *How to Test It:* The butter should be fluid and slightly warm.

SUGAR

As a sweet treat, cookies require sugar. But in addition to providing the requisite sweetness, sugar contributes to the moisture level, chew, structure, and browning of cookies. And sweeteners come in many forms, from conventional white sugar to sticky-sweet honey or molasses. These are the sweeteners we use in this book.

granulated sugar

White granulated sugar, made from either sugar cane or sugar beets, is the type of sugar used most often in our cookie recipes. It has a clean flavor and an evenly ground, loose texture that incorporates well with butter when creaming and dissolves easily into doughs.

superfine sugar

Finely processed white sugar, superfine sugar has extra-small crystals that dissolve quickly. Superfine sugar promotes a melt-in-the-mouth texture in delicate cookies such as Mexican Wedding Cookies (page 223). Superfine sugar can sometimes be hard to find; to make your own, simply process granulated sugar in a food processor for about 30 seconds.

confectioners' sugar

Also called powdered sugar, confectioners' sugar is the most finely ground sugar. It's most commonly used for dusting cookies and for making glazes and icings, but it can also be used in cookies where an ultrafine, tender crumb is desired, as with our Pecan Sandies (page 78). To prevent clumping, confectioners' sugar contains a small amount of cornstarch. You can approximate confectioners' sugar with this method: For 1 cup of confectioners' sugar, process 1 cup granulated sugar with 1 tablespoon of cornstarch in a blender (not a food processor) until fine, 30 to 40 seconds.

brown sugar

Brown sugar is granulated sugar that has been combined with molasses. If important, an ingredient list will indicate "light" or "dark" brown sugar; if either can be used, we simply call for "brown sugar." Store brown sugar in an airtight container to prevent it from drying out. (We pop in a Sugar Bears Inc. Brown Sugar Bear ($3.25), a clay bear that keeps the sugar soft.) If brown sugar does become hard, place it in a bowl with a slice of sandwich bread, cover, and microwave for 10 to 20 seconds to revive it.

To approximate 1 cup of light brown sugar, pulse 1 cup of granulated sugar with 1 tablespoon of mild molasses in a food processor until blended. Use 2 tablespoons molasses for dark brown sugar. Brown sugar is so moist and clumpy that it must be packed into a measuring cup to get an accurate reading. To do this, use your fingers or the bottom of a smaller cup to tap and press the sugar into the cup.

Brown Sugar Gives Cookies Chew

In addition to imparting a caramel flavor, brown sugar tends to make cookies more moist and chewy. Why? Molasses is an invert sugar. With invert sugars, sucrose breaks down into individual glucose and fructose molecules when heated with acid—as with molasses—or when treated with enzymes. Invert sugar is especially hygroscopic, pulling water from wherever it can be found—the best source being the air. Cookies made with brown sugar tend to stay chewy because the invert sugar pulls in moisture even after the cookies cool. The Chocolate Chunk Oatmeal Cookie with Pecans and Dried Cherries (page 33) on the left was made with dark brown sugar; it baked up chewy and easily bent around a rolling pin. The cookie on the right was made with granulated sugar; it emerged from the oven dry and snapped immediately when bent.

turbinado and demerara sugar

These coarse, caramel-colored (and caramel-flavored) sugars are also referred to as "raw" sugar. Their large crystals don't readily dissolve—a reason to avoid them in dough. Instead, we use them as a finishing touch the same way we'd use colorful sanding sugar or sprinkles, rolling logs of slice-and-bake dough into them (as with our Sablés on page 80).

corn syrup

Don't confuse corn syrup with high fructose corn syrup—a much sweeter product that is used in processed foods. Corn syrup, which is about 45 percent as sweet as sugar, is very thick and doesn't crystallize like maple syrup or honey, which is why it's often used in candy making. Corn syrup comes in light and dark varieties, with dark corn syrup having a deeper flavor. Manufacturers turn light corn syrup into dark by adding caramel color and a molasses-like product. Because it's extremely hygroscopic, we sometimes use corn syrup in recipes like our Chewy Chocolate Cookies (page 51) for the ultimate chew without the competing flavor of honey or molasses.

molasses

Molasses is a dark, thick syrup that's the by-product of sugarcane refining. It comes in three types: light or mild, dark or robust, and blackstrap. We prefer either light or dark molasses in baking and generally avoid using bitter blackstrap molasses. Store molasses in the pantry, not in the fridge where it turns into a thick sludge.

honey

This viscous liquid is made by bees from flower nectar; it's mechanically filtered and strained to remove wax and debris. Color generally indicates depth of flavor: Lighter shades will be more mellow and darker shades richer and even slightly bitter. Honey crystallizes in the refrigerator, so store it in the pantry.

If your honey is crystallized, put the opened jar in a saucepan filled with 1 inch of water, and heat the honey until it reaches 160 degrees. (Make sure the container is heatproof.)

maple syrup

This syrup is made by boiling down sap from maple trees. Maple syrup has a high moisture level, so refrigerating it not only helps it retain flavor but also prevents microorganisms from growing. Once opened, it will keep for six months to a year in the refrigerator. For long-term storage, maple syrup can be stored in the freezer. If it crystallizes in the freezer, a quick zap in the microwave will restore it.

EGGS

Eggs are indispensable in baking. Their yolks and whites have different properties and functions; together they can bind, thicken, emulsify, and leaven. Here's everything you need to know about this magical ingredient.

egg sizes and weights

Theoretically, eggs come in three grades (AA, A, and B), six sizes (from peewee to jumbo), and a rainbow of colors. But the only grade we could find in a standard supermarket was grade A, the only colors were brown and white, and the only sizes were jumbo, extra-large, large, and medium. After extensive tasting, we could not discern any consistent flavor differences among egg sizes or these two colors. For consistency's sake, however, the size (and volume) of the eggs used in recipes is important, particularly when baking. Thus, in all of our recipes, we use large eggs.

Medium	1.75 ounces
Large	2 ounces
Extra-Large	2.25 ounces
Jumbo	2.50 ounces

You can use this chart to make accurate calculations when substituting egg sizes. For example, four jumbo eggs are equivalent to five large eggs because their weight (10 ounces) is the same.

storing eggs

Properly stored eggs will last up to three months, but both the yolks and the whites will become looser and the eggs will begin to lose their structure-lending properties, which are paramount in baking. To be sure you have fresh eggs, check the sell-by date on the side of the carton. By law, the sell-by date must be no more than 30 days after the packing date. To ensure freshness, store eggs in the back of the refrigerator (the coldest area), not in the door (the warmest area), and keep them in the carton; it holds in moisture, keeps eggs from drying out, and protects the eggs from odors. Separated egg whites can be frozen, but in our tests we found that their rising properties were compromised, so frozen whites are best used in egg washes and not in recipes that depend on whipped whites, like Meringue Cookies (page 184).

egg substitutes

Egg substitutes are made with egg whites (some brands contain up to 99 percent whites) along with a mixture of vegetable gums, dairy products, vitamins and other nutrients, water, and coloring agents. We don't like any of these products in savory egg-based recipes such as omelets. But the substitutes fared much better in baking tests, and we couldn't distinguish between cakes, cookies, and brownies made with real eggs and those made with substitutes. You can use egg substitutes in any cookie recipe, replacing each whole egg in a recipe with ¼ cup of substitute.

liquid egg whites

Chances are good that you're tossing egg yolks when making recipes that call for egg whites only, so you might think liquid egg whites are a better option. But we've found that in baked goods most liquid egg whites came up short—literally. The pasteurization process they undergo compromises the whites' structure. As a result, they can't achieve the same volume as fresh whites when whipped. While we'd rather use conventional whites from whole eggs, **Eggology 100% Egg Whites** make satisfactory baked goods.

adding eggs to batters

A common step in cookie making after creaming the butter and sugar together is to mix in the eggs, adding them one at a time. Why the cautionary mixing? Like oil and vinegar, eggs and butter don't mix naturally. Butter is at least 80 percent fat, while eggs contain large amounts of water. So any time you add more than a single egg to creamed butter, it's best to do it slowly to give the mixture time to thicken and emulsify. In fact, when we added eggs to butter all at once when making cookies, the cookies spread, became misshapen, and were dense.

WHIPPING EGG WHITES

Perfectly whipped egg whites begin with a scrupulously clean bowl—fat will inhibit egg whites from whipping properly. Choosing the right bowl is essential, too. Bowls made from porous plastic retain an oily film even when washed carefully and should not be used for whipping egg whites. Glass and ceramic should be avoided as well, as their slippery surfaces make it harder for whites to billow up. The two best choices are stainless steel and, for those who have it, copper. First wash the bowl in soapy, hot-as-you-can-stand-it water, rinse with more hot water, and dry with paper towels. (A dish towel may have traces of oil within its fibers.) Start with eggs straight from the fridge—these will separate more easily than eggs at room temperature. Be careful not to puncture the yolk as you separate the eggs.

Egg whites whipped to stiff peaks lighten and leaven Ladyfingers (page 189), give Meringue Cookies (page 184) a delicate structure, and provide a confection-like filling for Old World Butter Horns (page 230)—so it's important to whip them right. If whipped shy of stiff peaks, their structure will be too weak in these applications; but if overwhipped, the same will be true.

Soft Peaks

Stiff Peaks

Overwhipped

The Cookie Cabinet: Staples, Mix-Ins, and Miscellany

Beyond The Big Four—flour, butter, sugar, and eggs—these are the ingredients that we like to stock so that baking cookies is an anytime activity.

CORNSTARCH

Cornstarch is made from the dried, ground corn endosperm (which contains starch and protein). Though cornstarch is most commonly used as a thickener, adding it to cookie dough in place of some of the flour can reduce gluten development; cornstarch doesn't contain the protein gluten so it contributes to tender cookies.

OATS

Oats are found in recipes from the iconic, like Classic Chewy Oatmeal Cookies (page 30) and Crunchy Granola Bars (page 276), to Cranberry-Oat Bars (page 297) and even Shortbread Cookies (page 102). While quick-cooking oats have their place (as in our Oatmeal Fudge Bars on page 317), and we love steel-cut oats for our morning bowl of oatmeal, we use old-fashioned rolled oats most often in our cookie kitchen. These are whole oats that are hulled, cleaned, steamed, and rolled. Their toasty flavor and hearty chew shine in cookies. When these same oats are also rolled very thinly to cook faster, they are called quick oats. Instant oats are cooked and dehydrated; they need no cooking and are easily reconstituted with hot water. Quick-cooking oats can often be used in place of old-fashioned oats, but cookies made with them will typically be less chewy and more cakey. You should avoid instant oats, which have a mushy texture when baked into cookies. Steel-cut oats are neither steamed nor rolled; they're simply whole oats that have been cut into smaller pieces. They're rarely used in baking, as they don't soften enough.

Our favorite old-fashioned oats are **Bob's Red Mill Old Fashioned Rolled Oats**, which boast a toasty flavor and tender texture and have just the right amount of chew. Note that Bob's Red Mill also makes Extra Thick Rolled Oats. A portion of these oats contains fewer per ounce than do the Old Fashioned Rolled Oats; this translates to cookies that spread too much during baking.

CORNMEAL

What's inside a bag of cornmeal may not be clear unless you understand the terms. Steel-cut cornmeal is cornmeal that's processed between steel rollers. This process breaks the corn kernels, resulting in a sharper-textured meal. Major brands like Quaker and Martha White are processed this way. Stone-ground cornmeal is ground between stones. Most of the meals we prefer are processed in this way. Stone-ground cornmeal has a more rustic texture because of the stone's rough grinding surface, and it has a fuller flavor because it contains both the hull and oil-rich germ of the corn kernel. Whole-grain cornmeal is ground whole, resulting in a meal made up of the bran, germ, and endosperm. Since the germ and bran contain the oil, this flavorful meal should be refrigerated or even frozen. Degerminated cornmeal has been stripped of its germ and bran before milling. Since the germ and bran contain the oil, this meal is drier and less flavorful than whole grain. Organic cornmeal has simply been milled from corn that has grown in a certified organic field. Our favorite cornmeal is **Arrowhead Mills Organic Yellow Cornmeal**. It is a whole-grain stone-ground cornmeal that works in all different applications.

CHEMICAL LEAVENERS

A majority of cookies include some kind of chemical leavener to help them rise during baking. Baking soda is an alkali and therefore requires an acidic ingredient in the dough, such as sour cream, molasses, or brown sugar, in order to produce carbon dioxide. The leavening action happens right after mixing, so you should bake right away. In addition to leavening, baking soda also promotes browning. Baking powder is a mixture of baking soda, a dry acid, and double-dried cornstarch. The cornstarch absorbs moisture and prevents the premature production of gas. Baking powder works twice—when it first comes in contact with a liquid, and again in response to heat. Once a container is opened, it will lose its effectiveness after six months. Our favorite baking powder is **Argo Double Acting Baking Powder**.

LEAVENERS—NOT JUST FOR LIFT

Why do so many cookies call for a combination of leaveners? The two work in tandem to create cookies that rise—and spread—to the right degree. Baking powder is responsible for lift since it's engineered to produce most of its gas after the cookies go into the oven, where the dough sets before the bubbles can burst. But too much lift can mean cookies that turn out domed and cakey. Here's where baking soda comes in: As long as there's an acidic ingredient in the dough for it to react with, a small amount of baking soda can even things out. Baking soda raises the pH of the dough (baking powder does too, but not as high), weakening gluten. Weaker gluten means less structure and cookies that spread nicely. It also allows for the crackly tops to form on cookies like our Chewy Sugar Cookies (page 36); the baking soda reacts immediately in the wet dough to produce large bubbles of carbon dioxide that can't all be contained by the weakened dough. Before the cookies can set in the oven, the bubbles rise to the top and burst, leaving fissures in their wake.

Baking Soda at Work

In our Gingersnaps (page 46), we use a dramatic amount of baking soda—a full 2 teaspoons—and no baking powder to create a cookie with extra snap and large fissures. The weaker gluten structure created in this environment means a more porous structure from which air bubbles and moisture can escape. It also means that the dough will collapse after its initial rise in the oven, leading to cracks that also allow more moisture to evaporate.

No Baking Soda   **½ Teaspoon Baking Soda**

1 Teaspoon Baking Soda   **1½ Teaspoons Baking Soda**

2 Teaspoons Baking Soda

VANILLA EXTRACT

Vanilla is the most commonly used flavoring in cookie baking. It's sold in pure and imitation varieties. Which should you buy? If you want to buy just one bottle of extract for all kitchen tasks, our top choice is a real extract—real vanilla has around 250 flavor compounds compared to imitation vanilla's one, giving it a complexity tasters appreciated when we tried it in cooked applications and in cold and creamy dessert. Our favorite pure vanilla is **McCormick Pure Vanilla Extract**. But if you use vanilla only for baking, we have to admit there's not much of a difference between a well-made synthetic vanilla and the real thing (the flavor and aroma compounds in pure vanilla begin to bake off at higher temperatures, so the subtleties are lost). Our top-rated imitation vanilla, CF Sauer Co. Gold Medal Imitation Vanilla Extract, has a well-balanced and full vanilla flavor—and a budget-friendly price to boot.

Want the ultimate vanilla extract? Try making your own by soaking a split vanilla bean in heated vodka (which contributes very little of its own flavor). After testing several ratios of vanilla beans to vodka, we arrived at 1 bean per ¾ cup of vodka as the proportion most closely resembling the potency of our favorite McCormick extract. We then tested our homemade extract against this supermarket product in sugar cookies, crème brûlée, and vanilla buttercream frosting. In each case, our extract outperformed the commercial version, boasting cleaner, more intense vanilla flavor. To make vanilla extract, split a fresh bean lengthwise and scrape out the seeds. Place the seeds and split pod in a 1-cup sealable container. Add ¾ cup hot vodka (we used Smirnoff—a premium brand is not necessary) and let the mixture cool to room temperature. Seal the container and store at room temperature for one week, shaking gently every day. Strain the extract, if desired, and store in a cool, dark place. The homemade extract, like store-bought versions, should keep indefinitely.

VANILLA BEANS

For recipes in which vanilla is the star—as with our Vanilla Bean–Apricot Sandwich Cookies on page 166—we've found that beans impart deeper flavor than extract. We tested five brands of vanilla beans, three mail-order and two from the supermarket. Although all of the samples were acceptable—including cheaper Spice Islands ($8.49 for two)—we recommend splurging on **McCormick Madagascar Vanilla Beans**, $15.99 for two, for their plump, seed-filled pods and complex caramel-like flavor.

1 To remove the seeds from vanilla bean pods first use a paring knife to cut the bean in half lengthwise.

2 Scrape the seeds out of the bean with the blade of the knife.

NUTS

We love the richness and texture nuts contribute to cookies, and you'll find nuts of all varieties throughout this book—ground into flour, chopped and mixed into doughs and batters, and sprinkled on top of baked cookies.

storing nuts

All nuts are high in oil and will become rancid rather quickly. In the test kitchen, we store nuts in the freezer in zipper-lock bags. Frozen nuts will keep for months, and there's no need to defrost before toasting or chopping.

toasting nuts

Toasting nuts enhances their flavor and gives them a satisfying, crunchy texture. We like to toast nuts when mixing them into doughs or batters, where they're prone to sogginess. We don't toast them when they're sprinkled on cookies before baking, as this could cause overbrowning or burning. (For more information on toasting nuts, see page 197.)

skinning hazelnuts

The skins from hazelnuts can impart a bitter flavor and undesirable texture.

To remove the skins, simply rub the hot toasted nuts inside a clean dish towel.

PEANUT BUTTER

Peanut butter is a beloved cookie ingredient found in everything from classics like candy-topped Peanut Blossom Cookies (page 130) to modern favorites like Salted Peanut Butter–Pretzel–Chocolate Chip Cookies (page 71). Peanut butter comes salted and unsalted; in creamy, chunky, and even extra-chunky varieties; and conventional and natural. Natural peanut butter refers either to butters made simply from ground peanuts without added partially hydrogenated fats or emulsifiers (these butters exhibit natural oil separation and require stirring) or to those with just the addition of palm oil (these do not require stirring). Sometimes the styles are interchangeable and other times they're not. Creamy and chunky butters both play a role in our cookie baking, but we always like the flavor boost provided by salt. We don't recommend using natural peanut butters made only from peanuts in cookies; they tend to turn out greasy, tough cookies that spread too much.

creamy peanut butter

We tasted 10 widely available peanut butters in the creamy category—some conventional and some natural—plain, in cookies, and in a satay sauce. Texture proved paramount. The peanut butters had to be smooth, creamy, and spreadable; they also had to have a good balance of sweet and salty flavors. The overall champ was a conventional peanut butter, **Skippy Peanut Butter**. Jif Natural Peanut Butter Spread, which tasters praised for its "dark-roasty flavor," was a very close runner-up.

chunky peanut butter

Would our favorite chunky peanut butter come from the same brand as our favorite creamy peanut butter? To find out, we sampled seven chunky spreads. Our lineup tracked closely with the results from the creamy tasting. The losers all suffered from texture flaws, with tasters condemning them for "grainy," "gritty," "soupy," or "viscous" consistencies. In some instances, their flavors were no help either; one brand's butter even tasted "fishy" in both creamy and chunky varieties. In the end our favorite chunky peanut butter was **Jif Natural Crunchy Peanut Butter Spread**. It has a "nice roasted-peanut flavor" and "well-balanced" sweetness that reminded tasters of "honey," and "good crunch."

BAKING SPICES

Warm spices are a great way to round out the flavor of a cookie or to give it a bolder profile. Preground spices are convenient, but their flavors fade fast. To make the most of your baking spices, we recommend following a few tips: Label them with the purchase date; store them in a cool, dry place; and use within 12 months. Otherwise, buy whole spices and grind them in a coffee grinder devoted solely to this purpose. We use the following spices most often in our cookie baking.

cinnamon

Given the number of options available at the supermarket, cinnamon seems to be Americans' favorite baking spice; while basic versions abound, you can also choose from among bottles labeled as "Vietnamese" or even "Saigon." Such cinnamons also command a higher price—up to about $4.00 per ounce, compared with as little as $0.90 per ounce for those with generic labeling. Does origin really matter? We found that cinnamons are indeed markedly different from each other. The Vietnamese cinnamons, for example, all fell on the spicier end of the spectrum, while the Indonesian cinnamons were mild. If you like a big, spicy flavor, we recommend springing for **Penzeys Vietnamese Cinnamon Ground**. At $4.09 per ounce, it was the most expensive product in our lineup, but it also had the highest percentage of volatile oils, which carry the flavor of cinnamon. If you prefer a milder, sweeter cinnamon, stick with cheaper cinnamons that make no claim to origin. Our favorite among these cinnamons was **Morton & Bassett Spices Ground Cinnamon**. The nuances are hard to detect in baking as opposed to in unheated applications.

nutmeg

Heady and potent, nutmeg is a hard, brown seed from a tropical tree. We compared fresh with preground and found that in recipes in which nutmeg is the sole spice, like Eggnog Snickerdoodles (page 384), grinding it yourself (we like to use a rasp-style grater) is important. But in foods with lots of spices, preground nutmeg is fine.

cardamom

Fragrant cardamom comes in pods, either green or black, each holding many tiny seeds. Seeds from the more common green pods are used in many Scandinavian baked goods—such as Danish Kleiner on page 229—and Indian sweets like Indian Tea Biscuits (page 121). Most of the highly aromatic flavors live in the seeds.

ground ginger

Ground ginger comes from the dried fresh root, but you can't substitute one for the other; they taste different (fresh is more floral; dry is spicier) and work differently in baking (fresh is moister). Our favorite dried ginger is **Spice Islands Ground Ginger**.

black pepper

Black pepper is more versatile than you might think; while we generally associate this spice with savory applications, it makes an intriguing addition to spiced cookies like Gingersnaps (page 46). Don't be tempted to buy preground, though; the flavor doesn't compare with fresh ground. The test kitchen's favorite peppercorns are mail-order: **Kalustyan's Indian Tellicherry Black Peppercorns**. Our favorite supermarket option is from **Morton & Bassett**.

spicing up spices

We love to use spices in our cookies but, depending on the amount used, they can taste a bit dusty right out of the jar. Sometimes we like to cook spices briefly in melted butter or whisk them into just-melted or just-browned butter in a cookie recipe; this technique, known as blooming, removes any raw flavor. It also releases their essential oils from a solid state into solution form, where they interact, producing a more complex flavor. Be careful to avoid burning them.

Blooming spices in hot butter releases their flavor.

COCONUT

Packaged coconut products all start as raw coconut meat that's then boiled, grated, and dried. Dried coconut comes in large flakes, shreds, or desiccated. There are two types of shredded coconut—sweetened and unsweetened. The dehydrated shreds are either immediately packaged and sold as unsweetened coconut or soaked in a liquid sugar solution and dried again to make sweetened coconut. We use both in our recipes, depending on whether we're looking to add sweetness or just deep coconut flavor. We rarely use flaked coconut in cookie baking because it's too large to incorporate into doughs, but it does make a good decoration.

the easiest way to toast coconut

There are a few ways to toast coconut; the two most common are in a skillet on the stovetop or spread on a baking sheet in a moderate oven. However, both of these methods require frequent stirring and a watchful eye to avoid burning the coconut. We've found that the microwave is actually the best place for toasting coconut, as this approach virtually eliminates the worry of burning.

Spread the coconut in an even layer on a large plate and microwave on high power until it's golden brown. The time will depend on the amount of coconut, but it usually takes a couple of minutes. Stir the coconut at 30-second intervals.

DRIED FRUIT

The process of drying fruit concentrates flavor and sugar, and these days, most fruits are available in dried form—from blueberries to cranberries to mangos. We use earthy-tasting raisins (regular and golden raisins can be used interchangeably), tart dried cranberries (they're infused with sweetened cranberry juice in the process of being dried), dried cherries (usually the tart variety for the biggest cherry punch), and dried figs (we often choose Calimyrna figs; this caramel-y fruit is the California version of the Turkish Smyrna fig) most often in our cookies. Sometimes we simply mix dried fruits into doughs, sometimes we cook them into a puree, and sometimes we plump them in the microwave with water or liquor to rehydrate them a bit before using.

TOFFEE BITS

Toffee is a common addition to cookies. Don't bother making your own and breaking it up; the stuff in the bags does the job well. It's most commonly sold as Heath Bits O' Brickle Toffee Bits. These crushed bits can be found in 8-ounce bags in the baking aisle of your supermarket near the chocolate chips. If a recipe calls for plain toffee bits, be sure to buy bits without any chocolate coating.

All About Chocolate

All chocolate begins as cacao beans found in large pods that grow on cacao trees. These beans are fermented, dried, and roasted and then the inner meat (or nib) of the bean is removed from the shell and ground into a paste called chocolate liquor (although it contains no alcohol), which consists of cocoa solids and cocoa butter. Chocolate liquor is then further processed and mixed with sugar and flavorings to make the various types of chocolate. White chocolate is made from just the cocoa butter and doesn't contain any cocoa solids. Milk, semisweet, and bittersweet chocolate go through a refining process known as conching where the chocolate liquor and the other ingredients are smeared against rollers until smooth. This conching action also drives off some of the volatile compounds responsible for chocolate's natural bitterness.

TYPES OF CHOCOLATE

The type and brand of chocolate you use in baking can make a big difference. Here's what you need to know.

cocoa powder

Cocoa powder is chocolate liquor that is processed to remove all but 10 to 24 percent of the cocoa butter. Cocoa powder comes in natural and Dutched versions. Dutching, which was invented in the 19th century by a Dutch chemist and chocolatier, raises the powder's pH, which neutralizes its acids and astringent notes and rounds out its flavor. (It also darkens the color.) We often "bloom" cocoa powder in a hot liquid such as water or coffee. This dissolves the remaining cocoa butter and disperses water-soluble flavor compounds for a deeper, stronger flavor. Our favorites? All-purpose: **Hershey's Natural Cocoa Unsweetened**. Dutched: **Droste Cocoa**.

unsweetened chocolate

Unsweetened chocolate is the traditional choice for recipes in which a bold hit of chocolate flavor is more important than a smooth or delicate texture (think brownies). If you don't have unsweetened chocolate, you can replace 1 ounce of unsweetened chocolate with 3 tablespoons of cocoa powder and 1 tablespoon of butter or oil. This substitution, however, is best for small quantities; it ignores the important differences between butter, oil, and cocoa butter. Our favorite? **Hershey's Unsweetened Baking Bar**.

semisweet and bittersweet chocolate

Semisweet and bittersweet chocolates, also called dark chocolate, must contain at least 35 percent chocolate liquor, although most contain more than 55 percent and some go as high as 99 percent. (Chocolates containing 70 percent or more cacao usually require recipe adjustments to get good results.)

For substitutions, we found that you can replace 1 ounce of bittersweet or semisweet chocolate with ⅔ ounce of unsweetened chocolate and 2 teaspoons of granulated sugar, yet because the unsweetened chocolate has not been conched it will not provide the same smooth, creamy texture as bittersweet or semisweet chocolate. Our favorite? **Ghirardelli 60% Cacao Bittersweet Chocolate Premium Baking Bar**.

milk chocolate

Milk chocolate must contain at least 10 percent chocolate liquor and 12 percent milk solids, with sweeteners and flavorings making up the balance. The result is a mellow, smooth flavor. Yet because of its relatively weak chocolate flavor (milk chocolate is usually more than 50 percent sugar), we don't use it in many recipes and mostly eat it out of hand. Our favorite? **Dove Silky Smooth Milk Chocolate**.

white chocolate

White chocolate is technically not chocolate since it contains no cocoa solids. Authentic white chocolate contains at least 20 percent cocoa butter, which provides its meltingly smooth texture. Many brands rely on palm oil in place of some or all of the cocoa butter and can't be labeled "chocolate." If the product is called "white chips" or "white confection," it is made with little or no cocoa butter. That said, since both styles derive their flavor from milk and sugar, not the fat, we find this distinction makes little difference in recipes. Our favorite? **Guittard Choc-Au-Lait White Chips**.

chocolate chips

While chocolate chips contain less cocoa butter than bar chocolate, they have stabilizers and emulsifiers that help them hold their shape better when baked. Our favorites? Dark chocolate: **Ghirardelli 60% Cacao Bittersweet Chocolate Chips**. Milk chocolate: **Hershey's Milk Chocolate Chips**.

STORING CHOCOLATE

Wrap open bars of chocolate tightly in plastic wrap and store them in a cool pantry. Avoid the refrigerator or freezer, as cocoa butter easily absorbs off-flavors from other foods and temperature changes can alter its crystal structure so it behaves differently in recipes. Unsweetened and dark chocolate, stored properly, will last about 2 years. The milk solids in white and milk chocolate give them a shorter shelf life; they last about 6 months.

WAKING UP CHOCOLATE FLAVOR

Sometimes we call for espresso powder in cookies even when coffee flavor is not the goal. Why? Just a pinch pumps up chocolate flavor considerably, making it more intense and complex without imparting a noticeable coffee presence. Our favorite instant espresso powder for brewing a demitasse or baking brownies is **Caffe D'Vita Imported Premium Instant Espresso**, which contributes dark, deep, fruity, roast-y notes to baked goods.

CHOPPING CHOCOLATE

There are two ways to chop a large block of chocolate into pieces.

To use a knife, hold a chef's knife at a 45-degree angle to one of the corners and bear down evenly. After cutting about an inch from the corner, repeat with the other corners.

Alternatively, you can use a sharp two-tined meat fork to break the chocolate into smaller pieces.

MELTING CHOCOLATE

Chocolate can burn easily, so it's best to use a gentle approach for melting. We've found two methods to be the best for melting chocolate: using an improvised double boiler or microwaving it at 50 percent power. Do not let the slightest amount of water get in melted chocolate or it will seize and turn grainy: The liquid forms a syrup with the sugar in the chocolate to which the cocoa particles will cling, creating clumps.

On the Stovetop

Chop the chocolate (so it melts evenly) and place it in a heatproof bowl set over a pot of barely simmering water. (Be sure the bowl is not touching the water or the chocolate could scorch.) Stir occasionally.

In the Microwave

Microwave the chopped chocolate at 50 percent power for the amount of time specified in the recipe. (This will depend on the amount of chocolate.) Stir the chocolate and continue microwaving until melted, stirring occasionally.

How a Cookie Crumbles: Manipulating Texture

Cookie texture is polarizing: Some prefer a chewy cookie like Brown Sugar Cookies (page 39), with crisp edges and a moist center that yields when you take a bite. The milk dunkers like things crispy, and enjoy the snap of Thin and Crispy Chocolate Chip Cookies (page 29). And then there are those who enjoy cookies that straddle the dessert line between cookie and little cake, like Lemon Sour Cream Cookies (page 64). Here's how we manipulate ingredients to achieve the result we desire.

VARIABLE	COOKIE TYPE		
	CHEWY	THIN AND CRISPY	CAKEY
Flour	Bread flour has a high protein content that gives breads chew, but it makes delicate cookies tough and dense so all-purpose flour is best for chewy cookies.	All-purpose flour works for most cookies.	Introducing some cake flour (or cutting all-purpose flour with cornstarch) makes baked goods, including cookies, more tender.
Fat	Using the right ratio of unsaturated fat (like oil) to saturated fat (like butter)—about 3:1—forms a more crystalline structure that translates to chew. Melting the butter makes its water available so it can readily interact with the flour, developing more gluten, which gives baked goods chew.	Using less butter creates a leaner cookie with less moisture so it's less soft. Melting the butter can boost chewiness, but it also contributes to a thin cookie. Melted butter cannot aerate the way creamed butter does so its structure can't lock in moisture.	Creaming the butter with sugar can open the cookie's crumb. Shortening has a higher melting point than butter so the structure sets before the cookie spreads much. With no water, shortening also tenderizes the crumb, making it crumbly, so cutting the butter with shortening can make a cakier cookie.
Sugar	Brown sugar is hygroscopic and holds onto moisture during and after baking so a cookie made with it will be chewier. This effect is even more extreme with liquid sweeteners like corn syrup or molasses.	Granulated sugar crystallizes as the cookie cools, making the cookie crunchier. It doesn't hold onto moisture readily.	Granulated sugar or a combination of granulated and brown sugars is appropriate for cakey cookies; using all brown sugar or a liquid sweetener would make the cookie too moist.
Eggs	Using more yolks than whites can create a chewier cookie, because whites tend to create a drier, cakier crumb. Since the white contains much of the egg's protein, any white that isn't fully absorbed dries out. An extra yolk also adds fat that keeps the cookie chewy after it's baked.	Using a small amount of egg (or even just yolk) will bind the cookie without adding a lot of moisture.	The more eggs called for, the more lift they provide.
Leavener	A combination of baking soda and baking powder ensures that the cookie rises and the crumb opens enough but then the cookie collapses a bit and spreads into the classic shape of a chewy cookie.	Extra baking soda helps dry out a cookie, giving it crispness; the rapid collapse it causes creates fissures that let out moisture. And more alkaline doughs brown better.	Most of the gas produced by baking powder is released once the cookie is in the oven, so using it alone (or in a higher amount than the baking soda) means the cookie rises and sets before the bubbles burst.
Liquid	Liquid, besides eggs, is not usually found in chewy cookies.	Adding some liquid to cookie dough—even just a couple of tablespoons—makes a looser dough that spreads in the oven.	Using more liquid than is customary in cookies can make a batter-like dough that has extra moisture; this moisture turns to steam in the oven for a more open, cakier crumb.
Cookie Size	Forming larger dough portions means the edges set before the centers, resulting in a chewier middle.	Larger dough portions won't spread enough to become thin and crisp.	Small dough portions will dry out too quickly to maintain a cakey texture.
Baking Time	Underbaking cookies slightly ensures they don't dry out; they set up during cooling.	Baking cookies until deep golden brown dries them out and crisps them.	

Storing, Shipping, and Sharing Cookies

Cookies are perfect for any occasion—holidays, bake sales, school lunches, everyday dessert—so it makes sense that you might need to make them ahead or pack them as gifts. Here's how we keep cookies at their best.

REFRIGERATING DOUGHS

If you're making cookies just for your family, you may want to refrigerate the dough and bake cookies a few at a time. Is this OK? It depends on the type of leavener in the cookies. We made four sugar cookie doughs: one with baking powder, one with baking soda, one with both, and the last (an icebox cookie) with neither. The dough with baking soda held well for two days but baked up a little flatter on the third. Cookies with both baking powder and soda began to lose lift after four days of dough storage (though we wouldn't recommend refrigerating a dough beyond 3 days so it doesn't pick up off flavors). The cookie dough with only baking powder maintained good lift for 7 days, with the same caveat. The unleavened cookies will hold just as long.

The dough with baking soda lasted for a shorter amount of time because soda is a single-acting leavener: It begins to produce lift-giving air bubbles as soon as it gets wet and comes in contact with an acid. Once started, this action continues until all the leavening power is spent—so there's a time limit. Baking powder is double acting, so it releases gas twice: once when it gets wet, and again when it heats up. So even if the first batch of air bubbles is spent, the second action will allow cookies to rise in the oven.

FREEZING DOUGHS

By keeping unbaked cookie dough in the freezer, you can satisfy your craving for freshly-baked cookies—just one or a whole batch—anytime. After making the dough, portion it out as you would for baking right away—either on parchment-lined baking sheets or on large plates—and place in the freezer until the dough is frozen solid, at least 30 minutes. Remove the frozen unbaked cookies from the sheet, arrange them in a zipper-lock bag or in layers in an airtight storage container and place them back in the freezer for up to two months. You may need to increase the recipe's baking time, but no defrosting is necessary.

STORING BAKED COOKIES

Many of the cookies in this book can be stored according to the methods below. Exceptions are noted in the recipes.

COOKIE TYPE	HOW TO STORE
Drop Cookies	About 3 days in an airtight container at room temperature.
Slice-and-Bake Cookies	About 1 week in an airtight container at room temperature.
Brownies and Blondies	About 5 days in an airtight container at room temperature. Topped brownies may require refrigeration. Uncut brownies last longer than cut brownies.

REVIVING STALE COOKIES

To restore cookies to just-baked freshness, recrisp them in a 425-degree oven for 4 to 5 minutes. Let the cookies cool on the sheet for a couple of minutes and serve them warm.

SHIPPING COOKIES

Cookies are the ultimate giftable confection. Here are our tips for shipping cookies so they arrive in perfect condition.

select wisely
Cookies that are baked until dried throughout, like gingersnaps, remained intact, crunchy, and fresh-tasting. Moist, dense brownies and bar cookies also fared well. But chewy cookies that started out moist ended up stale, and delicate lace cookies were reduced to shards.

combine like with like
Moist brownies turned crisp meringues to mush. Gingersnaps transferred their spicy flavors to mild spritz cookies.

stack bars
Place parchment between each bar, wrap small stacks tightly in plastic wrap, and enclose in zipper-lock bags.

pack with padding
Surround wrapped cookies with lightweight bulk: Packing peanuts, bubble wrap, and even popcorn work well. Place the most delicate items in the center of the box.

Cookie Troubleshooting

Here are the most common things that can go wrong during cookie baking—and how to fix them.

Problem Cookies don't add up to the correct yield

Solution Use a portion scoop

When cookies are portioned out larger or smaller than the recipe directs, they may not produce the intended texture. To ensure consistent size and the proper yield, we use a portion scoop.

Problem Cookies run together

Solution Bake in staggered rows

When scoops of dough are placed too close together on the sheet, the cookies can fuse together. To ensure enough space between cookies, alternate the rows. For example, place three cookies in the first row, two in the second, three in the third, and so on.

Problem Chewy cookies that aren't chewy

Solution Underbake

To ensure a chewy texture, take cookies out of the oven when they are still slightly underdone, which often means they'll droop over the end of a spatula. Crevices should appear moist and edges on smooth cookies should be lightly browned.

Problem Overly crisp edges

Solution Briefly chill dough and don't use a hot sheet

If cookies spread early in the oven, the edges can overcook. This can result from butter in the dough melting. If the dough seems too soft, chill it for 10 to 15 minutes before portioning. And let baking sheets cool completely between batches. To expedite cooling, rinse warm sheets under cold tap water.

Problem Cookies are overbaked

Solution Immediately transfer the cookies to a wire rack

Most recipes call for letting the cookies set up for a few minutes on the baking sheet before transferring them to a wire rack. But if you've overbaked your cookies, transfer them directly to a wire rack; otherwise, they'll keep cooking from the residual heat of the baking sheet.

Problem The last cookies always seem short on chips

Solution Reserve some morsels to add later

When chocolate chips, nuts, or raisins are in the mix, the last few cookies from a batch never seem to have as many of these goodies as the first few. To get around this, reserve some of the mix-ins and stir them into the dough after about half of it has been scooped out.

1

DROP
COOKIES

PERFECT CHOCOLATE CHIP COOKIES

Makes 16 cookies

1¾ cups (8¾ ounces) all-purpose flour

½ teaspoon baking soda

14 tablespoons unsalted butter

¾ cup packed (5¼ ounces) dark brown sugar

½ cup (3½ ounces) granulated sugar

2 teaspoons vanilla extract

1 teaspoon salt

1 large egg plus 1 large yolk

1¼ cups (7½ ounces) semisweet or bittersweet chocolate chips

¾ cup pecans or walnuts, toasted and chopped (optional)

Why This Recipe Works There's no question that the chocolate chip cookie is the most iconic American treat. While both crispy cookies and cakey ones have their place, we wanted a version reminiscent of the classic Toll House cookie, one with crisp edges and a chewy interior. But perhaps nostalgia has clouded our memory, because the Toll House recipe actually produces cookies that are a bit cakey and wan. We wanted a reliably moist and chewy cookie with crisp edges and deep butterscotch notes. The key ingredient was browned butter. Melting the butter made its water content readily available to interact with the flour, thus creating more gluten and a chewier texture. Continuing to cook the butter until it browned contributed deep caramel notes, as did dissolving the sugar in the melted butter. Using two egg yolks but only one white added richness without giving the cookies a cakey texture. Studded with gooey chocolate and boasting a complex toffee flavor, these are chocolate chip cookies, perfected. Light brown sugar can be used in place of the dark, but the cookies won't be as full-flavored.

1 Adjust oven rack to middle position and heat oven to 375 degrees. Line 2 baking sheets with parchment paper. Whisk flour and baking soda together in bowl.

2 Melt 10 tablespoons butter in 10-inch skillet over medium-high heat. Continue to cook, swirling skillet constantly, until butter is dark golden brown and has nutty aroma, 1 to 3 minutes. Transfer browned butter to large bowl and stir in remaining 4 tablespoons butter until melted. Whisk in brown sugar, granulated sugar, vanilla, and salt until incorporated. Whisk in egg and yolk until smooth and no lumps remain, about 30 seconds.

3 Let mixture stand for 3 minutes, then whisk for 30 seconds. Repeat process of resting and whisking 2 more times until mixture is thick, smooth, and shiny. Using rubber spatula, stir in flour mixture until just combined, about 1 minute. Stir in chocolate chips and pecans, if using.

4 Working with 3 tablespoons dough at a time, roll into balls and space them 2 inches apart on prepared sheets. (Dough balls can be frozen for up to 1 month; bake frozen dough balls in 300-degree oven for 30 to 35 minutes.)

5 Bake cookies, 1 sheet at a time, until golden brown and edges have begun to set but centers are still soft and puffy, 10 to 14 minutes, rotating sheet halfway through baking. Transfer baking sheet to wire rack. Let cookies cool completely before serving.

Baking a Bigger, Better Cookie

We pulled out lots of tricks to produce a cookie with the chew that's missing from the Toll House chocolate chip cookie recipe. But there's one particularly easy way to get a cookie with a gradation of textures: Simply make the cookie bigger. While the Toll House recipe calls for dropping rounded tablespoons of dough onto a baking sheet, we call for rolling 3 tablespoons of dough into a ball for each cookie. A larger diameter increases the contrast between the crispy edges and the chewy centers.

Less Dough
One tablespoon of dough per cookie creates a more uniform texture from edge to center.

More Dough
Three tablespoons of dough per cookie increase its crisp-chewy contrast.

THIN AND CRISPY CHOCOLATE CHIP COOKIES

Makes about 40 cookies

1½ cups (7½ ounces) all-purpose flour

¾ teaspoon baking soda

¼ teaspoon salt

8 tablespoons unsalted butter, melted and cooled

½ cup (3½ ounces) granulated sugar

⅓ cup packed (2⅓ ounces) light brown sugar

2 tablespoons light corn syrup

1 large egg yolk

2 tablespoons milk

1 tablespoon vanilla extract

¾ cup (4½ ounces) semisweet chocolate chips

Why This Recipe Works While our Perfect Chocolate Chip Cookies (page 27) are rich and buttery with an irresistibly chewy center, sometimes we get a hankering for another style: a thin, crisp cookie—one that's perfectly flat, almost praline in appearance, and that packs a big crunch. This style of cookie should feature the simple, gratifying flavors of butter and deeply caramelized sugar. While brown sugar gives chocolate chip cookies nice flavor, it also contributes moisture; substituting white sugar for some of the brown gave our cookies just the right balance of butterscotch flavor and good crunch. Adding some milk to our dough allowed it to spread in the oven, resulting in a thinner cookie. And instead of creaming the ingredients until fluffy, we simply beat them until combined for less aeration. Knowing that corn syrup browns at a lower temperature than sugar, we added a couple tablespoons for a shiny, crackly golden surface. Increasing the baking soda also improved browning. Baking the cookies one sheet at a time further encouraged spread so that the cookies flattened and cooled into thin, crisp disks—perfect for dunking. You can use either whole or low-fat milk here.

1 Adjust oven rack to middle position and heat oven to 375 degrees. Line 2 baking sheets with parchment paper. Whisk flour, baking soda, and salt together in bowl.

2 Using stand mixer fitted with paddle, beat melted butter, granulated sugar, brown sugar, and corn syrup on low speed until thoroughly blended, about 1 minute. Add egg yolk, milk, and vanilla and mix until fully incorporated and smooth, about 1 minute, scraping down bowl as needed. Slowly add flour mixture and mix until just combined. Using rubber spatula, stir in chocolate chips. Give dough final stir by hand to ensure that no flour pockets remain and ingredients are evenly distributed. (Dough can be covered tightly with plastic wrap and refrigerated for up to 2 days. Let refrigerated dough soften at room temperature for 30 minutes before portioning and baking.)

3 Working with 1 tablespoon dough at a time, roll into balls and space them 2 inches apart on prepared sheets. Bake, 1 sheet at a time, until deep golden brown and flat, about 12 minutes, rotating sheet halfway through baking.

4 Let cookies cool on sheet for 3 minutes, then transfer to wire rack. Let cookies cool completely before serving. (Cookies can be stored in zipper-lock bag for up to 1 week.)

CLASSIC CHEWY OATMEAL COOKIES

Makes 20 cookies

1 cup (5 ounces) all-purpose flour

¾ teaspoon salt

½ teaspoon baking soda

4 tablespoons unsalted butter

¼ teaspoon ground cinnamon

¾ cup (5¼ ounces) dark brown sugar

½ cup (3½ ounces) granulated sugar

½ cup vegetable oil

1 large egg plus 1 large yolk

1 teaspoon vanilla extract

3 cups (9 ounces) old-fashioned rolled oats

½ cup raisins (optional)

Why This Recipe Works Most oatmeal cookies have one place of origin: Quaker's Best Oatmeal Cookies recipe. But why are they ubiquitous when the result is usually dry, cakey, overly spiced rounds? We ran every variable through the wringer to achieve an oaty cookie with crisp edges and a dense, chewy middle. We took a big step in the right direction when we adjusted the fat content: Instead of using all butter, we introduced vegetable oil, an unsaturated fat that's fluid at room temperature. The right combination of unsaturated and saturated fats results in chewy baked goods; a ratio of nearly 3 parts unsaturated to 1 part saturated was the sweet spot. Decreasing the flour further mitigated cakiness, while adding an extra egg yolk boosted moisture. Blooming the cinnamon in the butter intensified its flavor so we didn't use excessive amounts. To avoid beating too much air into this dough, we mixed it by hand. Regular old-fashioned rolled oats work best in this recipe. Do not use extra-thick rolled oats; they will be tough. If you don't add the optional raisins, the recipe will yield 18 cookies.

1 Adjust oven rack to middle position and heat oven to 375 degrees. Line 2 baking sheets with parchment paper. Whisk flour, salt, and baking soda together in bowl.

2 Melt butter in 8-inch skillet over medium-high heat, swirling skillet occasionally. Continue to cook, stirring and scraping bottom of pan with heatproof spatula, until butter is dark golden brown and has nutty aroma, 1 to 2 minutes. Transfer browned butter to large bowl, scraping skillet with spatula, and stir in cinnamon.

3 Whisk brown sugar, granulated sugar, and oil into browned butter until combined. Whisk in egg and yolk and vanilla until smooth. Using wooden spoon or stiff rubber spatula, stir in flour mixture until fully combined, about 1 minute. Stir in oats and raisins, if using, until evenly distributed (mixture will be stiff).

4 Divide dough into twenty 3-tablespoon portions (or use #24 cookie scoop). Space dough balls 2 inches apart on prepared sheets, 10 per sheet. Using your dampened hand, press each dough ball until 2½ inches in diameter.

5 Bake cookies, 1 sheet at a time, until edges are set and lightly browned and centers are still soft but not wet, 8 to 10 minutes, rotating sheet halfway through baking. Let cookies cool on sheet for 5 minutes, then transfer to wire rack with wide metal spatula. Let cookies cool completely before serving.

For a Chewy Cookie, Cut the (Saturated) Fat

When our cookies were coming out cakey and tender rather than dense and chewy, we looked at the fat—specifically, the type of fat we were using. Saturated fat (e.g., butter) will produce baked goods with a tender texture, while unsaturated fat (e.g., vegetable oil) results in a chewier baked good. We were using all butter up to this point, so swapping in vegetable oil for some of that butter (and adding another egg yolk) gave us a ratio of about 3 parts unsaturated fat to 1 part saturated—and cookies that met our chewy, dense ideal.

CHOCOLATE CHUNK OATMEAL COOKIES WITH PECANS AND DRIED CHERRIES

Makes about 16 cookies

1¼ cups (6¼ ounces) all-purpose flour

¾ teaspoon baking powder

½ teaspoon baking soda

½ teaspoon salt

1¼ cups (3¾ ounces) old-fashioned rolled oats

1 cup pecans, toasted and chopped

1 cup (4 ounces) dried sour cherries, chopped coarse

4 ounces bittersweet chocolate, chopped into chunks about size of chocolate chips

12 tablespoons unsalted butter, softened

1½ cups packed (10½ ounces) dark brown sugar

1 large egg

1 teaspoon vanilla extract

Why This Recipe Works Oatmeal cookies provide an ideal backdrop for almost any addition. But in pursuit of the ultimate oatmeal cookie, it's easy to lapse into a kitchen-sink mentality, overloading the dough with a crazy jumble of ingredients. We wanted the perfect combination of oats, nuts, chocolate, and fruit in a superlatively chewy package. To achieve this, we used all brown sugar, leveling up to dark brown for deep molasses flavor and the chewiest texture. Making big cookies (a whopping ¼ cup of dough per cookie) and baking them just until set yet slightly underdone further ensured chewy cookies. And a combination of baking powder and baking soda produced a cookie that was light and crisp on the outside but chewy, dense, and soft in the center. For our carefully curated mix-ins we found that a combination of bittersweet chocolate chunks, toasted pecans, and tart dried sour cherries struck a perfect balance of flavors and textures. You can substitute walnuts or skinned hazelnuts for the pecans and dried cranberries for the cherries. Quick oats can be used in place of the old-fashioned oats, but they will yield a cookie with slightly less chew.

1 Adjust oven racks to upper-middle and lower-middle positions and heat oven to 350 degrees. Line 2 baking sheets with parchment paper. Whisk flour, baking powder, baking soda, and salt together in bowl. Stir oats, pecans, cherries, and chocolate together in second bowl.

2 Using stand mixer fitted with paddle, beat butter and sugar on medium speed until no sugar lumps remain, about 1 minute, scraping down bowl as needed. Reduce speed to medium-low, add egg and vanilla, and beat until fully incorporated, about 30 seconds, scraping down bowl as needed. Reduce speed to low, add flour mixture, and mix until just combined, about 30 seconds. Gradually add oat mixture until just incorporated. Give dough final stir by hand to ensure that no flour pockets remain and ingredients are evenly distributed.

3 Working with ¼ cup dough at a time, roll into balls and space them 2½ inches apart on prepared sheets. Using bottom of greased dry measuring cup, press each ball to 1-inch thickness.

4 Bake cookies until medium brown and edges have begun to set but centers are still soft (cookies will look raw between cracks and seem underdone), 20 to 22 minutes, switching and rotating sheets halfway through baking. Let cookies cool on sheets for 5 minutes, then transfer to wire rack. Let cookies cool completely before serving.

THIN AND CRISPY OATMEAL COOKIES

Makes 24 cookies

1 cup (5 ounces) all-purpose flour

¾ teaspoon baking powder

½ teaspoon baking soda

½ teaspoon salt

14 tablespoons unsalted butter, softened but still cool

1 cup (7 ounces) granulated sugar

¼ cup packed (1¾ ounces) light brown sugar

1 large egg

1 teaspoon vanilla extract

2½ cups (7½ ounces) old-fashioned rolled oats

Why This Recipe Works We wanted to refine the standard oatmeal cookie recipe to create a crisp, delicate cookie in which the flavor of buttery oats would really stand out. Scaling back the sugar reduced moisture so that even the center of the cookies was dry enough to develop a pleasant crunch. Increasing the amounts of baking powder and baking soda gave us cookies that were crisp but not tough. To ensure that the cookies baked evenly and were crisp throughout, we pressed them flat and baked them 1 sheet at a time until they were fully set and evenly browned from edge to center. Place them on the baking sheet in three rows, with three cookies in the outer rows and two cookies in the center row. We developed this recipe using Quaker Old Fashioned Rolled Oats. Other brands of old-fashioned oats can be substituted but may cause the cookies to spread more. Do not use quick or instant oats.

1 Adjust oven rack to middle position and heat oven to 350 degrees. Line 3 baking sheets with parchment paper. Whisk flour, baking powder, baking soda, and salt together in bowl.

2 Using stand mixer fitted with paddle, beat butter, granulated sugar, and brown sugar at medium-low speed until just combined, about 20 seconds. Increase speed to medium and continue to beat until pale and fluffy, about 1 minute longer, scraping down bowl as needed. Add egg and vanilla and beat on medium-low until fully incorporated, about 30 seconds, scraping down bowl as needed. Reduce speed to low, add flour mixture, and mix until just incorporated and smooth, about 10 seconds. With mixer running, gradually add oats and mix until well incorporated, about 20 seconds. Give dough final stir by hand to ensure that no flour pockets remain and ingredients are evenly distributed.

3 Working with 2 tablespoons dough at a time, roll into balls and space them 2½ inches apart on prepared sheets. Using your fingertips, gently press each ball to ¾-inch thickness.

4 Bake, 1 sheet at a time, until cookies are deep golden brown, edges are crisp, and centers yield to slight pressure when pressed, 13 to 16 minutes, rotating sheet halfway through baking. Transfer sheet to wire rack and let cookies cool completely before serving.

Salty Thin and Crispy Oatmeal Cookies

We prefer the texture and flavor of a larger-grained flake sea salt, such as Maldon or *fleur de sel*, but kosher salt can be used. If using kosher salt, reduce the amount sprinkled over the cookies to ¼ teaspoon.

Reduce amount of salt in dough to ¼ teaspoon. Lightly sprinkle ½ teaspoon flake sea salt evenly over flattened dough balls before baking.

Thin and Crispy Coconut Oatmeal Cookies

Decrease oats to 2 cups and add 1½ cups sweetened flaked coconut to dough with oats in step 2.

Thin and Crispy Orange-Almond Oatmeal Cookies

Beat 2 teaspoons grated orange zest with butter and sugars in step 2. Decrease oats to 2 cups and add 1 cup coarsely chopped toasted almonds to dough with oats in step 2.

CHEWY SUGAR COOKIES

Makes 24 cookies

2¼ cups (11¼ ounces) all-purpose flour

1 teaspoon baking powder

½ teaspoon baking soda

½ teaspoon salt

1½ cups (10½ ounces) sugar, plus ⅓ cup for rolling

2 ounces cream cheese, cut into 8 pieces

6 tablespoons unsalted butter, melted and still warm

⅓ cup vegetable oil

1 large egg

1 tablespoon whole milk

2 teaspoons vanilla extract

Why This Recipe Works The hallmark of a standout sugar cookie is satisfying chew. But sugar cookie recipes can be surprisingly fussy: If the butter temperature isn't just right or the measurements are a bit off, the resulting cookies are brittle. We wanted an approachable recipe for great sugar cookies that anyone could make. Knowing that the right proportions of saturated and unsaturated fats can enhance chewiness (for more information on this, see pages 10 and 30), we replaced some of the butter in the recipe with oil. The cookies had good chew but they were cloying. To mitigate the sweetness, we added an unconventional ingredient: cream cheese. A small amount contributed a slight tang that provided the perfect counterpoint to the sugar without compromising the cookie's texture. As a bonus, its acidic presence enabled us to include baking soda as an additional leavener, which gave the cookies a beautiful crackly surface. The final dough will be slightly softer than most cookie doughs. For the best results, handle the dough as briefly and as gently as possible; overworking the dough will result in flatter cookies.

1 Adjust oven rack to middle position and heat oven to 350 degrees. Line 2 baking sheets with parchment paper. Whisk flour, baking powder, baking soda, and salt together in bowl.

2 Place 1½ cups sugar and cream cheese in large bowl. Whisk in warm melted butter (some lumps of cream cheese will remain). Whisk in oil until incorporated. Whisk in egg, milk, and vanilla until smooth. Using rubber spatula, fold in flour mixture until soft, homogeneous dough forms.

3 Spread remaining ⅓ cup sugar in shallow dish. Working with 2 tablespoons dough at a time, roll into balls, then roll in sugar to coat; space dough balls 2 inches apart on prepared sheets. Using bottom of greased dry measuring cup, press each ball until 3 inches in diameter. Using sugar left in dish, sprinkle 2 teaspoons sugar over each sheet of cookies; discard extra sugar. (Raw cookies can be frozen for up to 1 month; bake frozen cookies in 350-degree oven for 17 to 22 minutes.)

4 Bake cookies, 1 sheet at a time, until edges are set and beginning to brown, 11 to 13 minutes, rotating sheet halfway through baking. Let cookies cool on sheet for 5 minutes, then transfer to wire rack. Let cookies cool completely before serving.

Chewy Chai Spice Sugar Cookies

Add ¼ teaspoon ground cinnamon, ¼ teaspoon ground ginger, ¼ teaspoon ground cardamom, ¼ teaspoon ground cloves, and pinch pepper to bowl with sugar and cream cheese in step 2. Reduce vanilla to 1 teaspoon.

Chewy Coconut-Lime Sugar Cookies

Whisk ½ cup finely chopped sweetened shredded coconut into flour mixture in step 1. Add 1 teaspoon finely grated lime zest to bowl with sugar and cream cheese in step 2. Substitute 1 tablespoon lime juice for vanilla.

Chewy Hazelnut–Browned Butter Sugar Cookies

Increase milk to 2 tablespoons and omit vanilla. Add ¼ cup finely chopped toasted hazelnuts to bowl with sugar and cream cheese. Substitute browned butter for melted butter; melt butter in 10-inch skillet over medium-high heat, then continue to cook, swirling skillet constantly, until butter is dark golden brown and has nutty aroma, 1 to 3 minutes. Immediately add browned butter to bowl with sugar and cream cheese.

BROWN SUGAR COOKIES

Makes 24 cookies

14 tablespoons unsalted butter

2 cups plus 2 tablespoons (10⅔ ounces) all-purpose flour

½ teaspoon baking soda

¼ teaspoon baking powder

1¾ cups packed (12¼ ounces) dark brown sugar, plus ¼ cup for rolling

½ teaspoon salt

1 large egg plus 1 large yolk

1 tablespoon vanilla extract

¼ cup (1¾ ounces) granulated sugar

Why This Recipe Works We love a plain sugar cookie, but we wanted to turn up the volume on this classic by swapping out mild granulated sugar for more robust brown sugar—and we wanted an oversize cookie to match its big flavor. Dark brown sugar gave us the biggest flavor boost, and we underscored its sweet caramel notes with a full tablespoon of vanilla and balanced it with a dash of salt. Browning the butter, as we do in many of our drop cookies, worked well here; the browned butter contributed butterscotch and toffee notes that complemented the brown sugar's rich molasses flavor. By itself, baking soda gave the cookies a nice, crackly top but made the crumb coarse; the addition of a little baking powder resulted in a finer crumb. For the signature crystalline sugar-cookie coating, we stuck with brown sugar but added a little white sugar to prevent clumping. Finally, the right baking technique proved crucial. We baked the cookies one sheet at a time and pulled them from the oven when a light touch from our fingers produced a slight indentation in the surface of the cookie. Use fresh, moist brown sugar for cookies with the best texture.

1 Melt 10 tablespoons butter in 10-inch skillet over medium-high heat. Continue to cook, swirling skillet constantly, until butter is dark golden brown and has nutty aroma, 1 to 3 minutes. Transfer browned butter to large bowl and stir in remaining 4 tablespoons butter until melted; let cool for 15 minutes.

2 Meanwhile, adjust oven rack to middle position and heat oven to 350 degrees. Line 2 baking sheets with parchment paper. Whisk flour, baking soda, and baking powder together in bowl.

3 Whisk 1¾ cups brown sugar and salt into cooled browned butter until smooth and no lumps remain, about 30 seconds. Whisk in egg and yolk and vanilla until incorporated, about 30 seconds. Using rubber spatula, stir in flour mixture until just combined, about 1 minute.

4 Combine remaining ¼ cup brown sugar and granulated sugar in shallow dish. Working with 2 tablespoons dough at a time, roll into balls, then roll in sugar to coat; space dough balls 2 inches apart on prepared sheets. (Dough balls can be frozen for up to 1 month; bake frozen dough balls on 1 baking sheet set inside second sheet in 325-degree oven for 20 to 25 minutes.)

5 Bake cookies, 1 sheet at a time, until edges have begun to set but centers are still soft, puffy, and cracked (cookies will look raw between cracks and seem underdone), 12 to 14 minutes, rotating sheet halfway through baking. Let cookies cool on sheet for 5 minutes, then transfer to wire rack. Let cookies cool completely before serving.

Building Big Brown Sugar Flavor

Dark brown sugar was an obvious place to begin our efforts to create a cookie with bold flavor. A whole tablespoon of vanilla helped, but it was browning the butter that had the greatest impact on the flavor of these cookies.

Dark Brown Sugar   **Lots of Vanilla**   **Browned Butter**

CHOCOLATE SUGAR COOKIES

Makes 24 cookies

⅓ cup granulated sugar

1½ cups plus 2 tablespoons (8⅛ ounces) all-purpose flour

¾ cup (2¼ ounces) unsweetened cocoa powder

½ teaspoon baking soda

¼ teaspoon baking powder

14 tablespoons unsalted butter

1¾ cups packed (12¼ ounces) dark brown sugar

1 tablespoon vanilla extract

½ teaspoon salt

1 large egg plus 1 large yolk

Why This Recipe Works Sugar cookies, with their crisp edges, chewy centers, and crunchy, crackled, glistening tops, are one of our favorite cookies, so it seemed like a no-brainer to create a chocolate version with all of the same features. We figured that simply adding some melted chocolate to our favorite chewy sugar cookie would give us the chocolate variation we sought; but by the time we had added enough chocolate to the dough to give the cookies the rich chocolaty flavor we wanted, the cookies lost their signature chew. Instead we replaced ¾ cup of the flour with cocoa powder; since cocoa is more intense than bar chocolate, the flavor was bold and the cookies retained their chew. Our chocolate sugar cookie recipe had come together nicely, but one problem remained: The results were inconsistent from batch to batch. After further testing, we determined that the melted butter was to blame; if it was too hot when we added it to the dough, the cookies spread too much. To ensure a foolproof recipe, we melted most of the butter and then stirred in the remaining cold butter to cool it down and to keep the temperature consistent every time we make these cookies—which will be quite often.

1 Adjust oven rack to middle position and heat oven to 350 degrees. Line 2 baking sheets with parchment paper. Spread granulated sugar in shallow dish; set aside. Whisk flour, cocoa, baking soda, and baking powder together in bowl.

2 Microwave 10 tablespoons butter, covered, in large bowl until melted, about 1 minute. Remove bowl from microwave and stir in remaining 4 tablespoons butter until melted. Let butter cool to 90 to 95 degrees, about 5 minutes.

3 Whisk brown sugar, vanilla, and salt into melted butter until no lumps remain, scraping down bowl as needed. Whisk in egg and yolk until smooth. Stir in flour mixture until just combined.

4 Working with 2 tablespoons dough at a time, roll into balls, then roll in granulated sugar to coat; space dough balls evenly on prepared sheets. Using bottom of greased dry measuring cup, press each ball until 2 inches in diameter. Evenly sprinkle remaining granulated sugar over cookies.

5 Bake, 1 sheet at a time, until cookies are slightly puffy and edges have begun to set (cookies will look raw between cracks and seem underdone), about 15 minutes, rotating sheet halfway through baking. Let cookies cool on sheet for 5 minutes, then transfer to wire rack. Let cookies cool completely before serving.

PEANUT BUTTER COOKIES

Makes 24 cookies

2½ cups (12½ ounces) all-purpose flour

1 teaspoon salt

½ teaspoon baking powder

½ teaspoon baking soda

1 cup salted dry-roasted peanuts

16 tablespoons unsalted butter, softened

1 cup packed (7 ounces) light brown sugar

1 cup (7 ounces) granulated sugar

1 cup extra-crunchy peanut butter

2 teaspoons vanilla extract

2 large eggs

Why This Recipe Works Peanut butter cookies fall into two camps: There are the cookies that are sweet and chewy but have minimal peanut butter flavor (which is obscured by significant amounts of sugar and butter), and there are the crumbly, sandy cookies that have strong peanut flavor owing to lots of peanut butter and not very much flour. We wanted a peanut butter cookie that was the best of both worlds—crisp around the edges and chewy in the center, with a buttery, sweet, and deeply peanutty flavor. We added peanut butter to our dough until we reached 1 cup; any more and the cookies were dense and heavy. To increase nuttiness without adding more peanut butter, we used extra-crunchy peanut butter and then mixed in a cup of salted dry-roasted peanuts, which we processed to fine crumbs. The extra peanuts and salt gave the cookie a strong roasted-nut flavor without sacrificing its wonderful texture. Finally, we thought of one last way we could further accentuate the cookie's nuttiness: sugar. We had been using granulated sugar, but a combination of granulated and brown sugars proved best. The white sugar yielded crisp-edged cookies, while the brown sugar's deep molasses notes underscored the peanut flavor. We prefer extra-crunchy peanut butter for these cookies, but crunchy peanut butter or creamy peanut butter also works.

1 Adjust oven racks to upper-middle and lower-middle positions and heat oven to 350 degrees. Line 2 baking sheets with parchment paper. Whisk flour, salt, baking powder, and baking soda together in bowl. Pulse peanuts in food processor to fine crumbs, about 14 pulses.

2 Using stand mixer fitted with paddle, beat butter, brown sugar, and granulated sugar on medium speed until pale and fluffy, about 3 minutes. Add peanut butter and beat until fully incorporated, about 30 seconds. Add vanilla, then eggs, one at a time, and beat until combined, about 30 seconds, scraping down bowl as needed. Reduce speed to low and slowly add flour mixture until combined, about 30 seconds. Mix in ground peanuts until incorporated. Give dough final stir by hand to ensure that no flour pockets remain.

3 Working with 3 tablespoons dough at a time, roll into balls and space them 2 inches apart on prepared sheets. Using fork, make crosshatch design on cookies. (Raw cookies can be frozen for up to 1 month; bake frozen cookies in 300-degree oven for 17 to 22 minutes.)

4 Bake cookies until edges are golden and centers have puffed but are beginning to deflate, 10 to 12 minutes, switching and rotating sheets halfway through baking. Let cookies cool on sheets for 10 minutes. Serve warm or transfer to wire rack and let cool completely.

Crosshatching Peanut Butter Cookies

Using fork, press crosshatch design into each cookie before baking.

MOLASSES SPICE COOKIES

Makes 24 cookies

2¼ cups (11¼ ounces) all-purpose flour

1 teaspoon baking soda

1½ teaspoons ground cinnamon

1½ teaspoons ground ginger

½ teaspoon ground cloves

¼ teaspoon ground allspice

¼ teaspoon pepper

¼ teaspoon salt

12 tablespoons unsalted butter, softened

⅓ cup packed (2⅓ ounces) dark brown sugar

⅓ cup (2⅓ ounces) granulated sugar, plus ½ cup for rolling

1 large egg yolk

1 teaspoon vanilla extract

½ cup mild or robust molasses

Why This Recipe Works The best molasses spice cookies combine a homespun crinkled appearance with a chewy texture and a deep, gently spiced molasses flavor. We tested the three main kinds of molasses in our dough and liked two of them equally: light (or mild) and dark (or robust). Light molasses imparted a mild flavor, while dark had a stronger presence, so the choice is up to you. (We found blackstrap molasses overpowering and bitter.) A modest amount of dark brown sugar boosted the sweetness and added strong caramel notes. To complement these assertive sweeteners, we needed a powerful yet balanced team of spices. Cinnamon, ginger, cloves, allspice, and black pepper provided warmth and just enough bite, and a spoonful of vanilla smoothed out any rough edges. When rolling the balls of dough, we found that dipping our hands in water prevented the dough from sticking to them and also helped the granulated sugar adhere to the dough balls. For the best texture and appearance, be sure to bake the cookies one sheet at a time and pull them from the oven when they still look substantially underdone. (They will continue to bake and harden as they cool, with the insides remaining soft and moist.)

1 Adjust oven rack to middle position and heat oven to 375 degrees. Line 2 baking sheets with parchment paper. Whisk flour, baking soda, cinnamon, ginger, cloves, allspice, pepper, and salt together in bowl.

2 Using stand mixer fitted with paddle, beat butter, brown sugar, and ⅓ cup granulated sugar on medium speed until pale and fluffy, about 3 minutes. Reduce speed to medium-low, add egg yolk and vanilla, and beat until combined, about 30 seconds. Beat in molasses until incorporated, about 30 seconds, scraping down bowl as needed. Reduce speed to low and slowly add flour mixture until combined, about 30 seconds (dough will be soft). Give dough final stir by hand to ensure that no flour pockets remain.

3 Spread remaining ½ cup granulated sugar in shallow dish. Working with 2 tablespoons dough at a time, roll into balls with your dampened hands, then roll in sugar to coat; space dough balls 2 inches apart on prepared sheets. (Dough balls can be frozen for up to 1 month; bake frozen dough balls in 300-degree oven for 30 to 35 minutes.)

4 Bake cookies, 1 sheet at a time, until edges are set but centers are still soft, puffy, and cracked (cookies will look raw between cracks and seem underdone), 10 to 12 minutes, rotating sheet halfway through baking. Let cookies cool on sheet for 10 minutes. Serve warm or transfer to wire rack and let cool completely.

Molasses Spice Cookies with Dark Rum Glaze
Whisk 1 cup confectioners' sugar and 3 tablespoons dark rum in bowl until smooth. Drizzle glaze over cooled cookies and let dry for 10 to 15 minutes before serving.

Molasses Spice Cookies with Orange Essence
Add 1 teaspoon grated orange zest to dough with molasses in step 2. Process ⅔ cup granulated sugar with 2 teaspoons grated orange zest in food processor until fragrant, about 10 seconds; substitute orange sugar for granulated sugar when rolling in step 3.

GINGERSNAPS

Makes 80 cookies

2½ cups (12½ ounces) all-purpose flour

2 teaspoons baking soda

½ teaspoon salt

12 tablespoons unsalted butter

2 tablespoons ground ginger

1 teaspoon ground cinnamon

¼ teaspoon ground cloves

¼ teaspoon pepper

Pinch cayenne pepper

1¼ cups packed (8¾ ounces) dark brown sugar

¼ cup molasses

2 tablespoons finely grated fresh ginger

1 large egg plus 1 large yolk

½ cup granulated sugar

Why This Recipe Works Most gingersnap recipes don't live up to their name on either account. Once you get past the brittle edges of those made from homemade recipes, the cookies turn soft and chewy. And they always fall short on flavor, lacking sufficient ginger and spice notes. We wanted freshly baked homemade gingersnaps to rival the snap and spice of the store-bought kind. The biggest obstacle to achieving snap was too much moisture in the dough. Cutting back on the brown sugar reduced moisture with little effort while browning the butter eliminated some of its water; tweaking these key ingredients resulted in noticeably drier and crunchier cookies. Using plenty of baking soda resulted in attractive fissures on the tops of our cookies, which also served as channels for moisture to escape. Finally, lowering the oven temperature and baking the cookies for longer than normal dried them out enough to yield our desired snappy texture. As for flavor, we wanted cookies with real bite, so we doubled the amount of dried ginger called for in most recipes and also added fresh ginger, black pepper, and a secret weapon: cayenne pepper. For efficiency, form the second batch of cookies while the first batch bakes. And no, the 2 teaspoons of baking soda is not a mistake; it's essential to getting the right texture.

1 Whisk flour, baking soda, and salt together in bowl; set aside.

2 Melt butter in 10-inch skillet over medium heat. Reduce heat to medium-low and continue to cook, swirling skillet frequently, until butter is just beginning to brown, 2 to 4 minutes. Transfer browned butter to large bowl and whisk in ground ginger, cinnamon, cloves, pepper, and cayenne. Let cool slightly, about 2 minutes.

3 Whisk brown sugar, molasses, and fresh ginger into butter mixture until combined. Whisk in egg and yolk until combined. Stir in flour mixture until just combined. Cover bowl tightly with plastic wrap and refrigerate until dough is firm, about 1 hour.

4 Adjust oven racks to upper-middle and lower-middle positions and heat oven to 300 degrees. Line 2 baking sheets with parchment paper. Spread granulated sugar in shallow dish.

Divide dough into heaping teaspoon portions; roll dough into 1-inch balls. Working in batches of 10, roll balls in sugar to coat; space dough balls evenly on prepared sheets, 20 dough balls per sheet.

5 Place 1 sheet on upper rack and bake for 15 minutes. Transfer partially baked top sheet to lower rack, rotating sheet, and place second sheet of dough balls on upper rack. Continue to bake until cookies on lower sheet just begin to darken around edges, 10 to 12 minutes longer. Remove lower sheet of cookies and transfer upper sheet to lower rack, rotating sheet; continue to bake until cookies begin to darken around edges, 15 to 17 minutes longer.

6 Slide baked cookies, still on parchment, onto wire rack and let cool completely before serving. Repeat with remaining dough balls.

ALL ABOUT DROP COOKIES

Drop cookies are American classics. Chocolate chip, oatmeal, sugar—these cookies typically have a lightly crisp outer edge and a soft, chewy middle. They are some of the easiest cookies to shape and bake. That said, we have some test kitchen tricks to ensure your drop cookies are better than the rest.

FORMING DROP COOKIES

Many recipes call for simply "dropping" (hence the name) a measurement of cookie dough onto the baking sheet, usually with two spoons. For the best cookies, we prefer to roll the dough between our hands into perfectly round balls. This creates cookies of uniform shape that bake evenly. The exception is for soft doughs or cakier cookies such as our Applesauce Cookies (page 58) that have loose batters, which makes it difficult to roll them between your hands.

AN EASIER WAY TO PORTION COOKIES

Spring-loaded ice cream scoops aren't our favorite for scooping ice cream, but we found a better use for them: portioning out cookie dough. These scoops are sized according to how many scoops will yield a quart. For example, a #8 scoop will render eight scoops per quart of ice cream (or dough or batter). Having a few means you can use them to portion out cookie doughs for a variety of cookie recipes.

But if you're going to have just one, we recommend getting one that holds about 3 tablespoons of dough, a serving size we use often for recipes like Classic Chewy Oatmeal Cookies (page 30) and Perfect Chocolate Chip Cookies (page 27). When testing out portion scoops (our favorite is the **OXO Good Grips Large Cookie Scoop** ($14.97) that features grippy handles and an inner spring with just the right amount of resistance), we wanted to see just how much easier they made the process, and we tested them against a tablespoon measure— the tool we'd use to measure out cookies if we were without scoops. Unsurprisingly, scoops were all neater and more consistent at portioning the cookies. But the difference in speed was most remarkable: It took an average of 2½ minutes to serve up uniform hemispheres of cookie dough compared with the 6 minutes it took the tablespoon to make messy mounds. It's a worthwhile tool.

Use a Portion Scoop for Even Cookies

FREEZING COOKIE DOUGH

Keeping some frozen dough on hand means you can bake just as many, or as few, cookies as you like whenever the feeling strikes. To freeze the dough, form it into balls, arrange the balls on a rimmed baking sheet, and place the sheet in the freezer. Once the individual balls are frozen solid, place them in a zipper-lock bag and store them in the freezer. To bake most frozen cookies, arrange the dough balls (do not thaw) on a parchment paper–lined baking sheet and bake as directed, increasing the baking time as needed.

We like our drop cookies to have a crisp outer edge that yields to a chewy middle. But if you overbake them—or even bake them until they appear just cooked through—the centers will be hard and crumbly rather than chewy. To ensure a chewy texture, take the cookies out of the oven when they still look raw between the cracks and seem underdone. The edges should be set, but the centers should still be soft and puffy.

It can be a bit trickier to figure out when dark cookies like our Brown Sugar Cookies (page 39) are ready to come out of the oven; you may not be able to see between the cracks. For these cookies, try pressing the middle with your fingers; gently press halfway between the edge and center of the cookie. When the cookie's done, it will form an indent with slight resistance. Check early and err on the side of underdone.

Because drop cookies are best when you slightly underbake them, they are very soft when they come out of the oven and won't hold together if manipulated. To avoid misshapen cookies, wait until they are firm enough that a spatula doesn't cause damage. Also, this step gives the residual heat in the baking sheet time to finish baking the cookies. However, if the cookies are slightly overbaked, don't let them cool on the sheet. Move cookies to a rack to cool quickly. (If the cookies are slightly burnt, you can try to scrape off burnt spots with a rasp-style grater. This isn't ideal, but it's better than serving cookies with burnt edges.)

To keep drop cookies chewy, you can't simply throw them in a cookie jar. To prevent cookies from turning dry and brittle, we recommend storing them in a zipper-lock bag with a half slice of sandwich bread.

Chocolate chips are the most commonly reached-for cookie mix-in, and the star of the most iconic drop cookie, of course. Not so long ago, most markets stocked one kind of chocolate chips: Nestlé Toll House Morsels. Nowadays, the shelves are full of different products. Does Nestlé still deserve to be the nation's best-selling morsel? To find out, we rounded up eight chips, including two from Nestlé. We then sampled them plain and in cookies.

While bars of dark chocolate typically boast cacao amounts starting at 60 percent, most of the chips we tasted contained far less: 42 to 47 percent. Less cacao means less cocoa butter, which means the chocolate will be less fluid when melted, making it easier for chips to hold their shape. Because cocoa butter is expensive, using less of it makes chips cheaper to produce than the average bar.

The absence of cocoa butter was clear when we tasted chips right out of the bag. Tasters found the chips gritty and grainy instead of creamy and smooth like bar chocolate, with one exception, our winner: intense, complex-tasting **Ghirardelli 60% Cacao Bittersweet Chocolate Chips**. The product that stood apart distinguished itself further when we baked the chips in cookies. Unlike the other chips, which kept their shape during baking, this chip melted into thin layers that spread throughout the cookie, ensuring gooey chocolate in every bite. Furthermore, when we examined its ingredient list, we found that this chip had the highest percentage of cacao in the lineup—60 percent, comparable to bar chocolate—and the most cocoa butter by far (44 percent, minus a tiny amount of milk fat). It was also wider and flatter than a standard chip, which enhanced its ability to melt into thin strata throughout the cookie.

CHEWY CHOCOLATE COOKIES

Makes 16 cookies

1½ cups (7½ ounces) all-purpose flour

¾ cup (2¼ ounces) Dutch-processed cocoa powder

½ teaspoon baking soda

⅜ teaspoon salt

½ cup dark corn syrup

1 large egg white

1 teaspoon vanilla extract

12 tablespoons unsalted butter, softened

⅓ cup packed (2⅓ ounces) dark brown sugar

⅓ cup (2⅓ ounces) granulated sugar, plus ½ cup for rolling

4 ounces bittersweet or semisweet chocolate, chopped into ½-inch pieces

Why This Recipe Works Cookies labeled with a "death-by-chocolate" description typically claim texture as their first victim. We set out to make an exceptionally rich chocolate cookie we could sink our teeth into without it falling apart. Our first batch, made with modest amounts of both cocoa powder and melted chocolate, baked up too tender. The bar chocolate was the culprit—its high fat content softened the dough too much. Using only cocoa powder—and plenty of it—gave our cookies bold chocolate flavor without compromising texture. And using just an egg white rather than a whole egg further boosted structure without adding fat. Cutting some of the white sugar with dark brown sugar meant a chewier cookie and deeper flavor, and adding dark corn syrup further enhanced the brown sugar's effects. For more richness, we folded in chopped bittersweet chocolate; the chunks stayed intact and added intense pockets of flavor. As a finishing touch, we dipped the dough balls in granulated sugar to give the cookies a sweet crunch and an attractive crackled appearance. Use a high-quality bittersweet or semisweet chocolate. Light brown sugar can be used in place of the dark, but the cookies won't be as full-flavored.

1 Adjust oven racks to upper-middle and lower-middle positions and heat oven to 375 degrees. Line 2 baking sheets with parchment paper. Whisk flour, cocoa, baking soda, and salt together in bowl. Whisk corn syrup, egg white, and vanilla together in second bowl.

2 Using stand mixer fitted with paddle, beat butter, brown sugar, and ⅓ cup granulated sugar on medium speed until pale and fluffy, about 3 minutes. Reduce speed to medium-low, add corn syrup mixture, and beat until fully incorporated, about 20 seconds, scraping down bowl as needed. Reduce speed to low, add flour mixture and chocolate, and mix until just incorporated, about 30 seconds. Give dough final stir by hand to ensure that no flour pockets remain. Cover bowl tightly with plastic wrap and refrigerate for 30 minutes.

3 Spread remaining ½ cup granulated sugar in shallow dish. Working with 2 tablespoons dough at a time, roll into balls, then roll in sugar to coat; space dough balls 2 inches apart on prepared sheets. (Dough balls can be frozen for up to 1 month; bake frozen dough balls in 325-degree oven for about 25 minutes.)

4 Bake cookies until edges have begun to set but centers are still soft, puffy, and cracked (cookies will look raw between cracks and seem underdone), 10 to 11 minutes, switching and rotating sheets halfway through baking. Let cookies cool on sheets for 5 minutes, then transfer to wire rack. Let cookies cool completely before serving.

The Right Size Chunk

Tiny pieces will melt and disappear when baked. Chunks (about ½-inch pieces) stay intact.

Too Small   **Just Right**

SNICKERDOODLES

Makes 24 cookies

2½ cups (12½ ounces) all-purpose flour

2 teaspoons cream of tartar

1 teaspoon baking soda

½ teaspoon salt

8 tablespoons unsalted butter, softened

8 tablespoons vegetable shortening

1½ cups (10½ ounces) sugar,
plus ¼ cup for rolling

2 large eggs

1 tablespoon ground cinnamon

Why This Recipe Works With their crinkly tops, slightly tangy flavor, and liberal coating of cinnamon sugar, chewy snickerdoodles are a New England favorite. We quickly determined that an oft-included ingredient, cream of tartar, is essential to these cookies. Not only is it responsible for their characteristic subtle tang, but, when combined with baking soda, it creates a short-lived leavening effect that causes the cookies to rise and fall quickly while baking, leaving them with a distinctive crinkly appearance. Some traditional snickerdoodle recipes contain vegetable shortening, and with good reason: Unlike butter, shortening contains no water, so cookies made with shortening tend to hold their shape rather than spread out. We found that using equal amounts of shortening and butter gave us the best of both worlds—thick, nicely shaped cookies that were chewy and rich-tasting. The final step was rolling the balls of dough in the traditional cinnamon sugar. For the best results, bake the cookies one sheet at a time and pull them from the oven just as they are beginning to brown but are still soft and puffy in the middle. They will continue to cook as they cool on the baking sheet.

1 Adjust oven rack to middle position and heat oven to 375 degrees. Line 2 baking sheets with parchment paper. Whisk flour, cream of tartar, baking soda, and salt together in bowl.

2 Using stand mixer fitted with paddle, beat butter, shortening, and 1½ cups sugar on medium speed until pale and fluffy, about 3 minutes. Add eggs, one at a time, and beat until incorporated, about 30 seconds, scraping down bowl as needed. Reduce speed to low and slowly add flour mixture until combined, about 30 seconds. Give dough final stir by hand to ensure that no flour pockets remain.

3 Combine remaining ¼ cup sugar and cinnamon in shallow dish. Working with 2 tablespoons dough at a time, roll into balls, then roll in sugar to coat; space 2 inches apart on prepared baking sheets. (Dough balls can be frozen for up to 1 month; bake frozen dough balls in 300-degree oven for 18 to 20 minutes.)

4 Bake cookies, 1 sheet at a time, until edges are just set and beginning to brown but centers are still soft, puffy, and cracked (cookies will look raw between cracks and seem underdone), 10 to 12 minutes, rotating sheet halfway through baking. Let cookies cool on sheet for 10 minutes, then transfer to wire rack. Let cookies cool completely before serving.

Essential Snickerdoodle Ingredients

Snickerdoodles are known for their subtle tang and spiced sugar coating. Two other defining features are the crinkled top and soft interior. To make sure these cookies are authentically crinkled and soft, most recipes rely on a combination of cream of tartar and baking soda. Cream of tartar is an acidic powder that acts as a flavoring agent, providing the characteristic tanginess to the cookies. When alkaline baking soda meets up with acidic cream of tartar, carbon and oxygen combine to form carbon dioxide. This in turn causes the cookie to rise and then collapse, a process that results in a crinkly top and cakey texture. The combination of the two is generally called for in recipes in which none of the other ingredients is acidic.

CHOCOLATE CRINKLE COOKIES

Makes 22 Cookies

1 cup (5 ounces) all-purpose flour

½ cup (1½ ounces) unsweetened cocoa powder

1 teaspoon baking powder

¼ teaspoon baking soda

½ teaspoon salt

1½ cups packed (10½ ounces) brown sugar

3 large eggs

4 teaspoons instant espresso powder (optional)

1 teaspoon vanilla extract

4 ounces unsweetened chocolate, chopped

4 tablespoons unsalted butter

½ cup granulated sugar

½ cup confectioners' sugar

Why This Recipe Works Rolled in powdered sugar before baking, chocolate crinkle cookies (often called earthquakes) feature chocolaty fissures that break through the bright white surface during baking. While striking in appearance, these cookies often fall short on taste. Using a combination of cocoa powder and unsweetened bar chocolate rather than bittersweet chocolate (which contains sugar) certainly upped the intensity, and swapping brown sugar for the granulated created a complex sweetness. At this point, the cookies had deep, rich flavor, but the exterior cracks were too few and too wide, and the cookies weren't spreading enough. Using a combination of baking soda and baking powder helped—the bubbles produced by the leaveners rose to the surface and burst, leaving fissures—but the cracks gapped. We had been refrigerating this fluid dough overnight before portioning and baking the cookies, but the cold dough didn't begin to spread very much until after that dried exterior had formed, forcing the cracks to open wide. The solution was to bake the cookies after letting the dough sit at room temperature for 10 minutes, which was just enough time for the dough to firm up to a scoopable consistency.

1 Adjust oven rack to middle position and heat oven to 325 degrees. Line 2 baking sheets with parchment paper. Whisk flour, cocoa, baking powder, baking soda, and salt together in bowl.

2 Whisk brown sugar; eggs; espresso powder, if using; and vanilla together in large bowl. Microwave chocolate and butter in bowl at 50 percent power, stirring occasionally, until melted, 2 to 3 minutes.

3 Whisk chocolate mixture into egg mixture until combined. Fold in flour mixture until no dry streaks remain. Let dough sit at room temperature for 10 minutes.

4 Spread granulated sugar in shallow dish. Spread confectioners' sugar in second shallow dish. Working in batches, drop 2-tablespoon mounds of dough (or use #30 scoop) directly into granulated sugar and roll to coat. Transfer dough balls to confectioners' sugar and roll to coat; space dough balls evenly on prepared sheets, 11 per sheet.

5 Bake cookies, 1 sheet at a time, until they are puffed and cracked and edges have begun to set but centers are still soft (cookies will look raw between cracks and seem underdone), about 12 minutes, rotating sheet halfway through baking. Let cookies cool on sheet for 5 minutes, then transfer to wire rack. Let cookies cool completely before serving.

Granulated Sugar Creates More Crinkle

Most cookies have top crusts that remain relatively soft and flexible as the cookies set during baking. However, if the top surface dries out before the cookie is finished spreading and rising, it hardens, cracks, and pulls apart. To encourage more cracks in our Chocolate Crinkle Cookies, we rolled the balls of dough in granulated sugar before the traditional confectioners'. As the coarse crystals of the granulated sugar absorb moisture, some—but not all—dissolve into a syrup. As the cookies continue to bake, the moisture evaporates, and the sugar begins to recrystallize, a process that's accelerated by the presence of undissolved sugar crystals. The upshot: a cookie with a faster-drying surface that is more prone to cracking.

CRANBERRY, WHITE CHOCOLATE, AND MACADAMIA COOKIES

Makes about 32 cookies

2 cups (10 ounces) all-purpose flour

½ teaspoon baking soda

½ teaspoon salt

12 tablespoons unsalted butter, melted and cooled slightly

1 cup packed (7 ounces) light brown sugar

½ cup (3½ ounces) granulated sugar

1 large egg plus 1 large yolk

2 teaspoons vanilla extract

1 cup (6 ounces) white chocolate chips

1 cup dried cranberries, chopped coarse

1 cup macadamia nuts, chopped

Why This Recipe Works Raisins, semisweet chocolate chips, and walnuts are all great additions to cookies, but sometimes we crave a different flavor combination. The key to incorporating mix-ins is balance. In this cookie, we achieved balance by pairing tart dried cranberries with sweet white chocolate. We then added macadamia nuts; their mild, almost creamy flavor paired well with the other elements. One cup each of cranberries, chocolate, and nuts made for cookies loaded with flavor and contrasting texture in every bite. Slightly underbaking the cookies and allowing them to finish cooking from the residual heat of the baking sheet ensured that they retained their fresh-baked chew once cool. You can recapture that just-baked texture after the cookies have been sitting around for a few days (though we can't guarantee they'll last that long!) by recrisping them in a 425-degree oven for 4 to 5 minutes and serving them warm.

1 Adjust oven rack to lower-middle position and heat oven to 325 degrees. Line 2 baking sheets with parchment paper. Whisk flour, baking soda, and salt together in bowl.

2 Using stand mixer fitted with paddle, beat melted butter, brown sugar, and granulated sugar on medium speed until smooth, 1 to 2 minutes. Add egg and yolk and vanilla and beat until combined, scraping down bowl as needed. Reduce speed to low, slowly add flour mixture, and mix until just combined. Add chocolate chips, cranberries, and macadamia nuts and mix until incorporated.

3 Working with 2 tablespoons dough at a time, roll into balls and space them 2 inches apart on prepared sheets. Bake, 1 sheet at a time, until edges are set but centers are still soft and puffy, 15 to 20 minutes, rotating sheet halfway through baking. Let cookies cool on sheet for 10 minutes, then transfer to wire rack. Let cookies cool completely before serving.

APPLESAUCE COOKIES

Makes 22 cookies

1½ cups (7½ ounces) all-purpose flour

½ cup walnuts, toasted and chopped

¾ teaspoon baking soda

½ teaspoon salt

8 tablespoons unsalted butter

¾ teaspoon plus ⅛ teaspoon
ground cinnamon

¾ cup unsweetened applesauce

¾ cup packed (5¼ ounces) light
brown sugar

1 large egg yolk

6 tablespoons (1½ ounces)
confectioners' sugar

2 tablespoons sour cream

Why This Recipe Works Applesauce spice cake is a comforting snack; we wanted to transform its flavors into a portable treat—one that would be perfect for the kids' lunch boxes or as a grown-up accompaniment to coffee or tea. But applesauce baked goods frequently are so overwhelmed with spices that they're apple in name only. In addition, they are typically weighed down by moisture, making them dense, wet, and gummy. We wanted a light, fluffy applesauce cookie loaded with apple flavor. To achieve our goal we needed to find ways to eliminate water in the dough without decreasing the applesauce. Because applesauce acts as a binder, we found we didn't need a lot of egg; just one yolk gave us structure and richness without added water from the white. Browning the butter, a technique we use for other cookies, further cut down on water and imparted a nutty depth, while blooming the cinnamon in the warm browned butter intensified its flavor. Finally, a healthy amount of baking soda gave the cookies lift, lightening the crumb; it also contributed to a nicely browned exterior. To give our soft, tender cookies some textural contrast, we mixed in crunchy toasted walnuts and drizzled the finished cookies with a tangy spiced glaze—a nod to our spice cake inspiration.

1 Adjust oven racks to upper-middle and lower-middle positions and heat oven to 375 degrees. Line 2 baking sheets with parchment paper. Whisk flour, walnuts, baking soda, and salt together in bowl.

2 Melt butter in 10-inch skillet over medium-high heat. Continue to cook, swirling skillet constantly, until butter is dark golden and has nutty aroma, 1 to 3 minutes. Add ¾ teaspoon cinnamon and continue to cook, stirring constantly, for 5 seconds. Transfer butter mixture to bowl; let cool for 15 minutes.

3 Whisk applesauce, brown sugar, and egg yolk together in large bowl. Add butter mixture and whisk until combined. Stir in flour mixture until smooth. Drop 2-tablespoon mounds of dough onto prepared sheets, spacing them about 1½ inches apart.

4 Bake cookies until edges are golden brown and centers are firm, 13 to 15 minutes, switching and rotating sheets halfway through baking. Let cookies cool on sheets for 10 minutes, then transfer to wire rack and let cool completely.

5 Whisk confectioners' sugar, sour cream, and remaining ⅛ teaspoon cinnamon in bowl until smooth. Drizzle cookies with glaze and let dry for at least 15 minutes before serving.

TRAIL MIX COOKIES

Makes 24 cookies

1 cup (3 ounces) old-fashioned rolled oats

½ cup (2¾ ounces) whole-wheat flour

¼ cup (1¼ ounces) all-purpose flour

½ teaspoon salt

¼ teaspoon ground cinnamon

¼ teaspoon baking soda

5 tablespoons unsalted butter, melted and cooled

1 large egg

2 teaspoons vanilla extract

1 cup packed (7 ounces) light or dark brown sugar

½ cup dried cherries, dried cranberries, or raisins

½ cup unsalted pumpkin or sunflower seeds, toasted

¼ cup pecans, walnuts, or almonds, toasted and chopped coarse

¼ cup semisweet chocolate chips

Why This Recipe Works Unlike cakes and pies, we tend to think of cookies as anytime treats. Still, enjoying cookies with some frequency is easier to justify when the cookie doesn't just taste good but is also good for you. In our quest to develop a more healthful cookie, we sought to pack a whole-grain dough with a variety of interesting mix-ins. A full cup of oats, combined with whole-wheat flour and a small amount of all-purpose flour for structure, formed our cookie's base. Taking a cue from trail mix—and its ideal blend of healthful yet tasty ingredients—we added dried fruit, seeds, nuts, and chocolate chips. Trail mix preferences vary, but we found that our cookie base was versatile enough to support any combination of nuts, seeds, and dried fruit that you enjoy. A small amount of cinnamon gave the cookies a rounder flavor, and using brown sugar rather than white gave us the biggest bang for our buck; its deeper flavor meant we didn't need to use an excessive amount of sugar. We needed just 5 tablespoons of melted butter, along with an egg, to bring the dough together. The result was a chunky, satisfying cookie filled with tasty goodness that you can enjoy whenever you like. We prefer the texture and flavor of old-fashioned rolled oats; however, quick oats can be substituted. Do not use instant oats.

1 Adjust oven rack to middle position and heat oven to 350 degrees. Line 2 baking sheets with parchment paper. Whisk oats, whole-wheat flour, all-purpose flour, salt, cinnamon, and baking soda together in bowl.

2 Whisk melted butter, egg, and vanilla together in large bowl. Stir in sugar until smooth, smearing any remaining clumps of sugar against side of bowl. Stir in oat mixture until just combined, then stir in cherries, pumpkin seeds, pecans, and chocolate chips.

3 Working with 1 heaping tablespoon dough at a time, roll into balls and space them 2 inches apart on prepared sheets. Bake, 1 sheet at a time, until edges are set and beginning to brown but centers are soft and puffy (cookies will look raw between cracks and seem underdone), 12 to 16 minutes, rotating sheet halfway through baking. Let cookies cool on sheet for 10 minutes. Serve warm or transfer to wire rack and let cool completely before serving.

CHOCOLATE CHEWIES

Makes 24 cookies

2¼ cups (9 ounces) confectioners' sugar

6 tablespoons (1⅛ ounces) unsweetened cocoa powder

2 tablespoons all-purpose flour

¼ teaspoon salt

3 large egg whites

¾ teaspoon vanilla extract

2 cups pecans, toasted and chopped fine

1 ounce bittersweet chocolate, grated

Why This Recipe Works Chocolate chewies are a rich, fudgy—almost brownie-like—cookie. These ultrachocolaty treats are inspired by a popular old recipe from Gottlieb's, a beloved bakery in Savannah, Georgia. While many versions of the chocolate chewy exist and can be found in bakeries across the country, we wanted a refined recipe for a simple-to-make cookie so we could get our chocolate fix any time. True chocoholics, we first worked to ramp up the cookies' fudgy character by using both cocoa powder and bittersweet chocolate. We grated the bar chocolate to give the cookies a velvety melt-in-the-mouth quality. Recipes for chewies usually include upwards of 3 cups of confectioners' sugar to bring the largely flourless cookies together. With the right combination of structure-building egg whites, cocoa, and a scant amount of flour, we were able to use just 2¼ cups of sugar; less sweetness allowed the fruity notes of the chocolate to come through more readily. A simple addition to the recipe—a little salt—also heightened the chocolate notes. Stirring in 2 cups of toasted, chopped pecans gave the soft, chewy cookies some heft and substance and introduced a welcome crunch.

1 Adjust oven rack to middle position and heat oven to 325 degrees. Line 2 baking sheets with parchment paper.

2 Whisk confectioners' sugar, cocoa, flour, and salt together in bowl of stand mixer fitted with paddle. With mixer running on medium speed, add egg whites to sugar mixture, one at a time. Add vanilla and beat for 3 minutes on high speed, scraping down sides of bowl as needed. Stir in pecans and chocolate. Drop 1-tablespoon portions of batter onto prepared sheets, spacing them 1 inch apart.

3 Bake cookies, 1 sheet at a time, until dry at edges but soft in centers, 15 to 18 minutes, rotating sheet halfway through baking. Slide cookies, still on parchment, onto wire rack. Repeat with remaining batter. Let cookies cool completely before peeling from parchment and serving.

LEMON SOUR CREAM COOKIES

Makes about 42 cookies

3 cups (15 ounces) all-purpose flour

1 teaspoon baking powder

½ teaspoon baking soda

½ teaspoon salt

16 tablespoons unsalted butter, softened

1½ cups (10½ ounces) granulated sugar

2 large eggs

1 cup sour cream

2 teaspoons grated lemon zest plus ¼ cup juice (2 lemons)

1 ounce cream cheese, softened

3 cups (12 ounces) confectioners' sugar

Why This Recipe Works We're all for the crispy edges, chewy middles, and buttery caramelized flavor of a chocolate chip cookie, but sometimes we get a hankering for a cookie that's more plush and tender. We loved the idea of a soft-baked lemon cookie that we could top with a tangy glaze. With their fluffy-yet-sturdy texture and a crumb that is simultaneously moist and light and airy, these cookies more than fit the bill. To achieve this unique texture, we reached for sour cream, and plenty of it; a full cup contributed moisture and richness, tenderized the cookies' crumb, and, in conjunction with the lemon juice in this recipe, reacted with the leavener to create fluffy lift. This generous amount of sour cream also added a pleasant tang, which we reinforced with a couple teaspoons of floral lemon zest. Creaming the butter and sugar and adding two whole eggs to the recipe also helped aerate the dough. While the cookies themselves were sufficiently tangy, they were a bit plain, so we turned to the topping. A lemon–cream cheese glaze was a nice finishing touch that delivered a second hit of clean citrusy flavor.

1 Whisk flour, baking powder, baking soda, and salt together in large bowl. Using stand mixer fitted with paddle, beat butter and granulated sugar on medium-high speed until pale and fluffy, about 3 minutes. Add eggs, one at a time, and beat until incorporated, about 30 seconds. Reduce speed to low, add sour cream and lemon zest, and beat until just combined. Add flour mixture until incorporated, about 30 seconds. Cover bowl tightly with plastic wrap and refrigerate for 1 hour.

2 Adjust oven racks to upper-middle and lower-middle positions and heat oven to 375 degrees. Line 2 baking sheets with parchment paper.

3 Drop heaping 1-tablespoon mounds of dough onto prepared sheets, spacing them about 2 inches apart. Bake until just golden around edges, about 15 minutes, switching and rotating sheets halfway through baking. Repeat with remaining dough. Let cookies cool completely on sheets.

4 Whisk lemon juice and cream cheese in bowl until combined. Add confectioners' sugar and whisk until smooth. Spread 1 teaspoon glaze onto each cooled cookie before serving.

COFFEE TOFFEE COOKIES

Makes 24 cookies

2 cups (10 ounces) all-purpose flour

¾ teaspoon baking soda

½ teaspoon salt

2 tablespoons instant espresso powder

1 tablespoon hot water

10 tablespoons unsalted butter, melted

1¼ cups (8¾ ounces) sugar

2 large eggs

1 teaspoon vanilla extract

¾ cup toffee bits

Why This Recipe Works Some of the best desserts feature coffee—think coffee ice cream and tiramisù. Coffee is also frequently paired with chocolate for a mocha flavor, but we've never seen it take a starring role in a cookie recipe. We wanted the coffee flavor in our cookies to be front and center, so we started with the strong stuff: espresso. Instant espresso powder gave our cookies a double shot of coffee flavor without adding excess moisture; we found that a full 2 tablespoons of espresso powder were necessary to satisfy our java craving. Only 1 tablespoon of hot water was needed to dissolve the espresso before whisking it into the melted butter (since espresso is water-soluble, it wouldn't effectively dissolve in just the warm butter). Surprisingly, coffee-flavored liqueur added neither flavor nor complexity to our cookies, but vanilla extract helped balance and soften the espresso's potent kick. The addition of toffee bits contributed buttery, caramel notes and a welcome texture to our cookies without overshadowing the coffee flavor. You can substitute espresso granules for the espresso powder; however, they might not dissolve as readily in the water. These cookies taste great at room temperature, but they're best when served still warm from the oven.

1 Adjust oven racks to upper-middle and lower-middle positions and heat oven to 350 degrees. Line 2 baking sheets with parchment paper. Whisk flour, baking soda, and salt together in bowl.

2 Whisk espresso powder and water in large bowl until espresso dissolves, then whisk in melted butter and sugar until incorporated. Whisk in eggs and vanilla until smooth. Using rubber spatula, gently stir in flour mixture until soft dough forms; fold in toffee bits.

3 Working with 2 tablespoons dough at a time, roll into balls and space them 2 inches apart on prepared sheets. Bake until edges are set but centers are still soft and puffy, about 16 minutes, switching and rotating sheets halfway through baking. Let cookies cool on sheets for 10 minutes. Serve warm or transfer to wire rack and let cool completely before serving.

Instant Espresso Powder

There's your average joe, and then there's freshly brewed espresso. The same gulf separates regular instant coffee from instant espresso, whose more concentrated flavor adds dimension and depth to our coffee toffee cookies. We tried three nationally available products in a test kitchen recipe for brownies to see if any product delivered a better flavor boost. Each powder performed comparably to produce brownies that tasted deeper, richer, and more complex without imparting an overt coffee taste, so there was no overall winner. That said, all three products made a below-average hot beverage, so our advice is to save the powder for baking recipes and take the time to brew real espresso for your demitasse.

POTATO CHIP COOKIES

Makes 24 cookies

¾ cup (3¾ ounces) all-purpose flour

1½ ounces reduced-fat potato chips, crushed fine (½ cup)

¼ cup pecans, toasted and chopped fine

¼ teaspoon salt

8 tablespoons unsalted butter, cut into 8 pieces, softened but still cool

¼ cup (1¾ ounces) granulated sugar

¼ cup (1 ounce) confectioners' sugar

1 large egg yolk

½ teaspoon vanilla extract

Why This Recipe Works Potato chip cookies are one in a long line of recipes invented by manufacturers to push their products on consumers—and, in this case, we're totally fine with that. These cookies bring together sugar, salt, and crunch for an addictive combination of flavors and textures. For the cookie base itself, we wanted something multitextured, with the right balance of shortness and chew. Using half granulated sugar and half confectioners' sugar gave us a cookie that was tender without being too delicate. Tasters preferred potato chip crumbs to the shards found in many recipes—all of the crunch without the sharp edges. During our testing, we thought the cookies tasted slightly of frying oil, and they were sporting edges that darkened too deeply. We had been making our recipe with the test kitchen's favorite potato chip: Lay's Kettle Cooked Original Potato Chips. To see if a different chip would produce a better cookie, we tried our recipe with baked, reduced-fat, fried, and kettle-fried chips. Batches made with reduced-fat chips were best; the hint of oil vanished, as did the overly dark edges that were forming as a result of too much fat. We liked the common addition of chopped pecans; they added a nutty crunch without obscuring the salty-sugary contrast. Cape Cod 40% Reduced Fat Potato Chips are the test kitchen favorite among reduced-fat chips.

1 Adjust oven rack to middle position and heat oven to 350 degrees. Line 2 baking sheets with parchment paper. Combine flour, potato chips, pecans, and salt in bowl.

2 Using stand mixer fitted with paddle, beat butter, granulated sugar, and confectioners' sugar on medium-high speed until pale and fluffy, about 3 minutes. Add egg yolk and vanilla and beat until combined. Reduce speed to low and slowly add flour mixture in 3 additions. Roll dough into 1-inch balls and space them 3 inches apart on prepared sheets. Using a floured dry measuring cup, press each ball to ¼-inch thickness.

3 Bake cookies, 1 sheet at a time, until just set and lightly browned on bottom, 10 to 13 minutes, rotating sheet halfway through baking. Let cookies cool completely on sheet, about 15 minutes, before serving.

Chocolate-Dipped Potato Chip Cookies

Microwave 10 ounces finely chopped bittersweet chocolate in bowl at 50 percent power, stirring occasionally, until melted, 2 to 4 minutes. Carefully dip half of each cooled cookie in chocolate, scraping off excess with finger, and place on parchment paper–lined baking sheet. Sprinkle flake sea salt over warm chocolate and refrigerate until chocolate sets, about 15 minutes. Serve.

SALTED PEANUT BUTTER–PRETZEL–CHOCOLATE CHIP COOKIES

Makes 24 cookies

1¼ cups (6¼ ounces) all-purpose flour

1 cup (3 ounces) quick oats

1 teaspoon baking soda

¼ teaspoon salt

12 tablespoons unsalted butter, softened

1¼ cups packed (8¾ ounces) light brown sugar

⅔ cup crunchy peanut butter

1 large egg

1 teaspoon vanilla extract

1 cup (6 ounces) bittersweet chocolate chips

1½ ounces pretzel sticks, coarsely crushed (⅔ cup)

Flake sea salt

Why This Recipe Works It's impossible to pick a favorite cookie—and with so many different styles, it's hard to even compare them. But the flavors and textures in this particular cookie might make it one of the very best. Peanut butter and pretzels are an irresistible salty snack combination. Add chocolate for compelling sweetness and richness and hearty oats for nuttiness and heft, and you have a cookie bursting at the seams with goodness. We made a simple peanut butter oatmeal cookie and sweetened it with brown sugar, which complemented the nutty peanut butter and oats. A generous amount of chocolate chips and coarsely crushed pretzel sticks gave the cookies great flavor and crunch without obscuring the peanut butter–oat base. As a finishing touch, we sprinkled the cookies with sea salt to hint at the flavors inside. We sprinkled the cookies with the salt after they came out of the oven so the salt flakes would remain crunchy, distinct, and glistening—a perfect finishing touch for this irresistible treat.

1 Combine flour, oats, baking soda, and salt in bowl. Using stand mixer fitted with paddle, beat butter and sugar on medium speed until smooth, about 1 minute. Add peanut butter, egg, and vanilla and mix until fully incorporated, about 30 seconds, scraping down bowl as needed. Reduce speed to low and slowly add flour mixture until just combined. Add chocolate chips and pretzels and mix until just incorporated. Cover bowl tightly with plastic wrap and refrigerate until dough is firm, about 1 hour.

2 Adjust oven racks to upper-middle and lower-middle positions and heat oven to 350 degrees. Line 2 baking sheets with parchment paper. Working with 2 tablespoons dough at a time, roll into balls and space them evenly on prepared sheets, 12 per sheet. Using bottom of greased dry measuring cup, press each ball to ¾-inch thickness.

3 Bake cookies until puffed and cracks just form on top, 11 to 13 minutes, switching and rotating sheets halfway through baking. Let cookies cool on sheets for 5 minutes. Sprinkle cookies with sea salt, then transfer to wire rack. Let cookies cool completely before serving.

SLICE & BAKE SWEETS

2

VANILLA ICEBOX COOKIES

Makes about 40 cookies

⅓ cup (2⅓ ounces) granulated sugar

2 tablespoons packed light brown sugar

½ teaspoon salt

12 tablespoons unsalted butter,
cut into pieces and softened

1 large egg yolk

2 teaspoons vanilla extract

1½ cups (7½ ounces) all-purpose flour

Why This Recipe Works Having slice-and-bake (or icebox) cookie dough in the refrigerator or freezer, ready to bake, is the ultimate sweet convenience. Essentially shortbread shaped into a log, these simple cookies have so few ingredients (just butter, sugar, salt, egg, vanilla, and flour) that imperfections are impossible to hide. With too much flour, the cookies are crisp but dry and bland; go overboard with the butter, sugar, or egg, and the cookies are rich but soft and misshapen. We set out to create a recipe for icebox cookies that would have both a crisp texture and rich buttery, vanilla flavor. First, we added as much butter as we could without the cookies losing their crisp edge; 12 tablespoons was as high as we could go. Most recipes use a whole egg, but we found that using only the yolk made the cookies firmer. We doubled the vanilla extract, but the flavor still lacked depth; replacing some of the granulated sugar with light brown sugar gave the cookies complexity. The cookies tasted great, but the texture wasn't quite right. We had been using the traditional creaming method, a process of beating the butter and sugar to incorporate air—not ideal when the goal is a dense shortbread texture. A better option was the food processor, which combined the ingredients in seconds without whipping in much air.

1 Process granulated sugar, brown sugar, and salt in food processor until no lumps of brown sugar remain, about 30 seconds. Add butter, egg yolk, and vanilla and process until smooth and creamy, about 20 seconds. Scrape down bowl, add flour, and pulse until cohesive dough forms, about 20 pulses.

2 Transfer dough to lightly floured counter and roll into 10-inch log. Wrap log tightly in plastic wrap and refrigerate until firm, at least 2 hours or up to 3 days.

3 Adjust oven racks to upper-middle and lower-middle positions and heat oven to 350 degrees. Line 2 baking sheets with parchment paper.

4 Slice chilled dough into ¼-inch-thick rounds and space them 1 inch apart on prepared baking sheets. Bake until edges are just golden, about 15 minutes, switching and rotating sheets halfway through baking. Let cookies cool on sheets for 10 minutes, then transfer to wire rack. Repeat with remaining dough. Let cookies cool completely before serving.

Brown Sugar–Walnut Icebox Cookies

Increase brown sugar to ¼ cup. Add 1 cup walnuts to food processor with sugars and salt in step 1 and process until walnuts are finely ground, about 1 minute.

Coconut–Lime Icebox Cookies

Add 2 cups sweetened shredded coconut and 2 teaspoons grated lime zest to food processor with sugars and salt in step 1.

Orange–Poppy Seed Icebox Cookies

Add ¼ cup poppy seeds and 1 tablespoon grated orange zest to food processor with sugars and salt in step 1.

CHECKERBOARD ICEBOX COOKIES

Makes about 36 cookies

16 tablespoons unsalted butter, softened

¾ cup (5¼ ounces) granulated sugar

½ cup (2 ounces) confectioners' sugar

½ teaspoon salt

2 large egg yolks

2 teaspoons vanilla extract

2¼ cups (11¼ ounces) all-purpose flour

1 ounce semisweet chocolate, melted

2 tablespoons Dutch-processed cocoa powder

Why This Recipe Works Like swirled soft-serve ice cream, this cookie is a gift to the indecisive, offering the best of two worlds: chocolate and vanilla. We puzzle together logs of chocolate and vanilla dough to form an attractive checkerboard shape that's as fun to make as it is to eat. To save ourselves the work of making two separate cookie doughs, we mixed up an easy basic vanilla dough, divided it in half, and then incorporated melted semisweet chocolate and cocoa powder into one portion. A combination of granulated and confectioners' sugars allowed the dough to hold its striking geometric pattern during baking, and created a cookie that was tender with just enough snap. These cookies may look intricate, but we found forming was a breeze. We molded our two easy-to-handle doughs into rectangles, then stacked the two rectangles and chilled the dough. Once firm, we cut the log in half lengthwise, rotated one half, and fused the logs back together to create the checkerboard pattern before slicing into squares. These cookies don't spread much, so we were able to space them closely together and bake them all at once.

1 Using stand mixer fitted with paddle, beat butter, granulated sugar, confectioners' sugar, and salt on medium-high speed until pale and fluffy, about 3 minutes. Add egg yolks and vanilla and beat until combined. Reduce speed to low, slowly add flour, and mix until combined. Set aside half of dough; add chocolate and cocoa to remaining dough in mixer bowl and mix on low until fully combined.

2 Transfer dough to counter and form each piece into 9 by 2-inch rectangle, about 1 inch thick. Stack rectangles to create 2-inch-square log. Wrap log tightly in plastic wrap and refrigerate for at least 2 hours or up to 3 days.

3 Adjust oven racks to upper-middle and lower-middle positions and heat oven to 325 degrees. Line 2 baking sheets with parchment paper.

4 Slice chilled dough in half lengthwise, rotating 1 half to create checkerboard pattern, then press gently to re-adhere halves. Slice dough into ¼-inch-thick squares and space them ¾ inch apart on prepared sheets. Bake until edges are light golden brown, 12 to 15 minutes, switching and rotating sheets halfway through baking. Let cookies cool on sheets for 5 minutes, then transfer to wire rack. Let cookies cool completely before serving.

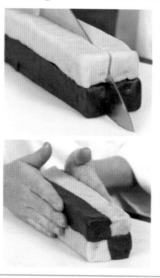

Creating Checkerboard Pattern

1 After refrigerating stacked dough log until it's firm, cut log in half lengthwise.

2 Rotate one of cut pieces to form checkerboard pattern, pressing pieces together gently so they adhere to each other.

PECAN SANDIES
Makes 32 cookies

2 cups pecans, toasted

½ cup packed (3½ ounces) light brown sugar

¼ cup (1 ounce) confectioners' sugar

1½ cups (7½ ounces) all-purpose flour

¼ teaspoon salt

12 tablespoons unsalted butter, cut into ½-inch pieces and chilled

1 large egg yolk

Why This Recipe Works Homemade versions of pecan sandies can run the gamut from greasy and bland to dry and crumbly. Here's what they should be: buttery shortbread cookies with a tender but crisp texture, a sandy melt-in-the-mouth character, and loads of nutty pecan flavor. Because it's in the name, nailing the sandy texture was key. Some recipes try to achieve that sandiness by substituting vegetable oil for butter; while oil did help limit the amount of air that formed in the cookie dough, the flavor was abysmal and the cookies were greasy, so we decided to stick with butter. For nice praline flavor—another hallmark of this cookie—we started by using all light brown sugar in our dough (dark brown sugar overpowered the buttery pecans), but the cookies were a bit tough. Swapping out a portion of the brown sugar for confectioners' sugar solved this problem, resulting in a more tender crumb. Toasting the pecans and then grinding them into a flour ensured rich nutty flavor in every bite. As a finishing touch, we placed a single pecan half in the center of each cookie to provide a visual hint of the flavor within.

1 Reserve 32 unbroken pecan halves for garnish. Process brown sugar, confectioners' sugar, and remaining pecans in food processor until pecans are finely ground, about 20 seconds. Add flour and salt and process until combined, about 10 seconds.

2 Scatter butter over top and process until mixture resembles damp sand and rides up sides of bowl, about 20 seconds. With processor running, add egg yolk and process until dough forms rough ball, about 20 seconds.

3 Transfer dough to counter, knead briefly, and divide in half. Roll each piece of dough into 6-inch log. Wrap logs tightly in plastic wrap and refrigerate until firm, at least 2 hours or up to 3 days.

4 Adjust oven racks to upper-middle and lower-middle positions and heat oven to 325 degrees. Line 2 baking sheets with parchment paper.

5 Working with 1 dough log at a time, slice chilled dough into ⅜-inch-thick rounds and space them 1 inch apart on prepared sheets. Gently press pecan half in center of each cookie.

6 Bake cookies until edges are golden brown, 20 to 25 minutes, switching and rotating sheets halfway through baking. Let cookies cool on sheets for 3 minutes, then transfer to wire rack. Let cookies cool completely before serving.

Almond Sandies
Substitute 2 cups whole blanched almonds, toasted, for pecans. Add ¼ teaspoon almond extract to dough with egg yolk.

SABLÉS

Makes about 40 cookies

1 large egg

10 tablespoons unsalted butter, softened

⅓ cup plus 1 tablespoon (2¾ ounces) granulated sugar

¼ teaspoon salt

1 teaspoon vanilla extract

1½ cups (7½ ounces) all-purpose flour

1 large egg white, lightly beaten with 1 teaspoon water

4 teaspoons turbinado sugar

Why This Recipe Works French butter cookies known as *sablés* offer an upgrade to the sturdy American butter cookie in sophistication and style—that is, if you can capture their elusive sandy texture (*sablé* is French for "sandy"). The moisture content of a cookie plays a big role in determining sandiness, or rather, lack thereof; liquid in the dough dissolves sugar crystals, and it's those sugar crystals that help create the perception of sandiness. Starting with a basic dough recipe using the creaming method to combine the butter and sugar (for more information on creaming, see page 3), we took incremental steps to decrease the liquid. Cutting back on butter (which is roughly 20 percent water) helped, but that still didn't give us the texture we sought. Another ingredient that has a lot of water? Egg whites. Switching from a whole egg to just the rich yolk was a giant step in the right direction, but we wanted to push our efforts even further to produce supremely sandy, crystalline sablés. When we came across recipes that called for a hard-cooked egg yolk, we had initially dismissed it. Our skepticism gave way to intrigue, however, so we hard-boiled an egg and added the mashed yolk during the creaming process. *Voilà!* This unusual step really was the key to eliminating that last bit of moisture and perfecting the texture of our cookies. For a final flourish, we brushed the dough rounds with a beaten egg white and sprinkled them with coarse turbinado sugar before baking.

1 Place egg in small saucepan, cover with water by 1 inch, and bring to boil over high heat. Remove pan from heat, cover, and let sit for 10 minutes. Meanwhile, fill small bowl with ice water. Using slotted spoon, transfer egg to ice water and let stand for 5 minutes. Crack egg and peel shell. Separate yolk from white; discard white. Press yolk through fine-mesh strainer into small bowl.

2 Using stand mixer fitted with paddle, beat butter, granulated sugar, salt, and cooked egg yolk on medium speed until pale and fluffy, about 4 minutes, scraping down bowl as needed. Reduce speed to low, add vanilla, and mix until incorporated. Stop mixer; add flour and mix on low speed until just combined, about 30 seconds. Using rubber spatula, press dough into cohesive mass.

3 Transfer dough to counter and divide in half. Roll each piece of dough into 6-inch log. Wrap logs tightly in plastic wrap and twist ends tightly to seal and chill until firm, about 2 hours in refrigerator or 45 minutes in freezer.

4 Adjust oven racks to upper-middle and lower-middle positions and heat oven to 350 degrees. Line 2 baking sheets with parchment paper.

5 Working with 1 dough log at a time, slice chilled dough into ¼-inch-thick rounds and space them 1 inch apart on prepared sheets. Using pastry brush, gently brush cookies with egg white mixture and sprinkle evenly with turbinado sugar.

6 Bake cookies until centers are pale golden brown and edges are slightly darker than centers, about 15 minutes, switching and rotating sheets halfway through baking. Let cookies cool on sheets for 5 minutes, then transfer to wire rack and let cool completely before serving.

Continued

Almond Sablés

Substitute 1½ teaspoons almond extract for vanilla. Add
⅓ cup finely ground almonds to dough with flour in step 2.
After brushing cookies with egg white mixture, press
3 almond slices in petal shape in center of each cookie
instead of sprinkling with turbinado sugar.

Chocolate Sablés

Reduce flour to 1⅓ cups and add ¼ cup Dutch-processed
cocoa with flour in step 2.

Black and White Spiral Cookies
Makes about 80 cookies

Make 1 batch Sablés cookie dough and 1 batch Chocolate
Sablés cookie dough (through step 2). Divide each dough in
half and roll each portion into 8 by 6-inch rectangle on parchment paper. Chill doughs briefly until easy to handle. Stack
1 rectangle plain dough on top of 1 rectangle chocolate dough
and roll into 9 by 6-inch rectangle. Starting at long end, roll
dough into tight pinwheel log. Repeat with remaining doughs.
Wrap logs in plastic and chill as directed before slicing
and baking.

Forming Black and White Spiral Cookies

1 Divide each batch of plain and chocolate dough in half.

2 Roll each dough portion into 8 by 6-inch rectangle on parchment paper. Chill doughs briefly until easy to handle.

3 Stack 1 rectangle plain dough on top of 1 rectangle chocolate dough.

4 Roll dough stack into 9 by 6-inch rectangle.

5 Starting at long end, roll dough into tight pinwheel log. Repeat with remaining doughs.

6 Wrap logs in plastic and chill. Slice dough logs.

Chocolate Sandwich Cookies

Slice cookies ⅛ inch thick in step 5, omit egg white mixture and turbinado sugar, and reduce baking time to 10 to 13 minutes. When all cookies are baked and cooled, microwave 3½ ounces chopped dark or milk chocolate at 50 percent power for 1 to 2 minutes; let cool slightly. Spread melted chocolate evenly over half of cookies, then top with second cookie. Let chocolate set before serving.

Lemon Sablés

Add 4 teaspoons grated lemon zest with vanilla in step 2. Omit egg white mixture and turbinado sugar. Dust cooled cookies with confectioners' sugar.

Toasted Coconut Sablés

Be sure to use untoasted coconut when sprinkling the cookies before baking.

Add ⅓ cup finely chopped toasted sweetened coconut to dough with flour in step 2. Omit turbinado sugar. After brushing cookies with egg white mixture, sprinkle with ⅓ cup finely chopped sweetened shredded coconut.

Vanilla Pretzel Cookies

Increase vanilla extract to 1 tablespoon and reduce refrigerator chilling time in step 3 to 30 minutes (dough will not be completely firm). Slice dough into ¼-inch-thick rounds and roll into balls. Roll each ball into 6-inch rope, tapering ends. Form ropes into pretzel shapes. Brush cookies with egg, sprinkle with turbinado sugar, and bake as directed.

Forming Pretzel Sablés

1 Slice slightly chilled dough into ¼-inch-thick rounds and roll into balls.

2 Roll each ball into 6-inch rope, tapering ends.

3 Pick up 1 end of rope and cross it over to form half of pretzel shape.

4 Bring second end over to complete pretzel shape.

ALL ABOUT SLICE-AND-BAKE COOKIES

Slice-and-bake cookies are often called icebox cookies. That's because they're typically rolled into logs and then conveniently stored in the refrigerator, or icebox, until you're ready to cut them into cookies and bake them. Whether the logs are round or squared off, we follow the same methods for most of our slice-and-bake sweets to ensure evenly baked, attractive-looking cookies.

1 Divide and Roll After mixing, transfer the dough to the counter and roll it into a log—the length will be specified in the recipe. (Some recipes may call for dividing the dough into pieces first.)

2 Twist and Chill Wrap the log of dough tightly in plastic wrap and twist the ends to help the dough hold its shape. Try to square off the ends as much as possible. Refrigerate the wrapped dough log until it's firm.

3 Slice the Dough Cut the chilled dough into slices as specified in the recipe. Cutting cookies of uniform thickness ensures they bake evenly.

4 Arrange and Bake Space the cookies evenly on a parchment paper–lined baking sheet. Icebox cookies don't spread very much, so you can fit more on the baking sheet than you would for drop cookies.

To help dough logs keep their shape in the refrigerator, you can place each wrapped log in a paper towel tube that's been cut open to form a large semicircle. This keeps the dough from flattening out on the refrigerator shelf. And when you cut the log, rotate the dough a quarter turn after each slice so that it won't become misshapen from the weight of the knife. If the dough seems sticky, transfer it back to the refrigerator to chill. This too will prevent misshapen cookies.

Most wrapped logs of dough can be refrigerated for up to 3 days. But you can also freeze the logs for up to 1 month. Simply wrap them in an additional layer of aluminum foil. Slice and bake frozen cookies as directed, increasing the time if needed.

CUTTING FROZEN DOUGH

Sometimes the knife can drag when slicing through logs of frozen cookie dough, making sloppy cuts. To prevent this, dip the blade of the knife in flour after every couple of cuts.

GUSSYING UP COOKIES

To add more flavor, texture, and visual appeal to slice-and-bake cookies, simply roll the chilled dough log in sprinkles, sugar, or finely chopped toasted nuts. You'll need about ½ cup of garnish for a 6-inch log. This works particularly well with Vanilla Icebox Cookies (page 75) and Sablés (page 80).

BAKING IN BATCHES

Because they're rolled into logs and sliced thin, slice-and-bake cookies often yield a lot of cookies. When a recipe calls for baking in batches, assuming you own only 2 rimmed baking sheets, be sure to always let the sheets cool before repeating. Baking cookies on warm sheets will cause them to spread too much during baking. Also, in most cases, it's best to line the sheets with new parchment paper to prevent sticking and excess grease.

A CHEF'S KNIFE THAT MAKES THE CUT

When you think of cookie baking, a sharp-blade chef's knife might not be the first tool to come to mind. But this kitchen essential isn't just for savory cooking. Chopping nuts and chocolate, breaking cookies into pieces, and, for slice-and-bake cookies, cleanly cutting dough logs into even-size coins. The best knife for this or any job: the inexpensive, Victorinox 8" Swiss Army Fibrox Pro Chef's Knife ($39.95) has been a test kitchen favorite for more than 20 years. We find that it maintains its edge long after its competitors have gone dull. The Victorinox effortlessly butchers chickens, dices onions, minces herbs, hacks through tough winter squash—and slices through cookie dough. Its textured grip feels secure for a wide range of hand sizes and is comfortable for a variety of different grips. You'll use it for everything.

WRAP IT UP

Plastic wrap is a slice-and-bake cookie essential. The logs of dough need to chill fully before you can slice through them neatly. Rolling them tightly in plastic helps them keep their shape and protects them from odors in the fridge. As it turns out, not all rolls of plastic are created equal; in fact, we could only recommend one that we tried: **Glad Cling Wrap Clear Plastic** ($1.20 per 100 square feet). This wrap is practically impermeable. Its box features well-placed, sharp teeth that easily tore the plastic, and "Glad Grab" (a 1-inch adhesive pad to hold the cut end of the wrap). One thing to note. This plastic is made from low-density polyethylene (LDPE), while there are others in our lineup that are made with food-safe PVC. The main difference? PVC clings but is not impermeable; LDPE is impermeable but has far less cling. Clingy PVC wraps are preferable if you are trans-porting food or are worried about spills and leaks, but to keep foods fresh longer—the more important property when making icebox cookies—select plastic wraps made from LDPE and reach for a box of our winner.

WASHBOARDS

Makes 36 cookies

2 cups (10 ounces) all-purpose flour

½ teaspoon baking powder

¼ teaspoon baking soda

¼ teaspoon salt

¼ teaspoon ground nutmeg

8 tablespoons unsalted butter, softened

1 cup packed (7 ounces) light brown sugar

1 large egg, room temperature

2 tablespoons milk

1 cup (3 ounces) sweetened shredded coconut

Why This Recipe Works We love the old-fashioned laundry washboard shape of these classic coconutty tea cookies. A good version is crisp, rich with coconut, and only mildly sweet—perfect as an afternoon snack to accompany a warm beverage. Most recipes call simply for granulated sugar, but we found that light brown sugar gave the cookies a rich, toasted depth that enhanced the coconut flavor. One cup of sweetened coconut was the perfect amount to give the cookies prominent coconut flavor while still allowing their buttery richness to shine through. To keep the cookies' texture light and crisp, we added just one egg, which was enough to hold the dough together without making it soft and cakey. These cookies may look artfully shaped, but forming them was just as easy as any other slice-and-bake cookie: We shaped the dough into a rectangular log, chilled it, and sliced the chilled log into thin cookies. To finish the cookies with their signature ridged top, we used a good, old-fashioned tool: a fork.

1 Whisk flour, baking powder, baking soda, salt, and nutmeg together in bowl. Using stand mixer fitted with paddle, beat butter and sugar on medium-high speed until pale and fluffy, about 2 minutes. Add egg and milk and beat until well combined. Reduce speed to low, add flour mixture and coconut, and mix until just incorporated.

2 Transfer dough to counter and, using your floured hands, roll dough into 15-inch log, then flatten top and sides to measure 3 inches by 1 inch. Wrap log tightly in plastic wrap and refrigerate until firm, at least 45 minutes or up to 3 days.

3 Adjust oven racks to upper-middle and lower-middle positions and heat oven to 350 degrees. Line 2 baking sheets with parchment paper.

4 Slice chilled dough into ¼-inch-thick rectangles and space them 1 inch apart on prepared sheets. Using floured fork, make crosswise indentations in dough slices. Bake until toasty brown, 15 to 18 minutes, switching and rotating sheets halfway through baking. Let cookies cool on sheets for 10 minutes, then transfer to wire rack. Let cookies cool completely before serving.

Shaping Washboards

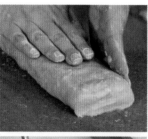

1 After shaping dough into 15-inch log, flatten its top and sides so that it measures 1 inch tall and 3 inches wide.

2 Arrange ¼-inch-thick rectangles 1 inch apart on parchment-lined baking sheets, then use floured tines of fork to gently press crosswise indentations into dough slices.

BUTTERSCOTCH COOKIES

Makes about 32 cookies

½ cup (3 ounces) butterscotch chips

3 tablespoons unsalted butter, plus 9 tablespoons cut into 9 pieces and chilled

2 teaspoons vanilla extract

¾ cup packed (5¼ ounces) dark brown sugar

½ teaspoon salt

1 large egg yolk

1¾ cups (8¾ ounces) all-purpose flour

1 teaspoon baking powder

Why This Recipe Works Few flavors are as recognizable as butterscotch. While it doesn't have the star power of chocolate and isn't as ubiquitous as vanilla, sweet, salty, complex butterscotch is a classic. Butterscotch is made by cooking brown sugar and butter together, but simply increasing the amounts of those ingredients in our icebox cookie dough wasn't enough to create a convincing butterscotch cookie. Exchanging light brown sugar for dark helped amplify the butterscotch notes, but only slightly. Although it felt a bit like cheating, we came to the conclusion that butterscotch chips have come to define the flavor for us, and adding ½ cup of them to the dough gave our recipe plenty of butterscotch punch. However, when we simply stirred the chips into the dough, the cookies were impossible to slice neatly. Instead, we melted the chips and creamed them with the butter and sugar. While most recipes that use the creaming method to combine butter and sugar call for softened butter, we started with chilled butter here so it didn't melt into a greasy mess when we added the melted butterscotch chips. Incorporating the chips this way made our cookies smooth and sliceable and provided bold butterscotch flavor throughout. Take that, chocolate.

1 Microwave butterscotch chips and 3 tablespoons butter in bowl at 50 percent power until melted, about 1 minute, stirring halfway through microwaving. Whisk in vanilla until mixture is smooth; let cool for 10 minutes.

2 Using stand mixer fitted with paddle, beat chilled butter, sugar, and salt on medium-high speed until pale and fluffy, about 3 minutes. Add cooled butterscotch mixture and beat until thoroughly combined, about 1 minute. Add egg yolk and beat until incorporated, about 30 seconds. Reduce speed to low, add flour and baking powder, and mix until dough forms, about 1 minute. Transfer dough to counter and roll into 9-inch log. Wrap log tightly in plastic wrap and refrigerate until firm, at least 2 hours or up to 3 days.

3 Adjust oven racks to upper-middle and lower-middle positions and heat oven to 325 degrees. Line 2 baking sheets with parchment paper.

4 Slice chilled dough into ¼-inch-thick rounds and space them 1 inch apart on prepared sheets. Bake until edges have darkened slightly, about 15 minutes, switching and rotating sheets halfway through baking. Let cookies cool on sheets for 10 minutes, then transfer to wire rack. Let cookies cool completely before serving.

CHERRY ICEBOX RIBBONS

Makes about 40 cookies

⅓ cup (2⅓ ounces) granulated sugar

2 tablespoons packed light brown sugar

½ teaspoon salt

12 tablespoons unsalted butter,
cut into 12 pieces and softened

1 large egg yolk

1½ teaspoons vanilla extract

½ teaspoon almond extract

1½ cups (7½ ounces) all-purpose flour

⅔ cup dried tart cherries

6 tablespoons cherry jam or preserves

Why This Recipe Works Layered with vibrant ribbons of cherry jam, these buttery cookies have a striking appearance. But while their stripy aesthetic may look difficult to achieve, these are actually simple slice-and-bake cookies. We started by making a basic dough, which we enhanced with a touch of light brown sugar and vanilla and almond extracts, both of which complement cherry flavor. After rolling out the dough we stuck it in the freezer to firm up, then we cut it into strips, spread the filling over the top, and stacked the strips. After another brief stint in the freezer, the dough was ready to be sliced and baked. There was just one problem: The jam seeped out of the layers during baking. To maintain distinct layers, we briefly cooked the jam to thicken it—a process that also concentrated its flavor. This helped, but the cookies still weren't holding together neatly. We found we could eliminate seeping altogether by adding dried tart cherries to the jam before heating. The dried cherries plumped and thickened the mixture beautifully while also fortifying the tangy cherry flavor.

1 Process granulated sugar, brown sugar, and salt in food processor until no lumps of brown sugar remain, about 30 seconds. Add butter, egg yolk, vanilla, and almond extract and process until smooth and creamy, about 20 seconds, scraping down bowl as needed. Add flour and pulse until cohesive dough forms, about 20 pulses. Transfer dough to counter and pat into 5-inch square. Wrap square tightly in plastic wrap and refrigerate until firm, about 1 hour.

2 Heat cherries and jam in small saucepan over medium heat until just bubbling; let cool completely, about 30 minutes. Process cherry mixture in clean, dry food processor until smooth, about 15 seconds.

3 Roll dough between 2 pieces of parchment paper into 10-inch square, about ¼ inch thick. Freeze dough until firm, about 15 minutes. Cut chilled dough into four 2½-inch-wide strips. Spread cherry mixture evenly over 3 strips and stack strips, cherry mixture side up; place plain strip on top. Wrap dough tightly in plastic and freeze until firm, about 15 minutes.

4 Adjust oven racks to upper-middle and lower-middle positions and heat oven to 350 degrees. Line 2 baking sheets with parchment. Slice chilled dough into ¼-inch-thick rectangles and space them 1 inch apart on prepared sheets. Bake until edges are just golden, 13 to 15 minutes, switching and rotating sheets halfway through baking. Immediately and carefully transfer cookies to wire rack. Repeat with remaining dough. Let cookies cool completely before serving.

Assembling Icebox Ribbons

1 Roll dough into 10-inch square, freeze it, then cut it into four 2½-inch-wide strips. Spread cherry mixture evenly over three strips of dough. Stack strips, placing plain strip on top.

2 Wrap stack in plastic wrap and freeze until firm. Slice chilled cookies into ¼-inch-thick rectangles.

CHOCOLATE-TOFFEE BUTTER COOKIES

Makes about 60 cookies

2⅓ cups (11⅔ ounces) all-purpose flour

½ teaspoon baking powder

½ teaspoon salt

16 tablespoons unsalted butter, softened

1 cup packed (7 ounces) light brown sugar

1 large egg

1 teaspoon vanilla extract

1 cup (5 ounces) plain toffee bits

1½ cups (9 ounces) semisweet chocolate chips

1 tablespoon vegetable oil

⅔ cup pecans, toasted and chopped fine

Why This Recipe Works Sweet and complex like caramel, crunchy, and deeply buttery, toffee is both an irresistible candy and a great addition to a cookie recipe. Conveniently sold in bits, toffee can be mixed into cookie dough just like chocolate chips; once baked, it melts slightly yet still keeps its firm but yielding texture and contributes an appealing chewy crunch to the finished cookie. The addition of light brown sugar to a simple butter cookie base contributed caramel notes that enhanced the toffee's flavor. Toffee plays nicely with chocolate, so we decided to give these cookies some decorative flair by adorning them with melted chocolate and complementary buttery pecans. The options for decorating these cookies are endless; we particularly like dipping the cookies in the melted chocolate, but you could also simply drizzle the chocolate on top for sophistication and ease. Or, fill a zipper-lock bag with the melted chocolate, snip off a small corner, and pipe a chocolaty design on top. Use your imagination!

1 Whisk flour, baking powder, and salt together in bowl. Using stand mixer fitted with paddle, beat butter and sugar on medium speed until pale and fluffy, 3 to 6 minutes. Add egg and vanilla and beat until combined, about 30 seconds, scraping down bowl as needed. Reduce speed to low and slowly add flour mixture until combined, about 30 seconds. Mix in toffee bits until just incorporated. Cover bowl with plastic wrap and refrigerate until dough is no longer sticky, 10 to 15 minutes.

2 Transfer dough to counter and shape into rectangular log about 15 inches long and 3 inches wide. Wrap log tightly in plastic and refrigerate until firm, at least 2 hours or up to 3 days.

3 Adjust oven racks to upper-middle and lower-middle positions and heat oven to 350 degrees. Line 2 baking sheets with parchment paper.

4 Slice chilled dough into ¼-inch-thick rectangles and space them 1 inch apart on prepared sheets. Bake until edges are browned, 12 to 16 minutes, switching and rotating sheets halfway through baking. Let cookies cool on sheets for 3 minutes, then transfer to wire rack. Repeat with remaining dough. Let cookies cool completely.

5 Microwave chocolate in bowl at 50 percent power, stirring occasionally, until melted, 2 to 3 minutes. Stir in oil until smooth. Dip part of each cookie into melted chocolate or drizzle chocolate over cookies with spoon. Sprinkle pecans over cookies and let chocolate set, about 1 hour, before serving.

CINNAMON SWIRL COOKIES

Makes about 48 cookies

2½ cups (12½ ounces) all-purpose flour

¾ cup (5⅔ ounces) superfine sugar

¼ teaspoon salt

16 tablespoons (2 sticks) unsalted butter, cut into ½-inch pieces and softened

2 tablespoons cream cheese, softened

2 teaspoons vanilla extract

3 tablespoons granulated sugar

½ teaspoon ground cinnamon

Why This Recipe Works For a cookie with cinnamon flavor from center to edge, we took an artful approach and spiraled a layer of cinnamon sugar into a butter cookie dough. After making a workable dough base—and chilling it to prevent sticking—we rolled it into a large rectangle. We then sprinkled the dough with our star ingredient, the cinnamon sugar, and sprayed the mixture lightly with water so it would adhere. We rolled up the dough into a log, jelly roll–style, and chilled it until it was firm enough to cut into cinnamon-spiraled rounds. You can replace the cinnamon sugar in this recipe with 2 tablespoons of colored sugar; or, for a flavorful variation, we also created a maple-pecan swirl cookie. To get the maple-pecan mixture to stick, we grind the nuts fine and mix the sticky maple syrup and pecans with an egg yolk to bind them together.

1 Using stand mixer fitted with paddle, mix flour, superfine sugar, and salt until combined. Add butter, 1 piece at a time, and mix until crumbly and slightly wet, 1 to 2 minutes. Add cream cheese and vanilla and mix until dough just begins to form large clumps, about 30 seconds. Knead dough in bowl by hand a few times until it forms large cohesive mass.

2 Transfer dough to counter and divide in half. Form each half into 5-inch square, wrap squares tightly in plastic wrap, and refrigerate until firm yet malleable, about 30 minutes. Meanwhile, whisk granulated sugar and cinnamon together in small bowl; set aside.

3 Working with 1 piece of dough at a time, roll between 2 large sheets of parchment paper to 12 by 7-inch rectangle. Remove top piece of parchment and sprinkle with half of cinnamon sugar, leaving ¼-inch border along edges. Spritz sugar lightly with water to dampen.

4 With short side facing you, roll dough into tight log, pat log to measure 7 inches, and smear seam with your fingers to seal. Wrap logs tightly in plastic wrap and refrigerate until firm, about 2 hours.

5 Adjust oven rack to middle position and heat oven to 375 degrees. Line 2 baking sheets with parchment paper. Trim and discard about ½ inch from both ends of logs. Slice chilled dough into ¼-inch-thick rounds and space them 1 inch apart on prepared sheets. Bake, 1 sheet at a time, until light golden brown, 12 to 15 minutes, rotating sheet halfway through baking. Let cookies cool on sheet for 3 minutes, then transfer to a wire rack. Let cookies cool completely before serving.

Maple-Pecan Swirl Cookies

Pulse ¾ cup toasted pecans in food processor until finely ground, about 10 pulses. Add 3 tablespoons maple syrup and 1 egg yolk and pulse to incorporate, about 4 pulses; substitute pecan mixture for cinnamon sugar; do not spritz filling with water.

Filling Cinnamon Swirl Cookies

1 Sprinkle dough rectangle with cinnamon sugar mixture, leaving ¼-inch border along edges.

2 Spray filling lightly with water and then, working from short side, roll dough into tight, round log and smear seam with your finger to seal.

DATE-FILLED ROLL-UPS

Makes about 32 cookies

Filling

1¾ cups walnuts or pecans, chopped fine

9 ounces pitted dates, chopped fine (1½ cups)

1 cup water

½ cup (3½ ounces) granulated sugar

Dough

3½ cups (17½ ounces) all-purpose flour

1 teaspoon baking soda

½ teaspoon salt

12 tablespoons unsalted butter, softened

1 cup packed (7 ounces) brown sugar

1 cup (7 ounces) granulated sugar

3 large eggs

1 teaspoon vanilla extract

Why This Recipe Works With flavor and a pleasant stickiness reminiscent of caramel, plump, moist dates are as sweet as candy—and we thought they would make a delicious filling for cookies. We cooked the dates with some water, a little sugar, and a generous amount of nuts for a filling that stayed put. We then paired our filling with a soft, cake-like cookie, spreading the filling over the dough and then rolling it up for a spiraled appearance. Using brown sugar in place of half of the white sugar in our dough contributed a subtle molasses note that perfectly underscored the caramel flavor of the dates. Plus, the brown sugar added moisture and softness to the dough. Three eggs gave our cookies the cakey crumb we were looking for. We used a sheet of parchment to help guide the soft dough as we rolled it into a log to prevent it from sticking or tearing. Plan ahead for these cookies: The dough needs time to fully chill twice. If the dough becomes soft when rolling or slicing the cookies, return it to the refrigerator until firm. Be sure to grease the parchment paper so these soft cookies don't stick.

1 For the filling Combine walnuts, dates, water, and sugar in small saucepan and bring to boil over medium heat. Cook, stirring frequently, until thickened, 3 to 5 minutes. Transfer to bowl and let cool completely, about 1 hour.

2 For the dough Whisk flour, baking soda, and salt together in bowl. Using stand mixer fitted with paddle, beat butter, brown sugar, and granulated sugar on medium-high speed until pale and fluffy, about 3 minutes. Add eggs, one at a time, and beat until combined. Add vanilla and beat until combined. Reduce speed to low, add flour mixture in 3 additions, and mix until just combined, scraping down bowl as needed. Transfer dough to counter and divide in half. Form each half into 6-inch square, wrap squares tightly in plastic wrap, and refrigerate for at least 1 hour or up to 2 days.

3 Roll 1 dough square into 13 by 9-inch rectangle on large sheet of floured parchment. Spread half of cooled filling evenly over dough. With long side facing you, use parchment to roll dough into log. Wrap log tightly with parchment and refrigerate until firm, about 2 hours. Repeat with remaining dough and filling.

4 Adjust oven racks to upper-middle and lower-middle positions and heat oven to 350 degrees. Line 2 baking sheets with parchment and grease parchment. Working with 1 log at a time, slice dough into ½-inch-thick rounds and space them 2 inches apart on prepared sheets. Bake until tops are golden brown, 18 to 22 minutes, switching and rotating sheets halfway through baking. Slide cookies, still on parchment, onto wire rack. Repeat with second dough log. Let cookies cool completely before serving.

Forming Date-Filled Roll-Ups

1 Roll 1 dough square into 13 by 9-inch rectangle on large sheet of floured parchment paper. Spread half of cooled filling evenly over dough.

2 With long side of dough facing you, use parchment to guide dough and roll it into log.

SPUMONI BARS

Makes 48 cookies

2 cups (10 ounces) all-purpose flour

¼ teaspoon baking powder

⅛ teaspoon salt

12 tablespoons unsalted butter, softened

⅔ cup (4⅔ ounces) sugar

3 large egg yolks

1 teaspoon vanilla extract

12 maraschino cherries, drained, stemmed, and chopped fine

¼ cup walnuts, toasted and chopped fine

¼ cup semisweet chocolate chips, melted and slightly cooled

Why This Recipe Works One of the best things about cookies is that they're a blank slate, just waiting for your creative contribution. These cookies are inspired by the frozen Italian dessert spumoni. Striped just like the slabs of ice cream, they feature three traditional flavors—nuts, chocolate, and cherry. Instead of emptying and washing the mixer three times for three flavored doughs, we streamlined the process by making one dough, dividing it into thirds, and simply stirring the flavorings into each batch of dough. Then, to shape the cookies, we formed the doughs into ropes and pressed a rope of each color together, rolled out the tricolored dough, and sliced it into bars. We refrigerated the dough as needed to keep the process from getting messy. In the end we had an eye-catching and colorful cookie featuring three delicious flavors. And the best part? Unlike ice cream, we could savor them for as long as we liked without them melting. If the ropes don't stick together well, lightly brush their sides with water to help them adhere.

1 Adjust oven racks to upper-middle and lower-middle positions and heat oven to 375 degrees. Line 2 baking sheets with parchment paper.

2 Whisk flour, baking powder, and salt together in bowl. Using stand mixer fitted with paddle, beat butter and sugar on medium-high speed until pale and fluffy, about 2 minutes. Add egg yolks and vanilla and beat until incorporated. Reduce speed to low, add flour mixture, and mix until just combined. Divide dough into 3 equal pieces and transfer each piece to separate bowl.

3 Add cherries to first bowl of dough and mix with wooden spoon until incorporated. Add walnuts to second bowl and mix until incorporated. Add melted chocolate to third bowl and mix until incorporated. Refrigerate until doughs are slightly firm, about 10 minutes.

4 Divide each dough in half. Roll each dough half into 12-inch rope on lightly floured counter. Place 1 rope of each color side-by-side and gently press together. Refrigerate dough ropes until slightly firm, about 10 minutes. Roll each set of ropes into 24 by 3-inch rectangle. Cut rectangles crosswise into 1-inch cookies and space them ¾ inch apart on prepared sheets.

5 Bake until just set but not browned, 12 to 14 minutes, switching and rotating sheets halfway through baking. Let cookies cool on sheets for 5 minutes, then transfer to wire rack. Let cookies cool completely before serving.

Assembling Spumoni Bars

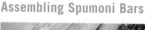

1 Roll each dough half into 12-inch rope.

2 Gently press one rope of each flavor together, then chill until slightly firm, about 10 minutes. Roll into single long rectangle on lightly floured counter, then cut crosswise into 1-inch cookies.

3

ROLLED, SHAPED & PRESSED

SHORTBREAD COOKIES

Makes 16 wedges

½ cup (1½ ounces) old-fashioned rolled oats

1½ cups (7½ ounces) all-purpose flour

⅔ cup (2⅔ ounces) confectioners' sugar

¼ cup (1 ounce) cornstarch

½ teaspoon salt

14 tablespoons unsalted butter, cut into ⅛-inch-thick slices and chilled

Why This Recipe Works Shortbread dates back to at least 12th-century Scotland and has earned a reputation as a favorite of royalty from Mary, Queen of Scots, to Elizabeth II. We wanted shortbread worthy of high-ranking palates: tawny brown cookies with a distinctive texture and pure buttery richness. We tinkered with the time-honored ratio of butter to flour, settling on slightly less butter than flour by weight, which yielded rich-tasting—but not greasy—shortbread. Neither cutting the butter into the flour, as one would for pie dough (the traditional method), nor creaming the butter with the sugar (the modern method) did the trick. The former method resulted in cookies that were crumbly in some spots and brittle in others; the latter incorporated too much air and resulted in cakey shortbread. Reverse creaming—mixing the flour and sugar before adding the butter—created less aeration and produced substantial shortbread. But the cookies were tough, so we needed to find a way to minimize gluten development. Replacing some of the flour with a combination of ground oats (which were traditional in early shortbread recipes) and cornstarch tenderized the shortbread. Originally, shortbread was made by leaving the dough in a still-warm oven heated only by dying embers. We found that the best baking method wasn't too far off: We baked the formed shortbread for 5 minutes in a hot 450-degree oven, after which we turned the temperature down to 250 degrees and baked the cookies for about 10 more minutes. Finally, we scored the shortbread and returned it to a turned-off oven, where it dried and finished cooking.

1 Adjust oven rack to middle position and heat oven to 450 degrees. Pulse oats in spice grinder or blender to fine powder, about 10 pulses. Using stand mixer fitted with paddle, mix flour, sugar, cornstarch, salt, and processed oats on low speed until combined. Add butter, 1 piece at a time, and mix until dough just forms and pulls away from sides of bowl, 5 to 10 minutes.

2 Place collar of 9- or 9½-inch springform pan on parchment paper–lined rimmed baking sheet (do not use springform pan bottom). Press dough evenly into collar, smoothing top of dough with back of spoon. Using 2-inch cutter, cut out center of dough, place extracted 2-inch cookie on sheet next to collar, and replace cutter in center of dough. Open springform collar, but leave it in place.

3 Bake for 5 minutes. Reduce oven temperature to 250 degrees and continue to bake until edges turn pale golden, 10 to 15 minutes.

4 Remove baking sheet from oven and turn off oven. Remove springform pan collar. Using knife, score surface of shortbread into 16 even wedges, cutting down halfway through shortbread. Using wooden skewer, poke 8 to 10 holes in each wedge. Return shortbread to oven, prop door open with handle of wooden spoon, and let shortbread dry in turned-off oven until center is firm but giving to touch, about 1 hour.

5 Remove shortbread from oven and let cool completely on sheet, about 2 hours. Cut shortbread at scored marks and serve.

Chocolate-Dipped Pistachio Shortbread

Add ½ cup shelled pistachios, toasted and finely chopped, to flour mixture in step 1. Once shortbread is cool, microwave 8 ounces finely chopped bittersweet chocolate in bowl at 50 percent power for 2 minutes. Stir chocolate and continue to microwave until melted, stirring once every minute. Stir in additional 2 ounces finely chopped bittersweet chocolate until smooth. Carefully dip base of each wedge in chocolate, allowing chocolate to come halfway up cookie. Scrape off excess with your finger and place on parchment paper–lined baking sheet. Refrigerate until chocolate sets, about 15 minutes.

Ginger Shortbread

Add ½ cup chopped crystallized ginger to flour mixture in step 1. Sprinkle shortbread with 1 tablespoon turbinado sugar after poking holes in shortbread in step 4.

Toasted Oat Shortbread

We prefer the texture and flavor of a coarse-grained flake sea salt like Maldon or *fleur de sel*, but kosher salt can be used.

Toast ½ cup additional oats in 8-inch skillet over medium-high heat until light golden brown, 5 to 8 minutes. Add toasted oats to flour mixture in step 1. Sprinkle ½ teaspoon flake sea salt evenly over surface of dough before baking.

Forming Shortbread Cookies

1 Press dough evenly into collar of springform pan, smoothing top of dough with back of spoon.

2 Cut out center of dough using 2-inch cutter.

3 Place extracted 2-inch cookie on sheet next to collar, then replace cutter in center of dough. Open springform collar, but leave it in place.

4 After baking, remove collar and score surface of shortbread into 16 wedges, cutting halfway through. Using wooden skewer, poke 8 to 10 holes in each wedge.

CHOCOLATE BUTTER COOKIES

Makes about 48 cookies

20 tablespoons (2½ sticks) unsalted butter, softened

½ cup (1½ ounces) unsweetened cocoa powder

1 teaspoon instant espresso powder

1 cup (7 ounces) sugar

¼ teaspoon salt

2 large egg yolks

1 tablespoon vanilla extract

2¼ cups (11¼ ounces) all-purpose flour

Why This Recipe Works On the butter cookie plate, the chocolate cookie, with its rich, dark color, is often the most alluring of the bunch. Sadly, though, a cookie that looks like it's made from chocolate doesn't necessarily taste like it's made from chocolate. We wanted to cram big chocolate flavor into a tender, crisp cookie. Cocoa powder has more cocoa solids than other forms of chocolate, so we figured it was the best candidate for producing deep, rich flavor. To really maximize the chocolate flavor, we doubled the amount of cocoa found in most recipes and bloomed it in hot melted butter, along with a teaspoon of instant espresso powder, before adding it to the dough. However, such a generous amount of cocoa powder resulted in dry cookies. To restore moisture, we cut back on the flour and added two egg yolks to the dough. A full tablespoon of vanilla extract enhanced the chocolate's aromatic qualities. An optional bittersweet chocolate glaze gives these sleek cookies a classy sheen and yet another dose of chocolate flavor. Espresso powder provides the most complexity here, but instant coffee powder can be substituted in a pinch. Do not reroll the scraps more than once; it will cause the cookies to be tough. Serve the cookies plain, dusted with confectioners' sugar, or with Bittersweet Chocolate Glaze (recipe follows) or Easy All-Purpose Glaze (page 370). Dust or glaze the cookies just before serving.

1 Melt 4 tablespoons butter in medium saucepan over medium heat. Add cocoa and espresso powder; stir until mixture forms smooth paste. Let cool for 15 to 20 minutes.

2 Using stand mixer fitted with paddle, beat remaining 16 tablespoons butter, sugar, salt, and cooled cocoa mixture on high speed until well combined and fluffy, about 1 minute, scraping down bowl as needed. Reduce speed to medium, add egg yolks and vanilla, and mix until thoroughly combined, about 30 seconds. Scrape down bowl. Reduce speed to low and add flour in 3 additions, waiting until each addition is incorporated before adding next and scraping down bowl after each addition. Continue to mix until dough forms cohesive ball, about 5 seconds. Transfer dough to counter and divide into 3 equal pieces. Form each piece into 4-inch disk, wrap disks tightly in plastic wrap, and refrigerate until dough is firm yet malleable, 45 minutes to 1 hour.

3 Adjust oven rack to middle position and heat oven to 375 degrees. Line 2 rimmed baking sheets with parchment paper. Working with 1 disk of dough at a time, roll ³⁄₁₆ inch thick between 2 large sheets of parchment. If dough becomes too soft and sticky to work with, slide rolled dough on parchment onto baking sheet and refrigerate until firm, about 10 minutes.

4 Remove top piece of parchment. Using 2-inch cookie cutter, cut dough into shapes; space shapes 1 inch apart on prepared sheets. Bake, 1 sheet at a time, until cookies show slight resistance to touch, 10 to 12 minutes, rotating sheet halfway through baking. (If cookies begin to darken on edges, they have overbaked.) Let cookies cool on sheets for 5 minutes, then transfer to wire rack. Let cookies cool completely before serving.

Chocolate-Orange Butter Cookies with Chocolate-Brandy Glaze

Beat 2 teaspoons grated orange zest with butter, sugar, and salt in step 2. Substitute 1 teaspoon brandy for vanilla extract. While cookies are cooling, make Bittersweet Chocolate Glaze (recipe follows), substituting 1 teaspoon brandy for vanilla. Glaze cookies and let dry for at least 20 minutes before serving.

Glazed Chocolate-Mint Butter Cookies

Substitute 2 teaspoons mint extract for vanilla extract. Glaze cookies with Bittersweet Chocolate Glaze (recipe follows) and let dry for at least 20 minutes. Melt 1 cup white chocolate chips and drizzle over glazed cookies. Let set for at least 20 minutes before serving.

Mexican Chocolate Butter Cookies

Toast ½ cup sliced almonds, 1 teaspoon ground cinnamon, and ⅛ teaspoon cayenne in 10-inch skillet over medium heat until fragrant, about 3 minutes; transfer to small bowl and let cool completely. Process cooled mixture in food processor until very fine, about 15 seconds. Whisk almond-spice mixture into flour before adding flour to dough in step 2. Sprinkle cookies evenly with ½ cup Demerara, turbinado, or sanding sugar before baking.

Salted Chocolate Caramel Butter Cookies

While cookies are cooling, heat 14 ounces soft caramels and ¼ cup heavy cream in medium saucepan over medium-low heat, stirring until melted and smooth. Spread each cookie with 1 heaping teaspoon caramel, sprinkle evenly with ½ teaspoon flake sea salt, and let caramel set for at least 30 minutes before serving.

BITTERSWEET CHOCOLATE GLAZE
Makes ⅔ cup

To glaze Chocolate Butter Cookies, use the back of a spoon to spread a scant teaspoon almost to the edge of each cookie. Be sure to let the glazed cookies dry for at least 20 minutes before serving.

4 ounces bittersweet chocolate, chopped
4 tablespoons unsalted butter
2 tablespoons corn syrup
1 teaspoon vanilla extract

Melt chocolate and butter in medium heatproof bowl set over saucepan filled with 1 inch barely simmering water, making sure that water does not touch bottom of bowl and stirring occasionally until butter and chocolate are melted. Remove bowl from saucepan; add corn syrup and vanilla and mix until smooth and shiny.

Determining Doneness

Properly baked cookies will show slight resistance when gently pressed. If they yield easily, they are underdone and need more time to become crisp; if they begin to darken at the edges, they have baked too long and will taste burnt and bitter.

SWEDISH WALNUT FINGERS

Makes 40 cookies

2¾ cups (13¾ ounces) all-purpose flour

Pinch salt

24 tablespoons unsalted butter, softened

¾ cup (5¼ ounces) plus 1 teaspoon sugar

1 large egg, separated

1 teaspoon almond or vanilla extract

½ cup walnuts, chopped fine

Why This Recipe Works These buttery, nut-topped Swedish cookies have a texture that's similar to sandy shortbread but they're lighter, crumbling delicately with each bite. Their exterior boasts a unique sweetness and crunch that comes from brushing them with a mixture of lightly beaten egg white and sugar. In addition to providing a flavor and texture boost, this mixture helps the walnuts adhere to the surface of the dough. The walnut topping toasts as the cookies bake, adding nutty contrast to the lightly sweet cookie. These cookies traditionally sport a rustic ridged surface, which further ensures that the walnuts stay in place. To create these grooves, we simply pat the cookie dough into a rectangle and dragged a floured fork across the surface. Our dough was packed with butter, which made it rich and gave it great flavor—but it also made it very sticky and difficult to maneuver. We found we needed to refrigerate the walnut-topped dough until it was firm before we cut it into rectangles for baking. To prevent the bottom of these delicate cookies from over-browning, we baked them slowly at a moderate 350 degrees and then let them sit on the baking sheet for only 1 minute—just enough time for them to set up before being transferred to a wire rack to cool.

1 Line baking sheet with parchment paper. Whisk flour and salt together in bowl. Using stand mixer fitted with paddle, beat butter and ¾ cup sugar on medium speed until pale and fluffy, 3 to 6 minutes. Add egg yolk and almond extract and beat until combined. Reduce speed to low, slowly add flour mixture, and mix until just combined.

2 Transfer dough to prepared sheet and press into 10 by 8-inch rectangle, about ½ inch thick. Using floured fork, press tines into dough and pull across rectangle to make washboard design. Lightly beat egg white with remaining 1 teaspoon sugar in small bowl, then brush evenly over dough. Sprinkle dough with walnuts, pressing gently to adhere. Cover baking sheet tightly with plastic wrap and refrigerate for 30 minutes.

3 Adjust oven racks to upper-middle and lower-middle positions and heat oven to 350 degrees. Slide dough, still on parchment, onto cutting board. Line baking sheet with fresh parchment; line second baking sheet with parchment.

4 Cut dough into 2 by 1-inch rectangles and space them 1½ inches apart on prepared sheets. Bake until lightly browned and set, 20 to 25 minutes, switching and rotating sheets halfway through baking. Let cookies cool on sheets for 1 minute, then transfer to wire rack. Let cookies cool completely before serving.

Forming Swedish Walnut Fingers

1 Press dough into 10 by 8-inch rectangle, about ½ inch thick, on parchment paper–lined baking sheet. Using floured fork, make washboard design.

2 Brush dough with egg white and sugar mixture and then sprinkle on walnuts. Once chilled, cut dough into 2 by 1-inch rectangles and bake.

GRAHAM CRACKERS
Makes 48 crackers

1½ cups (8¼ ounces) graham flour

¾ cup (3¾ ounces) all-purpose flour

½ cup (3½ ounces) sugar

1 teaspoon baking powder

1 teaspoon baking soda

½ teaspoon salt

¼ teaspoon ground cinnamon

8 tablespoons unsalted butter, cut into ½-inch pieces and chilled

5 tablespoons water

2 tablespoons molasses

1 teaspoon vanilla extract

Why This Recipe Works Homemade graham crackers boast a warmer, rounder wheaty graham flavor and heartier texture than store-bought versions. Supermarket crackers contain far more white flour than the coarse whole-wheat graham flour that gives them their name and signature flavor, so we started by reversing these proportions, using twice as much graham flour as all-purpose. To sweeten the crackers we opted for a combination of molasses for toasty, caramel flavor and granulated sugar for crispness. For flat crackers with an open, striated crumb, we mixed the dough like pie dough, using a food processor to pulse chilled butter into the flour. The crackers need to bake until they're fully crisp, but not so long that they dry out; check them as they bake and remove them from the oven when they are golden and firm around the edges. These graham crackers are also great for making s'mores or pie crusts. Graham flour is sold at well-stocked supermarkets and health food stores. Labeling may vary: Both Bob's Red Mill Whole Wheat Graham Flour and Arrowhead Mills Stone-Ground Whole Wheat Flour work well.

1 Adjust oven racks to upper-middle and lower-middle positions and heat oven to 375 degrees. Process graham flour, all-purpose flour, sugar, baking powder, baking soda, salt, and cinnamon in food processor until combined, about 3 seconds. Add butter and process until mixture resembles coarse cornmeal, about 15 seconds. Add water, molasses, and vanilla and process until dough comes together, about 20 seconds.

2 Transfer dough to counter and divide into 4 equal pieces. Working with 1 piece of dough at a time (keep remaining pieces covered with plastic wrap), roll into 11 by 8-inch rectangle, ⅛ inch thick, between 2 large sheets of parchment paper. Remove top piece of parchment and trim dough into tidy 10 by 7½-inch rectangle with knife, then score into twelve 2½-inch squares. Prick each square several times with fork.

3 Slide 2 pieces of rolled-out and scored dough, still on parchment, onto separate baking sheets. Bake until golden brown and edges are firm, about 15 minutes, switching and rotating sheets halfway through baking. Slide baked crackers, still on parchment, onto wire rack. Repeat with remaining 2 pieces of rolled-out dough. Let crackers cool completely. Transfer cooled crackers, still on parchment, to cutting board and carefully cut apart along scored lines. Serve. (Graham crackers can be stored at room temperature for up to 2 weeks.)

Cinnamon Graham Crackers
Increase amount of cinnamon in dough to ½ teaspoon. Toss ¼ cup sugar with 1 teaspoon ground cinnamon, then sprinkle mixture over scored crackers just before baking.

Cutting Graham Crackers

1 Using pastry cutter or sharp knife, score dough rectangle into twelve 2½-inch squares, making sure to cut all the way through dough.

2 Once baked crackers are completely cool, transfer them, still on parchment paper, to cutting board and carefully cut apart crackers along scored lines with chef's knife.

THIN CHOCOLATE-MINT COOKIES

Makes about 70 cookies

Cookies

1½ cups (7½ ounces) all-purpose flour

½ cup (1½ ounces) unsweetened cocoa powder

½ teaspoon salt

¼ teaspoon baking powder

¼ teaspoon baking soda

½ cup refined coconut oil, chilled

¾ cup (5¼ ounces) sugar

2 tablespoons milk

1 large egg

1 teaspoon vanilla extract

Chocolate Coating

1 pound semisweet couverture chocolate wafers

⅛ teaspoon peppermint oil

Why This Recipe Works Thin Mints—the best-selling Girl Scout cookie with a crisp chocolate coating and just the right amount of cool mint flavor—are a favorite of children and adults alike. We no longer wanted to count the days until the cookie season arrives, so we re-created them. To keep the mint flavor in check, we reserved the peppermint oil for use in the chocolate coating and omitted it from the cookie itself. Thin Mints get their crisp, short texture from palm kernel oil; coconut oil, which is in the same family, did the trick. Baking the cookies until they were thoroughly dry ensured the proper crunch. We wanted an attractive, crisp shell so we tempered the chocolate—a technique that stabilizes chocolate's structure, but one that also makes many home bakers wary. Though the process is exacting—it involves melting chocolate, agitating it, and cooling it to a specific temperature—it's not difficult to do. Our spin on Thin Mints doesn't just live up to our expectations; it exceeds them—scout's honor. We use wafers of *couverture* chocolate (also referred to as *feves* or *callets*) for the coating; this professional-quality chocolate is high in fat due to added cocoa butter. You can buy Guittard couverture chocolate wafers at Sur La Table, Williams-Sonoma, or some high-end supermarkets. You can also order it online at kingarthurflour.com.

1 For the cookies Whisk flour, cocoa, salt, baking powder, and baking soda together in bowl; set aside. Using stand mixer fitted with paddle, beat oil and sugar on medium-high speed until fluffy, about 2 minutes. Reduce speed to low, add milk, egg, and vanilla, and beat until combined, about 30 seconds. Slowly add flour mixture and beat until just combined, about 1 minute, scraping down bowl as needed. Divide dough in half. Form each half into 4-inch disk, wrap disks tightly in plastic wrap, and refrigerate until dough is firm yet malleable, about 45 minutes.

2 Adjust oven racks to upper-middle and lower-middle positions and heat oven to 350 degrees. Line 2 baking sheets with parchment paper. Working with 1 disk of dough at a time, roll into 11-inch circle, about ⅛ inch thick, between 2 large sheets of lightly floured parchment paper. Remove top piece of parchment. Using 1¾-inch round cookie cutter, cut dough into circles; space circles ½ inch apart on prepared sheets. Gently reroll scraps ⅛ inch thick, cut into rounds, and transfer to prepared sheets. Bake until very firm, 16 to 18 minutes, switching and rotating sheets halfway through baking. Let cookies cool on sheets for 5 minutes, then transfer to wire rack. Let cookies cool completely.

3 For the chocolate coating Line 2 baking sheets with parchment. Melt two-thirds of chocolate and oil in medium metal heatproof bowl set over small saucepan filled with 1 inch barely simmering water, stirring often, until chocolate registers 118 degrees. Remove bowl from heat and slowly add remaining chocolate, stirring constantly, until chocolate registers 82 degrees, 15 to 30 minutes. Briefly return bowl to saucepan and heat, stirring often, until mixture reaches 90 degrees, moving bowl on and off the heat every 15 seconds to prevent overheating.

4 To test for temper, dip tip of butter knife in chocolate and let sit for 10 minutes. Chocolate should harden and be glossy. Working with 1 cookie at a time, place cookie on fork and dip bottom of cookie in chocolate. Using offset spatula, spread chocolate over top of cookie, creating thin coating. Transfer cookie to prepared baking sheet and repeat with remaining cookies. Let cookies sit until chocolate sets, about 10 minutes, before serving. (Cookies can be stored at room temperature for up to 2 weeks.)

ALL ABOUT ROLLED COOKIES

Cutout cookies require a little more consideration to form than do those that are simply dropped onto a baking sheet, rolled into balls between your hands, or shaped into a log and sliced. The dough can become too soft to roll or it can tear, and the thin cookies can overbake. Here are the keys to achieving perfectly elegant, great-tasting rolled cookies.

REST THE DOUGH AND CHILL

Chilling the dough after mixing makes cookie rolling simple: First, it prevents the butter from getting too warm and the dough from becoming too sticky. Also, a refrigerator rest allows the flour to hydrate and the gluten that was formed during mixing to relax, so the dough isn't too tough to roll out or doesn't retract upon rolling. Wrap disks of dough tightly in plastic wrap, and refrigerate the dough until it's firm yet malleable.

START ROLLING AT THE CENTER

If areas of the dough are thicker than others, the cookies will bake at different rates. It helps to start at the center of the disk of dough and roll away from you, spinning the dough a quarter turn after each stroke. This helps ensure every inch of dough is of the same thickness. Apply even pressure as you roll.

ROLL BETWEEN PARCHMENT

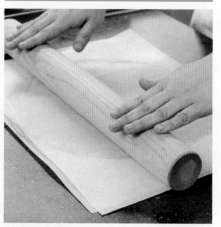

For sticky doughs, we call for rolling the dough between 2 large sheets of parchment paper rather than on the counter; this eliminates the need for dusting the dough with an excessive amount of flour, which can result in dry cookies. Rolling out dough between parchment minimizes sticking and makes it easier to transfer the cookies to the baking sheet; you simply remove the top piece of parchment, stamp out the cookies, and then transfer them to the sheet with a thin offset spatula instead of trying to coax the cookies off the counter.

MAKE THE FRIDGE YOUR FRIEND

If at any time the dough becomes too soft or sticky to roll, slide the dough, still between the parchment, onto a baking sheet and refrigerate until the dough is firm, about 10 minutes.

Minimize scraps by cutting shapes close together, starting from the outside and working your way to the middle. When making large and small cookies, we alternate cutters as we stamp to use as much dough as possible.

AVOID OVERBAKING

Thinly rolled cookies go from perfectly baked to overbaked in a matter of minutes, so it's important to watch—most cookies should show a slight resistance to the touch and start to become brown along the edges.

TEMPERING CHOCOLATE FOR COOKIES

We dip, drizzle, decorate, or coat many of the cookies in this book with chocolate. Chilling sets up this chocolate so it's hard, but at room temperature it will lack snap and shine. That's fine for some applications, but for our Thin Chocolate-Mint Cookies (page 112), we wanted the cookies to maintain the glossy, crisp coating of the Girl Scout originals. Tempering isn't as difficult as you think; use the below instructions to enrobe Thin Chocolate-Mint Cookies; or, use the technique to up your coating game for any number of cookies.

1 Melt two-thirds of chocolate with peppermint oil in metal heatproof bowl set over small saucepan filled with 1 inch of barely simmering water, stirring often, until chocolate registers 118 degrees.

2 Remove bowl from heat and slowly add remaining chocolate, stirring constantly, until chocolate registers 82 degrees, 15 to 30 minutes.

3 Briefly return bowl to saucepan and heat, stirring often, until mixture reaches 90 degrees, moving bowl on and off heat every 15 seconds to prevent overheating.

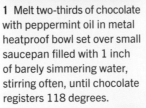
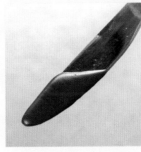

4 To test for temper, dip tip of butter knife in chocolate and let it sit for 10 minutes. Chocolate should harden and be glossy.

5 Working with 1 cookie at a time, place cookie on fork and dip bottom of cookie in chocolate.

6 Using offset spatula, spread chocolate over top of cookie, creating thin coating.

LEMON THINS

Makes about 40 cookies

Cookies

1½ cups (7½ ounces) all-purpose flour

2 tablespoons cornstarch

¼ teaspoon salt

¼ teaspoon baking powder

⅛ teaspoon baking soda

10 tablespoons unsalted butter, softened

½ cup (3½ ounces) granulated sugar

2 tablespoons lemon juice

1 large egg yolk

1½ teaspoons lemon extract

Glaze

1 cup (4 ounces) confectioners' sugar

1 teaspoon grated lemon zest plus 7 teaspoons juice, plus extra juice if needed

Pinch salt

Why This Recipe Works Small and delicate, lemon thins had legions of fans in times past, and grocery store shelves, particularly in the South, were crowded with regional versions. But the cookie zeitgeist now favors bigger, bolder biscuits. We wanted to bring back these pleasantly crisp cookies, and we wanted them to pack a serious lemon punch. When we tested existing recipes, we found them to be too thick and soft or too crumbly or too chewy—and all were desperately short on lemon flavor. Texture was the first puzzle to solve. Just out of the oven, our working recipe was thin and crisp; however, after they cooled, the cookies became tough. Baking the cookies for a shorter period of time left them soft. Enriching the dough with more butter made the dough too difficult to work with. We found the answer in an old test kitchen trick for making cookies lighter: Replacing a small amount of the flour with cornstarch made for incredibly tender yet crisp cookies—even after they cooled. Still missing? Bold lemon flavor. We were thrilled with the bright, sour sweetness of cookies using the zest of a whopping 10 lemons. Since zesting 10 lemons was too much work, we scaled back to a more modest amount of juice, and then added 1½ teaspoons of pure lemon extract. A light lemon glaze enforced the citrus flavor.

1 For the cookies Whisk flour, cornstarch, salt, baking powder, and baking soda together in bowl; set aside. Using stand mixer fitted with paddle, beat butter and sugar on medium-high speed until pale and fluffy, about 3 minutes. Add lemon juice, egg yolk, and lemon extract and beat until combined. Reduce speed to low and add flour mixture in 3 additions until just combined, scraping down bowl as needed. Transfer dough to counter and divide in half. Form each half into 5-inch disk, wrap disks tightly in plastic wrap, and refrigerate for at least 1 hour or up to 24 hours.

2 Adjust oven rack to middle position and heat oven to 325 degrees. Line 2 baking sheets with parchment paper. Remove 1 disk of dough from refrigerator and knead for 3 to 5 turns to make more pliable. On lightly floured counter, roll dough into 10-inch circle, about ¼ inch thick.

3 Using 2-inch round cookie cutter, cut 14 to 15 rounds from dough. Reroll scraps up to 2 times to similar thickness and cut out remaining 5 to 6 rounds to yield 20 cookies. Space cookies 1 inch apart on 1 prepared sheet.

4 Bake cookies until edges are lightly browned, 12 to 14 minutes, rotating sheet halfway through baking. Let cookies cool on sheet for 5 minutes, then transfer to wire rack and let cool completely. Repeat with remaining dough.

5 For the glaze Whisk sugar, lemon zest and juice, and salt together in bowl. Working with 1 cookie at a time, dip top of cookie into glaze, then drag top lightly against rim of bowl to remove excess glaze. (If glaze thickens as it sits, add extra lemon juice as needed to maintain proper consistency.) Let glaze dry before serving, about 15 minutes.

CORNMEAL-ORANGE COOKIES

Makes about 84 cookies

1½ cups (7½ ounces) all-purpose flour

1 cup (5 ounces) cornmeal

16 tablespoons unsalted butter, softened

1 cup (7 ounces) superfine sugar

1 teaspoon grated orange zest

½ teaspoon salt

1 large egg plus 1 large yolk

2 teaspoons vanilla extract

Why This Recipe Works We love rich, buttery shortbread-style cookies, but sometimes we want something a little more unique in terms of both flavor and texture to accompany our afternoon tea. These cornmeal-enhanced cookies fit the bill: They're a bit rustic, with a substantial texture from the addition of cornmeal to a basic shortbread dough. Besides introducing a pleasant grit to the short-and-sandy base cookie, the cornmeal imparts a warm, round, buttery-sweet flavor. We found that a 2:3 ratio of cornmeal to all-purpose flour provided big corn flavor without compromising the cookie's structure. These cookies were satisfying, but we wanted to introduce another flavor to complement the cornmeal, so we paired it with aromatic orange zest, which contributed subtle floral notes and a welcome burst of citrus. Just 1 teaspoon of orange zest provided plenty of citrus infusion without overshadowing the buttery corn flavor. Do not reroll the scraps more than once; it will cause the cookies to be tough. Do not use coarse-ground cornmeal for this recipe. This recipe yields a lot of cookies because the hardy stackable rounds hold up well for travel or being packaged and gifted.

1 Whisk flour and cornmeal together in bowl. Using stand mixer fitted with paddle, beat butter, sugar, orange zest, and salt on medium speed until pale and fluffy, about 3 minutes. Beat in egg yolk, then add whole egg and vanilla and continue to beat until well incorporated. Reduce speed to low, add flour mixture, and mix until just incorporated.

2 Transfer dough to counter and divide into 4 equal pieces. Form each piece of dough into disk, wrap disks tightly in plastic wrap, and refrigerate for 45 minutes.

3 Adjust oven racks to upper-middle and lower-middle positions and heat oven to 375 degrees. Line 2 baking sheets with parchment paper.

4 Roll 1 disk of dough ¼ inch thick on lightly floured counter, using offset spatula to loosen dough as needed to prevent it from sticking. Using 2-inch cookie cutter, cut dough into shapes; space shapes evenly on prepared sheets.

5 Bake cookies until evenly golden brown, 6 to 8 minutes, switching and rotating sheets halfway through baking. Let cookies cool on sheets for 5 minutes, then transfer to wire rack. Repeat with remaining dough. Let cookies cool completely before serving.

INDIAN TEA BISCUITS

Makes 36 cookies

2 cups (10 ounces) all-purpose flour

1 teaspoon ground cardamom

½ teaspoon baking powder

¼ teaspoon salt

16 tablespoons unsalted butter, softened

1 cup (4 ounces) confectioners' sugar

1½ tablespoons plain whole-milk or low-fat yogurt

¼ teaspoon vanilla extract

18 salted roasted cashews, split in half

Why This Recipe Works *Nankhatai* are eggless cardamom-scented cookies that are a favorite in India and Pakistan. One taste of these aromatic cookies and we knew they were a worthy addition to our repertoire. They're often made with semolina flour, rice flour, chickpea flour, or a combination of these along with the white flour, but we found we could make great-tasting biscuits with pantry staples. Though nankhatai are often thick and puffy, our version is rolled thin for dunking into chai. We wanted the flavor of cardamom to take center stage, so we started with a simple butter cookie base. To help bring the cookie dough together without egg, we enriched it with a small amount—just 1½ tablespoons—of plain yogurt, a common ingredient in Indian cooking. In addition to giving our dough just the right consistency, the yogurt provided a slight tang that befit these unique biscuits. For an elegant finish, we studded the middle of each cookie with a single cashew half. We like the appearance of fluted rounds for these cookies, but you can cut them into any shape you like. You can use plain whole-milk or low-fat yogurt for these cookies, but don't use nonfat yogurt; it will make the cookies too lean. Be sure to plan ahead, as the dough must chill for several hours.

1 Whisk flour, cardamom, baking powder, and salt together in bowl; set aside. Using stand mixer fitted with paddle, beat butter and sugar on medium-high speed until pale and fluffy, about 2 minutes. Add yogurt and vanilla and beat until incorporated, about 30 seconds. Reduce speed to low, add flour mixture in 3 additions, and mix until just combined. Transfer dough to counter and divide in half. Form each half into 5-inch disk, wrap disks tightly in plastic wrap, and refrigerate for at least 4 hours or up to 2 days.

2 Adjust oven racks to upper-middle and lower-middle positions and heat oven to 350 degrees. Line 2 baking sheets with parchment paper. Let chilled dough sit on counter to soften slightly, about 10 minutes. Working with 1 disk of dough at a time, roll dough ⅛ inch thick. Using 2½-inch cookie cutter, cut dough into shapes; space shapes 1 inch apart on prepared sheets. Gently reroll scraps once, cut into shapes, and transfer to prepared sheets. Gently press cashew half in center of each cookie.

3 Bake cookies until lightly browned, 14 to 18 minutes, switching and rotating sheets halfway through baking. Let cookies cool on sheets for 5 minutes, then transfer to wire rack. Let cookies cool completely before serving.

Yogurt

Yogurt is simply milk fermented with specific bacteria in order to thicken and sour it. We use plain whole-milk yogurt here in the test kitchen for its rich, round flavor and its ability to impart moistness to baked goods; however, plain low-fat yogurt is also fine to use. (Avoid nonfat yogurt, which will adversely affect texture.) Greek-style yogurt is simply American-style yogurt that's been drained of its watery whey, giving it a smoother, thicker texture with less moisture than American yogurt. Because of this difference, baked goods made with Greek-style yogurt usually taste slightly drier than those made with American yogurt. To substitute Greek-style for American-style yogurt in baked goods, replace two-thirds of the amount of yogurt called for with Greek yogurt and make up the rest with water.

CHOCOLATE SPICE COOKIES

Makes about 42 cookies

1¾ cups slivered almonds

1 cup (4 ounces) confectioners' sugar

4 ounces bittersweet chocolate, chopped

¼ cup (1¾ ounces) granulated sugar, plus ½ cup for coating

3 tablespoons unsweetened cocoa powder

1 teaspoon ground cinnamon

¼ teaspoon salt

2 large egg whites

1 teaspoon vanilla extract

Why This Recipe Works A holiday tradition in Switzerland, these delicately spiced chocolate cookies are soft and chewy, unlike many rolled cookies that are crisp from edge to edge. Containing no flour and naturally gluten-free (for more gluten-free recipes, see page 398), *basler brunsli* are loaded with chocolate and ground almonds and bound with just a couple egg whites. To make our flourless dough drier and therefore easier to work with, we employed powdery-fine confectioners' sugar in place of much of the granulated sugar. In addition, we skipped melting the chocolate; instead, we treated it like a dry ingredient, grinding it in the food processor along with the others. Three tablespoons of cocoa powder amped up the chocolate flavor without adding any moisture. It's traditional to roll out basler brunsli dough on a counter sprinkled with sugar, but this method prevented us from being able to reroll the delicious scraps; instead we dunked each side of the cut cookies in a dish of sugar. Rechill the dough scraps if necessary before rerolling in step 4.

1 Adjust oven racks to upper-middle and lower-middle positions and heat oven to 325 degrees. Line 2 baking sheets with parchment paper.

2 Process almonds and confectioners' sugar in food processor until almonds are very finely ground, about 45 seconds. Add chocolate, ¼ cup granulated sugar, cocoa, cinnamon, and salt and process until chocolate is finely ground, about 30 seconds. Add egg whites and vanilla and pulse until dough forms, about 10 pulses.

3 Transfer dough to piece of parchment paper and knead gently to form smooth ball. Let dough sit until no longer sticky, about 10 minutes. Top with second piece of parchment and roll dough ¼ inch thick. Transfer dough, still between parchment, to refrigerator and let chill for 10 minutes.

4 Spread remaining ½ cup granulated sugar in shallow dish. Using 2-inch star cutter, cut dough into stars, gathering and rerolling scraps as necessary. Dip both sides of each star in granulated sugar to coat; space stars 1 inch apart on prepared sheets. Bake until puffed and cracked but centers are still soft, 13 to 15 minutes, switching and rotating sheets halfway through baking. Let cookies cool on sheets for 15 minutes, then transfer to wire rack. Let cookies cool completely before serving.

Coating Chocolate Spice Cookies

1 Spread ½ cup of granulated sugar in shallow dish. After cutting chilled dough into shapes, dip both sides of each cookie in sugar to coat, handling dough gently so star retains its shape.

2 Carefully transfer each coated star to parchment paper–lined baking sheet, spacing them 1 inch apart.

PUMPKIN-PECAN COOKIES

Makes about 40 cookies

1 cup pumpkin puree

2¾ cups (13¾ ounces) all-purpose flour

¾ cup (5¼ ounces) superfine sugar

2 teaspoons ground cinnamon

½ teaspoon ground ginger

½ teaspoon ground nutmeg

¼ teaspoon salt

16 tablespoons unsalted butter, cut into 16 pieces and softened

1¼ cups pecans, toasted and chopped fine

1½ ounces cream cheese, softened

2 teaspoons vanilla extract

2 tablespoons milk

1½ cups (6 ounces) confectioners' sugar

Why This Recipe Works Try to add pumpkin puree to cookies, and they'll usually come out cakey and muffin-like. That's because pumpkin puree is laden with water; when pumpkin treats hit the oven, that extra moisture turns to steam and provides cakey lift. That's not necessarily a bad thing, but we wished for a pumpkin cookie that wasn't like the rest—one that was thin, crisp, and shortbread-like and baked up with a flat surface that we could coat with a flavorful glaze. For a cookie with the texture we sought, we needed to remove as much moisture as possible from the puree. We tried reducing it on the stovetop, but the cooked flavor was too pronounced. To remove moisture without heat, we developed a unique method of spreading the canned puree thin on the underside of a baking sheet and soaking up moisture with paper towels until 1 cup of puree reduced all the way down to ⅓ cup. Adding this paste to the dough resulted in a fine crumb once the cookies were baked.

1 Line rimmed baking sheet with triple layer of paper towels. Spread pumpkin puree over towels. Press with second triple layer of paper towels until towels are saturated. Peel off top layer of towels. Place second baking sheet inside first over pumpkin and flip. Remove top sheet and towels. Repeat if needed to reduce paste to ⅓ cup.

2 Using stand mixer fitted with paddle, mix flour, superfine sugar, 1½ teaspoons cinnamon, ginger, nutmeg, and salt on low speed until combined. Add butter, 1 piece at a time, and mix until dough looks crumbly and slightly wet, 1 to 2 minutes. Add pecans, pumpkin paste, 2 tablespoons cream cheese, and vanilla and beat until dough just begins to form large clumps, about 30 seconds. Transfer dough to counter; knead just until it forms cohesive mass and divide in half. Form each half into disk, wrap disks tightly in plastic wrap, and refrigerate for 30 minutes.

3 Adjust oven rack to middle position and heat oven to 375 degrees. Line 2 baking sheets with parchment paper. Working with 1 disk of dough at a time, roll dough ⅛ inch thick between 2 large sheets of parchment paper. Transfer dough, still between parchment, to refrigerator and let chill for 10 minutes. Using 2½-inch cutter, cut dough into shapes; space shapes 1½ inches apart on prepared sheets. Gently reroll scraps, cut into shapes, and transfer to prepared sheets.

4 Bake, 1 sheet at a time, until cookies are light golden brown, about 10 minutes, rotating sheet halfway through baking. Let cookies cool on sheet for 3 minutes, then transfer to wire rack and let cool completely. Whisk milk, remaining ½ teaspoon cinnamon, and remaining 1 tablespoon cream cheese together in bowl until combined. Add confectioners' sugar and whisk until smooth. Spread glaze evenly onto cookies and let dry for at least 30 minutes before serving.

Making Pumpkin Paste

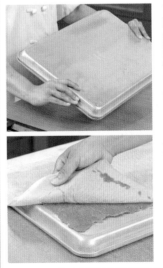

1 Line baking sheet with triple layer of paper towels. Spread pumpkin puree over towels. Press with second triple layer of towels until they're saturated. Peel off top layer. Place second baking sheet inside first over pumpkin and flip.

2 Remove top sheet and towels. Repeat if needed to reduce paste to ⅓ cup.

RUSSIAN CHEESE COOKIES

Makes about 48 cookies

1 tablespoons sugar, plus 1 cup for rolling

¾ teaspoon ground cardamom

2 teaspoons grated orange zest

2 cups (10 ounces) all-purpose flour

½ teaspoon baking powder

½ teaspoon salt

8 tablespoons unsalted butter, cut into ½-inch pieces and chilled, plus 6 tablespoons unsalted butter

1 cup (8 ounces) cottage cheese

Why This Recipe Works These humble yet delicious featherweight cookies hail from Russia. *Gusinie lapki* translates to "goose feet," and once you see the folded shape of these cookies, you'll understand why. Traditional recipes incorporate a beloved Russian ingredient, farmers' cheese, to achieve a light, flaky texture. We chose to make our version with a product that's easier to find stateside, cottage cheese, which had the signature texture and tang of Russian recipes. Mixing the dough in the food processor like pie dough and cutting cold butter into the flour before adding the cheese also helped achieve the traditional flaky texture. While they may look intricate, these cookies are easy to form: We simply rolled the dough thin, cut out circles, and folded the circles into quarters. Brushing the rounds with butter and coating them with sugar before folding gave them a crystalline sparkle and a touch of sweetness throughout. We made a departure from classic recipes by mixing in fragrant cardamom and orange zest; we love the touch of sophistication these flavors add, but they can be omitted if you desire a more traditional version.

1 Adjust oven racks to upper-middle and lower-middle positions and heat oven to 350 degrees. Line 2 baking sheets with parchment paper. Combine 1 cup sugar and cardamom in shallow bowl; set aside.

2 Process orange zest and remaining 1 tablespoon sugar in food processor until combined, about 10 seconds. Add flour, baking powder, and salt and process until combined, about 5 seconds. Scatter chilled butter over top and pulse until pea-size pieces of butter form, about 10 pulses. Add cottage cheese and process until dough forms, 20 to 30 seconds. Transfer dough to counter and divide in half. Form each half into disk, wrap disks tightly in plastic wrap, and refrigerate for 1 hour.

3 Working with 1 disk of dough at a time, roll into 14- to 15-inch circle ⅛ inch thick on lightly floured counter. Using 3-inch round cookie cutter, cut dough into circles. Gently reroll scraps and cut into circles. Melt remaining 6 tablespoons butter. Brush both sides of each dough circle with butter. Dip both sides of each circle in sugar-cardamom mixture to coat. Fold each circle into quarters, pinching gently at corner to adhere; space cookies 1 inch apart on prepared sheets.

4 Bake cookies until light golden brown, 18 to 20 minutes, switching and rotating sheets halfway through baking. Let cookies cool on sheets for 5 minutes, then transfer to wire rack. Let cookies cool completely before serving.

BISCOCHITOS

Makes about 40 cookies

1 cup (7 ounces) sugar

1 teaspoon ground cinnamon

1 tablespoon anise seeds

8 tablespoons unsalted butter, softened

8 tablespoons vegetable shortening, cut into 1-inch chunks

½ teaspoon salt

1 large egg yolk

1 teaspoon vanilla extract

2 cups (10 ounces) all-purpose flour

Why This Recipe Works Biscochitos find home in New Mexico, where they're served at any special celebration. These crisp shortbread cookies, which have Spanish roots, are scented with the licorice notes of anise seed and the warm spice of cinnamon. Biscochitos traditionally have a meltingly tender texture, thanks to the inclusion of lard. However, most bakers don't have lard at the ready, so we relied on a combination of equal parts butter and shortening for rich flavor and superlatively tender texture. The cookies come in many shapes and sizes, but we're partial to the diamond shape that's commonly used for weddings. To create this unique shape, we first rolled the dough into a circle and chilled it until it was firm. Then we cut the dough into strips (a pizza cutter made quick work of this step) and cut the strips diagonally into diamonds. To finish the cookies, we coated them in cinnamon sugar using the traditional method: We gently tossed the still-warm cookies in the sugary coating so it adhered and then let the cookies cool completely before serving them. Don't let the cookies cool on the baking sheets for longer than 5 minutes or the cinnamon-sugar mixture won't adhere.

1 Combine sugar and cinnamon in small bowl; spread ½ cup cinnamon sugar in shallow dish. Grind anise seeds in spice grinder until finely ground, about 10 seconds.

2 Using stand mixer fitted with paddle, beat butter, shortening, salt, remaining ½ cup cinnamon sugar, and ground anise on medium-high speed until pale and fluffy, about 3 minutes, scraping down bowl as needed. Add egg yolk and vanilla and beat until combined. Reduce speed to low, add flour, and mix until dough forms, about 10 seconds.

3 Roll dough into 9-inch circle, about ½ inch thick, on large sheet of parchment paper. Transfer dough, still on parchment, to large plate; cover with plastic wrap and refrigerate until firm, about 30 minutes.

4 Adjust oven racks to upper-middle and lower-middle positions and heat oven to 350 degrees. Line 2 baking sheets with parchment paper. Transfer dough, still on parchment, to cutting board. Using knife or pizza cutter, cut dough lengthwise into 1-inch-wide strips, then cut diagonally into 1-inch-wide strips to form diamonds; space diamonds evenly on prepared sheets, about 20 per sheet.

5 Bake cookies until set and just starting to brown, about 15 minutes, switching and rotating sheets halfway through baking. Let cookies cool on sheets for 5 minutes. Gently toss cookies, a few at a time, in reserved cinnamon sugar. Transfer cookies to wire rack. Let cookies cool completely before serving.

PEANUT BLOSSOM COOKIES

Makes about 48 cookies

1⅓ cups (6⅔ ounces) all-purpose flour

½ cup salted dry-roasted peanuts

¼ teaspoon baking powder

¼ teaspoon baking soda

¼ teaspoon salt

8 tablespoons unsalted butter, softened

⅓ cup packed (2⅓ ounces) dark brown sugar

⅓ cup (2⅓ ounces) granulated sugar

½ cup creamy peanut butter

1 large egg, room temperature

1 teaspoon vanilla extract

48–50 Hershey's Kisses, unwrapped

Why This Recipe Works Peanut blossom cookies first gained notoriety at the 1957 Pillsbury Bake-Off. They're simply a peanut butter cookie topped with a Hershey's Kiss. We started with the original recipe and made tweaks to it with the goal of achieving a more robust peanut flavor. Adding more peanut butter didn't do the trick. We tried swapping chunky peanut butter for the creamy, but tasters disliked the craggy texture it gave these cookies. We got the best peanut flavor when we replaced a portion of the flour with roasted peanuts, which we ground finely in the food processor so they wouldn't compromise the cookie's texture. Most recipes recommend pressing the kisses into the cookies immediately after baking, but the warm cookies softened the kisses too much, and they took 4 hours to firm up again—longer than we were willing to wait to indulge. Strangely enough, we found that placing the chocolates on the cookies during the last 2 minutes of baking helped them firm up more quickly. Why? It turns out that a little direct heat stabilizes and sets the exterior of the chocolate, and the kisses were firm enough to eat after the cookies had cooled for just 2 hours. Any Hershey's Kiss—dark, milk, white, or "Hugs"—works in this recipe.

1 Process ⅔ cup flour and peanuts in food processor until peanuts are finely ground, about 15 seconds; transfer to bowl and whisk in baking powder, baking soda, salt, and remaining ⅔ cup flour.

2 Using stand mixer fitted with paddle, beat butter, brown sugar, and granulated sugar until fluffy, about 2 minutes. Add peanut butter and beat until combined. Add egg and vanilla and beat until combined. Reduce speed to low, add flour mixture in 2 additions, and mix until just combined. Cover bowl tightly with plastic wrap and refrigerate for 30 minutes.

3 Adjust oven rack to middle position and heat oven to 350 degrees. Line 2 baking sheets with parchment paper. Roll dough into 1-inch balls and space them 2 inches apart on prepared sheets. Bake, 1 sheet at a time, until cookies are just set and beginning to crack, 9 to 11 minutes. Working quickly, remove sheet from oven and place 1 candy in center of each cookie, pressing down firmly. Return sheet to oven and bake until cookies are light golden, about 2 minutes longer. Let cookies cool on sheet for 5 minutes, then transfer to wire rack. Let cookies cool completely before serving.

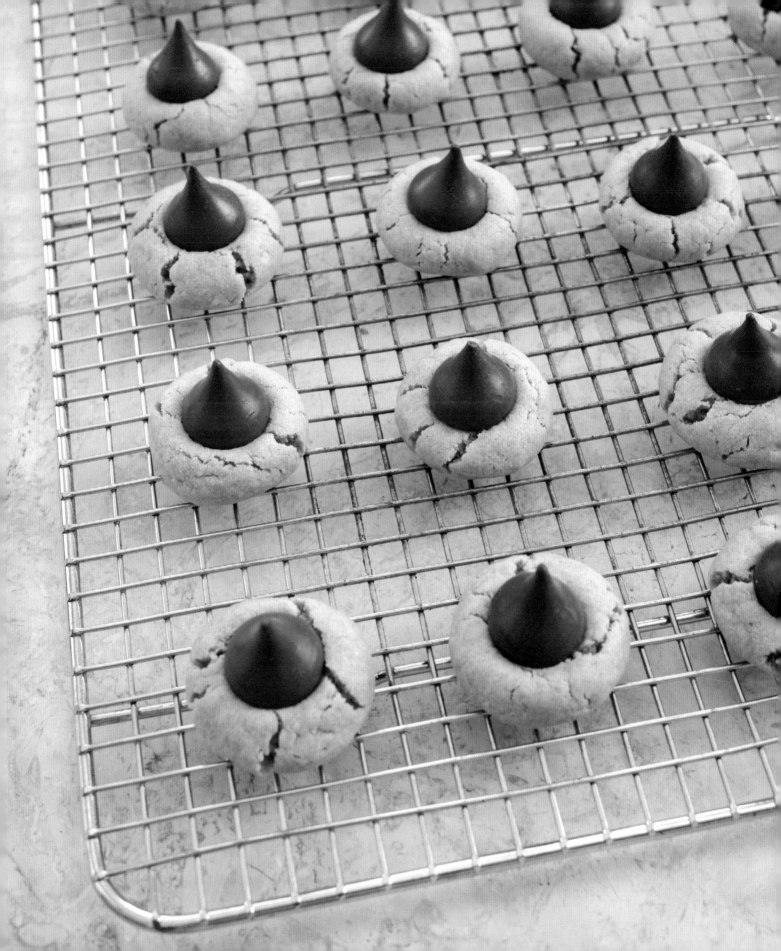

JAM THUMBPRINTS

Makes about 48 cookies

½ cup seedless jam

2¼ cups (11¼ ounces) all-purpose flour

½ teaspoon salt

½ teaspoon baking soda

¼ teaspoon baking powder

12 tablespoons unsalted butter, softened

⅔ cup (4⅔ ounces) sugar

3 ounces cream cheese, softened

1 large egg

1½ teaspoons vanilla extract

Why This Recipe Works A timeless favorite, jam thumbprints are a staple of bake sales and cookie swaps. Their jewel-like centers make them an eye-catching option, and the contrast between the fruity, plush jam and a rich, buttery, crisp cookie makes them hard to resist. Recipes traditionally call for plunging your thumb into balls of dough to make room for the filling, hence the name. We kept our thumbs out of our thumbprints and instead used the bottom of a greased 1-teaspoon measure to ensure even craters. When we added the jam to the indentations before baking, the sugars caramelized and the centers became sticky and leathery; but jam added after baking was too loose. After a bit of trial and error, we discovered the key to success: reshaping the thumbprints halfway through baking. Re-forming the indentations before the cookies were completely set meant we could fill them with a generous amount of jam, and adding the jam partway through baking resulted in a filling that was married to the cookie and set just enough. Any seedless jam can be used.

1 Adjust oven rack to middle position and heat oven to 350 degrees. Line 2 baking sheets with parchment paper.

2 Fill small zipper-lock bag with jam and set aside. Whisk flour, salt, baking soda, and baking powder together in medium bowl. Using stand mixer fitted with paddle, beat butter and sugar on medium speed until fluffy, 3 to 6 minutes. Add cream cheese, egg, and vanilla and beat until combined, about 30 seconds. Reduce speed to low, slowly add flour mixture, and mix until incorporated.

3 Working with 1½ teaspoons dough at a time, roll into balls and space them 1½ inches apart on prepared sheets. Using greased rounded 1-teaspoon measure, make indentation in center of each dough ball.

4 Bake cookies, 1 sheet at a time, until just beginning to set and lightly browned around edges, about 10 minutes. Remove sheet from oven and gently reshape indentation in center of each cookie with greased rounded 1-teaspoon measure. Snip small corner off zipper-lock bag and carefully fill each indentation with about ½ teaspoon jam. Rotate sheet and continue to bake until lightly golden, 12 to 14 minutes. Let cookies cool on sheet for 10 minutes, then transfer to wire rack. Let cookies cool completely before serving.

Forming and Filling Thumbprints

1 After baking cookies for 10 minutes, craters will have puffed up. Remove baking sheet from oven and use teaspoon measure to reshape original thumbprints.

2 Snip small corner off zipper-lock bag filled with jam.

3 Carefully fill each indentation with about ½ teaspoon jam.

HAZELNUT LEMON CURD THUMBPRINTS

Makes about 24 cookies

1 cup (5 ounces) all-purpose flour

¾ cup hazelnuts, toasted and skinned

Pinch salt

8 tablespoons unsalted butter, softened

⅓ cup (2⅓ ounces) granulated sugar

1 large egg yolk

¾ teaspoon vanilla extract

¼ cup lemon curd

Confectioners' sugar

Why This Recipe Works Jam thumbprints are appealing to kids and grownups alike: Who doesn't like a sweet surprise? But rarely do we see variations on the buttery cookie base and fruity jam filling. We thought this category of cookie was ripe for a new, sophisticated interpretation. For the filling, we immediately thought of another fruity spread, one that's richer and a bit more refined than jam: lemon curd, a custard-style sauce made from eggs, sugar, butter, and, of course, lemon juice. For the cookie base, we wanted an equally upscale flavor that would pair well with the lemon curd. A nut-based cookie seemed ideal, and the warm, round flavor of hazelnuts provided a nice contrast to the tart lemon filling. Toasting the hazelnuts before processing them with the flour and salt greatly enhanced their flavor. We love homemade lemon curd, but it's a lot of work, especially when we needed only ¼ cup to fill all the cookies. The convenience factor of the jarred variety was undeniable here; our favorite lemon curd is Wilkin & Sons Tiptree Lemon Curd. Many other varieties of jarred lemon curd taste cloying, so purchase carefully.

1 Adjust oven racks to upper-middle and lower-middle positions and heat oven to 350 degrees. Line 2 baking sheets with parchment paper.

2 Process flour, hazelnuts, and salt in food processor until finely ground, about 45 seconds. Using stand mixer fitted with paddle, beat butter and granulated sugar on medium-high speed until pale and fluffy, 3 to 6 minutes. Add egg yolk and vanilla and beat until incorporated. Reduce speed to low, slowly add flour mixture, and mix until just combined.

3 Working with 1 tablespoon dough at a time, roll into balls and space them 2 inches apart on prepared sheets. Using greased rounded 1-teaspoon measure, make indentation in center of each dough ball.

4 Bake cookies until just beginning to set, about 10 minutes. Remove sheets from oven and gently reshape indentation in center of each cookie with greased rounded 1-teaspoon measure. Fill each indentation with ½ teaspoon lemon curd. Bake until cookies are just beginning to brown around edges, 8 to 10 minutes, switching and rotating sheets halfway through baking. Let cookies cool on sheets for 5 minutes, then transfer to wire rack and let cool completely. Dust with confectioners' sugar before serving.

CHOCOLATE TURTLE COOKIES

Makes about 30 cookies

1 cup (5 ounces) all-purpose flour

⅓ cup (1 ounce) unsweetened cocoa powder

¼ teaspoon salt

8 tablespoons unsalted butter, softened

⅔ cup (4⅔ ounces) sugar

1 large egg, separated, plus 1 large white

2 tablespoons milk

1 teaspoon vanilla extract

1¼ cups pecans, chopped fine

14 soft caramels

3 tablespoons heavy cream

Why This Recipe Works Pecan turtles are so good because they pack multiple flavors and textures into every bite: Crunchy, buttery pecans are held together by chewy, sweet caramel, and the whole thing is coated with rich chocolate. We wanted to translate this into a cookie that would be as satisfying as the candy. A thumbprint cookie was the perfect vehicle for these ingredients; the hollowed-out center could conveniently hold a pour of gooey caramel. The rich chocolate dough gets its flavor from a generous amount of cocoa powder; using cocoa powder kept our cookies from being too sweet when paired with the caramel. For a dense, tender cookie, we omitted the egg white (and saved it for the coating) and added just one yolk. We rolled balls of the dough in chopped pecans, which toasted during baking and provided all-around crunch. To keep things simple, we used store-bought caramel candies for the filling and melted them down with heavy cream. We filled the cookie divots with caramel when the cookies were done baking so it set without becoming too hard or chewy. Be sure to microwave the caramel and cream in a bowl large enough to contain the mixture, and stir occasionally to prevent the mixture from bubbling over or scorching.

1 Whisk flour, cocoa, and salt together in bowl. Using stand mixer fitted with paddle, beat butter and sugar on medium-high speed until pale and fluffy, about 2 minutes. Add egg yolk, milk, and vanilla and beat until incorporated. Reduce speed to low, add flour mixture, and mix until just combined. Cover bowl tightly with plastic wrap and refrigerate until firm, about 1 hour.

2 Adjust oven racks to upper-middle and lower-middle positions and heat oven to 350 degrees. Line 2 baking sheets with parchment paper. Whisk egg whites in bowl until frothy. Place pecans in second bowl. Roll dough into 1-inch balls, dip in egg whites, then roll in pecans; space balls 2 inches apart on prepared sheets. Using greased rounded ½-teaspoon measure, make indentation in center of each dough ball. Bake until set, about 12 minutes, switching and rotating sheets halfway through baking.

3 Meanwhile, microwave caramels and cream in bowl, stirring occasionally, until melted and smooth, 1 to 2 minutes. When cookies are done baking, gently reshape indentation with ½-teaspoon measure. Fill each indentation with ½ teaspoon caramel mixture. Let cookies cool on sheets for 10 minutes, then transfer to wire rack and let cool completely before serving.

S'MORES BLOSSOM COOKIES

Makes 24 cookies

1¼ cups (6¼ ounces) all-purpose flour

½ teaspoon baking powder

¼ teaspoon baking soda

¼ teaspoon salt

8 tablespoons unsalted butter, softened

½ cup (3½ ounces) sugar

8 whole graham crackers, crushed into fine crumbs (1 cup)

1 large egg, room temperature

1 teaspoon vanilla extract

12 large marshmallows, halved crosswise

24 Hershey's Kisses, unwrapped

Why This Recipe Works S'mores may conjure memories of warm nights and sleep-away camp, but it doesn't need to be summertime to capture the flavors of this treat; the combination of wheaty graham crackers, rich chocolate, and sweet, gooey toasted marshmallow is good any time of year. We wanted to package s'mores into a neat blossom cookie, one that would give us all the flavor without the sticky, burned fingers. We made a basic butter cookie dough for the base and proceeded to boost its flavor by mixing in graham cracker crumbs. To really highlight the sweet, whole-wheat flavor of the grahams and to add some crunch, we also rolled the balls of cookie dough in more crushed graham crackers. A halved marshmallow sat neatly on top of the baked cookie and, once melted, took on the same size and shape as the cookies. To get a *brûlée* on the marshmallows without the burn, we ran the baked and topped cookies under the broiler until the marshmallows developed a toasty-roasty top. At last we turned to the crowning touch: the chocolate. Rather than use bar chocolate as with traditional s'mores, we thought we'd follow the dressed-up vibe of this cookie and top it with a Hershey's Kiss hat for the same chocolate flavor with a touch of flair. This cookie might just be better than the classic s'more—and there's no campfire required.

1 Adjust oven rack to middle position and heat oven to 350 degrees. Line 2 baking sheets with parchment paper. Whisk flour, baking powder, baking soda, and salt together in bowl.

2 Using stand mixer fitted with paddle, beat butter, sugar, and ½ cup graham cracker crumbs on medium-high speed until pale and fluffy, about 3 minutes. Add egg and vanilla and beat until incorporated. Reduce speed to low, slowly add flour mixture, and mix until just combined.

3 Spread remaining ½ cup graham cracker crumbs in shallow dish. Working with 1 tablespoon dough at a time, roll into balls, then toss in graham cracker crumbs to coat;

space dough balls evenly on prepared sheets. Bake, 1 sheet at a time, until just set and beginning to crack on sides, 10 to 12 minutes. Let cookies cool on sheets for 5 minutes.

4 Adjust oven rack 10 inches from broiler element and heat broiler. Place 1 marshmallow half, cut side down, in center of each cookie. Broil cookies until marshmallows are deep golden brown, 30 to 45 seconds, rotating sheet halfway through broiling for even browning if needed. Transfer sheet to wire rack and immediately place 1 candy in center of each marshmallow, pressing down gently. Repeat with remaining cookies, marshmallows, and kisses. Let cookies cool completely before serving.

TRIPLE-COCONUT MACAROONS

Makes 48 cookies

1 cup cream of coconut

4 large egg whites

2 tablespoons light corn syrup

2 teaspoons vanilla extract

½ teaspoon salt

3 cups (9 ounces) unsweetened shredded coconut

3 cups (9 ounces) sweetened shredded coconut

Why This Recipe Works Coconut macaroons are easy to find but usually quick to disappoint. What should be a sweet, chewy treat with unmistakable coconut flavor has deteriorated into a lackluster mound of beaten egg whites or sweetened condensed milk and coconut shreds. We set out to make a great version, one with a chewy texture and plenty of coconut flavor. Recipes call for either sweetened or unsweetened shredded coconut; using all sweetened coconut led to an overly sticky cookie, while using only unsweetened created a bland-tasting one. So we used both, for a cookie with appealing texture and flavor. But what really set our macaroons apart was the addition of cream of coconut, which provided one more layer of big flavor. A few egg whites, plus some corn syrup, ensured that the macaroons held together and baked up moist and chewy. Be sure to use cream of coconut (such as Coco López) and not coconut milk. Unsweetened coconut is commonly sold in natural foods stores and Asian markets. For larger macaroons, shape haystacks from a generous ¼ cup of batter and increase the baking time to 20 minutes.

1 Adjust oven racks to upper-middle and lower-middle positions and heat oven to 375 degrees. Line 2 baking sheets with parchment paper.

2 Whisk cream of coconut, egg whites, corn syrup, vanilla, and salt together in bowl; set aside. Toss unsweetened coconut and sweetened coconut together in large bowl, breaking up clumps with your fingertips. Pour cream of coconut mixture over coconut and mix until evenly moistened; transfer bowl to refrigerator for 15 minutes.

3 Drop 1-tablespoon mounds of dough onto prepared sheets, spacing them 1 inch apart. Using your moistened fingertips, form dough into loose haystacks. Bake until light golden brown, about 15 minutes, switching and rotating sheets halfway through baking.

4 Let cookies cool on sheets until slightly set, about 2 minutes, then transfer cookies to wire rack and let cool completely before serving.

Chocolate-Dipped Triple-Coconut Macaroons

Let baked macaroons cool completely. Line 2 baking sheets with parchment paper. Chop 10 ounces semisweet chocolate. Microwave 8 ounces chocolate at 50 percent power, stirring occasionally, until melted, 2 to 4 minutes. Remove melted

chocolate from microwave and stir in remaining 2 ounces chocolate until smooth. Holding macaroon by pointed top, dip bottom ½ inch up sides in chocolate, scrape off excess, and place macaroon on prepared baking sheet. Repeat with remaining macaroons. Refrigerate until chocolate sets, about 15 minutes, before serving.

Shaping Macaroons

1 Drop 1-tablespoon mounds of dough onto parchment paper–lined baking sheets, spacing mounds 1 inch apart.

2 Using your moistened fingertips, form dough mounds into loose haystacks.

HERMIT COOKIES

Makes about 20 cookies

1 cup raisins

2 tablespoons finely chopped crystallized ginger

8 tablespoons unsalted butter

1 teaspoon ground cinnamon

¼ teaspoon ground allspice

2 cups (10 ounces) all-purpose flour

½ teaspoon baking soda

½ teaspoon salt

¾ cup packed (5¼ ounces) dark brown sugar

½ cup molasses

2 large eggs

¾ cup (3 ounces) confectioners' sugar

1½ tablespoons orange juice

Why This Recipe Works A New England specialty, hermits are a chewy raisin-molasses-spice cookie with a sweet glaze. We had fond memories of these cookies, but most recipes we tried baked up more hard and dry than soft, were peppered with tough raisins, and tasted overly spiced. Hermits typically involve creaming softened butter, but we knew that melted butter generally makes cookies moister and chewier. Taking this a step further, we browned the butter to add nutty flavor. Pureeing the raisins and ginger into a rough paste and steeping them in the browned butter softened them, distributed their flavor in every bite, and provided the cookies with more chew. Opinions are divided as to how hermits should be shaped. One camp calls for dropping balls of dough to form round cookies; the other calls for the dough to be shaped into logs, baked, and then cut into individual cookies. A side-by-side test revealed that the hermits baked in logs and then cut were much chewier and moister, as the larger mass of dough better held its moisture during baking.

1 Process raisins and ginger in food processor until mixture sticks together and only small pieces remain, about 10 seconds. Transfer mixture to large bowl.

2 Melt butter in small saucepan over medium-low heat, swirling saucepan occasionally, until nutty brown in color, about 10 minutes. Stir in cinnamon and allspice and cook until fragrant, about 15 seconds. Stir butter mixture into raisin mixture until well combined; let cool completely.

3 Whisk flour, baking soda, and salt together in bowl. Stir brown sugar, molasses, and eggs into cooled butter-raisin mixture until incorporated. Using rubber spatula, fold in flour mixture (dough will be very sticky). Cover bowl with plastic wrap and refrigerate until dough is firm, at least 1½ hours or up to 24 hours.

4 Adjust oven racks to upper-middle and lower-middle positions and heat oven to 350 degrees. Line 2 baking sheets with parchment paper. Transfer dough to counter and divide into quarters. Roll 1 piece of dough into 10-inch log on lightly floured counter. Transfer log to prepared sheet and use ruler to neatly square off sides (each sheet will contain 2 logs). Repeat with remaining dough. Bake until only slight indentation remains on edges when touched (center will appear slightly soft), 15 to 20 minutes, switching and rotating sheets halfway through baking. Let cookies cool on sheets for 5 minutes, then slide cookies, still on parchment, onto wire rack. Let cookies cool completely.

5 Whisk confectioners' sugar and orange juice in small bowl until smooth. Drizzle glaze onto cooled cookies and let sit until glaze dries, about 15 minutes. Cut cookies into 2-inch bars before serving. (Hermits can be stored at room temperature for up to 5 days.)

Forming Hermits

1 Roll each dough quarter into 10-inch log, transfer to baking sheet, then use ruler to neatly square off sides before baking.

2 Once completely cooled, drizzle baked hermits with glaze before slicing into individual bars.

CASHEW-CARAMEL TASSIES

Makes 24 cookies

1 cup cashews, toasted

⅓ cup (1⅓ ounces) confectioners' sugar

2 tablespoons packed light brown sugar

1 cup (5 ounces) all-purpose flour

Salt

7 tablespoons unsalted butter,
cut into ½-inch pieces and chilled

1 large egg yolk

3¾ ounces soft caramels

2½ tablespoons heavy cream

Why This Recipe Works Pecan tassies are pecan pie in cookie form, with a buttery cookie "cup" holding a generous amount of sticky-sweet filling—and if you haven't had one, you've been missing out. But we couldn't help wondering why we never see any variations on this delightful bite-size treat. For a riff on pecan tassies, we combined creamy caramel and chopped cashews in a mini tart-like shell. To streamline the process for our glossy caramel-nut filling, we decided to use store-bought caramels. We melted them with cream to make a luxurious sauce, and the addition of a little salt cut the sweetness and complemented the nuts. Once the caramel was ready, we stirred in the cashews. But when added plain, the cashews' flavor didn't come through. Toasting the cashews before adding them to the caramel made their flavor shine. The filling was great, but we thought the cookies could use a little nutty flavor to liven them up, so we ground some cashews and added them to the buttery cookie dough shell. Using confectioners' sugar as the sweetener (along with a couple of tablespoons of brown sugar for deeper flavor) gave our cookie crusts a short, tart-like texture. Chilling the dough before baking helped it hold its shape and bake up tender and crisp.

1 Adjust oven rack to middle position and heat oven to 350 degrees. Grease one 24-cup, or two 12-cup, mini muffin tin(s).

2 Process ½ cup cashews, confectioners' sugar, and brown sugar in food processor until cashews are finely ground, about 20 seconds. Add flour and ¼ teaspoon salt and process until combined, about 10 seconds. Scatter butter over top and process until mixture resembles damp sand, about 20 seconds. Add egg yolk and process until dough forms ball, about 25 seconds. Working with 1 tablespoon dough at a time, press dough into bottom and sides of each prepared muffin cup. Refrigerate muffin tin(s) until dough is firm, about 20 minutes.

3 Bake shells until golden, 13 to 17 minutes, rotating muffin tin(s) halfway through baking. Let shells cool in muffin tin(s) on wire rack for 20 minutes. Gently remove shells from muffin tin(s) and let cool completely.

4 Coarsely chop remaining ½ cup cashews. Heat caramels, cream, and ⅛ teaspoon salt in small saucepan over medium-low heat, stirring constantly, until melted and smooth. Stir in chopped cashews. Fill each cookie shell with scant 1 teaspoon caramel mixture. Let filling cool until set, about 30 minutes, before serving.

Forming Cookie Shells

Working with 1 tablespoon dough at a time, press dough into bottom and sides of each prepared muffin cup.

FUDGY PEANUT BUTTER MOUSSE CUPS

Makes about 36 cookies

1 (17.5-ounce) package sugar
cookie mix

1 cup pecans, toasted

2 tablespoons all-purpose flour

8 tablespoons unsalted butter, melted

1¼ cups heavy cream

1 cup chunky peanut butter,
room temperature

8 ounces cream cheese, softened

1 cup (4 ounces) confectioners' sugar

1 teaspoon vanilla extract

1 cup (6 ounces) semisweet
chocolate chips

Why This Recipe Works These elegant cookie cups are a complete dessert in miniature. Filling a pecan shortbread cookie crust with a layer of chocolate and a plume of peanut butter mousse sounds like a lot of work, but these eye-catching cookies are much simpler to make than they appear. Since we'd be making a decadent peanut butter mousse, we decided to take a shortcut with our shortbread crust by modifying a store-bought sugar cookie mix. We combined the cookie mix, buttery toasted pecans, and some flour (for additional structure) in the food processor and pulsed the mixture until the dough was cohesive and the pecans were finely ground. Peanut butter—we liked chunky for the bold flavor and crunchy texture it contributed—and cream cheese formed the base of the filling, and we folded in whipped cream to lighten it to an airy mousse. Using a pastry bag made quick work of filling the cooled cookie shells with our rich mousse.

1 Adjust oven rack to middle position and heat oven to 350 degrees. Grease one 24-cup, or two 12-cup, mini muffin tin(s). Pulse cookie mix, pecans, and flour in food processor until pecans are finely ground. Transfer to large bowl and add butter, stirring until mixture resembles wet sand. Working with 1 rounded tablespoon dough mixture at a time, press dough into bottom and sides of each prepared muffin cup. Bake until golden, about 10 minutes. Let shells cool in muffin tin(s) for 20 minutes. Gently remove shells from muffin tin(s). Repeat with remaining dough. Let shells cool completely.

2 Using stand mixer fitted with whisk, whip 1 cup cream on medium-high speed to stiff peaks, about 2 minutes. Transfer to bowl. Mix peanut butter, cream cheese, sugar, and vanilla in now-empty mixer bowl on medium speed until smooth, about 1 minute; fold in whipped cream.

3 Microwave chocolate and remaining ¼ cup cream in small bowl at 50 percent power, stirring occasionally, until melted and smooth, about 1 minute. Portion ½ teaspoon chocolate mixture into each cookie cup, then fill cups with 1 tablespoon peanut butter mixture. Pipe remaining chocolate over peanut butter mixture and refrigerate until set, about 1 hour, before serving. (Cups can be refrigerated for up to 3 days.)

Filling Peanut Butter Mousse Cups

Fit pastry bag with ½-inch round tip and fill cooled cups with 1 tablespoon peanut butter mousse.

FAIRY GINGERBREAD

Makes 60 cookies

1½ teaspoons ground ginger

¾ cup plus 2 tablespoons (4⅜ ounces)
all-purpose flour

½ teaspoon baking soda

¼ teaspoon salt

5 tablespoons unsalted butter, softened

9 tablespoons packed (4 ounces) light
brown sugar

4 teaspoons grated fresh ginger

¾ teaspoon vanilla extract

¼ cup whole milk, room temperature

Why This Recipe Works We were intrigued by original recipes for fairy gingerbread, a cookie popular in the 19th century; with no eggs, no leavener, and batter spread paper-thin on an inverted baking sheet, these cookies were unlike ordinary gingerbread. The cookies we tried melted in our mouths—but they were also bland, so we tackled the flavor issue first. A bit of vanilla extract and salt helped boost the warm ginger notes, but these cookies were still lacking in spice. Doubling the ground ginger called for in most recipes added a much-needed kick, but it made the cookies taste like a dusty spice cupboard. We cut back a little and toasted the ginger to bring out its flavor. Adding fresh grated ginger to the batter added even more intense ginger flavor. While these cookies traditionally lack leavener, a little baking soda helped them retain their airy crispness after baking. These cookies were indeed dainty as a fairy. Use baking sheets that measure at least 15 by 12 inches. Don't be disconcerted by the scant amount of batter: You really are going to spread the batter very thin. Use the edges of the parchment paper as your guide, covering the entire surface thinly and evenly. For easier grating, freeze a 2-inch piece of peeled ginger for 30 minutes and then use a rasp-style grater.

1 Adjust oven racks to upper-middle and lower-middle positions and heat oven to 325 degrees. Spray 2 rimless baking sheets (or inverted rimmed baking sheets) with vegetable oil spray and cover each with 15 by 12-inch sheet parchment paper. Heat ground ginger in small skillet over medium heat until fragrant, about 1 minute. Combine flour, baking soda, salt, and toasted ginger in medium bowl.

2 Using stand mixer fitted with paddle, beat butter and sugar on medium-high speed until light and fluffy, about 2 minutes. Add fresh ginger and vanilla and mix until incorporated. Reduce speed to low and add flour mixture in 3 additions, alternating with milk in 2 additions; scrape down bowl as needed.

3 Evenly spread ¾ cup batter to cover parchment on each prepared sheet (batter will be very thin). Bake until deep golden brown, 16 to 20 minutes, switching and rotating sheets halfway through baking. Immediately score cookies into 3 by 2-inch rectangles. Let cool completely, about 20 minutes. Using tip of paring knife, separate cookies along score marks and serve.

CHOCOLATE CHIP SKILLET COOKIE

Serves 8

1¾ cups (8¾ ounces) all-purpose flour

½ teaspoon baking soda

12 tablespoons unsalted butter

¾ cup packed (5¼ ounces) dark brown sugar

½ cup (3½ ounces) granulated sugar

2 teaspoons vanilla extract

1 teaspoon salt

1 large egg plus 1 large yolk

1 cup (6 ounces) semisweet chocolate chips

Why This Recipe Works A cookie in a skillet? We admit this Internet phenom made us skeptical . . . until we tried it. Unlike making a traditional batch of cookies, this treatment doesn't require scooping, baking, and cooling multiple sheets of treats; the whole thing bakes at once in a single skillet. Plus, the hot bottom and tall sides of a well-seasoned cast-iron pan create a great crust on the cookie. And this treat can go straight from the oven to the table for a fun, hands-on dessert—or you can slice it and serve it like a tart for a more elegant presentation. What's not to like? We cut back on butter and chocolate chips from our usual cookie dough recipe to ensure that the skillet cookie remained crisp on the edges and baked through in the middle while staying perfectly chewy. We also increased the baking time to accommodate the giant size, but otherwise this recipe was simpler and faster than baking regular cookies. Top with ice cream for an extra-decadent treat.

1 Adjust oven rack to upper-middle position and heat oven to 375 degrees. Whisk flour and baking soda together in bowl.

2 Melt 9 tablespoons butter in 12-inch cast-iron skillet over medium heat. Continue to cook, stirring constantly, until butter is dark golden brown and has nutty aroma, about 5 minutes. Transfer browned butter to large bowl and stir in remaining 3 tablespoons butter until melted. Whisk in brown sugar, granulated sugar, vanilla, and salt until incorporated. Whisk in egg and yolk until smooth with no lumps, about 30 seconds.

3 Let mixture stand for 3 minutes, then whisk for 30 seconds. Repeat process of resting and whisking 2 more times until mixture is thick, smooth, and shiny. Using rubber spatula stir in flour mixture until just combined, about 1 minute. Stir in chocolate chips.

4 Wipe skillet clean with paper towels. Transfer dough to now-empty skillet and press into even layer with spatula. Bake until cookie is golden brown and edges are set, about 20 minutes, rotating skillet halfway through baking. Using potholders, transfer skillet to wire rack and let cookie cool for 30 minutes. Slice cookie into wedges and serve.

Making a Chocolate Chip Skillet Cookie

To ensure a uniformly baked cookie, transfer dough to skillet and press into even layer with spatula.

4

SUBLIME
SANDWICH
COOKIES

CHOCOLATE SANDWICH COOKIES

Makes about 40 sandwich cookies

Cookies

3 tablespoons unsalted butter, melted and cooled, plus 5 tablespoons softened

¼ cup (¾ ounce) black cocoa powder

2 tablespoons Dutch-processed cocoa powder

½ teaspoon instant espresso powder

½ cup (3½ ounces) granulated sugar

¼ teaspoon salt

1 large egg yolk

1½ teaspoons vanilla extract

1 cup (5 ounces) all-purpose flour

Filling

2 tablespoons unsalted butter, softened

2 tablespoons vegetable shortening

1 cup (4 ounces) confectioners' sugar

½ teaspoon vanilla extract

Pinch salt

Why This Recipe Works Given the tagline "milk's favorite cookie," it's no surprise Oreos unfailingly appeal to the kid in everyone, ourselves included. But at the risk of offending diehard Oreo fans, we have to admit that nostalgia may have clouded our memory, as we've come to realize that the flavor of Oreos is, in fact, pretty bland. However, once we figured out a few secrets, re-creating—and improving—these iconic cookies proved straightforward. For that midnight-black color of an Oreo, we turned to black cocoa powder. Black cocoa has almost no fat in it, so we cut it with some Dutch-processed cocoa to prevent our cookies from crumbling. A little espresso powder, in combination with the cocoas, gave our cookies the deep chocolaty punch we wanted. An all-butter filling was too similar to buttercream—much richer and softer than the filling of a classic Oreo. But one made from all shortening had no flavor; it just tasted sweet. A combination of butter and shortening resulted in a rich, round flavor and a melt-away texture. Whether you're a dunker or you prefer to twist and lick, you'll find these homemade cookies have supreme flavor and texture that make the effort worthwhile. It is important to slice these cookies exactly to size so they bake evenly and are thin enough to have the classic Oreo snap.

Black Cocoa Powder

For Chocolate Sandwich Cookies with authentic color and big chocolate flavor, we started our testing with black cocoa powder. Black cocoa powder is cocoa that has been heavily Dutched. (Dutching involves washing the cocoa beans in a potassium solution to lower their acidity before grinding.) This process causes the color to darken. Black cocoa contains very little fat, so to avoid a crumbly texture we cut it with some regular Dutch-processed cocoa and then added a little espresso powder to deepen chocolate flavor. Combining the cocoas and espresso powder with melted butter allowed their flavors to bloom and helped them blend easily with the other cookie ingredients. You can buy true black cocoa powder from kingarthurflour.com or use Hershey's Special Dark cocoa powder, which is also heavily Dutched.

1 For the cookies Stir melted butter, black cocoa, Dutch-processed cocoa, and espresso powder in bowl until combined and smooth.

2 Using stand mixer fitted with paddle, beat remaining 5 tablespoons butter, sugar, salt, and cocoa mixture on medium-high speed until fluffy, about 2 minutes, scraping down bowl as needed. Add egg yolk and vanilla and beat until combined, about 30 seconds. Reduce speed to low and slowly add flour in 3 additions, mixing well after each addition and scraping down bowl as needed. Continue to mix until dough forms cohesive ball, about 30 seconds.

3 Divide dough in half. Roll each half into 6-inch log. Wrap logs tightly in plastic wrap, twisting ends to firmly compact dough into tight cylinder, and refrigerate until firm, at least 1 hour or up to 3 days.

4 Adjust oven racks to upper-middle and lower-middle positions and heat oven to 325 degrees. Line 2 baking sheets with parchment paper. Trim ends of dough logs, then slice into ⅛-inch-thick rounds and space them ½ inch apart on prepared sheets.

5 Bake until cookies are firm and reveal slight indentation when pressed with your finger, 14 to 16 minutes, switching and rotating sheets halfway through baking. Let cookies cool on sheets for 5 minutes, then transfer to wire rack. Let cookies cool completely.

6 For the filling Using clean, dry mixer bowl and paddle, mix butter, shortening, sugar, vanilla, and salt on medium-low speed until combined, about 1 minute. Increase speed to medium-high and beat until light and fluffy, about 2 minutes.

7 Place rounded ½ teaspoon filling in center of bottom of half of cookies, then top with remaining cookies, pressing gently until filling spreads to edges. Serve. (Cookies can be stored at room temperature for up to 1 week.)

Making Chocolate Sandwich Cookies

1 Divide dough in half and roll each half into 6-inch log.

2 Wrap logs tightly in plastic wrap, twisting ends to firmly compact dough into tight cylinder; refrigerate logs until firm, at least 1 hour or up to 3 days.

3 Trim ends of dough logs, then slice logs into ⅛-inch-thick rounds (marking the slices makes it easy) and space them ½ inch apart on prepared baking sheets.

4 Bake until cookies are firm; cookies should reveal slight indentation when pressed with your finger, 14 to 16 minutes, switching and rotating sheets halfway through baking.

5 Place rounded ½ teaspoon filling in center of bottom of 40 cooled cookies.

6 Top cookie bottoms with remaining cookies and squeeze gently until filling is evenly distributed.

PEANUT BUTTER SANDWICH COOKIES

Makes 24 sandwich cookies

Cookies

1¼ cups raw or dry-roasted peanuts, toasted and cooled

¾ cup (3¾ ounces) all-purpose flour

1 teaspoon baking soda

½ teaspoon salt

3 tablespoons unsalted butter, melted

½ cup creamy peanut butter

½ cup (3½ ounces) granulated sugar

½ cup (3½ ounces) light brown sugar

3 tablespoons whole milk

1 large egg

Filling

¾ cup creamy peanut butter

3 tablespoons unsalted butter

1 cup (4 ounces) confectioners' sugar

Why This Recipe Works We love a thick, chewy peanut butter cookie, but we also have an undeniable soft spot for peanut butter sandwich cookies. Our ideal sandwich would feature thin, crunchy cookies and a smooth filling, both packed with peanut flavor—basically a Nutter Butter made better. The first task: giving the cookie rounds big flavor. In addition to the obvious inclusion of peanut butter in the dough, we cut a portion of the flour with finely chopped peanuts—a simple substitution that boosted flavor dramatically. To make the cookies thin and crisp, we added some milk; the increased moisture made a thinner dough that spread more readily during baking. This was a great start, but baking soda took our intentions further. Adding a full teaspoon to the recipe encouraged the air bubbles within the dough to inflate so rapidly that they burst before the cookies set, leaving the cookies flat. A creamy filling of peanut butter, confectioners' sugar, and butter tasted great but was too thick to spread without breaking the cookies. We didn't want to lose any peanut flavor in an effort to soften the filling, so we warmed the peanut butter and butter in the microwave to make the filling easy to sandwich. Do not use unsalted peanut butter. Take care when processing the peanuts—you want to chop them, not turn them into a paste.

Substituting Nut Butters

Either because of allergy or preference, we wondered if you can substitute other nut butters for peanut butter in cookie recipes. We tested substituting almond and cashew butter for peanut butter in cookies. The cashew butter cookies were very similar in texture and appearance to those made with peanut butter, but the cashew flavor was so subtle that it was easy to miss. The almond butter cookies fared worse: The almond skins made the cookies taste noticeably bitter, and the cookies also spread more than their peanut and cashew counterparts. It turns out that almonds contain not only slightly more fat than peanuts and cashews (which share a similar fat percentage) but also a much higher proportion of unsaturated fat. Because unsaturated fat has a lower melting point than the saturated kind, cookies made with almond butter are more fluid, allowing the batter to spread before their structure is set. In a nutshell: A direct substitution with cashew or almond butter won't produce the same results.

1 For the cookies Adjust oven racks to upper-middle and lower-middle positions and heat oven to 350 degrees. Line 2 baking sheets with parchment paper. Pulse peanuts in food processor until finely chopped, about 8 pulses. Whisk flour, baking soda, and salt together in bowl. Whisk melted butter, peanut butter, granulated sugar, brown sugar, milk, and egg together in second bowl. Using rubber spatula, stir flour mixture into peanut butter mixture until combined. Stir in chopped peanuts until evenly distributed.

2 Using 1-tablespoon measure or #60 scoop, drop 12 mounds evenly onto each prepared sheet. Using your dampened hand, press each mound until 2 inches in diameter.

3 Bake cookies until deep golden brown and firm to touch, 15 to 18 minutes, switching and rotating sheets halfway through baking. Let cookies cool on sheets for 5 minutes, then transfer to wire rack. Repeat with remaining dough. Let cookies cool completely.

4 For the filling Microwave peanut butter and butter until melted and warm, about 40 seconds. Using rubber spatula, stir in confectioners' sugar until combined.

5 Place 1 tablespoon (or #60 scoop) warm filling in center of bottom of half of cookies, then top with remaining cookies, pressing gently until filling spreads to edges. Let filling set for 1 hour before serving.

Peanut Butter Sandwich Cookies with Honey-Cinnamon Filling

Omit butter from filling. Stir 5 tablespoons honey and ½ teaspoon ground cinnamon into warm peanut butter before adding confectioners' sugar.

Peanut Butter Sandwich Cookies with Milk Chocolate Filling

Reduce peanut butter to ½ cup and omit butter from filling. Stir 6 ounces finely chopped milk chocolate into warm peanut butter until melted, microwaving for 10 seconds at a time if necessary, before adding confectioners' sugar.

Forming Peanut Butter Sandwich Cookies

1 Using 1-tablespoon measure or #60 scoop, drop 12 mounds evenly onto each prepared sheet. Using your dampened hand, press each mound until 2 inches in diameter.

2 Microwave peanut butter and butter until melted and warm, about 40 seconds. Using rubber spatula, stir in confectioners' sugar until combined.

3 Using 1-tablespoon measure or #60 scoop, portion warm filling onto bottoms of half of baked cookies.

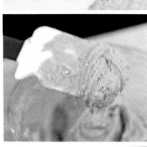

4 Rather than smearing filling with knife or offset spatula, top with second cookie and press gently until filling spreads to edges.

ALMOND-RASPBERRY SANDWICH COOKIES

Makes about 24 sandwich cookies

2 cups (10 ounces) all-purpose flour

1¼ cups slivered almonds

½ cup (3½ ounces) granulated sugar, plus ½ cup for coating

16 tablespoons unsalted butter, cut into ½-inch pieces and chilled

1 teaspoon vanilla extract

½ cup raspberry jam

Why This Recipe Works Almond and raspberry are a winning combination, especially in these tender, sugar-coated cookie sandwiches. The generous amount of almonds in the dough doesn't just flavor the cookies; it also tenderizes them for a rich melt-in-the-mouth texture. Sandwiched with sweet-tart raspberry jam, these cookies were delicious, but we went one step further to make them extra-special: We coated the sandwiches in granulated sugar for a sweet crunch and bit of sparkle. Filling the cookies with jam and coating them with the sugar while they were still warm helped the sugar stick to the baked cookies once they had cooled. The dough scraps can be gathered and rerolled; wrap them and refrigerate them briefly if they become too difficult to work with. Jams and preserves have superior berry flavor; do not fill the cookies with jelly. Our favorite is Smucker's Red Raspberry Preserves. Sliced blanched almonds can be substituted for the slivered almonds.

1 Adjust oven racks to upper-middle and lower-middle positions and heat oven to 350 degrees. Line 2 baking sheets with parchment paper. Process 1 cup flour and almonds in food processor until almonds are finely ground, about 1 minute. Add ½ cup sugar and remaining 1 cup flour and process until combined. Add butter and vanilla and pulse until dough forms.

2 Transfer dough to lightly floured counter and roll to ¼ inch thickness. Using 2-inch round cookie cutter, cut dough into circles; space circles 2 inches apart on prepared sheets. Gently reroll scraps, cut into circles, and transfer to prepared sheets. Bake until edges are light brown, about 15 minutes, switching and rotating sheets halfway through baking. Let cookies cool on sheets for 5 minutes, then transfer to wire rack.

3 Place remaining ½ cup sugar in bowl. Working quickly, spread 1 teaspoon jam over bottom of half of warm cookies, then top with remaining cookies, pressing lightly to adhere. Gently toss cookies in sugar to coat and transfer to wire rack. Let cookies cool completely before serving.

Making Almond-Raspberry Sandwich Cookies

1 While cookies are still very warm, spread 1 teaspoon jam over bottom of half of cookies, then top with remaining cookies, pressing lightly to adhere.

2 Give warm sandwiches a few flips in sugar in bowl so it adheres.

HAZELNUT ESPRESSO TRUFFLE COOKIES

Makes 30 sandwich cookies

1 cup hazelnuts, toasted and skinned

2½ cups (12½ ounces) all-purpose flour

½ teaspoon salt

½ teaspoon baking powder

16 tablespoons unsalted butter, softened

1¼ cups (8¾ ounces) superfine sugar

1 large egg plus 1 large yolk

4 teaspoons instant espresso powder

2 teaspoons vanilla extract

¾ cup heavy cream

3 cups (18 ounces) bittersweet chocolate chips

Why This Recipe Works The classic Italian combinations of hazelnut and chocolate and hazelnut and coffee are well-known and well-loved. We wanted to bring together all three flavors in one extra-special cookie. The hazelnut and coffee we incorporated into the cookie itself by mixing a generous amount of ground hazelnuts (toasted before grinding for depth) and instant espresso powder into the dough. We then made a smooth, rich, dark ganache from bittersweet chocolate and cream, which set up to the perfect consistency when sandwiched between the cookies—just like the center of the most luxurious dark chocolate truffle. A final drizzle of more dark chocolate gave these cookies an appearance as sophisticated as their complex flavor. There's a lot of chocolate in this recipe—a whopping 18 ounces; to streamline prep, we use chocolate chips, which don't require chopping. Both the dough and the filling need to chill. Use a thin spatula to help move these thin cookies from the counter to the baking sheets.

1 Process hazelnuts in food processor until finely ground, about 30 seconds. Whisk flour, salt, baking powder, and ground hazelnuts together in bowl. Using stand mixer fitted with paddle, beat butter and sugar on medium-high speed until pale and fluffy, about 3 minutes. Add egg and yolk, one at a time, espresso powder, and vanilla and beat until combined. Reduce speed to low and add flour mixture in 3 additions until just combined, scraping down bowl as needed. Transfer dough to counter and divide in half. Form each half into 5-inch disk, wrap disks tightly in plastic wrap, and refrigerate for 1 hour.

2 Adjust oven racks to upper-middle and lower-middle positions and heat oven to 375 degrees. Line 2 baking sheets with parchment paper. Let chilled dough sit on counter to soften slightly, about 10 minutes. Roll 1 disk of dough into 14-inch circle, about ⅛ inch thick, on lightly floured counter. Using 2¼-inch round cookie cutter, cut out 30 circles; space circles ½ inch apart on prepared sheets. Gently reroll scraps once, cut into circles, and transfer to prepared sheets. Bake until edges are slightly browned, about 7 minutes, switching and rotating sheets halfway through baking. Let cookies cool on sheets for 5 minutes, then transfer to wire rack. Repeat with second disk of dough. Let cookies cool completely.

3 Heat cream in small saucepan over medium heat until simmering. Place 1¾ cups chocolate chips in bowl. Pour hot cream over chocolate chips; cover and let sit for 5 minutes. Whisk chocolate mixture until smooth. Refrigerate ganache, uncovered, stirring occasionally, until thickened, about 40 minutes.

4 Spread 2 teaspoons ganache over bottom of half of cookies, then top with remaining cookies, pressing lightly to adhere. Microwave remaining 1¼ cups chocolate chips in bowl at 50 percent power, stirring occasionally, until melted, 2 to 4 minutes. Drizzle chocolate over cookies and let set, about 30 minutes, before serving.

MOLASSES SPICE–LEMON COOKIES

Makes about 42 sandwich cookies

Cookies

2 cups (10 ounces) all-purpose flour

2 teaspoons baking soda

1 teaspoon ground cinnamon

1 teaspoon ground ginger

¾ teaspoon salt

¼ teaspoon ground cloves

12 tablespoons unsalted butter, melted and cooled

2 cups (14 ounces) granulated sugar

¼ cup robust or full molasses

1 large egg

Filling

3 tablespoons unsalted butter, softened

2 cups (8 ounces) confectioners' sugar

3 tablespoons lemon juice

Why This Recipe Works Molasses and ginger are frequent companions in many desserts, but rarely are they paired with anything else. Sure, they provide a distinct, strong flavor combination, but they actually work beautifully with ingredients such as chocolate and cream cheese. However, our favorite combination—and one of the most intriguing, we think—is molasses and lemon. The contrast between a tart lemon filling and a warmly spiced molasses cookie makes for a supremely satisfying treat. While many sandwich cookies feature crunchy cookies, we loved the idea of a chewy cookie here for a soft-baked treat. Overbaking turned our cookies from chewy to crisp, so we made sure to pull the cookies from the oven when they'd puffed and were just starting to crack on the top; they sank to a perfectly flat sandwich-cookie shape as they cooled. For the best flavor, we used robust or full molasses; we found it best to avoid blackstrap varieties, which made the cookies bitter. The lemon filling for our cookies is essentially a tangy frosting. We whisked butter, lemon juice, and confectioners' sugar into a smooth spread and then generously filled the cookies for a flavor-packed treat.

1 For the cookies Whisk flour, baking soda, cinnamon, ginger, salt, and cloves together in bowl. Whisk melted butter, 1½ cups granulated sugar, molasses, and egg in second bowl until combined. Stir flour mixture into molasses mixture until incorporated. Cover bowl tightly with plastic wrap and chill until firm, about 1 hour.

2 Adjust oven racks to upper-middle and lower-middle positions and heat oven to 375 degrees. Line 2 baking sheets with parchment paper. Spread remaining ½ cup granulated sugar in shallow dish.

3 Roll dough into ¾-inch balls, then roll in granulated sugar to coat; space dough balls 2 inches apart on prepared sheets. Bake until tops are just beginning to crack, 8 to 10 minutes, switching and rotating sheets halfway through baking. Let cookies cool on sheets for 5 minutes, then transfer to wire rack. Repeat with remaining dough. Let cookies cool completely.

4 For the filling Whisk butter, confectioners' sugar, and lemon juice in bowl until smooth. Spread heaping 1-teaspoon filling over bottom of half of cookies, then top with remaining cookies, pressing lightly to adhere. Let filling set, about 1 hour, before serving.

VANILLA BEAN–APRICOT SANDWICH COOKIES

Makes 20 sandwich cookies

2½ cups (12½ ounces) all-purpose flour

¾ cup (5¼ ounces) superfine sugar

¼ teaspoon salt

16 tablespoons unsalted butter, cut into 16 pieces and softened

2 vanilla beans

1 ounce cream cheese, softened

2 teaspoons vanilla extract

¾ cup apricot preserves

Why This Recipe Works Filling cookies with jam is always a hit, but sometimes we tire of the classic butter cookie sandwiching any jam of the red variety. Searching for new inspiration, we decided to flavor the dough with vanilla and fill the cookies with often overlooked apricot preserves. For the cleanest, clearest vanilla flavor that would distinguish these cookies from plain butter cookies, we added both extract and vanilla bean seeds to the dough. Baking muted the vanilla flavor, so we found that we needed the seeds from two whole vanilla beans to properly perfume a batch of cookies. The floral notes of the vanilla complemented those of the apricot preserves. We loved the preserves' orange hue, so we cut a window into the top cookie with a small cookie cutter to allow for a peek at the bright filling inside. You can use any shape cutter you like for these cookies. For an elegant finishing touch, try decorating these cookies with icing.

1 Using stand mixer fitted with paddle, mix flour, sugar, and salt on low speed until combined. Add butter, 1 piece at a time, and mix until crumbly, 1 to 2 minutes. Cut vanilla beans in half lengthwise. Using tip of paring knife, scrape out seeds. Add vanilla bean seeds, cream cheese, and vanilla and mix until dough begins to form large clumps, about 30 seconds. Transfer dough to counter, knead briefly to form cohesive mass, and divide in half. Form each piece into disk, wrap disks in plastic wrap, and refrigerate for 30 minutes.

2 Adjust oven rack to middle position and heat oven to 375 degrees. Line 2 baking sheets with parchment paper. Roll each disk of dough ⅛ inch thick between 2 large sheets of parchment. Transfer dough rounds, still between parchment, to refrigerator for 10 minutes.

3 Remove top piece of parchment. Using 2½-inch cookie cutter, cut dough into shapes; space shapes 1½ inches apart on prepared sheets. Using ¾-inch cutter, cut out centers of half of dough shapes. Gently reroll scraps once, cut into shapes, transfer to prepared sheets, and cut out centers of half of dough shapes. Bake, 1 sheet at a time, until cookies are light golden brown, about 10 minutes, rotating sheet halfway through baking. Let cookies cool on sheet for 3 minutes, then transfer to wire rack. Let cookies cool completely.

4 Spread bottom of each solid cookie with 1 teaspoon preserves, then top with cutout cookie, pressing lightly to adhere, before serving.

COCONUT DROPS

Makes about 72 sandwich cookies

19 tablespoons unsalted butter, softened

1 cup (7 ounces) granulated sugar

¼ cup packed (1¾ ounces) light brown sugar

1 large egg plus 1 large yolk

1 teaspoon coconut extract

1 teaspoon vanilla extract

2 cups (10 ounces) all-purpose flour

2 cups (6 ounces) sweetened shredded coconut

½ cup whole blanched almonds, chopped fine

¾ cup (4½ ounces) semisweet chocolate chips

Why This Recipe Works If you like coconut macaroons and buttery short-bread, you'll love these cookies that combine the two in a rich, tender sandwich. To give the shortbread cookies as much coconut flavor as a macaroon, we used a lot of the sweet, shredded stuff—for equal parts flour and coconut—and we added coconut extract. In addition, we tossed a handful of finely chopped almonds into the dough for nuttiness. We wanted these cookies to be ultrarich and even more tender than traditional shortbread. We achieved this by enriching the dough with a whopping 16 tablespoons of butter. This made for a very soft dough; cutting the chilled dough into preportioned squares that we could then quickly roll into balls helped us turn out shapely dough portions without much hassle. Of course, melted chocolate was the perfect filling to sandwich these cookies together. With the irresistible combination of almonds, coconut, and chocolate in these small sandwich cookies, we felt like we were eating an Almond Joy—only better. A food processor makes quick work of finely chopping the nuts.

1 Using stand mixer fitted with paddle, beat 16 tablespoons butter, granulated sugar, and brown sugar on medium-high speed until fluffy, about 2 minutes. Add egg and yolk, coconut extract, and vanilla and beat until combined. Reduce speed to low; add flour, coconut, and almonds; and mix until just combined. Transfer dough to counter and divide in half. Form each half into 1-inch-thick square, wrap squares in plastic wrap, and refrigerate for 1 hour.

2 Adjust oven racks to upper-middle and lower-middle positions and heat oven to 350 degrees. Line 2 baking sheets with parchment paper. Cut 1 dough square into ½-inch squares. Roll squares into ¾-inch balls; space balls 1 inch apart on prepared sheets. Bake until edges are just golden, 12 to 14 minutes, switching and rotating sheets halfway through baking. Let cookies cool on sheets for 10 minutes, then transfer to wire rack. Repeat with remaining dough. Let cookies cool completely.

3 Microwave chocolate and remaining 3 tablespoons butter in bowl at 50 percent power, stirring frequently, until melted, about 2 minutes. Spread ½ teaspoon chocolate mixture over bottom of half of cookies, then top with remaining cookies, pressing lightly to adhere, before serving.

Forming Coconut Drops

Divide dough in half. Shape halves into 1-inch-thick squares; wrap squares in plastic and refrigerate for 1 hour. Using chef's knife, cut 1 chilled square into small ½-inch squares; quickly roll each square into ¾-inch ball. Repeat with remaining square.

DULCE DE LECHE AND CINNAMON SANDWICH COOKIES

Makes 24 sandwich cookies

Cookies

2 cups (10 ounces) all-purpose flour

1 teaspoon baking soda

½ teaspoon salt

½ teaspoon ground anise

16 tablespoons unsalted butter, softened

1 cup (7 ounces) sugar, plus ½ cup for rolling

1 large egg

1 teaspoon vanilla extract

1 teaspoon ground cinnamon

Filling

1 tablespoon unsalted butter

½ teaspoon ground cinnamon

½ teaspoon ground anise

1½ cups dulce de leche

Why This Recipe Works Dulce de leche, a rich and creamy South American caramel made from cooked milk, is the star of these deceptively simple sandwich cookies. Spicing the buttery cookies with cinnamon was a delicious start, and adding anise to the mix took the cookies over the top. The anise enhanced the flavor of the warm cinnamon, and both complemented the milky caramel filling—so much so that we decided to add both spices to the dulce de leche as well. Slow cooking milk for homemade dulce de leche can take a gruelingly long time, so to keep our cookies simple we turned to store-bought and doctored it with a tablespoon of butter for added richness. Melting the butter before adding it to the caramel allowed us to briefly cook the spices in it to bloom their flavor, and the melted butter easily blended into the filling. This made for a fragrant cookie, but we wanted the warm spice flavor to be even more prominent, so we took the cinnamon out of the dough and instead rolled the cookies in cinnamon sugar before baking. Not only did this ensure unmistakable cinnamon flavor in every bite, but the sugary coating—along with the rich amber hue of the filling—made for an attractive presentation.

1 For the cookies Adjust oven rack to middle position and heat oven to 350 degrees. Line baking sheet with parchment paper. Whisk flour, baking soda, salt, and anise together in bowl.

2 Using stand mixer fitted with paddle, beat butter and 1 cup sugar on medium-high speed until pale and fluffy, about 3 minutes. Add egg and vanilla and beat until combined. Reduce speed to low and add flour mixture in 3 additions until just combined, scraping down bowl as needed.

3 Combine cinnamon and remaining ½ cup sugar in shallow dish. Working with 2 teaspoons dough at a time, roll into 16 balls and space them 2 inches apart on prepared sheet. Bake until edges are firm, 10 to 12 minutes, rotating sheet halfway through baking. Let cookies cool on sheet for 1 minute, place in cinnamon sugar, and turn to coat evenly; transfer cookies to wire rack. Repeat twice more with remaining dough. Let cookies cool completely.

4 For the filling Melt butter in small saucepan over medium heat. Whisk in cinnamon and anise and cook until fragrant, about 1 minute. Off heat, stir in dulce de leche until incorporated. Spread 1½ teaspoons filling over bottom of half of cookies, then top with remaining cookies, pressing lightly to adhere, before serving.

Dulce de Leche

Dulce de leche is a South American caramel made by slowly heating sweetened milk (or sometimes condensed milk, coconut milk, or goat's milk; if the last, it's called *cajeta*). In Latin America, dulce de leche, sometimes translated as "milk jam," is used in many sweets or simply spread on toast or pancakes. It reached the United States in a big way more than a decade ago when Häagen-Dazs used it for a new ice cream flavor. Look for dulce de leche in the international or baking aisle of your grocery store.

SPICED SHORTBREAD BUTTONS

Makes about 30 sandwich cookies

2½ cups (12½ ounces) all-purpose flour

¾ cup (5¼ ounces) superfine sugar

1 teaspoon ground cinnamon

1 teaspoon ground ginger

½ teaspoon ground allspice

¼ teaspoon salt

16 tablespoons unsalted butter,
cut into 16 pieces and softened

1 ounce cream cheese, softened

2 teaspoons vanilla extract

1 teaspoon grated lemon zest

6 ounces white chocolate, chopped

Why This Recipe Works Unlike cakes, cupcakes, or brownies, which take the shape of the pans or tins in which they're baked, cookies allow for plenty of creativity in shaping. And these button-shaped cookies are as cute as, well, a button. After cutting out rounds of dough, we simply poked holes in the center of the circles so the cookies resembled buttons. Using a basic plastic straw made the task easy and created even-size holes. Scoring the cookies with a smaller round cookie cutter gave them a realistic edge. For a flavor profile as rustic as these buttons' appearance, we liked a combination of cinnamon, ginger, and allspice; a bright hint of lemon zest paired perfectly with these warm spices. Sweet white chocolate made an ideal filling, and its stark white color made for a striking appearance. A plastic straw is all you need to cut out button holes; as the straw fills with dough, simply trim off the end with scissors. You may need 2 to 3 straws in total.

1 Using stand mixer fitted with paddle, mix flour, sugar, cinnamon, ginger, allspice, and salt on low speed until combined. Add butter, 1 piece at a time, and mix until dough looks crumbly and slightly wet, 1 to 2 minutes. Add cream cheese, vanilla, and lemon zest and beat until dough just begins to form large clumps, about 30 seconds. Transfer dough to counter; knead just until it forms cohesive mass and divide in half. Form each half into disk, wrap disks in plastic wrap, and refrigerate for 30 minutes.

2 Adjust oven rack to middle position and heat oven to 375 degrees. Line 2 baking sheets with parchment paper. Roll each disk of dough ⅛ inch thick between 2 large sheets of parchment. Transfer dough rounds, still between parchment, to refrigerator for 10 minutes.

3 Using 2-inch round cutter, cut dough into circles; space circles ½ inch apart on prepared sheets. Gently reroll scraps once, cut into circles, and transfer to prepared sheets. Using 1½-inch round cutter, press cutter halfway through half of cookies and, using plastic straw, cut out 4 small holes in centers of same cookies.

4 Bake cookies, 1 sheet at a time, until edges are light golden brown, about 10 minutes, rotating sheet halfway through baking. Let cookies cool on sheet for 3 minutes, then transfer to wire rack. Let cookies cool completely.

5 Microwave chocolate at 50 percent power, stirring occasionally, until melted, 1 to 2 minutes. Spread 1 teaspoon melted chocolate over bottoms of whole cookies, then top with cut cookies, pressing lightly to adhere. Let chocolate set, about 30 minutes, before serving.

BACI DI DAMA

Makes 40 sandwich cookies

1 cup hazelnuts, toasted and skinned

½ cup (2½ ounces) all-purpose flour

¼ cup (1¾ ounces) sugar

2 tablespoons cornstarch

¼ teaspoon salt

5 tablespoons unsalted butter, cut into ½-inch pieces and chilled

½ teaspoon vanilla extract

½ cup (3 ounces) bittersweet chocolate chips

Why This Recipe Works Hailing from Italy's Piedmont region, *baci di dama* have a darling name (they translate to "lady's kisses") and an even more darling appearance. The sandwiches consist of two diminutive hazelnut cookies surrounding a rich chocolate filling. Baci di dama are a textural marvel, at once crisp and meltingly tender. The hazelnut cookies get their texture from rice flour, which gives baked goods crispness—and since it doesn't contain the protein gluten like wheat flour does, doughs made with it don't run the risk of becoming tough if overworked. But we don't usually have rice flour on hand, so to replicate the crisp texture with staples, we used a combination of all-purpose flour and cornstarch. We also found that cutting cold butter into the dry ingredients rather than creaming the butter and sugar resulted in a crispier cookie (and a dough that was easier to handle). We used chocolate chips for the filling rather than bar chocolate; chocolate chips contain emulsifiers so once they're melted, they have a thicker consistency—making them an ideal filling for holding the tiny, bulbous cookies together.

1 Adjust oven racks to upper-middle and lower-middle positions and heat oven to 350 degrees. Line 2 baking sheets with parchment paper.

2 Process hazelnuts, flour, sugar, cornstarch, and salt in food processor until finely ground, about 30 seconds. Add butter and vanilla and process until dough comes together, about 30 seconds.

3 Transfer dough to counter and divide into 4 equal pieces. Working with 1 piece of dough at a time, press and roll into 10-inch-long by 1-inch-wide rope. Using bench scraper or sharp knife, cut rope into 20 lengths, then roll lengths into balls with your hands and space them 1 inch apart on prepared sheets. Repeat with remaining dough. Bake until edges are lightly browned, 16 to 18 minutes, switching and rotating sheets halfway through baking. Let cookies cool completely on sheets.

4 Microwave chocolate chips in small bowl at 50 percent power, stirring occasionally, until melted, 1 to 2 minutes. Spread ¼ teaspoon chocolate over bottom of half of cookies, then top with remaining cookies, pressing lightly to adhere. Let chocolate set, about 15 minutes, before serving.

Shaping Baci di Dama

1 Press and roll 1 piece dough into rope that measures about 10 inches long and 1 inch wide.

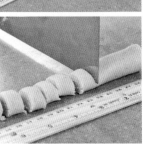

2 Using bench scraper or sharp knife, cut rope into 20 even lengths and then roll lengths into balls between your hands.

WHOOPIE PIES

Makes 6 sandwich cookies

Cakes

2 cups (10 ounces) all-purpose flour

½ cup (1½ ounces) Dutch-processed cocoa powder

1 teaspoon baking soda

½ teaspoon salt

8 tablespoons unsalted butter, softened

1 cup packed (7 ounces) light brown sugar

1 large egg, room temperature

1 teaspoon vanilla extract

1 cup buttermilk

Filling

12 tablespoons unsalted butter, softened

1¼ cups (5 ounces) confectioners' sugar

1½ teaspoons vanilla extract

⅛ teaspoon salt

2½ cups marshmallow crème

Why This Recipe Works Made up of two cookie-like chocolate cakes stuffed to the gills with fluffy marshmallow filling, the whoopie pie is a sweet indulgence. For the cake component, we drew inspiration from devil's food cake, creaming butter with sugar, adding eggs and buttermilk for tenderness, and using all-purpose flour and baking soda for the right amount of structure. For the chocolate flavor, we preferred the darker color and flavor that Dutch-processed cocoa provided. One-half cup of cocoa delivered a balanced flavor, especially when boosted with a splash of vanilla extract. We tried replacing some of the granulated sugar with brown sugar, and found that it deepened flavor and added moisture. In fact, we liked the results so much we wound up using all brown sugar. Using a ⅓-cup dry measuring cup, we portioned the batter onto two baking sheets to give the cakes plenty of room to spread. For the filling, we eschewed the traditional sugar and lard in favor of marshmallow crème, which we enriched with butter for a mixture that was fluffy yet firm. Don't be tempted to bake all the cakes on one baking sheet; the batter needs room to spread while it bakes.

1 For the cakes Adjust oven racks to upper-middle and lower-middle positions and heat oven to 350 degrees. Line 2 baking sheets with parchment paper. Whisk flour, cocoa, baking soda, and salt together in bowl.

2 Using stand mixer fitted with paddle, beat butter and sugar on medium speed until pale and fluffy, about 3 minutes. Add egg and beat until incorporated, scraping down bowl as needed. Add vanilla and mix until incorporated. Reduce speed to low and add flour mixture in 3 additions, alternating with buttermilk in 2 additions. Give batter final stir by hand to ensure that no flour pockets remain. Using ⅓-cup dry measuring cup, scoop 6 mounds of batter onto each prepared sheet, spaced about 3 inches apart. Bake until centers spring back when lightly pressed, 15 to 18 minutes, switching and rotating sheets halfway through baking. Let cakes cool completely on sheets.

3 For the filling Using stand mixer fitted with paddle, beat butter and sugar on medium speed until fluffy, about 3 minutes. Beat in vanilla and salt. Add marshmallow crème and mix until combined, about 2 minutes. Refrigerate until slightly firm, about 30 minutes. (Filling can be refrigerated for

up to 2 days.) Place ⅓ cup filling on bottom of half of cakes, then top with remaining cakes, pressing to spread filling to edge. Serve. (Whoopie pies can be refrigerated for up to 3 days.)

Baking and Filling Whoopie Pies

1 Using ⅓-cup dry measuring cup, drop 6 mounds of batter onto each prepared sheet, spaced about 3 inches apart.

2 Once cakes are baked and cooled, dollop ⅓ cup filling in center of flat side of 6 cakes, then top with flat side of remaining 6 cakes, pressing gently until filling spreads to edge of cake.

MINI PUMPKIN WHOOPIE PIES

Makes 24 sandwich cookies

1 cup (5 ounces) all-purpose flour

1½ teaspoons pumpkin pie spice

1 teaspoon baking soda

¾ teaspoon salt

2 large eggs

¾ cup (5¼ ounces) granulated sugar

1 cup canned unsweetened
pumpkin puree

6 tablespoons unsalted butter, melted
and cooled, plus 4 tablespoons softened

1 cup (4 ounces) confectioners' sugar,
plus extra for dusting (optional)

4 ounces cream cheese,
cut into 4 pieces and softened

Why This Recipe Works Whoopie pies are a fun treat—a portable dessert that's part cookie, part frosted cake. But whoopie pies are typically over-sized; we wanted to make a smaller version we could enjoy more often, and we wanted to create a flavorful variation on the traditional choco-late cakes. We settled on pumpkin spice for our reimagined whoopies. For ease, we didn't take measures to reduce the moisture in the pumpkin puree; instead we added the canned pumpkin as is and skipped adding another liquid ingredient to our cakes. Pairing the pumpkin with a marsh-mallow crème filling was fine, but our favorite spice cakes are slathered with cream cheese frosting, so we followed suit. The tangy frosting is a welcome contrast to the moist, warm-spiced cake. A pastry bag makes quick work of forming even cakes, but the batter can be dropped with a spoon instead if you like.

Canned Pumpkin Puree

To be sure we were opening the best canned pumpkin puree for our Mini Pumpkin Whoopie Pies, we selected three widely available pumpkin purees and tasted them plain, baked into pumpkin cake, and whipped into pumpkin chiffon pie. We were flummoxed by the variety of textures and colors. One yellow puree was a pulpy paste and reminiscent of baby food; it made a too-thick pie filling and an overly dense cake. Another product was fibrous when sampled plain and therefore created a gritty pie filling. Both of these products contained 33 percent more fiber than our top-ranking puree, **Libby's 100% Pure Pumpkin**, which had a silky consistency and subtle sweetness. Fortunately, it's also the easiest to find.

1 Adjust oven racks to upper-middle and lower-middle posi-tions and heat oven to 350 degrees. Line 2 baking sheets with parchment paper.

2 Whisk flour, pumpkin pie spice, baking soda, and salt together in medium bowl. Using stand mixer fitted with whisk, whip eggs and granulated sugar on medium-high speed until pale and fluffy, about 3 minutes. Reduce speed to low, add pumpkin and melted butter, and mix until incorporated. Slowly add flour mixture and mix until just combined, about 30 seconds.

3 Using pastry bag, pipe 1-tablespoon mounds of batter onto prepared sheets, spacing them about 1 inch apart. Bake until cakes are set, 10 to 12 minutes, switching and rotating sheets halfway through baking. Let cakes cool on sheets for 5 min-utes, then transfer to wire rack. Let cakes cool completely.

4 Using clean, dry bowl and whisk attachment, whip soft-ened butter and confectioners' sugar on medium-high speed until pale and fluffy, about 2 minutes. Add cream cheese, 1 piece at a time, and mix until no lumps remain. Spread scant tablespoon filling over bottom of half of cakes, then top with remaining cakes, pressing lightly to adhere. Dust with confectioners' sugar, if using, before serving.

5
LET'S GET FANCY

SPRITZ COOKIES

Makes about 72 cookies

1 large egg yolk

1 tablespoon heavy cream

1 teaspoon vanilla extract

16 tablespoons unsalted butter, softened

⅔ cup (4⅔ ounces) sugar

¼ teaspoon salt

2 cups (10 ounces) all-purpose flour

Why This Recipe Works Spritz cookies are beautiful in appearance with their golden swirled shape, but in terms of flavor they frequently fall short—a bland, gummy, tasteless disappointment. This Scandinavian treat has fallen victim to failed recipe modifications, such as the use of vegetable shortening instead of butter, an overload of eggs, and an excess of starchy confectioners' sugar. We set out to spruce up spritz and make them the light, crisp, buttery treats they were meant to be. For rich flavor, we used all butter and lots of it—16 tablespoons. Since these cookies are pressed or piped, the dough needs to be smooth. Adding a little heavy cream made the dough workable. Some recipes for spritz cookies call for whole eggs, while others use just yolks or even no eggs at all. Cookies made without eggs were too tender and crumbly, with an ill-defined shape. A whole egg made for chewy, tough cookies. Using just one yolk made spritz that were tender and crisp yet sturdy. You can use a cookie press or a pastry bag fitted with a star tip to create these cookies. (For more information on piping Spritz Cookies, see page 197.)

1 Adjust oven rack to middle position and heat oven to 375 degrees. Line 2 baking sheets with parchment paper. Whisk egg yolk, cream, and vanilla in small bowl until combined; set aside.

2 Using stand mixer fitted with paddle, beat butter, sugar, and salt on medium-high speed until pale and fluffy, about 3 minutes, scraping down bowl as needed. Reduce speed to medium, add egg yolk mixture, and beat until incorporated, about 30 seconds. Reduce speed to low and gradually add flour until combined, scraping down bowl as needed. Give dough final stir by hand. (Dough can be wrapped in plastic wrap and refrigerated for up to 4 days. Before using, let sit on counter until softened, about 45 minutes.)

3 If using cookie press to form cookies, follow manufacturer's instructions to fill press. If using pastry bag, fill pastry bag fitted with star tip with half of dough. Push dough down toward tip and twist top of bag tightly. Holding bag at base of twist and holding tip at 90-degree angle ½ inch above baking sheet, pipe cookies, spacing them about 1½ inches apart. Refill cookie press or pastry bag as needed. Bake, 1 sheet at a time, until cookies are light golden brown, 10 to 12 minutes, rotating sheet halfway through baking. Let cookies cool on sheets for 10 to 15 minutes, then transfer to wire rack. Let cookies cool completely before serving.

Almond Spritz Cookies

Grind ½ cup sliced almonds with 2 tablespoons flour called for in Spritz Cookies in food processor until almonds are powdery and evenly fine, about 1 minute; combine almond mixture with remaining flour before adding to dough in step 2. Substitute ¾ teaspoon almond extract for vanilla.

Lemon Spritz Cookies

Add 1 teaspoon lemon juice to yolk mixture in step 1 and 1 teaspoon finely grated lemon zest with butter, sugar, and salt in step 2.

Cookie Presses

A cookie press works like a dough "gun": You place a perforated disk for the desired cookie shape at the bottom of the barrel, fill the tube with cookie dough, and squeeze the trigger to release a spritz of dough—hence the cookie name. We tested five models priced from nearly $13 to nearly $30. After forming and baking multiple batches of buttery cookies, we rated each press on how easy it was to fill, use, and clean. The **Wilton Cookie Pro Ultra II** ($24.99) has a nonslip base, was easy to load, and turned out perfect cookies every time.

MERINGUE COOKIES

Makes about 48 cookies

¾ cup (5¼ ounces) sugar

2 teaspoons cornstarch

4 large egg whites

¾ teaspoon vanilla extract

⅛ teaspoon salt

Why This Recipe Works Precise timing is required to achieve a classic meringue, one that emerges from the oven glossy white, with a shattering texture that dissolves instantly once you bite into it. If you're not careful, you'll end up with meringue that's as dense as Styrofoam. When whipping the egg whites, it's important to add the sugar at just the right time. Add it too early, and it will interfere with the cross-linked egg white proteins that uphold the meringue; add it too late and there isn't enough water in which the sugar can dissolve, resulting in a gritty meringue. We found the sweet spot by adding the sugar just before the whites reached soft peak stage, when they have gained some volume but still have enough water for the sugar to dissolve. We wanted our cookies to be slightly less sweet than your typical meringue, but scaling back on sugar caused them to collapse, so we cut it with an ingredient that isn't often found in meringues: cornstarch. The meringues may be a little soft immediately after being removed from the oven but will stiffen as they cool. To minimize stickiness on humid or rainy days, let the meringues cool in a turned-off oven for an additional hour (2 hours total) without opening the door, then transfer them immediately to airtight containers and seal.

1 Adjust oven racks to upper-middle and lower-middle positions and heat oven to 225 degrees. Line 2 baking sheets with parchment paper. Whisk sugar and cornstarch together in small bowl.

2 Using stand mixer fitted with whisk attachment, whip egg whites, vanilla, and salt on high speed until very soft peaks start to form (peaks should slowly lose their shape when whisk is removed), 30 to 45 seconds. Reduce speed to medium and slowly add sugar mixture in steady stream down side of mixer bowl (process should take about 30 seconds). Stop mixer and scrape down bowl. Increase speed to high and whip until glossy, stiff peaks form, 30 to 45 seconds.

3 Working quickly, fill pastry bag fitted with ½-inch plain tip or large zipper-lock bag with ½ inch of corner cut off with meringue. Pipe 1¼-inch-wide mounds about 1 inch high on prepared sheets, 4 rows of 6 meringues on each sheet. Bake meringues for 1 hour, switching and rotating sheets halfway through baking. Turn off oven and let meringues cool in oven for at least 1 hour. Transfer sheets to wire rack and let meringues cool completely before serving. (Meringues can be stored at room temperature for up to 2 weeks.)

Chocolate Meringue Cookies

Gently fold 2 ounces finely chopped bittersweet chocolate into meringue mixture at end of step 2.

Espresso Meringue Cookies

Whisk 2 teaspoons instant espresso powder into sugar mixture in step 1.

Orange Meringue Cookies

Whisk 1 teaspoon grated orange zest into sugar mixture in step 1.

Toasted Almond Meringue Cookies

Substitute ½ teaspoon almond extract for vanilla extract. In step 3, sprinkle meringues with ⅓ cup almonds, toasted and coarsely chopped, and 1 teaspoon flake sea salt (optional) before baking.

MADELEINES

Makes 24 cookies

1 cup (4 ounces) cake flour

¼ teaspoon salt

2 large eggs plus 1 large yolk

½ cup (3½ ounces) sugar

1 tablespoon vanilla extract

10 tablespoons unsalted butter, melted and cooled

Why This Recipe Works Some know the madeleine as a symbol of involuntary memory, laid out by French writer Marcel Proust in *Swann's Way*, the first volume of his famous novel, *In Search of Lost Time.* The light, airy treats are unlike any other cookie; they're sponge cakes in cookie form, with a beautiful ridged exterior formed by the shell-shaped tins in which they are baked. But despite their appeal, madeleines aren't easy to find. Fortunately, this French treat is easy to prepare, so we felt confident that making them in our American kitchen would be a simple task. For madeleines with a light, tight crumb, we used downy-soft cake flour rather than all-purpose flour, which made our madeleines too tough. To cool the baked madeleines without ruining their ridged exteriors, we let them sit in the greased molds for 10 minutes after baking to set their exteriors before transferring them to a wire rack. This way, the rack didn't imprint lines on our cookies as they cooled. This recipe calls for a 12-cookie madeleine mold; even if you have two molds, be sure to bake them one at a time.

1 Adjust oven rack to middle position and heat oven to 375 degrees. Grease 12-cookie madeleine mold. Whisk flour and salt together in small bowl.

2 Using stand mixer fitted with paddle, beat eggs and yolk on medium-high speed until frothy, 3 to 5 minutes. Add sugar and vanilla and beat until very thick, 3 to 5 minutes. Using rubber spatula, gently fold in flour mixture, followed by melted butter.

3 Spoon half of batter into prepared mold, filling mold to rim. Bake until madeleines are golden and spring back when pressed lightly, about 10 minutes, rotating mold halfway through baking.

4 Let cookies cool in mold for 10 minutes. Remove madeleines from mold and transfer to wire rack. Repeat with remaining batter. Let madeleines cool completely before serving.

Almond Madeleines
Reduce vanilla to 2 teaspoons and add 1 teaspoon almond extract.

Chocolate Madeleines
Substitute ¼ cup sifted Dutch-processed cocoa for ¼ cup flour and add 2 teaspoons instant espresso powder to flour mixture in step 1.

Citrus Madeleines
Add 1 tablespoon grated lemon zest or orange zest with sugar and vanilla in step 2.

Rosewater Madeleines
Substitute 2 teaspoons rosewater for vanilla extract.

LADYFINGERS

Makes about 48 cookies

½ cup (3½ ounces) granulated sugar

¼ cup (1 ounce) confectioners' sugar

4 large eggs, separated

⅛ teaspoon salt

1 teaspoon vanilla

¾ cup (3¾ ounces) all-purpose flour

Why This Recipe Works For many, ladyfingers are known only as those hard (and often stale) packaged cookies that get soaked in espresso for tiramisù. But fresh, homemade ladyfingers are quite unlike the store-bought variety, with a lightly sweet flavor and soft texture that allow them to stand on their own. The key to airy ladyfingers is creating a sponge cake–like batter that can be easily piped without deflating. To achieve this, we found that using all-purpose flour was a must. Batter made with cake flour didn't have enough structure to support the whipped egg whites that we folded in, and the cakes collapsed and became dense. When whipping the egg whites, we added a portion of the sugar once they'd reached very soft peaks; this helped ensure that we didn't overbeat the whites. While many sponge cake recipes call for folding the batter after the addition of each component, we folded the whipped egg whites, yolks, and dry ingredients together at once to keep the batter aerated. A light dusting of confectioners' sugar was enough to make these ladyfingers ready for dessert.

1 Adjust oven racks to upper-middle and lower-middle positions and heat oven to 350 degrees. Line 2 baking sheets with parchment paper and spray with vegetable oil spray.

2 Whisk ¼ cup granulated sugar and 2 tablespoons confectioners' sugar together in small bowl. Using stand mixer fitted with whisk attachment, whip egg whites and salt on high speed until very soft peaks form (peaks should slowly lose their shape when whisk is removed), 30 to 45 seconds. Reduce speed to medium and gradually add sugar mixture. Increase speed to high and whip until glossy, stiff peaks form, about 30 seconds. Gently transfer whites to large bowl.

3 Fit stand mixer with paddle and beat egg yolks, vanilla, and remaining ¼ cup granulated sugar until thick and pale yellow, about 5 minutes. Pour yolk mixture on top of whites in bowl, then sift flour over top. Using rubber spatula, gently fold until combined.

4 Fill pastry bag fitted with ½-inch plain tip halfway with batter. Pipe batter into 3-inch by 1-inch strips, spacing them 1 inch apart on prepared sheets. Sift remaining 2 tablespoons confectioners' sugar over strips. Bake until edges are golden, 20 to 24 minutes, switching and rotating sheets halfway through baking. Let cookies cool on sheets for 5 minutes, then transfer to wire rack. Let cookies cool completely before serving.

TUILE CIGARS

Makes 28 cookies

¾ cup (3¾ ounces) all-purpose flour

1 tablespoon cornstarch

¼ teaspoon salt

4 tablespoons unsalted butter, softened

½ cup (3½ ounces) sugar

3 large egg whites, room temperature

½ teaspoon vanilla extract

6 ounces milk, semisweet, or bittersweet chocolate, chopped (optional)

½ cup nuts, toasted and chopped fine (optional)

Why This Recipe Works Also called pirouettes, these delicate, lightly sweet cookies get their name from their rolled-up shape. The cookie batter is easy to make; the success of these cookies lies in the shaping. First, we spread small portions of the batter onto baking sheets. Then, once the cookie disks were done baking, we quickly lifted an edge of the warm cookies with our trusty offset spatula and used our fingers to roll them into a tight cigar. The rolling might take some practice at first, but the cookies can be returned to the oven to resoften if needed, so cigar success is guaranteed. Once cooled, an optional dip in melted chocolate and finely chopped nuts (any varieties you like) gives the cigars party appeal. While we typically prefer to line our baking sheets with parchment paper, we found that the DeMarle Silpat Silicone Baking Mat worked best with these cookies, since it doesn't move when you spread the batter, and it created a smoother bottom on the cookies. (For more information on silicone baking mats, see page 8.) If you can't find a baking mat, lightly greased parchment secured to the baking sheets with vegetable oil spray will work. To keep the cookies crisp, store them in an airtight container at room temperature.

1 Adjust oven rack to middle position and heat oven to 350 degrees. Line 2 baking sheets with reusable baking mats. (Alternatively, lightly spray 2 baking sheets with vegetable oil spray, line with parchment paper, and lightly spray again.) Whisk flour, cornstarch, and salt together in small bowl.

2 Using stand mixer fitted with paddle, beat butter and sugar on medium-high speed until pale and fluffy, about 2 minutes. With mixer running, slowly add egg whites and vanilla and mix until well incorporated, scraping down bowl as needed. Reduce speed to low, add flour mixture, and mix until just combined.

3 Drop 2-teaspoon portions of batter onto prepared sheets, spaced at least 6 inches apart. Using small offset spatula, spread each into 5-inch circle of even thickness. Bake, 1 sheet at a time, until edges are golden brown, 5 to 7 minutes.

4 Working quickly, lift edge of each cookie with offset spatula and roll tightly into cigar shape; place seam side down on wire rack. If cookies become too stiff to roll, return to oven for 30 seconds to soften. Repeat with remaining batter. Let cookies cool completely.

5 Microwave chocolate, if using, at 50 percent power, stirring occasionally, until melted, 1 to 2 minutes. Dip about one-quarter of each cookie into chocolate, wiping away excess. Sprinkle evenly with nuts, if using; transfer to parchment-lined baking sheet; and let chocolate set, about 30 minutes, before serving.

Forming Tuile Cigars

1 Drop 2-teaspoon portions of batter onto prepared sheets, spacing them at least 6 inches apart.

2 Using small offset spatula, spread each portion of batter into 5-inch circle of even thickness.

3 Bake, 1 sheet at a time, until edges are golden brown, 5 to 7 minutes.

4 Working quickly, lift edge of each cookie with metal spatula.

5 Roll cookies tightly into cigar shape.

6 Place cigars seam side down on wire rack and let cool completely.

7 Dip about one-quarter of each cookie into melted chocolate, wiping away excess.

8 Sprinkle chocolate-dipped cigars evenly with chopped nuts.

9 Transfer cigars to parchment-lined baking sheet, and let chocolate set before serving.

FLORENTINE LACE COOKIES

Makes 24 cookies

2 cups slivered almonds

¾ cup heavy cream

4 tablespoons unsalted butter, cut into 4 pieces

½ cup (3½ ounces) sugar

¼ cup orange marmalade

3 tablespoons all-purpose flour

1 teaspoon vanilla extract

¼ teaspoon grated orange zest

¼ teaspoon salt

4 ounces bittersweet chocolate, chopped fine

Why This Recipe Works By making just a few tweaks to the recipes that the pros use for these wafer-thin citrus-flavored almond cookies, we were able to achieve foolproof, fantastic Florentines for the home kitchen. Our main challenge was making the batter thin enough that it would spread before becoming rock hard. Processing the almonds until they were coarsely ground gave the cookies a flatter profile, and upping the cream encouraged spread. But the Florentines still lacked crispness and a delicate filigreed appearance. Two quick fixes solved these problems: A few extra minutes in the oven allowed the cookies to crisp and turn deep golden brown from edge to edge, and a touch less flour helped them spread even thinner. It's important to cook the cream mixture in the saucepan until it's thick and starting to brown at the edges; undercooking will result in a dough that is too runny to portion. Don't be concerned if some butter separates from the dough. For the most uniform cookies, make sure that your parchment paper lies flat. When melting the chocolate, pause the microwave and stir the chocolate often to ensure that it doesn't get much warmer than body temperature.

1 Adjust oven racks to upper-middle and lower-middle positions and heat oven to 350 degrees. Line 2 baking sheets with parchment paper. Process almonds in food processor until they resemble coarse sand, about 30 seconds.

2 Bring cream, butter, and sugar to boil in medium saucepan over medium-high heat. Cook, stirring frequently, until mixture begins to thicken, 5 to 6 minutes. Continue to cook, stirring constantly, until mixture begins to brown at edges and is thick enough to leave trail that doesn't immediately fill in when spatula is scraped along pan bottom, 1 to 2 minutes longer (it's OK if some darker speckles appear in mixture). Remove pan from heat and stir in almonds, marmalade, flour, vanilla, orange zest, and salt until combined.

3 Drop six 1-tablespoon portions of dough onto each prepared sheet, spaced at least 3½ inches apart. When cool enough to handle, use your dampened fingers to press each portion into 2½-inch circle.

4 Bake cookies until deep brown from edge to edge, 15 to 17 minutes, switching and rotating sheets halfway through baking. Transfer cookies, still on parchment, to wire racks. Repeat with remaining dough. Let cookies cool completely.

5 Microwave 3 ounces chocolate in bowl at 50 percent power, stirring frequently, until about two-thirds melted, 1 to 2 minutes. Remove bowl from microwave, add remaining 1 ounce chocolate, and stir until melted, returning to microwave for no more than 5 seconds at a time to complete melting if necessary. Transfer chocolate to small zipper-lock bag and snip off corner, making hole no larger than ¹⁄₁₆ inch.

6 Pipe zigzag of chocolate over each cookie on wire racks, distributing chocolate evenly among all cookies. Refrigerate until chocolate is set, about 30 minutes, before serving. (Cookies can be stored at cool room temperature for up to 4 days.)

Making Florentine Lace Cookies

1 Bring cream, butter, and sugar to boil in medium saucepan over medium-high heat. Stir frequently until mixture begins to thicken, 5 to 6 minutes.

2 Cook and stir constantly until mixture browns at edges and leaves trail when spatula is scraped along pan bottom, 1 to 2 minutes.

3 Off heat, stir in ground almonds, marmalade, flour, vanilla, orange zest, and salt until combined.

4 Drop six 1-tablespoon portions of dough at least 3½ inches apart onto each prepared sheet.

5 When dough is cool enough to handle, use your dampened fingers to press each portion into 2½-inch circle.

6 Bake until deep brown from edge to edge, 15 to 17 minutes, switching and rotating sheets halfway through baking.

Decorating Florentine Lace Cookies

1 Transfer melted chocolate to small zipper-lock bag and snip off corner, making the hole no larger than 1/16 inch.

2 Pipe zigzag of chocolate over each cookie on wire racks, distributing chocolate evenly among all cookies. Refrigerate until chocolate is set, about 30 minutes, before serving.

ALL ABOUT ADVANCED PLACEMENT COOKIES

Many cookies—as seen in the chapters of this book—line up in neat categories, from rolled and cutout to brownies and bar cookies. But some cookies expand on these techniques and are a bit fancier—perfect for gifts, celebrations, or any time you want to impress. Here are some tricks and techniques for sharpening your baking skills and turning out superior cookies with ease.

BROWNING BUTTER

For recipes that call for melted butter, we sometimes take an extra step and brown it. Browned butter has a deeper flavor than butter that has simply been melted; as the milk solids brown they take on the flavor of toasted nuts. Browned butter can also improve the texture of cookies where too much moisture is a problem, as the process of browning causes some of the water in the butter to evaporate. Use a skillet with a light interior so you can judge the color of the butter.

1 Melt the butter in a skillet over medium-high heat.

2 Continue to cook, swirling the skillet constantly, until the butter is dark golden brown and has a nutty aroma.

3 Immediately transfer the butter to a bowl so it doesn't burn.

DO A DOUBLE-DIP

While most recipes call for simply rolling baked cookies in sugar and serving, we often take two steps for a thick coating with no bald patches.

1 Roll the cookies, while still warm, in sifted confectioners' sugar. The sugar will melt to create a frosted exterior on the cookie.

2 Roll the cooled cookies in sugar once again (or dust them for a more scant coating), so the cookie stays pretty and white.

TOP-NOTCH TOOL

Often thought of as a cake-decorating tool, a small offset spatula can be used at various stages of the cookie-making process to create professional-looking cookies like those you find in bakeries. These moderately priced, blunt-edged, offset metal pastry blades—which average about 4½ inches long—provide a better angle for neatly frosting cookies like our Chocolate-Mint Cookies (page 216) and bars like our Italian Rainbow Cookies (page 204), or for filling sandwich cookies like Almond-Raspberry Sandwich Cookies (page 161) with jam. They work better than a clunky rubber spatula for smoothing brownie batter into an even layer. And you can even ensure that cutout cookies hold their shape, no matter how sticky the dough or intricate the design, by using the thin blade to transfer the dough shapes from the counter to a baking sheet.

We tested five offset spatula models and, to our surprise, found significant differences. Thin blades wobbled and wooden handles absorbed odors. Our top choice, the **Wilton 9-inch Angled Spatula** ($4.79), has a sturdy, round-tipped blade and an easy-to-grip polypropylene handle that offers great control. Sleek, sturdy, and comfortable, this blade was just about flawless.

Tool of the Trade

WORKING WITH PIPING BAGS

For some fancy cookies, like our Meringue Cookies (page 184) or Ladyfingers (page 189), we deposit the dough or batter onto the baking sheets with a piping bag for added flair or height. You can also decorate cookies with frosting from a piping bag. While there are many different tips you can buy, most bags come with only the most basic one or two shapes.

1 Holding the pastry bag in one of your hands, fold the top of the pastry bag down about halfway. Insert the tip into the point of the bag and press it securely in place.

2 Scrape the dough, batter, frosting, or filling into the bag until the bag is half full.

3 Pull up the sides of the bag, push down the filling, and twist tightly. Push down on the bag to squeeze the air out and push the contents into the tip.

4 To pipe, grip the bag at the base, twist, and squeeze to form a shape. If the tip gets clogged during piping, move the tip over a bowl and apply more pressure to release the blockage.

PIPING DIFFERENT SPRITZ SHAPES

If you choose to use a pastry bag rather than a cookie press to form Spritz Cookies (page 183) on the baking sheet, you have some shaping options. Try the standard star, or have fun with the following elegant shapes. For stars, a ½- to ⅝-inch tip (measure the diameter of the tip at the smallest point) works best. For rosettes and S shapes, use a ⅜-inch tip. If you make an error while piping, the dough can be scraped off the baking sheet and re-piped.

1 To create stars Hold the pastry bag at a 90-degree angle to the baking sheet and pipe the dough straight down, until it is about 1 inch in diameter.

2 To create rosettes Pipe the dough while moving the bag in a circular motion, ending at the center; the rosettes should be about 1¼ inches in diameter.

3 To create S shapes Pipe the dough following the curves of a compact S; they should be about 2 inches long and 1 inch wide.

TOASTING NUTS AND SEEDS

Toasting deepens the flavor of nuts and seeds, and it ensures they retain their crunch when baked into dough. To toast a small amount of nuts or seeds (1 cup or less), cook them in a dry skillet over medium heat, shaking the skillet occasionally to prevent scorching, until they are lightly browned and fragrant, 3 to 8 minutes. To toast a larger quantity, bake nuts or seeds in a single layer on a rimmed baking sheet in a 350-degree oven, shaking the sheet every few minutes to promote even toasting, until lightly browned and fragrant, 5 to 10 minutes.

RUGELACH WITH RAISIN-WALNUT FILLING

Makes 32 rugelach

Dough

2¼ cups (11¼ ounces) all-purpose flour

1½ tablespoons sugar

¼ teaspoon salt

16 tablespoons unsalted butter,
cut into ¼-inch pieces and chilled

8 ounces cream cheese,
cut into ½-inch pieces and chilled

2 tablespoons sour cream

Filling

⅔ cup apricot preserves

1 cup (7 ounces) sugar

1 tablespoon ground cinnamon

1 cup golden raisins

2 cups walnuts, chopped fine

Glaze

2 large egg yolks

2 tablespoons milk

Why This Recipe Works Part cookie, part pastry, rugelach are a traditional Jewish party snack. Their tight curls can contain a variety of bounteous sweet fillings, from nuts and jam to dried fruit and even chocolate. The dough is made with tangy cream cheese and bakes up tender and flaky; however, many rugelach doughs are sticky and hard to work with, so solving this problem was our first order of business. We started by adding more flour to the dough than traditional recipes call for, which helped make it more workable. A couple of tablespoons of sour cream in addition to the cream cheese gave the cookies more tang and tenderized them further. For the filling, we settled on a generous combination of apricot preserves, raisins, and walnuts. To abate leaking, we finely chopped the nuts; smaller pieces were less likely to tear the dough. We also processed the preserves in a food processor to eliminate any large chunks. Be sure to stop processing the dough when the mixture resembles moist crumbs. If the dough gathers into a cohesive mass around the blade of the food processor, you've overprocessed it. If at any point during the cutting and rolling of the crescents the sheet of dough softens and becomes hard to roll, slide it onto a baking sheet and freeze it until it is firm enough to handle. Feel free to substitute chopped pitted prunes, chopped dried apricots, or dried cranberries for the raisins in the filling.

1 For the dough Pulse flour, sugar, and salt in food processor until combined, about 3 pulses. Add butter, cream cheese, and sour cream; pulse until dough comes together in small, uneven pebbles the size of cottage cheese curds, about 16 pulses. Transfer dough to counter, press into 9 by 6-inch log, and divide log into 4 equal pieces. Form each piece into 4½-inch disk. Place each disk between 2 sheets of plastic wrap and roll into 8½-inch circle. Stack dough circles, between parchment, on plate; freeze for 30 minutes.

2 For the filling Meanwhile, process apricot preserves in food processor until smooth, about 10 seconds. Combine sugar and cinnamon in small bowl; set aside. Line 2 rimmed baking sheets with parchment paper. Working with 1 dough circle at a time, remove dough from freezer and spread with 2½ tablespoons preserves. Sprinkle 2 tablespoons cinnamon sugar, ¼ cup raisins, and ½ cup walnuts over preserves and pat down gently with your fingers. Cut circle into 8 wedges. Roll each wedge into crescent shape; space crescents 2 inches apart on prepared sheets. Freeze crescents on sheets for 15 minutes.

3 For the glaze Adjust oven racks to upper-middle and lower-middle positions and heat oven to 375 degrees. Whisk egg yolks and milk in bowl. Brush crescents with glaze. Bake until rugelach are pale golden and slightly puffy, 21 to 23 minutes, switching and rotating sheets halfway through baking. Sprinkle each cookie with scant teaspoon cinnamon sugar. Transfer rugelach to wire rack with metal spatula. Let rugelach cool completely before serving. (Rugelach can be stored at room temperature for up to 4 days.)

To make ahead In step 2, space formed crescents ½ inch apart on parchment-lined baking sheet. Cover baking sheet loosely with plastic wrap and freeze cookies until firm, about 1¼ hours. Once frozen, transfer cookies to airtight container and freeze for up to 6 weeks. To bake frozen rugelach, place on parchment-lined baking sheets and glaze and bake immediately, increasing baking time by 6 to 7 minutes.

Chocolate-Raspberry Rugelach

Substitute ⅔ cup raspberry preserves for apricot preserves and substitute 1 cup mini semisweet chocolate chips for raisins.

PALMIERS

Makes 24 palmiers

Dough

3 cups (15 ounces) all-purpose flour

1½ tablespoons sugar

1½ teaspoons salt

2 teaspoons lemon juice

1 cup ice water

Butter Square

24 tablespoons (3 sticks) unsalted butter, chilled

2 tablespoons all-purpose flour

Sugar Coating

1 cup (7 ounces) sugar

Why This Recipe Works Whether you call them palmiers (*à la francaise*), elephant ears, butterflies, pig's ears, Prussians, or angel wings, they are all the same: flat heart-shaped sheets of coiled puff pastry coated thickly with a crunchy glaze. The best are crisp and lightly caramelized, tasting of nothing but pure butter, browned wheat, and golden sugar. Forming the cookies isn't hard, but making the puff pastry does take some time: An elastic dough is wrapped tightly around a thin sheet of butter and folded time and time again, which exponentially develops alternating layers of dough and butter. When baked, the moisture in the butter converts into steam, causing the layers of dough to puff and separate into flaky sheets. That said, as long as you chill the dough between turns and follow the directions, the long process isn't difficult. Our puff pastry is particularly forgiving because we add a drop of lemon juice to it; the acid inhibits excess gluten development, keeping the dough tender during rolling. Rolling out the puff pastry in sugar before forming the palmiers ensures that each layer gets a sweet, caramelized touch. In the end, the lengthy process (much of which is hands off) is worth it. If the dough or butter ever feels soft while you're working with it, cover it with plastic wrap and refrigerate it for a few minutes. For the crispiest pastry, it's crucial to prevent the butter from melting.

1 For the dough Process flour, sugar, and salt in food processor until combined, about 5 seconds. With processor running, add lemon juice, followed by ¾ cup ice water, in slow, steady stream. Add remaining ¼ cup water as needed, 1 tablespoon at a time, until dough comes together and no floury bits remain.

2 Transfer dough to sheet of plastic wrap. Form dough into 6-inch square, wrap square tightly in plastic, and refrigerate for 1 hour.

3 For the butter square Lay butter sticks side by side on sheet of parchment paper. Sprinkle flour over butter and cover with second sheet of parchment. Using rolling pin, gently pound butter until softened and flour is fully incorporated, then roll into 8-inch square. Wrap butter square in plastic and refrigerate until chilled, about 1 hour.

4 Roll chilled dough into 11-inch square on lightly floured counter. Place chilled butter square diagonally in center of dough. Fold corners of dough up over butter square so that corners meet in middle and pinch dough seams to seal.

5 Using rolling pin, gently tap dough, starting from center and working outward, until square becomes larger and butter begins to soften. Gently roll dough into 14-inch square, dusting with extra flour as needed to prevent sticking. Fold dough into thirds like business letter, then fold rectangle into thirds to form square. Wrap dough in plastic and refrigerate for 2 hours.

6 Repeat step 5 twice and let dough rest in refrigerator for 2 more hours. (Dough can be wrapped in plastic and refrigerated for up to 2 days or frozen for up to 1 month. Let dough thaw completely in refrigerator, about 12 hours, before using.)

7 For the sugar coating Sprinkle ½ cup sugar over counter and lay puff-pastry dough on top of sugar. Roll dough into 24 by 12-inch rectangle, about ¼ inch thick, dusting with remaining ½ cup sugar as needed to prevent sticking.

8 Roll short sides of dough toward center, so they meet in middle. Wrap dough log in plastic, transfer to baking sheet, and freeze until firm, about 20 minutes.

Making Puff Pastry Dough

1 Lay butter sticks side by side on sheet of parchment paper. Sprinkle flour over butter and cover with second sheet of parchment.

2 Using rolling pin, gently pound flour into butter until softened. Roll into 8-inch square. Wrap and refrigerate for 1 hour.

3 Roll chilled dough into 11-inch square on lightly floured counter. Place chilled butter square diagonally in center of dough.

4 Fold corners of dough square over butter square so that corners meet in middle and pinch dough seams to seal.

5 Roll dough into 14-inch square, then fold dough in thirds like a business letter.

6 Fold rectangle into thirds to form square; wrap and refrigerate for 2 hours. Roll, fold, and chill 2 more times and refrigerate.

9 Adjust oven rack to middle position and heat oven to 375 degrees. Line second baking sheet with parchment paper.

10 Slice half of dough log into ½-inch-thick cookies with long, thin-bladed slicing knife and space them 1 inch apart on prepared sheet; wrap remaining unsliced dough and keep frozen until ready to bake. Bake until palmiers begin to brown and firm up, 15 to 20 minutes.

11 Flip palmiers, rotate sheet, and continue to bake until golden and crisp, 5 to 10 minutes longer. Immediately transfer palmiers to wire rack. Repeat with remaining dough. Let palmiers cool completely before serving. (Palmiers can be stored at room temperature for up to 3 days.)

To make ahead Shaped dough log can be wrapped tightly in plastic wrap and frozen for up to 1 month. To bake, slice frozen dough into cookies and bake as directed.

Shaping Palmiers

1 After rolling out chilled dough square, roll short sides of dough rectangle toward center so they meet in middle. Wrap dough log in plastic and freeze until firm.

2 To cut cookies, slice dough log into ½-inch-thick pieces with long, thin-bladed slicing knife.

ITALIAN RAINBOW COOKIES

Makes 60 cookies

2 cups (8 ounces) cake flour

½ teaspoon baking powder

1½ cups (10½ ounces) sugar

8 ounces almond paste,
cut into 1-inch pieces

7 large eggs

1 teaspoon vanilla extract

½ teaspoon salt

8 tablespoons unsalted butter,
melted and cooled slightly

⅛ teaspoon red food coloring

⅛ teaspoon green food coloring

⅔ cup seedless raspberry jam

1 cup (6 ounces) bittersweet
chocolate chips

Why This Recipe Works Rainbow cookies, Napoleon cookies, tricolor cookies, seven layer cookies, or Venetian cookies: Whatever you call them, these multilayered treats are part cake, part cookie, part confection, and unabashedly sweet. With their green, white, and red stripes, these Italian American cookies are meant to look like miniature Italian flags. Each colorful layer is made from an almond paste–enhanced sponge cake, for a sturdy, slightly dense confection that's easy to stack, slice, and eat in cookie form. For tricolored cake layers, we made just one batter and then separated it into thirds, adding red and green food coloring to two of the portions. We baked each batter separately and then once the layers cooled we spread them with raspberry jam and stacked them. For a crowning touch, we spread a generous amount of melted chocolate over the surface, taking the final layer of these cookies over the top. Running a fork through the melted chocolate in waves once it had set and thickened for a few minutes provided the final flourish. After the chocolate coating was completely set, we trimmed the sides and cut the cookies into beautifully layered bars packed with almond, raspberry, and chocolate flavor in every bite.

1 Adjust oven rack to middle position and heat oven to 350 degrees. Grease 13 by 9-inch baking pan. Make parchment paper sling by folding 1 long sheet of parchment 13 inches wide and laying across width of pan, with extra parchment hanging over edges of pan. Push parchment into corners and up sides of pan, smoothing parchment flush to pan. Grease parchment.

2 Combine flour and baking powder and sift into bowl; set aside. Process sugar and almond paste in food processor until combined, 20 to 30 seconds. Transfer sugar mixture to bowl of stand mixer; add eggs, vanilla, and salt. Fit mixer with whisk attachment and whip mixture on medium-high speed until pale and thickened, 5 to 7 minutes. Reduce speed to low and add melted butter. Slowly add flour mixture until just combined.

3 Transfer 2 cups batter to prepared pan and spread in even layer with offset spatula. Bake until top is set and edges are just starting to brown, 10 to 12 minutes. Let cool in pan for 5 minutes. Using parchment overhang, remove cake from pan and transfer to wire rack. Let cake and pan cool completely.

4 Divide remaining batter between 2 bowls. Stir red food coloring into first bowl and green food coloring into second bowl. Make new parchment sling for now-empty pan and repeat baking with each colored batter, letting pan cool after each batch.

5 Invert red layer onto cutting board and gently remove parchment. Spread ⅓ cup jam evenly over top. Invert plain layer onto red layer and gently remove parchment. Spread remaining ⅓ cup jam evenly over top. Invert green layer onto plain layer and gently remove parchment.

6 Microwave chocolate chips in bowl at 50 percent power, stirring occasionally, until melted, 2 to 4 minutes. Spread chocolate evenly over green layer. Let set for 2 minutes, then run fork in wavy pattern through chocolate. Let chocolate set, 1 to 2 hours. Using serrated knife, trim away edges. Cut lengthwise into 5 equal strips (about 1½ inches wide) and then crosswise into 12 equal strips (about 1 inch wide). Serve.

Assembling Rainbow Cookies

1 Invert red layer onto cutting board and gently remove parchment.

2 Spread ⅓ cup jam evenly over top of cake.

3 Invert plain cake layer onto red layer and gently remove parchment.

4 Spread remaining ⅓ cup jam evenly over plain layer.

5 Invert green layer onto plain layer and gently remove parchment.

6 Spread melted chocolate evenly over top of cake and let it set for 2 minutes.

7 Run fork in wavy pattern through chocolate and let it sit until set, 1 to 2 hours.

8 Using serrated knife, trim away edges.

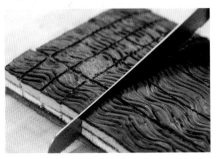

9 Cut cookies lengthwise into 5 equal strips (about 1½ inches wide) and then crosswise into 12 equal strips (about 1 inch wide).

ALMOND BISCOTTI

Makes 30 cookies

1¼ cups whole almonds, lightly toasted

1¾ cups (8¾ ounces) all-purpose flour

2 teaspoons baking powder

¼ teaspoon salt

2 large eggs, plus 1 large white beaten with pinch salt

1 cup (7 ounces) sugar

4 tablespoons unsalted butter, melted and cooled

1½ teaspoons almond extract

½ teaspoon vanilla extract

Vegetable oil spray

Why This Recipe Works Biscotti means "twice-baked"; the dough is formed into a loaf and baked and then sliced on the bias into planks, which are returned to the oven to dry. The result: nutty cookies that are perfect alongside coffee or a glass of vin santo. Italians like their biscotti dry and hard, whereas Americans tend to favor a buttery, tender version. We wanted a cookie that fell in between, one that had plenty of crunch but wasn't tooth-breaking. Batches of biscotti made with little (or no) fat were rocks, while doughs enriched with a full stick of butter baked up too soft. Four tablespoons of butter struck just the right balance, for a cookie that was both crunchy and tender. Whipping the eggs before adding the other ingredients provided lift, and swapping out ¼ cup of flour for an equal amount of ground almonds made the cookies more tender by breaking up the crumb and interrupting gluten development. The almonds will continue to toast during baking, so toast them just until they're fragrant.

1 Adjust oven rack to middle position and heat oven to 325 degrees. Using ruler and pencil, draw two 8 by 3-inch rectangles, spaced 4 inches apart, on piece of parchment paper. Grease baking sheet and place parchment on it, marked side down.

2 Pulse 1 cup almonds in food processor until coarsely chopped, 8 to 10 pulses; transfer to bowl and set aside. Process remaining ¼ cup almonds in now-empty food processor until finely ground, about 45 seconds. Add flour, baking powder, and salt; process to combine, about 15 seconds. Transfer flour mixture to second bowl. Process 2 eggs in now-empty food processor until lightened in color and almost doubled in volume, about 3 minutes. With processor running, slowly add sugar until thoroughly combined, about 15 seconds. Add melted butter, almond extract, and vanilla and process until combined, about 10 seconds. Transfer egg mixture to medium bowl. Sprinkle half of flour mixture over egg mixture and, using spatula, gently fold until just combined. Add remaining flour mixture and chopped almonds and gently fold until just combined.

3 Divide dough in half. Using floured hands, form each half into 8 by 3-inch rectangle, using lines on parchment as guide. Spray each loaf lightly with oil spray. Using rubber spatula lightly coated with oil spray, smooth tops and sides of loaves. Gently brush tops of loaves with egg white beaten with salt.

4 Bake until loaves are golden and just beginning to crack on top, 25 to 30 minutes, rotating sheet halfway through baking. Let loaves cool on sheet for 30 minutes, then transfer to cutting board. Using serrated knife, slice each loaf on slight bias into ½-inch-thick pieces. Set wire rack in rimmed baking sheet. Space slices, cut side down, about ¼ inch apart on prepared rack. Bake until crisp and golden brown on both sides, about 35 minutes, flipping slices halfway through baking. Let cool completely before serving. (Biscotti can be stored at room temperature for up to 1 month.)

Anise Biscotti
Add 1½ teaspoons anise seeds to flour mixture in step 2. Substitute anise-flavored liqueur for almond extract.

Hazelnut-Rosemary-Orange Biscotti
Substitute lightly toasted and skinned hazelnuts for almonds. Add 2 tablespoons minced fresh rosemary to flour mixture in step 2. Substitute orange-flavored liqueur for almond extract and add 1 tablespoon grated orange zest to egg mixture with butter in step 2.

Pistachio-Spice Biscotti
Substitute shelled pistachios for almonds. Add 1 teaspoon ground cardamom, ½ teaspoon ground cloves, ½ teaspoon pepper, ¼ teaspoon ground cinnamon, and ¼ teaspoon ground ginger to flour mixture in step 2. Substitute 1 teaspoon water for almond extract. Increase vanilla to 1 teaspoon.

FROSTED WALNUT DROPS

Makes about 30 cookies

1¾ cups walnuts, toasted

1 cup (5 ounces) all-purpose flour

½ teaspoon salt

10 tablespoons unsalted butter, softened

⅓ cup (2⅓ ounces) granulated sugar

1 large egg yolk

¾ teaspoon vanilla extract

2 ounces cream cheese, softened

½ cup (2 ounces) confectioners' sugar

Why This Recipe Works Sometimes walnuts are stirred into brownie batter or sprinkled over shortbread, but when it comes to nut-based cookies, it seems like peanuts, almonds, and pecans have all the fun. We wanted a cookie that featured buttery, earthy-tasting walnuts, one where they would be more than just a mix-in. To do this, we finely ground a generous amount of walnuts to form the base of a rich butter-cookie dough. Using the ground nuts in place of much of the flour allowed their flavor to permeate the dough, but we went a step further by mixing even more chopped walnuts into the dough for textural contrast. Toasting the walnuts before grinding and chopping enhanced their nutty presence. The high proportion of nuts in the dough made these cookies fragile, so we added an egg yolk to help hold them together. Our walnut cookies were delicate, ultratender, and elegant, but to up their sophistication even more, we topped them with a silky cream cheese frosting—the perfect counterpart to these rich, buttery cookies—and sprinkled them with more chopped walnuts for visual appeal.

1 Adjust oven racks to upper-middle and lower-middle positions and heat oven to 350 degrees. Line 2 baking sheets with parchment paper.

2 Process 1 cup walnuts, flour, and salt in food processor until walnuts are finely ground, about 30 seconds. Add ½ cup walnuts and pulse until finely chopped, about 8 pulses. Using stand mixer fitted with paddle, beat 8 tablespoons butter and granulated sugar on medium-high speed until pale and fluffy, about 3 minutes. Add egg yolk and ½ teaspoon vanilla and beat until combined. Reduce speed to low, slowly add flour mixture, and mix until just combined.

3 Working with 1 tablespoon dough at a time, roll into balls and space them 1½ inches apart on prepared sheets. Bake until edges are just beginning to brown, 16 to 18 minutes, switching and rotating sheets halfway through baking. Let cookies cool on sheets for 5 minutes, then transfer to wire rack. Let cookies cool completely.

4 Using clean, dry mixer bowl and paddle, mix cream cheese, remaining 2 tablespoons butter, and remaining ¼ teaspoon vanilla on medium-low speed until smooth. Add confectioners' sugar and beat until fluffy, about 2 minutes. Process remaining ¼ cup walnuts in food processor until very finely chopped, 10 to 15 seconds. Spread frosting evenly over cookies, sprinkle with walnuts, and serve.

BAKLAVA

Makes 32 to 40 pieces

Sugar Syrup

1¼ cups (8¾ ounces) sugar

¾ cup water

⅓ cup honey

3 (2-inch) strips lemon zest plus 1 tablespoon juice

1 cinnamon stick

5 whole cloves

⅛ teaspoon salt

Nut Filling

1¾ cups slivered almonds

1 cup walnuts

2 tablespoons sugar

1¼ teaspoons ground cinnamon

¼ teaspoon ground cloves

⅛ teaspoon salt

Pastry

5 tablespoons extra-virgin olive oil

1 pound (14 by 9-inch) phyllo, thawed

Why This Recipe Works We wanted a recipe for classic baklava featuring a crisp, flaky pastry that was light yet rich, a filling loaded with fragrant nuts and spices, and just enough assertive sweetness to pair with a Turkish coffee. To achieve this goal, we sprinkled phyllo dough with three separate layers of nuts (tasters liked a combination of almonds and walnuts) flavored with cinnamon and cloves. We brushed the phyllo layers with just enough olive oil to make them crisp and flaky, but not so much that the result was greasy. We found that cutting the baklava through rather than just scoring it before baking helped it absorb the sugar syrup. Finally, letting the baklava sit overnight before serving dramatically improved its flavor. A straight-sided traditional metal baking pan (not nonstick and not a glass baking dish) works best for making baklava. Phyllo dough is also available in larger 18 by 14-inch sheets; if using, cut them in half to make 14 by 9-inch sheets. Do not thaw the phyllo in the microwave; let it sit in the refrigerator overnight or on the counter for 4 to 5 hours. While working with the phyllo, cover the sheets with plastic wrap and then a damp dish towel to prevent drying. Use the nicest, most intact phyllo sheets for the bottom and top layers; use sheets with tears or ones that are smaller than the size of the pan in the middle layers, where their imperfections will go unnoticed.

1 For the sugar syrup Bring all ingredients to boil in small saucepan over medium-high heat and cook, stirring occasionally, until sugar has dissolved, about 5 minutes. Transfer syrup to 2-cup liquid measuring cup and let cool completely. Discard spices and zest; set aside.

2 For the nut filling Pulse almonds in food processor until very finely chopped, about 20 pulses; transfer to bowl. Pulse walnuts in food processor until very finely chopped, about 15 pulses; transfer to bowl with almonds and toss to combine. Measure out 1 tablespoon nuts and set aside for garnish. Add sugar, cinnamon, cloves, and salt to nut mixture and toss well to combine.

3 For the pastry Adjust oven rack to lower-middle position and heat oven to 300 degrees. Lay 1 phyllo sheet in bottom of greased 13 by 9-inch baking pan and brush thoroughly with oil. Repeat with 7 more phyllo sheets, brushing each with oil (you should have total of 8 layers of phyllo).

4 Sprinkle 1 cup nut filling evenly over phyllo. Cover nut filling with 6 more phyllo sheets, brushing each with oil, then sprinkle with 1 cup nut filling. Repeat with 6 phyllo sheets, oil, and remaining 1 cup nut filling.

5 Cover nut filling with 8 more phyllo sheets, brushing each layer, except final layer, with oil. Working from center outward, use palms of your hands to compress layers and press out any air pockets. Spoon remaining oil (about 2 tablespoons) on top layer and brush to cover surface.

6 Using serrated knife with pointed tip, cut baklava into diamonds. Bake until golden and crisp, about 1½ hours, rotating pan halfway through baking. Immediately pour all but 2 tablespoons cooled syrup over cut lines (syrup will sizzle when it hits hot pan). Drizzle remaining 2 tablespoons syrup over surface. Garnish center of each piece with pinch reserved ground nuts. Let baklava cool completely in pan, about 3 hours, then cover with aluminum foil and let sit at room temperature for 8 hours before serving.

TAHINI COOKIES WITH SESAME SEEDS

Makes 32 cookies

2½ cups (12½ ounces) all-purpose flour

1 teaspoon baking powder

½ teaspoon baking soda

½ teaspoon salt

12 tablespoons unsalted butter, softened

¾ cup (5¼ ounces) granulated sugar

¾ cup packed (5¼ ounces) light brown sugar

1 cup tahini

2 large eggs

1 teaspoon vanilla extract

1 tablespoon sesame seeds, lightly toasted

Why This Recipe Works If you're using tahini just for hummus, you're missing out; this sesame paste is like any other nut or seed butter—rich, creamy, and tasty spread on toast, used in sauces, or eaten off a spoon. Though a bit more savory and earthy than peanut butter, it also works well in desserts. In the Middle East, tahini cookies are common, but the treats are a simple affair—more shortbread than American cookie. We wanted to create a tahini cookie with a texture that more closely resembles that of a chewy peanut butter cookie. This required the addition of eggs and leaveners (we used both baking powder and baking soda), ingredients that are absent from most Israeli tahini cookies, to provide the lift and spread we were after. We also incorporated another ingredient not found in traditional recipes: brown sugar. Equal parts brown and granulated sugar resulted in cookies with crisp edges and the perfect interior chew, along with a complex sweetness that complemented the tahini's nuttiness. Just as with peanut butter cookies, take care not to overbake these cookies or they will lose their soft, slightly chewy centers.

1 Adjust oven racks to upper-middle and lower-middle positions and heat oven to 375 degrees. Line 2 baking sheets with parchment paper. Whisk flour, baking powder, baking soda, and salt together in bowl.

2 Using stand mixer fitted with paddle, beat butter, granulated sugar, and brown sugar on medium-high speed until fluffy, about 3 minutes. Add tahini, eggs, and vanilla and beat until well incorporated, scraping down bowl as needed. Reduce speed to low and slowly add flour mixture, mixing until just combined.

3 Working with 2 tablespoons dough at a time, roll into balls and space them 1½ inches apart on prepared sheets. Sprinkle each dough ball with pinch sesame seeds.

4 Bake until cookies are puffed and edges are just beginning to brown, 12 to 14 minutes, switching and rotating sheets halfway through baking. Let cookies cool on sheets for 5 minutes, then transfer to wire rack. Let cookies cool completely before serving.

ALMOND MACAROONS

Makes 24 cookies

3 cups (12 ounces) slivered almonds

1½ cups (10½ ounces) sugar

3 large egg whites

1 teaspoon almond extract

Why This Recipe Works Almond macaroons, commonly found in European-style bakeries, are flourless—and so, gluten-free—treats that rely on egg whites for both structure and leavening. They're sweet but not too sweet, and they taste strongly of their namesake ingredient. We wanted to develop a great macaroon recipe so we could make these cookies at home, and we were happy to discover that this task was surprisingly simple. To start, we finely ground slivered almonds and sugar in a food processor. Then we added the egg whites and a little almond extract to the work-bowl and processed the ingredients until the mixture formed a stiff but cohesive dough. To form macaroons into their traditional round shape, some recipes call for a pastry bag, but we simply rolled the dough into balls. We baked the macaroons at a relatively low temperature (325 degrees) for a sufficient amount of time (20 to 25 minutes) for cookies that were crunchy-chewy on the outside but still moist and soft on the inside. Be sure to line your baking sheets with parchment paper; the cookies will stick to unlined baking sheets and spread on greased ones.

1 Adjust oven racks to upper-middle and lower-middle positions and heat oven to 325 degrees. Line 2 baking sheets with parchment paper.

2 Process almonds in food processor until finely ground, about 1 minute. Add sugar and process for 15 seconds longer. Add egg whites and almond extract and process just until paste forms. Scrape down bowl and continue to process until stiff but cohesive, malleable paste (similar in consistency to marzipan or pasta dough) forms, about 5 seconds longer. If mixture is crumbly or dry, add water by drops and process until proper consistency is reached.

3 Working with 2 tablespoons dough at a time, roll into balls and space them 1½ inches apart on prepared sheets. Bake until golden brown, 20 to 25 minutes, switching and rotating sheets halfway through baking. Transfer macaroons, still on parchment, to wire racks. Let cookies cool completely before serving.

Fudgy Almond Macaroons

These macaroons are done when they have cracked lightly across the top.

Decrease almonds to 1½ cups and add 1 cup Dutch-processed cocoa and ¼ teaspoon salt with sugar in step 2.

Lemon Almond Macaroons

Add 2 tablespoons grated lemon zest with sugar in step 2 and process 10 seconds longer.

Pine Nut–Crusted Almond Macaroons

Lightly beat 3 egg whites in small bowl. Spread 3 cups pine nuts in shallow dish. Dip each dough ball into beaten egg white, then roll in pine nuts, pressing lightly with your finger-tips, before placing on prepared baking sheets. Flatten dough balls slightly with your fingers, making 1-inch-wide buttons.

CHOCOLATE-MINT COOKIES

Makes about 45 cookies

12 tablespoons unsalted butter, softened

1½ cups packed (10½ ounces) brown sugar

2 tablespoons water

2 cups (12 ounces) semisweet chocolate chips

2½ cups (12½ ounces) all-purpose flour

1¼ teaspoons baking soda

½ teaspoon salt

2 large eggs

45 Crème de Menthe Andes Mints, unwrapped

Why This Recipe Works For a play on one of our favorite treats, Andes chocolate mints, we didn't just pair chocolate and mint in a cookie; we turned to the candy itself to give our cookies that unmistakable Andes flavor and meltingly smooth texture. We knew we wanted the base to be a chewy, decadent chocolate cookie, so we used all melted chocolate (we chose chocolate chips for their quick melting abilities) rather than a combination of melted chocolate and cocoa powder; this made the cookies ultramoist and rich. Next, we thought about ways to incorporate the Andes mints. Chopping them up and mixing them into the dough was a possibility, but we were looking for a more unique approach. We thought about pressing a single mint into each cookie midway through baking, but this meant the flavor would be limited to a confined area. But that gave us another idea: What if we let the mint melt on the cookies and then spread it like frosting? After removing the cookies from the oven, we topped each one with an Andes mint. The residual heat melted the candy, turning it into a spreadable "frosting." After setting up, these treats were a perfect fusion of cookie and candy. You'll need two packages of Andes Mints for this recipe.

1 Combine butter, sugar, and water in medium saucepan and cook over low heat, stirring occasionally, until butter is melted, about 3 minutes. Add chocolate chips and stir constantly until chips are melted. Transfer mixture to bowl of stand mixer and let cool for 10 minutes. Whisk flour, baking soda, and salt together in separate bowl.

2 Fit mixer with paddle, add eggs to bowl with chocolate mixture, and beat on medium-high speed until smooth, about 2 minutes. Reduce speed to low, add flour mixture in 3 additions, and mix until just combined, scraping down bowl as needed. Cover bowl tightly with plastic wrap and refrigerate until dough is firm, at least 1 hour or up to 2 days.

3 Adjust oven racks to upper-middle and lower-middle positions and heat oven to 350 degrees. Line 2 baking sheets with parchment paper. Working with 1 heaping tablespoon dough at a time, roll into balls and space them 2 inches apart on prepared sheets. Bake until just set, 7 to 9 minutes, switching and rotating sheets halfway through baking. After removing cookies from oven, immediately place 1 candy in center of each cookie. Let stand until chocolate is softened,

about 5 minutes, then spread chocolate over tops of cookies. Transfer cookies to wire rack. Repeat with remaining dough and candies. Let cookies cool completely before serving.

Frosting Chocolate-Mint Cookies

1 When cookies are just set, remove baking sheet from oven and immediately place 1 candy in center of each cookie.

2 Let cookies stand until mint is softened, about 5 minutes. Then, using offset spatula, evenly spread melted candy over tops of cookies.

CORNMEAL OLIVE OIL COOKIES

Makes 24 cookies

1½ cups (7½ ounces) all-purpose flour

½ cup (2½ ounces) cornmeal

1 teaspoon baking powder

¼ teaspoon salt

½ cup (3½ ounces) granulated sugar

½ cup olive oil

2 eggs

1 teaspoon minced fresh rosemary

1 cup (4 ounces) confectioners' sugar, plus extra as needed

Why This Recipe Works Cookies don't always have to include traditional sweet ingredients such as chocolate, caramel, and nuts. We wanted a grown-up cookie that would work as dessert or alongside a cup of tea, one that would feature a pleasing contrast between sweet and savory. A cornmeal and olive oil dough seemed like a good start, and we decided to enhance it with some fresh, aromatic rosemary and only a modest amount of sugar for a decidedly savory base. Unlike our Cornmeal Orange Cookies (page 118), which have a texture similar to shortbread, we wanted this treat to be on the cakier side. A full teaspoon of baking powder and two whole eggs gave the cookies lift. A half cup of olive oil provided a fruity flavor without making the cookies greasy. To finish these special cookies, we coated them with confectioners' sugar to balance their earthy, savory notes and dress them up a bit. We found it best to give the cookies a double coating—once while warm and again just before serving—to ensure that the sugar wouldn't melt or brush off. Extra-virgin olive oil can be substituted for the regular olive oil; however, the cookies will have a more pronounced olive oil flavor.

1 Adjust oven racks to upper-middle and lower-middle positions and heat oven to 375 degrees. Line 2 baking sheets with parchment paper. Whisk flour, cornmeal, baking powder, and salt together in bowl.

2 Whisk granulated sugar and oil together in large bowl. Whisk in eggs and rosemary until smooth. Using rubber spatula, gently stir in flour mixture until soft dough forms. Drop 1-tablespoon portions of dough onto prepared sheets, spaced about 2 inches apart.

3 Bake cookies until edges are lightly golden and centers are puffy and split open, about 13 minutes, switching and rotating sheets halfway through baking. Let cookies cool on sheets for 5 minutes. Meanwhile, spread confectioners' sugar in shallow dish.

4 Working with several warm cookies at a time, roll in sugar to coat. Before serving, dust with extra confectioners' sugar. Serve warm or at room temperature.

ITALIAN ANISE COOKIES

Makes about 32 cookies

2 cups (10 ounces) all-purpose flour

½ cup (3½ ounces) granulated sugar

2 teaspoons baking powder

½ teaspoon salt

4 tablespoons unsalted butter,
cut into ½-inch pieces and chilled

4 tablespoons vegetable shortening,
cut into ½-inch pieces and chilled

2 large eggs

1¼ teaspoons anise extract

1 teaspoon vanilla extract

1 teaspoon grated lemon zest
plus 2 tablespoons juice

1½ cups (6 ounces) confectioners' sugar

Multicolored nonpareils (optional)

Why This Recipe Works *Angeletti*, also known as anisette cookies, are a staple at any big Italian celebration. Cakey, with a little heft, they share similarities with a scone or a biscuit. To achieve their unique texture, we used shortening in addition to butter. The shortening gave the cookies a lighter texture and an appealing crisp edge, while butter contributed plenty of flavor. A combination of 4 tablespoons of shortening and 4 tablespoons of butter struck the right balance, giving us cookies with both ethereal texture and rich flavor. A couple teaspoons of baking powder provided just enough lift. Lemon zest and juice ably complemented the refreshing hit of anise. To ensure the anise flavor fully permeated our cookies, we used extract in both the cookie dough and the glaze. These cookies are traditionally decorated with cheery multicolored nonpareils after their bright white glaze is applied, but feel free to use any sprinkles you like. Just be sure to glaze and decorate only a few cookies at a time so the sprinkles stick before the glaze dries.

1 Adjust oven racks to upper-middle and lower-middle positions and heat oven to 375 degrees. Line 2 baking sheets with parchment paper.

2 Process flour, granulated sugar, baking powder, and salt in food processor until combined, about 5 seconds. Scatter butter and shortening over top and pulse until mixture appears sandy, 10 to 12 pulses. Add eggs, 1 teaspoon anise extract, vanilla, and lemon zest and process until dough forms, 20 to 30 seconds.

3 Working with 1 tablespoon dough at a time, roll into balls and space them 2 inches apart on prepared sheets. Bake until tops have puffed and cracked and bottoms are light golden brown, 14 to 16 minutes, switching and rotating sheets halfway through baking. Let cookies cool on sheets for 5 minutes, then transfer to wire rack. Let cookies cool completely.

4 Whisk confectioners' sugar, lemon juice, and remaining ¼ teaspoon anise extract in bowl until smooth. Working with few cookies at a time, spread each cookie with glaze and decorate with nonpareils, if using. Let glaze dry for at least 30 minutes before serving.

MEXICAN WEDDING COOKIES

Makes 48 cookies

2 cups pecans or walnuts

2 cups (10 ounces) all-purpose flour

¾ teaspoon salt

16 tablespoons unsalted butter, softened

⅓ cup (2⅓ ounces) superfine sugar

1½ teaspoons vanilla extract

1½ cups (6 ounces) confectioners' sugar

Why This Recipe Works Mexican wedding cookies, also known as Russian tea cakes, have a delicate, fine, melt-in-your-mouth texture—not unlike shortbread—plus a rich, deeply nutty flavor. In order to really reinforce the nut flavor in our dough, we found it necessary to use equal amounts of nuts (we liked pecans or walnuts) and flour. But with all of those nuts, we found it hard to get the dough to hold together. We tried adding eggs but even one made these cookies too cakey. The trick, it turned out, was to grind some of the nuts very finely into crumbs (almost to a butter) to release their natural oil. When we tried grinding all of the nuts this fine, the cookies tasted great but were too dense; grinding half the nuts was just right. The cookie dough was cohesive, the texture of the cookies was delicate, and each bite still included the pleasing crunch of the coarsely chopped nuts. The thick confectioners' sugar coating is a defining characteristic of Mexican wedding cookies. As with our Cornmeal–Olive Oil Cookies (page 218), we found it best to roll the cookies in powdered sugar twice to ensure a thorough coating.

1 Adjust oven racks to upper-middle and lower-middle positions and heat oven to 325 degrees. Line 2 baking sheets with parchment paper. Process 1 cup pecans in food processor until texture of coarse cornmeal, 10 to 15 seconds; transfer pecans to bowl. Process remaining 1 cup pecans in now-empty food processor until coarsely chopped, about 5 seconds; transfer to bowl with ground pecans. Stir flour and salt into pecans.

2 Using stand mixer fitted with paddle, beat butter and super-fine sugar at medium speed until pale and fluffy, about 3 minutes. Beat in vanilla. Reduce speed to low and slowly add nut mixture until combined, about 30 seconds. Scrape down bowl and continue to mix on low speed until dough is cohesive, about 7 seconds. Give dough final stir by hand to ensure that no dry pockets of flour remain.

3 Working with 1 tablespoon dough at a time, roll into balls and space them 1 inch apart on prepared sheets. Bake until tops are pale golden and bottoms are just beginning to brown, about 18 minutes, switching and rotating sheets halfway through baking. Let cookies cool on sheets for 5 minutes, then transfer to wire rack. Let cookies cool completely.

4 Spread confectioners' sugar in shallow dish. Working with several cookies at a time, roll in sugar to coat. Before serving, reroll cookies in confectioners' sugar and gently shake off excess.

GREEK HONEY CAKES

Makes about 36 cookies

2¼ cups (11¼ ounces) all-purpose flour

¾ teaspoon baking soda

¾ teaspoon ground cinnamon

½ teaspoon salt

¼ teaspoon ground cloves

1½ cups (10½ ounces) sugar

1 tablespoon grated orange zest plus ½ cup juice

¾ cup olive oil

¾ cup water

½ cup honey

½ cup walnuts, toasted and chopped fine

Why This Recipe Works Called *melomakarona*, these moist, oval-shaped Greek cookies are soaked in a floral honey syrup, and are made without egg for a sturdy, biscuit-like texture that holds up well to their honey dip. The dough combines bright orange juice and zest with the warm spice of cinnamon and cloves, for a comfortingly familiar flavor combination typical of many Greek sweets. Another Mediterranean ingredient that makes these cookies unique: olive oil, which we simply blended with sugar in the food processor before mixing in the remaining dry ingredients by hand—no cutting, creaming, or melting of butter required. After carefully submerging the egg-shaped cookies in honey syrup so they were fully soaked—but not soggy—we decided to give them a decorative finish of chopped toasted walnuts. But the surface of the cookies wasn't tacky enough to allow the walnuts to adhere, so we mixed the walnuts with some soaking syrup to help them stay put. Adding some cinnamon to the nut-syrup mixture underscored the spice flavor of these fragrant cookies.

1 Adjust oven racks to upper-middle and lower-middle positions and heat oven to 350 degrees. Line 2 baking sheets with parchment paper.

2 Whisk flour, baking soda, ½ teaspoon cinnamon, salt, and cloves together in large bowl. Process ½ cup sugar and orange zest in food processor until moist and fragrant, about 30 seconds. Add oil and orange juice and process until slightly thickened, about 45 seconds. Transfer sugar mixture to bowl with flour mixture and stir together until dough forms. Working with 1 tablespoon dough at a time, roll into ovals and space them 1½ inches apart on prepared sheets. Bake until light golden brown, 16 to 18 minutes, switching and rotating sheets halfway through baking. Let cookies cool on sheets for 5 minutes.

3 Meanwhile, bring water, honey, and remaining 1 cup sugar to boil in medium saucepan over medium-high heat, stirring frequently to dissolve sugar. Remove saucepan from heat and let syrup cool slightly. Combine walnuts, 3 tablespoons syrup, and remaining ¼ teaspoon cinnamon in small bowl. Working in batches, drop cookies into warm syrup in saucepan for about 1 minute, gently flipping them halfway through soaking. Transfer cookies to wire rack and top each with ½ teaspoon walnut mixture. Let cookies cool completely before serving.

Soaking Greek Honey Cakes

1 Working in small batches, soak cookies in warm syrup for about 1 minute (cookies will float near top). Carefully flip each cookie after about 30 seconds of soaking.

2 Transfer cookies to wire rack so syrup can finish soaking in. Top cookies with mixture of walnuts, syrup, and cinnamon.

ORANGE-CARDAMOM TWISTS

Makes about 48 twists

½ cup walnuts

6 tablespoons (2⅔ ounces) sugar

½ teaspoon ground cardamom

¼ teaspoon salt

1 teaspoon grated orange zest

2 (9½ by 9-inch) sheets puff pastry, thawed

1 large egg, lightly beaten

Why This Recipe Works Crisp and delicate yet tender, puff pastry twists are a great addition to any cookie spread. These cookies are typically sprinkled with cinnamon sugar, but for a twist on twists, we switched the spice to fragrant cardamom and added some complementary orange zest. To keep our recipe simple, we used store-bought puff pastry dough, which we sprinkled with a spiced sugar and walnut mixture. To help the nut-spice mixture stick to the dough, we brushed the pastry with a lightly beaten egg before gently pressing the spice mixture into it with a rolling pin. A dusting of granulated sugar underneath the pastry added some sparkle and shine. We cut the puff pastry into even strips using a pizza wheel, which didn't stick or drag through the dough, and then gently twisted each strip into its requisite shape. A 20-minute stint in the oven was all these distinctive treats needed to brown and caramelize. To thaw frozen puff pastry, let it sit either in the refrigerator for 24 hours or on the counter for 30 minutes to 1 hour.

1 Adjust oven racks to upper-middle and lower-middle positions and heat oven to 375 degrees. Line 2 baking sheets with parchment paper.

2 Process walnuts, ¼ cup sugar, cardamom, and salt in food processor until walnuts are finely ground, about 10 seconds. Add orange zest and pulse until combined, about 5 pulses.

3 Sprinkle 1 tablespoon sugar over counter. Lay 1 sheet of puff pastry on sugar and brush lightly with beaten egg. Sprinkle half of walnut mixture evenly over dough. Gently roll into 10 by 9-inch rectangle. Using pizza cutter, cut dough in half crosswise to create two 9 by 5-inch rectangles, then cut each rectangle crosswise into ¾-inch strips. Twist each strip and space them 2 inches apart on prepared sheets.

4 Bake until twists are puffed and golden brown, about 20 minutes, switching and rotating sheets halfway through baking. Transfer twists to wire rack. Repeat with remaining 1 tablespoon sugar, remaining 1 sheet of puff pastry, remaining beaten egg, and remaining walnut mixture. Let twists cool completely before serving.

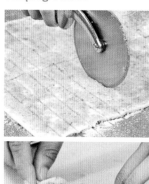

Shaping Twists

1 Cut each 9 by 5-inch rectangle crosswise into ¾-inch strips.

2 Using your fingers, gently twist each strip and space them 2 inches apart on parchment paper–lined baking sheets.

DANISH KLEINER

Makes about 60 cookies

3¾ cups (18¾ ounces) all-purpose flour

1 teaspoon baking powder

½ teaspoon salt

8 tablespoons unsalted butter

1½ teaspoons ground cardamom

1 cup (7 ounces) granulated sugar

3 large eggs

¼ cup heavy cream

1 teaspoon vanilla extract

4 cups vegetable shortening or vegetable oil

Confectioners' sugar (optional)

Why This Recipe Works These cookies are extra unique—and extra delicious—because they're deep-fried. *Kleiner* is the Danish version of a cookie that exists with slight variations all over Europe, but common to all is a diamond shape with one end pulled through a hole in the center. We like Danish kleiner because while fried and crisp, they maintain an interior texture that's somewhere between a cookie and a cake, unlike other European versions which can resemble fried wonton skins. Using cardamom in the dough infused the cookies with authentic flavor. Frying the cookies in vegetable shortening gave them the crispest exterior, but you can also fry in vegetable oil. If you don't have a diamond cookie cutter, cut the dough into 4 by 2¾-inch diamonds. You can also find kleiner/klejner cutters, also called *fattigman* cutters after the Norwegian variation, online.

1 Whisk flour, baking powder, and salt together in bowl. Microwave butter and cardamom in second bowl until melted and fragrant, about 1 minute.

2 Using stand mixer fitted with paddle, beat granulated sugar and eggs on medium speed until smooth, 1 to 2 minutes. Add melted butter mixture, cream, and vanilla and beat until combined, about 30 seconds, scraping down bowl as needed. Reduce speed to low and slowly add flour mixture until just combined.

3 Transfer dough to counter and divide into 4 equal pieces. Form each piece into 4-inch square, wrap squares tightly in plastic wrap, and refrigerate until firm, about 1 hour.

4 Line 2 rimmed baking sheets with parchment paper. Working with 1 dough square at a time (keep remaining dough refrigerated), roll into 12 by 10-inch rectangle, about ⅛ inch thick, on well-floured counter. Using 4 by 2¾-inch diamond cookie cutter, cut dough into diamonds. Cut 1½-inch-long slit, lengthwise, in center of each diamond, then carefully pull 1 tip of cookie through slit. Place cookies on prepared sheets and refrigerate until ready to fry.

5 Heat shortening in Dutch oven over medium-high heat to 350 degrees. Fry 8 cookies until golden brown, about 30 seconds per side. Adjust burner as necessary to maintain oil temperature of 350 degrees.

6 Transfer cookies to wire rack set in rimmed baking sheet to drain. Repeat with remaining cookies. Dust with confectioners' sugar, if using, and serve.

Forming Danish Kleiner

1 Cut 1½-inch-long slit, lengthwise, in center of each dough diamond.

2 Carefully pull 1 tip of diamond through slit.

OLD WORLD BUTTER HORNS

Makes 48 cookies

4 cups (20 ounces) all-purpose flour

2¼ teaspoons instant or rapid-rise yeast

½ teaspoon salt

18 tablespoons (2¼ sticks) unsalted butter, cut into ½-inch pieces and chilled

½ cup sour cream

2 large eggs, separated, plus 2 large yolks

1¾ teaspoons vanilla extract

¾ cup walnuts, toasted and chopped fine

⅛ teaspoon ground cinnamon

⅛ teaspoon cream of tartar

⅔ cup (4⅔ ounces) granulated sugar

Confectioners' sugar (optional)

Why This Recipe Works Butter horns originated in Italy and remain a favorite among Italian American bakers. Recipes for the filling and dough vary, but all butter horns feature a lightly crisp yet tender and yeasty dough that packages a softer center. Some recipes call for mixing spices and nuts with heavy cream to make the filling, but we wanted something with a little more substance, so we went the route of a cinnamon-scented meringue. After whipping egg whites to stiff peaks, we folded in toasted and chopped walnuts for a mixture that started off sticky but became sweet, soft, and a little chewy after baking. To envelop the filling with dough, we cut the dough into wedges, placed a dollop of meringue in the center of each wedge, and pinched the triangular edges together around the filling. Using just egg yolks rather than whole eggs (which made the dough too soft) in the dough and letting the cookies sit before baking ensured that these delicate cookies held their shape.

1 Adjust oven racks to upper-middle and lower-middle positions and heat oven to 400 degrees. Line 2 baking sheets with parchment paper. Process flour, yeast, and salt in food processor until combined, about 30 seconds. Scatter butter over top and pulse until mixture resembles coarse meal, 10 to 12 pulses. Add sour cream, 4 egg yolks, and 1 teaspoon vanilla and pulse until dough forms, about 10 pulses. Divide dough into 8 equal pieces. Form each piece into 4-inch disk, wrap disks in plastic wrap, and refrigerate while making filling.

2 Combine walnuts and cinnamon in bowl. Using stand mixer fitted with whisk attachment, whip egg whites and cream of tartar on medium-low speed until foamy, about 1 minute. Increase speed to medium-high and whip whites to soft, billowy mounds, about 1 minute. Gradually add granulated sugar and remaining ¾ teaspoon vanilla and whip until stiff, glossy peaks form, 2 to 3 minutes. Using rubber spatula, fold in nut mixture.

3 Working with 1 disk of dough at a time, roll into 7-inch circle on counter. Cut dough circle into 6 equal wedges. Place 1 heaping teaspoon of egg white mixture into center of each wedge and pinch points of dough together to seal; space cookies 1 inch apart on prepared sheets. Let shaped cookies stand for 15 minutes.

4 Bake cookies until lightly browned, 12 to 14 minutes, switching and rotating sheets halfway through baking. Let cookies cool on sheets for 5 minutes, then transfer to wire rack. Repeat with remaining dough and filling. Let cookies cool completely. Dust with confectioners' sugar (if using) and serve.

Forming Butter Horns

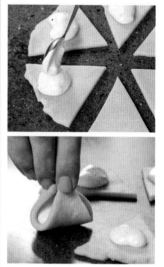

1 Place heaping teaspoon of egg white mixture into center of each dough wedge.

2 Pinch points of dough together to seal around filling.

RASPBERRY ALMOND TORTE COOKIES

Makes 36 cookies

Topping

½ cup sliced almonds

2 tablespoons turbinado sugar

1 tablespoon water

Cookies

3 cups (15 ounces) all-purpose flour

1 teaspoon baking powder

⅛ teaspoon salt

16 tablespoons unsalted butter, softened

1 cup (7 ounces) granulated sugar

3 ounces cream cheese, softened

1 large egg

2 tablespoons sour cream

½ teaspoon vanilla extract

Frosting and Filling

8 tablespoons unsalted butter, softened

2 cups (8 ounces) confectioners' sugar

3 tablespoons heavy cream

¼ teaspoon almond extract

6 tablespoons seedless raspberry jam

Why This Recipe Works With the sophistication of individual little cakes, these multicomponent cookies are sure to impress—perfect for special occasions or to cap off an upscale afternoon tea. The cookies are tender and almost biscuit-like, making them an ideal base for the raspberry filling and ensuring the jam stays put with each bite. To carefully slice the tops off the cookies without marring their elegant appearance, we used a serrated knife. After filling the cookies with jam and replacing their tops, we spread them with a basic frosting that's made light and billowy with the addition of a little cream and fragranced with almond extract. Since almonds and raspberries are a natural pairing, we gave the cookies a second dose of almond flavor, crowning them with a crunchy praline-like almond topping that tasted as good as it looked. Making the topping was easy; we simply tossed sliced almonds with a bit of caramel-y turbinado sugar and water and baked the mixture until lightly browned. We then broke the candied nut mixture into small pieces perfect for topping our petite desserts. Chilling the dough for 20 minutes helps this butter-rich dough firm up so that it is easier to work with.

1 For the topping Adjust oven racks to upper-middle and lower-middle positions and heat oven to 350 degrees. Line 2 baking sheets with parchment paper. Combine almonds, sugar, and water in bowl. Spread almond mixture in single layer on 1 prepared sheet. Bake on upper rack until lightly browned, 10 to 12 minutes. Let topping cool completely on sheet. Break into small pieces; transfer to bowl. (Leave parchment on sheet.)

2 For the cookies Increase oven temperature to 375 degrees. Whisk flour, baking powder, and salt together in bowl. Using stand mixer fitted with paddle, beat butter, sugar, and cream cheese on medium-high speed until pale and fluffy, about 3 minutes. Add egg, sour cream, and vanilla and beat until combined. Reduce speed to low and add flour mixture in 3 additions until just combined, scraping down bowl as needed. Cover bowl with plastic wrap and refrigerate until dough is slightly firm, about 20 minutes.

3 Working with 2 tablespoons dough at a time, roll into balls and space them 1 inch apart on prepared sheets. Bake cookies until dry on top but not browned, 10 to 12 minutes, switching and rotating sheets halfway through baking. Let cookies cool on sheets for 5 minutes, then transfer to wire rack. Let cookies cool completely.

4 For the frosting and filling Using stand mixer fitted with paddle, beat butter on medium-high speed until fluffy, about 30 seconds. Reduce speed to low and add sugar in 2 additions until combined. Increase speed to medium-high and beat until pale and fluffy, about 2 minutes, scraping down bowl as needed. Reduce speed to medium-low, add cream and almond extract, and mix until combined. Using serrated knife, cut off tops of cookies and reserve. Spread ½ teaspoon jam over 1 cookie bottom and replace top. Spread 1 heaping teaspoon frosting on cookie top and sprinkle with almond topping. Repeat with remaining cookies. Serve.

CHERRY CHEESECAKE COOKIES

Makes about 54 cookies

3½ cups (17½ ounces) all-purpose flour

2 teaspoons baking powder

1 teaspoon salt

1 pound cream cheese, softened

20 tablespoons (2½ sticks) unsalted butter, softened

1½ cups (10½ ounces) sugar

2 large eggs

2 teaspoons vanilla extract

8 whole graham crackers, crushed into crumbs (1 cup)

3 (20-ounce) cans cherry pie filling, drained

Why This Recipe Works Cheesecake is delicious, but its decadence comes at a price; it's one of the fussiest desserts to prepare. Once the delicate custard-based cake emerges from the oven—and its water bath—it needs to cool completely and then chill in the refrigerator for even more time. The creamy cake is a pain to transport and slice, and if it stays out of the fridge for long it becomes too soft to cut. Our solution: these attractive treats, which walk the line between cookie and cake and include all the flavor of the slices in an easy-to-make, portable form. The dough contains a full pound of cream cheese to ensure that tangy cheesecake flavor, while the addition of flour stabilizes the mixture and guarantees it will hold its shape when baked. To suggest the crust element of cheesecake, we rolled each dough ball in fine graham cracker crumbs, which gave the crackled cookies a handsome exterior finish. The most iconic accompaniment for cheesecake is a cherry topping, so we made an indentation in the center of each cookie and filled it with a few cherries from canned cherry pie filling. Draining the cherries kept moisture to a minimum and prevented the cookie base from becoming soggy.

1 Whisk flour, baking powder, and salt together in bowl. Using stand mixer fitted with paddle, beat cream cheese, butter, and sugar until smooth and creamy, about 2 minutes. Add eggs and vanilla and mix until incorporated. Reduce speed to low, add flour mixture, and mix until just combined. Cover bowl tightly with plastic wrap and refrigerate until firm, about 30 minutes.

2 Adjust oven racks to upper-middle and lower-middle positions and heat oven to 350 degrees. Line 2 baking sheets with parchment paper. Spread graham cracker crumbs in shallow dish.

3 Roll dough into 1½-inch balls, then roll in graham cracker crumbs; space dough balls 2 inches apart on prepared sheets. Using 1-tablespoon measure, make indentation in center of each dough ball. Place 3 cherries in each indentation. Bake until golden around edges, 12 to 14 minutes, switching and rotating sheets halfway through baking. Let cookies cool for 5 minutes on sheets, then transfer to wire rack. Let cookies cool completely before serving. (Cookies can be refrigerated for up to 2 days.)

Shaping Cheesecake Cookies

1 To make room for cherries, use 1-tablespoon measure to make large indentation in center of each dough ball. (If spoon sticks to cookie dough, dip it in crumbs to coat before pressing.)

2 Place 3 cherries in each indentation.

BLACK AND WHITE COOKIES

Makes 12 cookies

Cookies

1¾ cups (8¾ ounces) all-purpose flour

½ teaspoon baking powder

¼ teaspoon baking soda

⅛ teaspoon salt

10 tablespoons unsalted butter, softened

1 cup (7 ounces) granulated sugar

1 large egg

2 teaspoons vanilla extract

⅓ cup sour cream

Glaze

5 cups (20 ounces) confectioners' sugar, sifted

7 tablespoons whole milk

2 tablespoons corn syrup

1 teaspoon vanilla extract

½ teaspoon salt

3 tablespoons Dutch-processed cocoa powder, sifted

Why This Recipe Works These gigantic, tender, cakey cookies, a mainstay of New York City bakeries, are flavored with vanilla and sport a two-toned coat of icing—half chocolate and half vanilla. To create a black and white cookie worthy of its iconic status, we started with a basic creamed batter, then swapped in sour cream for the milk to add tenderness and rich flavor. We figured cake flour would further enhance tenderness, but it proved to be too much of a good thing, making the cookies crumbly; all-purpose flour provided enough structure to hold the cookies together. We dialed back the baking soda and baking powder to produce just enough lift while keeping the texture fine and even. For the icing, we had two major decisions to make: Should it be creamy or hard, and should it coat the round tops or flat undersides of the cookies? The second question was quickly settled; the flat undersides were far easier to frost. As for the texture, we discovered we could have it both ways: We made a simple glaze with confectioners' sugar, milk, vanilla, and corn syrup that formed a crisp shell as it dried yet stayed creamy underneath. Creating the chocolate glaze was as simple as adding cocoa to the vanilla glaze. You'll get neater cookies if you spread on the vanilla glaze first. This recipe provides a little extra glaze, just in case.

1 For the cookies Adjust oven racks to upper-middle and lower-middle positions and heat oven to 350 degrees. Line 2 baking sheets with parchment paper. Whisk flour, baking powder, baking soda, and salt together in bowl.

2 Using stand mixer fitted with paddle, beat butter and sugar on medium speed until pale and fluffy, about 3 minutes. Add egg and vanilla and beat until combined. Reduce speed to low and add flour mixture in 3 additions, alternating with sour cream in 2 additions, scraping down bowl as needed. Give dough final stir by hand to ensure that no dry pockets of flour remain. Using greased ¼-cup dry measuring cup, drop mounds of dough 3 inches apart on prepared sheets. Bake until edges are lightly browned, 15 to 18 minutes, switching and rotating sheets halfway through baking. Let cookies cool on sheets for 5 minutes, then transfer to wire rack. Let cookies cool completely.

3 For the glaze Whisk sugar, 6 tablespoons milk, corn syrup, vanilla, and salt together in bowl until smooth. Transfer 1 cup glaze to small bowl; reserve. Whisk cocoa and remaining 1 tablespoon milk into remaining glaze until combined.

4 Working with 1 cookie at a time, spread 1 tablespoon vanilla glaze over half of flat side of cookie. Refrigerate until glaze is dry, about 15 minutes. Glaze other half of cookie with 1 tablespoon chocolate glaze. Let glaze dry for at least 1 hour before serving.

Glazing Black and White Cookies

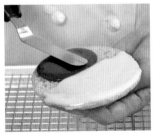

Once vanilla glaze is fully dry, glaze other half of cookie with chocolate glaze and let cookies sit until chocolate glaze is dry.

FROSTED RED VELVET COOKIES

Makes about 22 cookies

1¾ cups (8¾ ounces) all-purpose flour

1 tablespoon natural unsweetened cocoa powder

½ teaspoon baking soda

¼ teaspoon salt

12 tablespoons unsalted butter, softened

1 cup (7 ounces) granulated sugar

1 large egg

1 tablespoon (½ ounce) red food coloring

1½ teaspoons vanilla extract

¼ cup sour cream

4 ounces cream cheese, softened

1¼ cups (5 ounces) confectioners' sugar

Why This Recipe Works In addition to traditional red velvet cake, we've seen red velvet cupcakes, red velvet whoopie pies, and even red velvet doughnuts. This iconic flavor is popular for a reason, and we wanted to incorporate it into a soft, brilliantly colored cookie to get our fix. Like the cake, the red color of these cookies comes first from the natural cocoa powder in the recipe. It's a scant amount, but it's just enough to tinge the dough and give it a light cocoa flavor without making the cookie taste like chocolate. We found that the best way to bolster the color was also the easiest and most common: adding some red food coloring. Just as important as the cake itself is the creamy, dreamy cream cheese frosting. To fully satisfy our red velvet cake cravings, we topped each cookie with a generous amount of fluffy frosting, the tang of which brightened and complemented the light cocoa flavor of the cookie itself. With portable red velvet at our fingertips, we might never fuss with a layer cake again. If you want to dress up these cookies, you can sprinkle them with colored sugar, but with their bright red base and stark white frosting, these cookies look the part—and taste it, too.

1 Adjust oven racks to upper-middle and lower-middle positions and heat oven to 350 degrees. Line 2 baking sheets with parchment paper.

2 Whisk flour, cocoa, baking soda, and salt together in bowl. Using stand mixer fitted with paddle, beat 8 tablespoons butter and granulated sugar on medium-high speed until pale and fluffy, about 2 minutes. Add egg, food coloring, and 1 teaspoon vanilla and beat until combined, about 30 seconds. Reduce speed to low and add half of flour mixture, followed by sour cream, then remaining flour mixture until combined. Drop 2-tablespoon mounds of dough onto prepared sheets, spacing them about 2 inches apart.

3 Bake cookies until centers are set, 16 to 18 minutes, switching and rotating sheets halfway through baking. Let cookies cool on sheets for 5 minutes, then transfer to wire rack. Let cookies cool completely.

4 Using clean, dry mixer bowl and paddle, mix cream cheese, remaining 4 tablespoons butter, and remaining ½ teaspoon vanilla on medium-low speed until combined, about 30 seconds. Reduce speed to low, slowly add confectioners' sugar, and mix until smooth, about 1 minute. Increase speed to medium-high and beat until light and fluffy, 1 to 2 minutes. Spread 1 tablespoon frosting evenly on each cookie before serving.

6

BROWNIES & BLONDIES

FUDGY BROWNIES

Makes 36 brownies

5 ounces bittersweet or semisweet chocolate, chopped

2 ounces unsweetened chocolate, chopped

8 tablespoons unsalted butter, cut into 4 pieces

3 tablespoons unsweetened cocoa powder

1¼ cups (8¾ ounces) sugar

3 large eggs

2 teaspoons vanilla extract

½ teaspoon salt

1 cup (5 ounces) all-purpose flour

Why This Recipe Works Brownies are controversial territory to chart: Some like them cakey and light in flavor—more of a snack than a rich dessert; some like them moist and chewy; and others, the biggest chocoholics, like them to be purely decadent—almost as dense as fudge and deliciously dark. We wanted to make sinfully rich brownies that would be a chocolate lover's dream, so we started by using three forms of chocolate: unsweetened chocolate for intensity, cocoa powder for complexity, and bittersweet or semisweet chocolate for moisture and well-rounded flavor. Melting butter along with the chocolate was the key to a fudgy texture, and a generous three eggs contributed richness and structure. In addition to providing a clean sweetness, granulated sugar gave the baked brownies a delicate, shiny, crackly top crust. We found it best to cut these brownies into small bites rather than big bake-sale squares—a little goes a long way. Tasters preferred the more complex flavor of bittersweet chocolate over semisweet chocolate, but either type works well here, as does 5 ounces of bittersweet or semisweet chocolate chips in place of the bar chocolate.

1 Adjust oven rack to middle position and heat oven to 350 degrees. Make foil sling for 8-inch square baking pan by folding 2 long sheets of aluminum foil so each is 8 inches wide. Lay sheets of foil in pan perpendicular to each other, with extra foil hanging over edges of pan. Push foil into corners and up sides of pan, smoothing foil flush to pan. Grease foil.

2 Microwave bittersweet and unsweetened chocolates in bowl at 50 percent power for 2 minutes. Stir in butter and continue to microwave, stirring often, until melted. Whisk in cocoa and let mixture cool slightly.

3 Whisk sugar, eggs, vanilla, and salt in large bowl until combined. Whisk chocolate mixture into sugar mixture until smooth. Using rubber spatula, stir in flour until no dry streaks remain. Transfer batter to prepared pan and smooth top. Bake until toothpick inserted in center comes out with few moist crumbs attached, 35 to 40 minutes, rotating pan halfway through baking.

4 Let brownies cool completely in pan on wire rack, about 2 hours. Using foil overhang, remove brownies from pan. (Uncut brownies can be refrigerated for up to 3 days.) Cut into 36 squares before serving.

Fudgy Triple-Chocolate Espresso Brownies

Whisk in 1½ tablespoons instant espresso powder or instant coffee powder along with cocoa in step 2.

CHEWY BROWNIES

Makes 24 brownies

⅓ cup (1 ounce) Dutch-processed cocoa powder

1½ teaspoons instant espresso powder (optional)

½ cup plus 2 tablespoons boiling water

2 ounces unsweetened chocolate, chopped fine

½ cup plus 2 tablespoons vegetable oil

4 tablespoons unsalted butter, melted

2 large eggs plus 2 large yolks

2 teaspoons vanilla extract

2½ cups (17½ ounces) sugar

1¾ cups (8¾ ounces) all-purpose flour

¾ teaspoon salt

6 ounces bittersweet chocolate, cut into ½-inch pieces

Why This Recipe Works While box-mix brownies may not offer superior chocolate flavor, there's no denying their chewy appeal. Determined to crack the code for perfectly chewy brownies, we discovered that the key was fat—specifically, the right proportions of saturated and unsaturated fats. After much testing and many adjustments, we decided that an almost 1:3 ratio of saturated fat (butter) to unsaturated fat (vegetable oil) produced the chewiest brownies. With these amounts settled, we turned to fine-tuning the other sources of fat—eggs and chocolate—to preserve this careful balance. Two whole eggs plus two extra yolks emulsified the batter, preventing the brownies from turning greasy. We whisked unsweetened cocoa, along with a little espresso powder, into boiling water and then stirred in unsweetened chocolate. The heat unlocked the chocolate's flavor compounds, boosting its impact. For the chewiest texture, it's important to let the brownies cool thoroughly before cutting. If you use a glass baking dish instead of a metal baking pan, let the brownies cool for 10 minutes and then remove them promptly from the pan (otherwise, the superior heat retention of glass can lead to overbaking).

1 Adjust oven rack to lowest position and heat oven to 350 degrees. Make foil sling for 13 by 9-inch baking pan by folding 2 long sheets of aluminum foil; first sheet should be 13 inches wide and second sheet should be 9 inches wide. Lay sheets of foil in pan perpendicular to each other, with extra foil hanging over edges of pan. Push foil into corners and up sides of pan, smoothing foil flush to pan. Grease foil.

2 Whisk cocoa, espresso powder, if using, and boiling water in large bowl until smooth. Add unsweetened chocolate and whisk until chocolate is melted. Whisk in oil and melted butter. (Mixture may look curdled.) Whisk in eggs and yolks and vanilla until smooth and homogeneous. Whisk in sugar until fully incorporated. Using rubber spatula, stir in flour and salt until combined. Fold in chocolate pieces.

3 Transfer batter to prepared pan and smooth top. Bake until toothpick inserted halfway between edge and center comes out with few moist crumbs attached, 30 to 35 minutes, rotating pan halfway through baking. Let brownies cool in pan on wire rack for 1½ hours. Using foil overhang, remove brownies from pan. Transfer to wire rack and let cool completely, about 1 hour. Cut into 24 pieces before serving.

Chewy Chocolate Frosted Brownies

After brownies have cooled in pan for 1 hour, microwave 1⅓ cup chocolate chips and 2 tablespoons vegetable oil in bowl at 50 percent power, stirring often, until chocolate is melted, 2 to 4 minutes. Let mixture cool until barely warm, about 5 minutes, then spread over brownies with spatula. Continue to let brownies cool until topping sets, 1 to 2 hours.

Chewy German Chocolate Brownies

When brownies come out of oven, sprinkle with 2 cups butterscotch chips and let sit until chips soften but are not melted, about 5 minutes. Smooth softened chips into even layer, then sprinkle with 1 cup sweetened shredded coconut, toasted. Let brownies cool until topping sets, 1 to 2 hours.

Chewy White Chocolate and Peppermint Brownies

Pulse ⅔ cup peppermint candies in food processor until finely chopped. When brownies come out of oven, sprinkle with 2 cups white chocolate chips and let sit until chocolate softens but is not melted, about 5 minutes. Smooth softened chocolate into even layer, then sprinkle with chopped peppermint candies. Let brownies cool until topping sets, 1 to 2 hours.

CHOCOLATE-CHERRY BROWNIES

Makes 24 brownies

1½ cups (6 ounces) dried cherries, chopped

¼ cup plus ⅓ cup water

1 teaspoon almond extract

2 ounces unsweetened chocolate, chopped fine

4 tablespoons unsalted butter, cut into 4 pieces

6 tablespoons vegetable oil

⅓ cup (1 ounce) Dutch-processed cocoa powder

2 large eggs plus 2 large yolks

2 teaspoons vanilla extract

2¼ cups (15¾ ounces) sugar

¾ teaspoon salt

1¾ cups (8¾ ounces) all-purpose flour

Why This Recipe Works Chocolate and cherries are a common pairing—think Black Forest cake or cherry cordials. We wanted to find the best way to add bright cherry flavor to chocolaty brownies. The biggest challenge was incorporating the moist cherries without ruining the texture of the brownies. First we tried sprinkling chopped fresh cherries with sugar and leaving them to drain off some of their liquid before stirring them into the batter. Unfortunately, even after draining, the fresh cherry bits made the brownies wet. Dried cherries added a concentrated hit of fruit flavor and solved the moisture issue, but their texture was leathery. To plump and soften the dried cherries we rehydrated them with water in the microwave, but this dulled their flavor. Replacing the water with juice or liquor made the cherries too sweet or medicinal-tasting. The solution was to add a teaspoon of potent almond extract to the brew. This made sense: Almonds share similar flavor compounds with stone fruits—including cherries. Once stirred into the batter (with their liquid), these cherries gave the brownies a deep, fruity complexity. Either sweetened or unsweetened dried cherries can be used in this recipe.

1 Adjust oven rack to lowest position and heat oven to 350 degrees. Make foil sling for 13 by 9-inch baking pan by folding 2 long sheets of aluminum foil; first sheet should be 13 inches wide and second sheet should be 9 inches wide. Lay sheets of foil in pan perpendicular to each other, with extra foil hanging over edges of pan. Push foil into corners and up sides of pan, smoothing foil flush to pan. Grease foil.

2 Combine cherries, ¼ cup water, and almond extract in small bowl. Microwave, covered, until hot, about 1 minute. Let stand, covered, until cherries have softened, about 5 minutes. Microwave chocolate and butter in large bowl at 50 percent power, stirring occasionally, until melted, about 45 seconds. Whisk in oil, cocoa, and remaining ⅓ cup water. (Mixture may look curdled.)

3 Whisk eggs and yolks and vanilla into chocolate mixture until smooth and homogeneous. Whisk in sugar and salt until fully incorporated. Using rubber spatula, stir in flour until just combined. Stir in softened cherries and their liquid.

4 Transfer batter to prepared pan and smooth top. Bake until slightly puffed and toothpick inserted in center comes out with few moist crumbs attached, 25 to 30 minutes, rotating pan halfway through baking.

5 Let brownies cool in pan on wire rack for 1 hour. Using foil overhang, remove brownies from pan. Transfer to wire rack and let cool completely, about 1 hour. Cut into 24 pieces before serving.

CREAM CHEESE BROWNIES

Makes 16 brownies

Cream Cheese Filling

4 ounces cream cheese, cut into 8 pieces

½ cup sour cream

2 tablespoons sugar

1 tablespoon all-purpose flour

Brownies

⅔ cup (3⅓ ounces) all-purpose flour

½ teaspoon baking powder

½ teaspoon salt

4 ounces unsweetened chocolate, chopped fine

8 tablespoons unsalted butter

1¼ cups (8¾ ounces) sugar

2 large eggs

1 teaspoon vanilla extract

Why This Recipe Works A good cream cheese brownie serves up a perfectly matched duet of velvety cheesecake and fudgy brownie, swirled together yet each maintaining its identity. We started by making a brownie base that was slightly cakey, knowing that the cream cheese filling would add plenty of moisture, for a bar that was perfectly fudgy—not wet. Mixed with just an egg and a bit of sugar, the cream cheese flavor in the filling was too muted to hold its own; a half-cup of sour cream provided a refreshing tang that reinforced the flavor of the cream cheese. To compensate for the extra moisture from the sour cream, we ditched the egg and stirred in a tablespoon of flour. When we spooned the cream cheese mixture over the brownie batter and swirled it in, the cream cheese layer weighed down the chocolate. Instead, we spread most of the brownie batter in the pan and smoothed the cream cheese filling evenly over it. Then, we dolloped the last bit of brownie batter on top and swirled everything together. This ensured our brownies had cream cheese in every bite. To accurately test doneness, be sure to stick the toothpick through part of the brownie and not the cream cheese.

Swirling Technique Matters

Simply dumping a cream cheese mixture over a full pan of brownie batter and attempting to swirl the two together results in brownies with two distinct layers: An overwhelming cream cheese topping and a wet, weighed-down brownie base. We take a three-layer approach before swirling, setting aside some of the brownie batter to dollop on top of the cream cheese and then swirling everything together. Warming the reserved batter makes it easy to swirl.

Cream Cheese Collapse
Most cream cheese brownies suffer from a wet center weighed down by too much cream cheese.

Swirled Champion
Our version is well-balanced and fudgy through and through.

1 Adjust oven rack to middle position and heat oven to 325 degrees. Make foil sling for 8-inch square baking pan by folding 2 long sheets of aluminum foil so each is 8 inches wide. Lay sheets of foil in pan perpendicular to each other, with extra foil hanging over edges of pan. Push foil into corners and up sides of pan, smoothing foil flush to pan. Grease foil.

2 For the cream cheese filling Microwave cream cheese in bowl until soft, 20 to 30 seconds. Whisk in sour cream, sugar, and flour.

3 For the brownies Whisk flour, baking powder, and salt together in bowl. Microwave chocolate and butter in second bowl at 50 percent power, stirring often, until melted, 1 to 2 minutes. Whisk sugar, eggs, and vanilla together in third bowl. Whisk chocolate mixture into sugar mixture until incorporated. Using rubber spatula, fold in flour until combined.

4 Spread all but ½ cup brownie batter in even layer in prepared pan. Spread cream cheese mixture evenly over top. Microwave remaining brownie batter until warm and pourable, 10 to 20 seconds. Using spoon, dollop softened batter over cream cheese filling (6 to 8 dollops). Using butter knife, swirl brownie batter through cream cheese topping, making marbled pattern and leaving ½-inch border around edges.

5 Bake brownies until toothpick inserted in center comes out with few moist crumbs attached, 35 to 40 minutes, rotating pan halfway through baking. Let brownies cool in pan on wire rack for 1 hour.

6 Using foil overhang, remove brownies from pan. Transfer to wire rack and let cool completely, about 1 hour. Cut into 16 squares before serving.

Making Cream Cheese Brownies

1 Transfer ½ cup brownie batter to bowl used to melt chocolate.

2 Spread remaining batter in prepared pan.

3 Spread cream cheese mixture evenly over brownie batter.

4 Microwave remaining brownie batter until it's warm and pourable, 10 to 20 seconds.

5 Using spoon, dollop softened brownie batter over cream cheese filling.

6 Using knife, swirl brownie batter through cream cheese topping, making marbled pattern and leaving ½-inch border around edges.

ULTIMATE TURTLE BROWNIES

Makes 25 brownies

Caramel

6 tablespoons heavy cream

¼ teaspoon salt

¼ cup water

2 tablespoons light corn syrup

1¼ cups (8¾ ounces) sugar

2 tablespoons unsalted butter

1 teaspoon vanilla extract

Brownies

8 tablespoons unsalted butter, cut into 8 pieces

4 ounces bittersweet chocolate, chopped

2 ounces unsweetened chocolate, chopped

¾ cup (3¾ ounces) all-purpose flour

½ teaspoon baking powder

2 large eggs, room temperature

1 cup (7 ounces) sugar

2 teaspoons vanilla extract

¼ teaspoon salt

⅔ cup chopped pecans, plus 25 toasted pecan halves

⅓ cup (2 ounces) semisweet chocolate chips (optional)

Why This Recipe Works Dark chocolate brownies, rich and chewy caramel, and sweet pecans—it's hard to go wrong with turtle brownies. But many recipes for this treat call for box mixes and jarred caramel sauce; unsurprisingly, these shortcuts yield lackluster and sickly sweet results. We wanted a brownie reminiscent of the classic turtle candy: rich, chewy, and chocolaty, with bittersweet, gooey caramel and an abundance of crunchy pecans. Whole eggs, a modest amount of all-purpose flour, and baking powder gave us brownies with a structure that was partway between cakey and chewy—perfect for supporting a blanket of caramel. Garnishing each brownie with a pecan half made them look like turtles, but they didn't taste as nutty as authentic turtles until we stirred chopped pecans into the brownie batter as well. We wanted a thick, shiny caramel topping that wouldn't drip off the brownies—but that also wouldn't tug at our teeth when we took a bite. Caramel made with cream, butter, and sugar was pleasantly chewy and gooey. We added corn syrup to keep the caramel from crystallizing or turning gritty. Swirling the caramel into the batter and pouring more over the top ensured plenty of rich, gooey caramel in every bite of these brownies. If the caramel is too cool to be fluid, reheat it in the microwave.

1 For the caramel Combine cream and salt in small bowl; stir well to dissolve salt. Combine water and corn syrup in 2- to 3-quart saucepan; pour sugar into center of saucepan, taking care not to let sugar granules touch sides of saucepan. Gently stir with spatula to moisten sugar thoroughly. Cover and bring to boil over medium-high heat and cook, covered and without stirring, until sugar is completely dissolved and liquid is clear, 3 to 5 minutes. Uncover and continue to cook, without stirring, until bubbles show faint golden color, 3 to 5 minutes longer. Reduce heat to medium-low and continue to cook (swirling saucepan occasionally) until caramel is light amber and registers about 360 degrees, 1 to 3 minutes longer. Off heat, carefully add cream mixture to center of saucepan; stir (mixture will bubble and steam vigorously) until cream is fully incorporated and bubbling subsides. Stir in butter and vanilla until combined. Transfer caramel to liquid measuring cup or bowl; set aside.

2 For the brownies Adjust oven rack to lower-middle position and heat oven to 325 degrees. Make foil sling for 9-inch square baking pan by folding 2 long sheets of aluminum foil so each is 9 inches wide. Lay sheets of foil in pan perpendicular to each other, with extra foil hanging over edges of pan. Push foil into corners and up sides of pan, smoothing foil flush to pan. Grease foil.

3 Melt butter, bittersweet chocolate, and unsweetened chocolate in heatproof bowl set over saucepan filled with 1 inch barely simmering water, making sure that water does not touch bottom of bowl and stirring occasionally until chocolate and butter are melted; set aside and let cool slightly. Meanwhile, whisk flour and baking powder together in small bowl; set aside. Whisk eggs in large bowl to combine; add sugar, vanilla, and salt and whisk until incorporated. Add cooled chocolate mixture to egg mixture and whisk until combined. Using rubber spatula, stir in flour mixture until almost combined. Stir in chopped pecans and chocolate chips, if using, until incorporated and no flour streaks remain.

4 Spread half of brownie batter in even layer in prepared pan. Using ¼-cup dry measuring cup that's been sprayed with vegetable oil spray, drizzle ¼ cup caramel over batter. Using spoon, dollop remaining batter in large mounds over caramel layer and spread into even layer. Using butter knife, swirl brownie batter through caramel. Bake until toothpick inserted in center comes out with few moist crumbs attached, 35 to 40 minutes, rotating pan halfway through baking. Let brownies cool completely in pan on wire rack, about 1½ hours.

5 Heat remaining caramel (you should have about ¾ cup) in microwave until warm and pourable but still thick (do not boil), 45 to 60 seconds, stirring once or twice; pour caramel over brownies. Spread caramel to cover surface. Refrigerate brownies, uncovered, for 2 hours.

6 Using foil overhang, remove brownies from pan, loosening sides with paring knife if needed. Using chef's knife, cut brownies into 25 squares. Press pecan half onto surface of each brownie. Serve chilled or at room temperature. (Brownies can be wrapped in plastic wrap and refrigerated for up to 3 days.)

Putting Caramel to Work

1 Drizzle ¼ cup caramel over half of batter. Dollop the remaining batter over top.

2 Swirl caramel and brownie batter layers together with butter knife.

3 Microwave remaining caramel until warm and pourable but still thick (do not boil), 45 to 60 seconds, stirring once or twice.

4 Pour remaining caramel over cooled brownies; refrigerate, uncovered, for 2 hours.

ROCKY ROAD BROWNIES

Makes 16 brownies

8 tablespoons unsalted butter

3 ounces unsweetened chocolate, chopped coarse

⅔ cup (3⅓ ounces) all-purpose flour

½ teaspoon baking powder

¼ teaspoon salt

1 cup (7 ounces) sugar

2 large eggs

1 teaspoon vanilla extract

½ cup walnuts or pecans, toasted and chopped

1½ cups marshmallow crème

Why This Recipe Works Looking to rocky road ice cream for inspiration for these decadent treats, we topped our brownie base with a liberal amount of sweet marshmallow crème and then swirled it through the batter with a knife. While these brownies look gooey and messy with their shiny marshmallow swirl, we made the base nice and sturdy so it could support its delicious topping, and so the brownies could easily be packed for lunch or taken on a picnic. Unsweetened chocolate—rather than bittersweet or semisweet—kept the sweetness of these marshmallow-enhanced brownies in check. Swirling the marshmallow on top rather than hiding it as a layer within the brownie batter ensured this star ingredient wasn't overwhelmed by the chocolate. Toasted walnuts (or pecans if you prefer) provided crunch and the requisite rockiness. The result is a textural masterpiece: dense, chocolaty brownie; crunchy, toasty chopped nuts; and rivers of smooth, gooey marshmallow.

1 Adjust oven rack to middle position and heat oven to 350 degrees. Make foil sling for 8-inch square baking pan by folding 2 long sheets of aluminum foil so each is 8 inches wide. Lay sheets of foil in pan perpendicular to each other, with extra foil hanging over edges of pan. Push foil into corners and up sides of pan, smoothing foil flush to pan. Grease foil.

2 Microwave butter and chocolate in bowl at 50 percent power, stirring often, until melted, 1 to 3 minutes; let cool slightly.

3 Whisk flour, baking powder, and salt together in second bowl. Whisk sugar, eggs, and vanilla together in large bowl. Whisk chocolate mixture into sugar mixture until combined. Using rubber spatula, stir in flour mixture until just incorporated.

4 Transfer batter to prepared pan, smooth top, and sprinkle with walnuts. Using spoon, place small dollops of marshmallow crème over brownie batter. Using butter knife, swirl marshmallow through brownie batter. Bake until toothpick inserted in center comes out with few moist crumbs attached, 22 to 27 minutes, rotating pan halfway through baking.

5 Let brownies cool completely in pan on wire rack, about 2 hours. Using foil overhang, remove brownies from pan. Cut into 16 squares before serving.

PEANUT BUTTER SWIRL BROWNIES

Makes 16 brownies

8 tablespoons unsalted butter

3 ounces unsweetened chocolate, chopped coarse

⅔ cup (3⅓ ounces) all-purpose flour

½ teaspoon baking powder

¼ teaspoon salt

1 cup (7 ounces) sugar

2 large eggs

1 teaspoon vanilla extract

⅓ cup creamy or chunky peanut butter

Why This Recipe Works Nothing quite satisfies salty-sweet cravings better than the classic pairing of peanut butter and chocolate, and the richness of both ingredients makes for an unequivocally decadent treat. We wanted a brownie reminiscent of everyone's favorite peanut butter cup, with swirls of peanut butter running throughout a chocolaty brownie base. We started with a basic chocolate brownie that comes together by hand. Dolloping large mounds of peanut butter over the batter before swirling it in resulted in unbalanced brownies; some bites were overloaded with sticky peanut butter while others contained no peanut butter at all. That's because unlike cream cheese or marshmallow crème, peanut butter doesn't readily move with the knife. Dropping small dollops over the batter before swirling was much more successful, with pockets of peanut butter evenly distributed throughout every brownie. We like both the smoothness of creamy peanut butter and the crunch of chunky peanut butter in these brownies, so you can choose your favorite. If you store your peanut butter in the refrigerator, note that room temperature peanut butter is much easier to work with.

1 Adjust oven rack to middle position and heat oven to 350 degrees. Make foil sling for 8-inch square baking pan by folding 2 long sheets of aluminum foil so each is 8 inches wide. Lay sheets of foil in pan perpendicular to each other, with extra foil hanging over edges of pan. Push foil into corners and up sides of pan, smoothing foil flush to pan. Grease foil.

2 Microwave butter and chocolate in bowl at 50 percent power, stirring often, until melted, 1 to 3 minutes; let cool slightly.

3 Whisk flour, baking powder, and salt together in second bowl. Whisk sugar, eggs, and vanilla together in large bowl. Whisk chocolate mixture into sugar mixture until combined. Using rubber spatula, stir in flour mixture until just incorporated.

4 Transfer batter to prepared pan and smooth top. Using spoon, dollop small mounds of peanut butter over brownie batter. Using butter knife, swirl peanut butter through brownie batter. Bake until toothpick inserted in center comes out with few moist crumbs attached, 22 to 27 minutes, rotating pan halfway through baking.

5 Let brownies cool completely in pan on wire rack, about 2 hours. Using foil overhang, remove brownies from pan. Cut into 16 squares before serving.

S'MORES BROWNIES

Makes 16 brownies

Crust

6 whole graham crackers, crushed into crumbs (¾ cup)

4 tablespoons unsalted butter, melted

1 tablespoon sugar

Brownies

8 tablespoons unsalted butter

3 ounces unsweetened chocolate, chopped coarse

⅔ cup (3⅓ ounces) all-purpose flour

½ teaspoon baking powder

¼ teaspoon salt

1 cup (7 ounces) sugar

2 large eggs

1 teaspoon vanilla extract

2 cups marshmallows

Why This Recipe Works We can never get enough s'more-themed desserts, so while we love our S'mores Blossom Cookies (page 139), we couldn't resist adding another s'mores treat to our repertoire: these multilayered s'mores brownies. For a taste of the campfire, we topped the baked brownies with marshmallows and then ran the whole thing under the broiler until the marshmallows were gooey and uniformly kissed with a toasty-brown top. Because these brownies had a hefty topping, we wanted to make sure the base was particularly sturdy, so we employed the same workhorse brownie base that we used in our Rocky Road Brownies (page 255) and Peanut Butter Swirl Brownies (page 256). The only thing left to add was the graham cracker component. We decided to make a buttery bottom crust for these brownies, which we parbaked before adding the batter so it wouldn't turn soggy. The crisp cracker base was a nice foil to the decadent chocolate brownie "filling" and soft toasted marshmallow top. Prepare the brownie batter while the crust bakes. You will need 6 whole graham crackers to yield ¾ cup crumbs when finely ground in a food processor.

1 Adjust oven rack to middle position and heat oven to 350 degrees. Make foil sling for 8-inch square baking pan by folding 2 long sheets of aluminum foil so each is 8 inches wide. Lay sheets of foil in pan perpendicular to each other, with extra foil hanging over edges of pan. Push foil into corners and up sides of pan, smoothing foil flush to pan. Grease foil.

2 **For the crust** Using your fingers, combine graham cracker crumbs, melted butter, and sugar in bowl until evenly moistened. Sprinkle mixture into prepared pan and press firmly into even layer. Bake until firm and lightly browned, 8 to 10 minutes; set aside crust.

3 **For the brownies** While crust is baking, microwave butter and chocolate in bowl at 50 percent power, stirring often, until melted, 1 to 3 minutes; let cool slightly.

4 Whisk flour, baking powder, and salt together in second bowl. Whisk sugar, eggs, and vanilla together in large bowl. Whisk chocolate mixture into sugar mixture until combined. Using rubber spatula, stir in flour mixture until just incorporated.

5 Transfer batter to pan with crust and smooth top. Bake until toothpick inserted in center comes out with few moist crumbs attached, 22 to 27 minutes, rotating pan halfway through baking. Remove pan from oven and heat broiler.

6 Sprinkle brownies evenly with single layer of marshmallows. Return brownies to oven and broil until marshmallows are lightly browned, 1 to 3 minutes. (Watch oven constantly; marshmallows will melt slightly but should hold their shape.) Immediately remove pan from oven. Let brownies cool completely in pan on wire rack, about 2 hours.

7 Using foil overhang, remove brownies from pan. Slide foil out from under brownies. Spray knife with vegetable oil spray to prevent marshmallows from sticking. Cut into 16 squares before serving.

ALL ABOUT **BROWNIES**

At their most basic, brownies are easy to make: Simply stir together the ingredients, transfer the batter to a pan, and bake—no stand mixer or shaping required. But that doesn't mean that a little know-how can't make the process even more foolproof.

For the best-textured brownies and blondies, gently fold or stir in the flour and don't overmix. Properly mixed batter bakes into compact, tender brownies, while overmixed brownies bake up taller, tougher, and cakier. And what happens if you make brownies in a stand mixer? The effects of overmixing are even more noticeable, and the brownies taste less chocolaty. Mixing batter leads to gluten development. The overmixed brownies develop a strong gluten network that can trap the extra air created through fierce mixing.

Perfectly Mixed

Stirred Too Much

Mixed in a Stand Mixer

Achieving a glossy, crackly top on a brownie can be an elusive goal, but we finally discovered the trick: The type of sweetener you use matters. You can achieve this sheen only with granulated sugar. Brown sugar forms crystals on the surface of a cooling brownie; when they reflect light, they create a matte surface. The pure sucrose in granulated sugar creates a glass-like, noncrystalline surface that produces a shiny effect. As for the crackly crust, its formation depends on sugar molecules rising to the surface of the batter and drying out during baking. Brown sugar has too much moisture; the surface can never dry enough to become crisp. The number of eggs you use in the recipe can also affect moisture.

Brownies Made with Brown Sugar   **Brownies Made with White Sugar**

Overbaked brownies are dry and chalky and the chocolate flavor is diminished. To determine doneness, insert a toothpick in the center of the brownies. If the brownies are perfectly baked, the toothpick should emerge with a few moist crumbs clinging to it. If it comes out clean, the brownies are overbaked.

Our brownie and blondie recipes call for a metal baking pan rather than a glass baking dish. Can the two be used interchangeably? Yes and no. Yes, you can bake brownies in a glass baking dish, but we've found that the results are noticeably drier once cooled. Why? Glass retains heat well—almost too well. Brownies and blondies baked in glass dishes continue to cook from residual heat held by the pan after it has been removed from the oven. In addition, glass baking dishes have rounded edges and corners, and we like the clean lines provided by a straight-sided baking pan for our brownies and blondies.

MATCHING THE CHEW OF BOXED BROWNIES

Fat can be divided into two broad types: saturated and unsaturated. Predominantly saturated fats, such as butter and shortening, consist of long chains of carbon atoms strung together, each of which has the maximum amount of hydrogen atoms attached; the hydrogen atoms provide support, keeping the carbon chains rigid and packed together like a box of pencils. What does that mean? These fats are solid, even at room temperature. Unsaturated fats, such as vegetable oils, have fewer hydrogen atoms providing support, resulting in carbon chains that don't stick together tightly and a fat that is liquid at room temperature. The right combination of rigid and flexible chains is what gives box brownies their unique texture.

Boxed brownie mixes already come with the saturated-fat component, which is broken down into tiny, powdery crystals. When a cook then adds unsaturated vegetable oil to this mix, the liquid fat and powdered solid fat combine in a ratio designed to deliver maximum chew.

By using both butter (a predominantly saturated fat) and vegetable oil (an unsaturated fat) in our Chewy Brownies (page 245) we were able to approximate the same 1:3 ratio found in commercially engineered specimens to mimic their satisfying chew.

Fat's Role in Brownies

	SATURATED FAT	UNSATURATED FAT
Box Formula	28%	72%
Classic Formula	64%	36%
Our Formula	29%	71%

Box Formula
Besides containing the optimal ratio of different fat types, box brownies make use of highly processed powdered shortening to achieve their chewy texture.

Classic Formula
The classic version of brownies is made with all butter (and no vegetable oil) for a high proportion of solid, saturated fat that leads to a tender texture, versus a chewy one.

Our Formula
Our Chewy Brownies (page 245) contain a low-tech combo of butter and vegetable oil that creates a chewy texture similar to box brownies, but with a far richer taste.

We're not brownie style loyalists, and we think different brownies serve different purposes. An unadulterated chocolate brownie is delicious when dense, dark, and fudgy, while sometimes we like something a bit more subdued and with a bit more lift to stand up to a swirl of a sweet or rich topping.

Manipulating the types of chocolate we use in our brownies allows us to make treats for all occasions. The amount of flavor a chocolate variety can provide depends on the amount of cocoa solids it contains. That's why nearly all brownie recipes calling for bar chocolate include unsweetened chocolate, which contains just cocoa butter and chocolate solids. Many brownie recipes also use bittersweet chocolate; it contains more fat and sugar, so while it contributes less chocolate flavor it can help deliver a moist texture.

But when we want to pack a brownie with the most chocolate punch, we turn to cocoa powder: Ounce for ounce, cocoa powder has more cocoa solids—and thus more chocolate flavor—than any other type of chocolate (for more information on cocoa powder, see page 19). In order to equal the amount of chocolate solids in 1 ounce of cocoa powder, we had to use 1.63 ounces of unsweetened bar chocolate, or 3.8 ounces of bittersweet chocolate.

The takeaway: While we never use just cocoa powder in our brownies (with all of the starch and without the fat of cocoa butter, it can make dry brownies), adding some to the recipe can give it a big chocolate boost without weighing it down. You'll see that we often keep the cocoa out of the equation in recipes that have rich swirls or additions: The strongest chocolate flavor could overshadow the cream cheese, caramel, peanut butter, or marshmallow flourishes that make these brownies great.

GINGERBREAD BROWNIES

Makes 24 brownies

1½ cups (7½ ounces) all-purpose flour

¼ cup (¾ ounce) Dutch-processed cocoa powder

½ teaspoon salt

½ teaspoon baking powder

¼ teaspoon baking soda

4 ounces semisweet chocolate, chopped

8 tablespoons unsalted butter

1 tablespoon ground ginger

1 cup packed (7 ounces) light brown sugar

2 large eggs

⅓ cup molasses

Why This Recipe Works Gingerbread and brownies: What at first might sound like an unlikely pairing is actually a logical success. Chocolate and spice work well together; plus, both of these desserts have a dense, cakey chew, so we figured melding the two would be relatively easy. With so many bold ingredients we needed to find just the right balance of flavors, so we used only the most essential players: ginger and molasses from the gingerbread, and cocoa powder and melted chocolate from the brownies. (Other gingerbread additions such as cinnamon and cloves, or brownie enhancers such as espresso powder, overwhelmed these bars.) While we frequently enjoy the deepest, darkest of brownies, we settled on semisweet chocolate as the best complement to the gingerbread flavor. A small amount of smoky molasses resulted in brownies with superlative chew and sweet complexity. Adding ginger right to the batter made the brownies taste flat; for piquant flavor, we melted the butter that we were using for our brownies and bloomed the ground ginger in it. These brownies taste best when completely cool, so try to be patient.

1 Adjust oven rack to middle position and heat oven to 325 degrees. Make foil sling for 13 by 9-inch baking pan by folding 2 long sheets of aluminum foil; first sheet should be 13 inches wide and second sheet should be 9 inches wide. Lay sheets of foil in pan perpendicular to each other, with extra foil hanging over edges of pan. Push foil into corners and up sides of pan, smoothing foil flush to pan. Grease foil.

2 Whisk flour, cocoa, salt, baking powder, and baking soda together in bowl; set aside. Place chocolate in second bowl. Melt butter in 8-inch skillet over medium-high heat. Add ginger and cook, stirring constantly, for 15 seconds. Pour butter mixture over chocolate and let sit for 5 minutes. Whisk chocolate mixture until smooth.

3 Whisk sugar, eggs, and molasses in large bowl until combined. Stir chocolate mixture into sugar mixture and whisk until incorporated. Using rubber spatula, stir in flour mixture until just incorporated. Transfer batter to prepared pan and spread into even layer. Bake until toothpick inserted in center comes out with few moist crumbs attached, 22 to 25 minutes, rotating pan halfway through baking. Let brownies cool completely in pan on wire rack. Using foil overhang, remove brownies from pan. Cut into 24 pieces before serving.

PEPPERMINT SURPRISE BROWNIE BITES

Makes 36 small brownies

8 tablespoons unsalted butter

2 ounces unsweetened chocolate

¾ cup (3¾ ounces) all-purpose flour

½ teaspoon baking powder

¼ teaspoon salt

1 cup (7 ounces) granulated sugar

2 large eggs

1 teaspoon vanilla extract

16 (1½-inch) York Peppermint Patties, unwrapped

Why This Recipe Works Fans of the smooth, cool flavor of York Peppermint Patties will flip for these candy-packed treats. We already had a reliable brownie base, so we needed only to determine the best method for incorporating the candy. Chopping the patties and folding them into the batter was a flop; the small bits melted into the batter, and while the brownies tasted minty, we wanted a stronger candy presence in each bite. Tucking whole peppermint patties between layers of brownie batter worked much better. The candies melted into a minty layer during baking, and once the brownies cooled, the softened patties set up a bit, so slicing these brownies into squares resulted in clean lines of black and white, giving the brownies a bold striped appearance for an aesthetically pleasing treat. The simplest method for serving is to cut these brownies into small bites (they're rich!), but you can use cookie cutters for alternate shapes (we like stars and crescents). Since the candy layer becomes gooey during baking, inserting a toothpick into the center of the brownies is not a reliable method for determining doneness.

1 Adjust oven rack to middle position and heat oven to 350 degrees. Make foil sling for 8-inch square baking pan by folding 2 long sheets of aluminum foil so each is 8 inches wide. Lay sheets of foil in pan perpendicular to each other, with extra foil hanging over edges of pan. Push foil into corners and up sides of pan, smoothing foil flush to pan. Grease foil.

2 Microwave butter and chocolate in bowl at 50 percent power, stirring often, until melted, 1 to 3 minutes; let cool slightly. Whisk flour, baking powder, and salt together in second bowl. Whisk sugar, eggs, and vanilla together in large bowl. Whisk chocolate mixture into sugar mixture until combined. Using rubber spatula, stir in flour mixture until just incorporated.

3 Spread all but 1 cup batter in even layer in prepared pan. Space candies ½ inch apart on top of batter. Gently spread remaining batter over candies and smooth top. Bake until just set in center, 30 to 35 minutes, rotating pan halfway through baking. Let brownies cool in pan on wire rack for 2 hours. Using foil overhang, remove brownies from pan. Cut into 36 squares before serving.

Making Peppermint Layer

1 Space candies ½ inch apart on top of bottom layer of brownie batter so they have room to melt together.

2 Gently spread remaining brownie batter over candies, covering them with even layer.

MISSISSIPPI MUD BROWNIES

Makes 24 brownies

Brownies

6 ounces unsweetened chocolate, chopped

16 tablespoons unsalted butter

1½ cups (7½ ounces) all-purpose flour

⅓ cup (1 ounce) Dutch-processed cocoa powder

½ teaspoon salt

3 cups (21 ounces) sugar

5 large eggs

¾ cup pecans, chopped

Topping

¾ cup marshmallow crème

¼ cup semisweet chocolate chips

2 teaspoons vegetable oil

Why This Recipe Works Mississippi mud desserts typically take the form of pie, cake, or brownies. The brownies are usually laced with pecans, topped with mini marshmallows once the base is set but still moist, briefly returned to the oven, and then covered with chocolate frosting once cooled—phew! We love the idea but many recipes are overwhelmed by an overload of sugar; we wanted a version that would lose the tooth-aching sweetness but keep the rich decadence intact. We started from the bottom up. We wanted an ultrachocolaty brownie (these are called Mississippi "mud," after all), so in addition to bittersweet chocolate we used cocoa powder. Three-quarters cup of chopped pecans added plenty of textural interest. Next, we ditched the mini marshmallows in favor of a thin layer of marshmallow crème spread evenly over the brownies. And did we really need the frosting? We decided the brownies were chocolaty enough; they needed just a drizzle of chocolate for a dressed-up look. We melted some chocolate chips and added a little oil to keep the chocolate flowing from the spoon as we swirled it over the brownies. Be careful not to overbake these brownies; they should be moist and fudgy.

1 For the brownies Adjust oven rack to middle position and heat oven to 325 degrees. Make foil sling for 13 by 9-inch baking pan by folding 2 long sheets of aluminum foil; first sheet should be 13 inches wide and second sheet should be 9 inches wide. Lay sheets of foil in pan perpendicular to each other, with extra foil hanging over edges of pan. Push foil into corners and up sides of pan, smoothing foil flush to pan. Grease foil.

2 Melt chocolate and butter in large bowl set over medium saucepan filled with ½ inch of barely simmering water (don't let bowl touch water), stirring occasionally, until smooth, 5 to 7 minutes; let cool slightly. Whisk flour, cocoa, and salt together in bowl. Whisk sugar and eggs in second bowl until combined. Whisk chocolate mixture into sugar mixture until smooth. Using rubber spatula, stir flour mixture into chocolate mixture until no streaks of flour remain. Fold in pecans. Transfer batter to prepared pan and smooth top.

3 Bake brownies until toothpick inserted in center comes out with few moist crumbs attached, about 35 minutes. Transfer pan to wire rack.

4 For the topping Using spoon, dollop marshmallow crème over hot brownies and let sit until softened, about 1 minute. Meanwhile, microwave chocolate chips and oil in small bowl until smooth, 30 to 60 seconds. Spread marshmallow crème evenly over brownies, then drizzle with chocolate. Let brownies cool completely in pan, about 2 hours. Using foil overhang, remove brownies from pan. Cut into 24 pieces before serving.

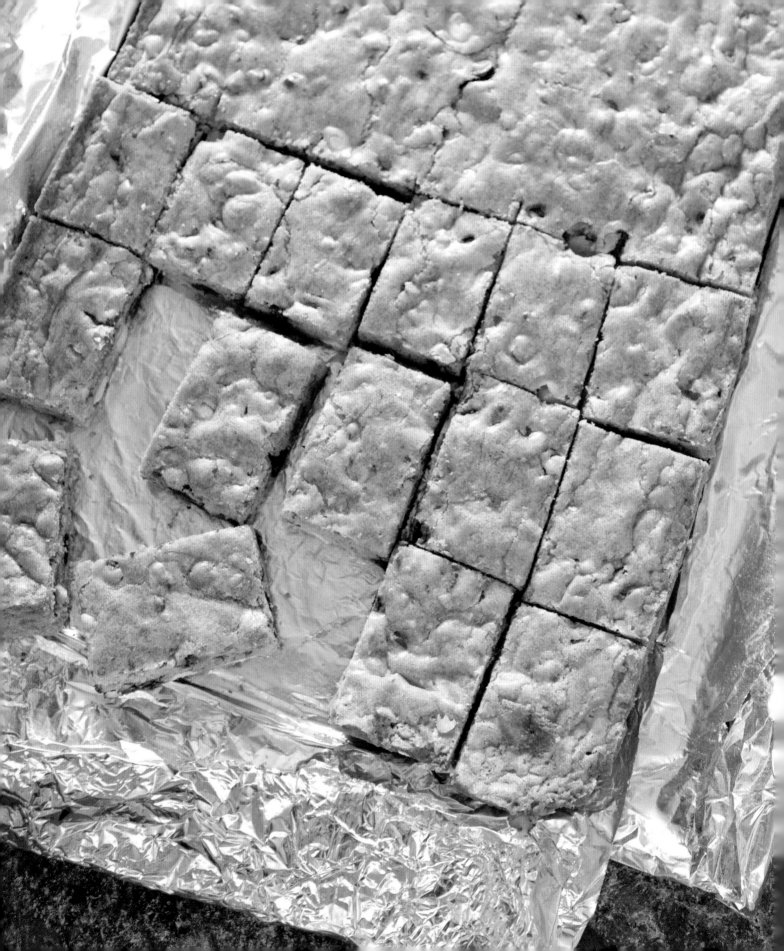

BLONDIES

Makes 36 blondies

1½ cups (7½ ounces) all-purpose flour

1 teaspoon baking powder

½ teaspoon salt

1½ cups packed (10½ ounces) light brown sugar

12 tablespoons unsalted butter, melted and cooled

2 large eggs

1½ teaspoons vanilla extract

1 cup pecans or walnuts, toasted and chopped coarse

½ cup (3 ounces) semisweet chocolate chips

½ cup (3 ounces) white chocolate chips

Why This Recipe Works Although blondies are baked in a pan like brownies, their flavor is closer to that of chocolate chip cookies—with even more of a butterscotch punch. Our ideal blondie is chewy (not cakey but not too dense), sweet but not cloying, and loaded with nuts and chocolate. Many recipes for blondies cream the butter, but we found that the creaming process incorporated too much air into the batter and resulted in a cakey bar. The secret to blondies with the ideal amount of chew was using melted butter. For sweetening, granulated sugar produced a flat-tasting blondie; light brown sugar lent the perfect amount of dimension. When we combined the brown sugar with a substantial amount—1½ teaspoons—of vanilla extract and salt, the blondies developed the rich butterscotch flavor we were after. A generous amount of chocolate chips and pecans contributed creamy richness and crunch to the chewy bars. Butterscotch chips overpowered the butterscotch notes in the blondie base, but white chocolate chips added a sweet milkiness and produced the best blondies yet. Be sure to check the blondies early so you don't overbake them.

1 Adjust oven rack to middle position and heat oven to 350 degrees. Make foil sling for 13 by 9-inch baking pan by folding 2 long sheets of aluminum foil; first sheet should be 13 inches wide, and second sheet should be 9 inches wide. Lay sheets of foil in pan perpendicular to each other, with extra foil hanging over edges of pan. Push foil into corners and up sides of pan, smoothing foil flush to pan. Grease foil.

2 Whisk flour, baking powder, and salt together in bowl. Whisk sugar and melted butter in second bowl until combined. Whisk eggs and vanilla into sugar mixture until combined. Using rubber spatula, fold in flour mixture until just combined. Fold in pecans, semisweet chocolate chips, and white chocolate chips.

3 Transfer batter to prepared pan and smooth top. Bake until top is shiny and cracked and feels firm to touch, 22 to 25 minutes, rotating pan halfway through baking. Let blondies cool completely in pan on wire rack, about 2 hours. Using foil overhang, lift blondies from pan. Cut into 36 pieces before serving.

Congo Bars

Add 1½ cups unsweetened shredded coconut, toasted, to batter with chocolate chips and nuts.

PEANUT BUTTER BLONDIES

Makes 24 blondies

1½ cups (7½ ounces) all-purpose flour

1 teaspoon baking powder

½ teaspoon salt

1½ cups packed (10½ ounces) light brown sugar

8 tablespoons unsalted butter, melted and cooled

2 large eggs

4 teaspoons vanilla extract

½ cup chunky peanut butter

½ cup (3 ounces) peanut butter chips

¼ cup salted dry-roasted peanuts, chopped

Why This Recipe Works Peanut butter has the potential to make just about everything better, and blondies are no exception: The rich, nutty flavor of peanut butter is a perfect complement to the butterscotch notes of this classic bar cookie. But making a peanut butter blondie wasn't as simple as stirring some peanut butter into our classic blondie base. By the time we added enough for super-nutty flavor, our blondies were dense and heavy from all the added fat. We maxed out at ½ cup of peanut butter, and even then we had to decrease the amount of butter to accommodate this amount. Chunky peanut butter packed double the peanut flavor of creamy, and we didn't mind the texture it added, either. But we wanted still more peanut butter flavor. Stirring some toasted and chopped nuts into the batter gave our blondies an earthy crunch, but it still wasn't enough. The only peanut product we had left to test: peanut butter chips. We didn't think the candies would help—and we couldn't have been more wrong. They provided pockets of concentrated peanut butter flavor for the blondies of our dreams. If you store your peanut butter in the refrigerator, note that room temperature peanut butter will combine more easily with the batter.

1 Adjust oven rack to middle position and heat oven to 350 degrees. Make foil sling for 13 by 9-inch baking pan by folding 2 long sheets of aluminum foil; first sheet should be 13 inches wide and second sheet should be 9 inches wide. Lay sheets of foil in pan perpendicular to each other, with extra foil hanging over edges of pan. Push foil into corners and up sides of pan, smoothing foil flush to pan. Grease foil.

2 Whisk flour, baking powder, and salt together in bowl. Whisk sugar and melted butter in second bowl until combined. Whisk eggs and vanilla into sugar mixture until combined. Whisk in peanut butter until combined. Using rubber spatula, fold in flour mixture until just combined. Fold in peanut butter chips and peanuts.

3 Transfer batter to prepared pan and smooth top. Bake until toothpick inserted in center comes out with few moist crumbs attached, 30 to 35 minutes, rotating pan halfway through baking. Using foil overhang, remove blondies from pan. Cut into 24 pieces before serving.

Chocolate Peanut Butter Blondies
Although we prefer bittersweet chips here, semisweet chocolate chips can be substituted.

Add 1 cup bittersweet chocolate chips with peanut butter chips and peanuts in step 2.

BUTTERSCOTCH MERINGUE BARS

Makes 24 bars

2 cups (10 ounces) all-purpose flour

1 teaspoon baking powder

½ teaspoon baking soda

½ teaspoon salt

16 tablespoons unsalted butter, softened

2 cups packed (14 ounces) light brown sugar

½ cup (3½ ounces) granulated sugar

2 large eggs, separated

1 tablespoon water

1 teaspoon vanilla extract

2 cups (12 ounces) semisweet chocolate chips

Why This Recipe Works When it comes to meringue, we all know meringue cookies, but the cloud-like confection can—and should—be used for more than just those sweet, pearly-white bites. Here we use meringue as a topping for a rich, chewy, multilayered blondie bar, a cookie with an intriguing contrast of textures. An ultrachewy brown sugar blondie base was our starting point. Instead of mixing chocolate chips into the batter, we pressed them on top before baking; this way, the chocolate got its own fudgy layer. For the final layer, we brought in the meringue, spreading a fluff of the sweet, glossy whites over the chocolate chips. During baking the interior of the meringue stayed soft and airy, while the top developed a lightly crunchy crackle that we loved. To emphasize the blondies' butterscotch flavor, we used brown sugar rather than white sugar in the meringue. The result? A unique, chewy, three-layer blondie with butterscotch flavor from top to bottom.

1 Adjust oven rack to lower-middle position and heat oven to 350 degrees. Make foil sling for 13 by 9-inch baking pan by folding 2 long sheets of aluminum foil; first sheet should be 13 inches wide and second sheet should be 9 inches wide. Lay sheets of foil in pan perpendicular to each other, with extra foil hanging over edges of pan. Push foil into corners and up sides of pan, smoothing foil flush to pan. Grease foil.

2 Whisk flour, baking powder, baking soda, and salt together in large bowl. Using stand mixer fitted with paddle, beat butter, 1 cup brown sugar, and granulated sugar on medium-high speed until light and fluffy, about 2 minutes. Add egg yolks, water, and vanilla and mix until incorporated. Reduce speed to low and add flour mixture, mixing until combined. Transfer batter to prepared pan and spread into even layer. Press chocolate chips lightly into dough.

3 Using clean, dry mixer bowl and whisk attachment, whip egg whites at medium-high speed until stiff peaks form, about 3 minutes. Reduce speed to medium-low and slowly add remaining 1 cup brown sugar, mixing until smooth and shiny. Gently spread egg white mixture over chocolate chip layer.

4 Bake bars until golden brown, 25 to 30 minutes. Let bars cool completely in pan on wire rack, about 2 hours. Using foil overhang, remove bars from pan. Cut into 24 pieces before serving.

Assembling Butterscotch Meringue Bars

1 Gently press even layer chocolate chips into bottom layer of batter.

2 Spread meringue over top.

7
BAR
COOKIES

CRUNCHY GRANOLA BARS

Makes 36 bars

7 cups (21 ounces) old-fashioned rolled oats

½ cup vegetable oil

½ teaspoon salt

¾ cup honey

¾ cup packed (5¼ ounces) light brown sugar

1 tablespoon vanilla extract

2 teaspoons ground cinnamon (optional)

1½ cups almonds, pecans, peanuts, or walnuts, chopped coarse

Why This Recipe Works Great granola bars put the flavor of the oats at the forefront while supporting players back them up with a mellow sweetness. We found that toasting the oats with a little oil and salt before mixing them with the other ingredients really deepened their flavor. Honey provided plenty of stickiness to hold the bars together. We kept the other flavors simple: a little brown sugar for extra sweetness, aromatic vanilla and cinnamon, and chopped nuts for additional crunch. After multiple attempts at baking the bars resulted in a crumbly mess, we realized the key to making granola bars that held their shape was to spread the mixture onto a rimmed baking sheet and then firmly press on it with a greased metal spatula. Do not substitute quick or instant oats in this recipe. Don't use a baking sheet smaller than 18 by 13 inches or the bars will be too thick and won't bake evenly. Be sure to let the granola bars cool for 15 minutes before cutting. If any of the bars should fall apart during cutting, just press them back together; as they cool they will firm up and stick together.

1 Adjust oven rack to middle position and heat oven to 375 degrees. Toss oats, oil, and salt together in medium bowl. Spread mixture over rimmed baking sheet and toast, stirring often, until pale golden, 20 to 25 minutes.

2 Meanwhile, line 18 by 13-inch rimmed baking sheet with aluminum foil and grease foil. Cook honey and sugar in small saucepan over medium heat, stirring frequently, until sugar is fully dissolved, about 5 minutes. Off heat, stir in vanilla and cinnamon, if using.

3 Transfer toasted oat mixture to large bowl. Reduce oven temperature to 300 degrees. Add honey mixture and almonds to oat mixture and toss until well combined. Transfer mixture to prepared sheet and press firmly into even layer with greased metal spatula.

4 Bake bars until golden, 35 to 40 minutes, rotating sheet halfway through baking. Let bars cool completely in sheet on wire rack for 15 minutes, then cut into 36 pieces. Let cool completely, then remove individual bars from sheet with spatula. Serve. (Bars can be stored at room temperature for up to 2 weeks.)

Crunchy Granola Bars with Coconut and Sesame
Add ½ cup sesame seeds and ½ cup unsweetened shredded coconut to granola mixture with nuts.

Crunchy Granola Bars with Dried Cranberries and Ginger
Microwave 1 cup dried cranberries with ½ cup water in bowl until softened, about 4 minutes; drain and pat dry. Add softened cranberries and ¼ cup chopped crystallized ginger to granola mixture with nuts.

Pressing Granola Bars

Spread granola mixture over prepared sheet and press into even layer using greased spatula.

ULTRANUTTY PECAN BARS

Makes 24 bars

Crust

1¾ cups (8¾ ounces) all-purpose flour

6 tablespoons (2⅔ ounces) granulated sugar

½ teaspoon salt

8 tablespoons unsalted butter, melted

Topping

¾ cup packed (5¼ ounces) light brown sugar

½ cup light corn syrup

7 tablespoons unsalted butter, melted and hot

1 teaspoon vanilla extract

½ teaspoon salt

4 cups (1 pound) pecan halves, toasted

½ teaspoon flake sea salt (optional)

Why This Recipe Works Most pecan bars consist of a single layer of nuts dominated by a thick, gooey, ultrasweet filling sitting atop the crust—essentially, pecan pie in bar form. Our ideal pecan bar would feature a buttery crust piled high with the star ingredient. The pecans would be held in place by a not-too-sweet glaze that enhanced their flavor and glued them to the crust. We tried making glazes from a variety of sweeteners, but most were problematic: Corn syrup coated the nuts nicely but had a flat flavor; maple syrup dried out and crystallized; and honey had a flavor that overwhelmed the pecans. The best glaze was made with a combination of brown sugar and corn syrup, melted butter, vanilla, and salt. Into the glaze we stirred a whole pound of pecans; with that many pecans, the nuts were layered on top of one another, allowing for a variety of textures—some nuts were slicked with glaze and chewy, while those sitting on top were crisp. Since the topping wasn't wet, we didn't need to parbake our crust. The edges will be slightly firmer than the center. If desired, trim ¼ inch from the edges before cutting into bars.

1 **For the crust** Adjust oven rack to lowest position and heat oven to 350 degrees. Make foil sling for 13 by 9-inch baking pan by folding 2 long sheets of aluminum foil; first sheet should be 13 inches wide, and second sheet should be 9 inches wide. Lay sheets of foil in pan perpendicular to each other, with extra foil hanging over edges of pan. Push foil into corners and up sides of pan, smoothing foil flush to pan. Grease foil.

2 Whisk flour, sugar, and salt together in bowl. Stir in melted butter with wooden spoon until dough begins to form. Using your hands, continue to combine until no dry flour remains and small portion of dough holds together when squeezed in palm of your hand. Evenly scatter 1-tablespoon pieces of dough over surface of pan. Using your fingertips and palm of your hand, press and smooth dough into even thickness in bottom of pan.

3 **For the topping** Whisk sugar, corn syrup, melted butter, vanilla, and salt in bowl until smooth (mixture will look separated at first but will become homogeneous), about 20 seconds. Fold pecans into sugar mixture until nuts are evenly coated.

4 Pour topping over crust and spread into even layer with spatula, pushing to edges and into corners (there will be bare patches). Bake until topping is evenly distributed and rapidly bubbling across entire surface, 23 to 25 minutes.

5 Transfer pan to wire rack and sprinkle bars with sea salt, if using. Let bars cool completely in pan, about 1½ hours. Using foil overhang, remove bars from pan. Cut into 24 pieces before serving. (Bars can be stored at room temperature for up to 5 days.)

LEMON BARS

Makes 16 bars

Crust

1¼ cups (6¼ ounces) all-purpose flour

½ cup (2 ounces) confectioners' sugar

½ teaspoon salt

8 tablespoons unsalted butter,
cut into 8 pieces and softened

Filling

2 large eggs plus 7 large yolks

1 cup (7 ounces) plus 2 tablespoons
granulated sugar

¼ cup grated lemon zest plus ⅔ cup
juice (4 lemons)

Pinch salt

4 tablespoons unsalted butter,
cut into 4 pieces

3 tablespoons heavy cream

Confectioners' sugar

Why This Recipe Works For bright citrus flavor, successful lemon bars depend on ample amounts of fresh lemon juice, yes, but also a generous amount of lemon zest, which provides round, floral notes. We used four lemons for our lemon curd filling, which yielded a whopping ⅔ cup of juice and ¼ cup of zest. The other major ingredient for lemon curd is eggs, and lots of them. Two whole eggs and seven yolks gave us a luxurious curd with good thickening properties. To tame the curd's pucker power and make it ultracreamy, we added a small amount of heavy cream and some butter. Confectioners' sugar contributed a tender texture to the crust. We found that it was important to pour the warm filling over a still-hot crust to ensure that the filling cooked through evenly; you can prepare the filling while the crust bakes. Humidity tends to make the sugar melt and turn splotchy, so if you live in a humid climate dust the lemon bars with the confectioners' sugar right before serving.

1 Adjust oven rack to middle position and heat oven to 350 degrees. Make foil sling for 9-inch square baking pan by folding 2 long sheets of aluminum foil so each is 9 inches wide. Lay sheets of foil in pan perpendicular to each other, with extra foil hanging over edges of pan. Push foil into corners and up sides of pan, smoothing foil flush to pan. Grease foil.

2 **For the crust** Process flour, sugar, and salt in food processor until combined, about 3 seconds. Sprinkle butter over top and pulse until mixture is pale yellow and resembles coarse meal, about 8 pulses. Sprinkle mixture into prepared pan and press firmly into even layer. Bake until crust begins to brown, about 20 minutes, rotating pan halfway through baking. (Crust must still be hot when filling is added.)

3 **For the filling** Meanwhile, whisk eggs and yolks together in medium saucepan. Whisk in granulated sugar until combined, then whisk in lemon zest and juice and salt. Add butter and cook over medium-low heat, stirring constantly, until butter is melted and mixture thickens slightly and registers 170 degrees, about 5 minutes.

4 Immediately strain mixture through fine-mesh strainer into bowl and stir in cream. Pour warm lemon curd evenly over hot crust. Bake until filling is shiny and opaque and center jiggles slightly when shaken, 10 to 15 minutes, rotating pan halfway through baking.

5 Let bars cool completely in pan on wire rack, about 2 hours. Using foil overhang, remove bars from pan. Cut into 16 pieces and dust with confectioners' sugar before serving. (Bars can be refrigerated for up to 2 days.)

KEY LIME BARS

Makes 16 bars

Crust

5 ounces (2½ cups) animal crackers

3 tablespoons packed light brown sugar

Pinch salt

4 tablespoons unsalted butter,
melted and cooled

Filling

2 ounces cream cheese, softened

1 tablespoon grated lime zest
plus ½ cup juice (4 limes)

Pinch salt

1 (14-ounce) can sweetened
condensed milk

1 large egg yolk

¾ cup (2¼ ounces) sweetened
shredded coconut, toasted (optional)

Why This Recipe Works To get big lime flavor into our lime bars, we avoided weak, bitter-tasting bottled juice and went with the fresh stuff. But fresh lime juice alone didn't give us a taste of the Florida Keys; we also added lime zest. We found that regular supermarket, or Persian, limes worked just fine in the filling, and it took only four (as opposed to 20 Key limes) to yield the right amount of juice. For these bars to slice and eat neatly, we needed the filling to be firmer than that of a typical Key lime pie, so we supplemented the usual sweetened condensed milk and egg yolk with cream cheese. Our crust needed to be sturdier, too, and this meant using more crumbs. We had been using graham crackers, but when we increased the amount in the crust their flavor overpowered the filling. Animal crackers had just the right vanilla flavor, and light brown sugar added subtle caramel notes. Key limes can be substituted for the regular limes here, although they have a more delicate flavor; you'll need about 20 to make ½ cup of juice. Do not substitute bottled Key lime juice. Be sure to zest the limes before juicing them.

1 Adjust oven rack to middle position and heat oven to 325 degrees. Make foil sling for 8-inch square baking pan by folding 2 long sheets of aluminum foil so each is 8 inches wide. Lay sheets of foil in pan perpendicular to each other, with extra foil hanging over edges of pan. Push foil into corners and up sides of pan, smoothing foil flush to pan. Grease foil.

2 **For the crust** Process animal crackers, sugar, and salt in food processor to fine crumbs, about 15 seconds. Add melted butter and pulse to combine, about 10 pulses. Sprinkle mixture into prepared pan and press firmly into even layer. Bake until crust is fragrant and deep golden brown, 18 to 20 minutes, rotating pan halfway through baking.

3 **For the filling** Stir cream cheese, lime zest, and salt in bowl until combined. Whisk in condensed milk until smooth. Whisk in egg yolk and lime juice until combined.

4 Pour filling evenly over crust. Bake until bars are set and edges begin to pull away slightly from sides of pan, 15 to 20 minutes, rotating pan halfway through baking.

5 Let bars cool completely in pan on wire rack, about 2 hours, then refrigerate until thoroughly chilled, about 2 hours. Using foil overhang, remove bars from pan. Cut into 16 pieces and top with toasted coconut, if using, before serving. (Uncut bars can be frozen for up to 1 month; let wrapped bars thaw at room temperature for 4 hours before serving.)

Triple-Citrus Bars

Reduce lime zest to 1½ teaspoons and combine with 1½ teaspoons grated lemon zest and 1½ teaspoons grated orange zest. Reduce lime juice to 6 tablespoons and combine with 1 tablespoon lemon juice and 1 tablespoon orange juice.

PEACH SQUARES

Makes 24 squares

1¾ cups sliced almonds

1½ cups (7½ ounces) all-purpose flour

⅓ cup (2⅓ ounces) granulated sugar

⅓ cup packed (2⅓ ounces) plus
1 tablespoon packed light brown sugar

Salt

12 tablespoons unsalted butter,
cut into 12 pieces and softened

1½ pounds (6 cups) frozen peaches,
thawed and drained

½ cup peach jam

½ teaspoon grated lemon zest
plus 1 teaspoon juice

Why This Recipe Works Combining sweet, juicy fruit with rich, tender short-bread creates an appealing contrast of flavors and textures. We wanted to make a bar cookie featuring peaches, but quickly realized their challenge: Peaches contain so much moisture that they required precooking or the bars would be too wet. Frozen peaches were more convenient than fresh (no peeling and pitting) and their quality proved more consistent; perhaps most importantly, they're available year-round. We processed the thawed peaches with peach jam and cooked them in a large skillet to rapidly drive off moisture. The jam intensified the peach flavor, and a little lemon zest and juice brightened it further. Almonds are a natural pairing with peaches, so we ground a generous amount for the crust and also added sliced almonds to the streusel topping. Our recipe worked so well that we made a version with frozen cherries, and another featuring dried apricots. To drain the thawed peaches, we spread them on a dish towel.

1 Adjust oven rack to middle position and heat oven to 375 degrees. Make foil sling for 13 by 9-inch baking pan by folding 2 long sheets of aluminum foil; first sheet should be 13 inches wide and second sheet should be 9 inches wide. Lay sheets of foil in pan perpendicular to each other, with extra foil hanging over edges of pan. Push foil into corners and up sides of pan, smoothing foil flush to pan. Grease foil.

2 Process 1¼ cups almonds, flour, granulated sugar, ⅓ cup brown sugar, and ½ teaspoon salt in food processor until combined, about 5 seconds. Scatter butter over top and pulse until mixture resembles coarse meal with few pea-size pieces, about 20 pulses. Set aside ½ cup mixture in bowl for topping.

3 Sprinkle remaining flour mixture into prepared pan and press firmly into even layer. Bake until crust is fragrant and golden brown, about 15 minutes, rotating pan halfway through baking. (Crust must still be hot when filling is added.)

4 Meanwhile, mix remaining 1 tablespoon brown sugar and reserved flour mixture together, and pinch mixture between your fingers into clumps of streusel.

5 Pulse peaches and jam in food processor until peaches are cut into rough ¼-inch chunks, 5 to 7 pulses. Transfer peach mixture to 12-inch nonstick skillet and cook over high heat until mixture has thick, jam-like consistency, about 10 minutes. Off heat, stir in lemon zest and juice and pinch salt.

6 Spread cooked peach mixture evenly over hot crust, then sprinkle with streusel and remaining ½ cup almonds. Bake until almonds are golden brown, about 20 minutes, rotating pan halfway through baking. Let bars cool completely in pan on wire rack, about 2 hours. Using foil overhang, remove bars from pan. Cut into 24 pieces before serving.

Apricot Squares

Substitute 1 pound dried apricots for frozen peaches, and apricot jam for peach jam. Add 1 cup water to food processor with apricots in step 5.

Cherry Squares

Substitute 1½ pounds frozen pitted cherries for frozen peaches and cherry jam for peach jam. Omit lemon zest and reduce lemon juice to ½ teaspoon. Add ¼ teaspoon vanilla extract to peach mixture with lemon juice in step 5.

RASPBERRY STREUSEL BARS

Makes 24 bars

2½ cups (12½ ounces) all-purpose flour

⅔ cup (4⅔ ounces) granulated sugar

½ teaspoon salt

18 tablespoons (2¼ sticks) unsalted butter, cut into 18 pieces and softened

½ cup (1½ ounces) old-fashioned rolled oats

½ cup pecans, toasted and chopped fine

¼ cup packed (1¾ ounces) light brown sugar

¾ cup raspberry jam

3¾ ounces (¾ cup) fresh raspberries

1 tablespoon lemon juice

Why This Recipe Works For the very best raspberry bars, we needed to strike just the right balance between bright, tangy fruit filling; tender, buttery shortbread crust; and rich, crumbly topping. To streamline our recipe, we made a butter-rich shortbread dough that did double duty as both the bottom crust and the base for our streusel topping. After pressing part of the mixture into the pan, we added oats, brown sugar, nuts, and a little extra butter to the rest and pinched it into clumps to create our topping. These additions made a topping that was light and dry enough to adhere to the filling. For a fresh-tasting fruity filling that stayed neatly sandwiched between the base and topping, we combined fresh raspberries with raspberry jam. Adding a squeeze of lemon juice to the berries brightened the mix. Frozen raspberries can be substituted for fresh, but be sure to defrost them before using. Quick oats will work, but the bars will be less chewy and flavorful; do not use instant oats.

1 Adjust oven rack to middle position and heat oven to 375 degrees. Make foil sling for 13 by 9-inch baking pan by folding 2 long sheets of aluminum foil; first sheet should be 13 inches wide and second sheet should be 9 inches wide. Lay sheets of foil in pan perpendicular to each other, with extra foil hanging over edges of pan. Push foil into corners and up sides of pan, smoothing foil flush to pan. Grease foil.

2 Whisk flour, granulated sugar, and salt together in bowl of stand mixer. Fit mixer with paddle and beat in 16 tablespoons butter, 1 piece at a time, on medium-low speed until mixture resembles damp sand, 1 to 1½ minutes. Set aside 1¼ cups mixture in bowl for topping.

3 Sprinkle remaining flour mixture into prepared pan and press firmly into even layer. Bake until edges of crust begin to brown, 14 to 18 minutes, rotating pan halfway through baking. (Crust must still be hot when filling is added.)

4 Meanwhile, stir oats, pecans, and brown sugar into reserved topping mixture. Add remaining 2 tablespoons butter and pinch mixture between your fingers into clumps of streusel. Using fork, mash jam, raspberries, and lemon juice in small bowl until few berry pieces remain.

5 Spread berry mixture evenly over hot crust, then sprinkle with streusel. Bake until filling is bubbling and topping is deep golden brown, 22 to 25 minutes, rotating pan halfway through baking.

6 Let bars cool completely in pan on wire rack, about 2 hours. Using foil overhang, remove bars from pan. Cut into 24 pieces before serving. (Uncut bars can be frozen for up to 1 month; let wrapped bars thaw at room temperature for 4 hours before serving.)

Blueberry Streusel Bars
Thawed frozen blueberries will also work here.
   Substitute blueberry jam and ¾ cup fresh blueberries for the raspberry jam and raspberries.

Strawberry Streusel Bars
Thawed frozen strawberries will also work here.
   Substitute strawberry jam and ¾ cup chopped fresh strawberries for the raspberry jam and raspberries.

STRUDEL BARS

Makes 24 bars

1 cup dried apple slices

¾ cup packed (5¼ ounces) light brown sugar

½ cup dried tart cherries or cranberries

½ cup water

½ teaspoon ground cinnamon

¼ teaspoon salt

2 cups pecans, toasted

1 large egg plus 2 large whites

7½ tablespoons unsalted butter, melted

¼ cup (1¾ ounces) plus 2 teaspoons granulated sugar

20 (14 by 9-inch) phyllo sheets, thawed

Why This Recipe Works Strudel is a filled and rolled treat that features ultracrisp pastry and a fruit or nut filling—and it typically takes all day to prepare. We wanted to transform this intricate dessert into an easy bar cookie. We used phyllo dough for the pastry, layering the thin sheets with melted butter and a little sugar. On top of this base, we spread a thick paste made from rich nuts, dried fruits—we liked the contrast of sweet apple and tart sour cherries—and warm cinnamon. We cooked the fruits with sugar and water and then combined the syrupy mix in the food processor with a generous amount of pecans, one whole egg, and a couple of egg whites to bring it together. The filling was rich and full-flavored, but the pièce de résistance was the topping. We took more phyllo, rolled it up, and cut it into ribbons that baked up supercrisp, providing a crackly contrast to the moist filling. Phyllo dough is also available in larger 18 by 14-inch sheets; if using, cut them in half to make 14 by 9-inch sheets. Don't thaw the phyllo in the microwave; let it sit in the refrigerator overnight or on the counter for 4 to 5 hours. While working with the phyllo, cover the sheets with plastic wrap and then a damp dish towel to prevent drying. Walnuts can be substituted for the pecans.

1 Cook apples, brown sugar, cherries, water, cinnamon, and salt in medium saucepan over medium-high heat until syrup has thickened, 6 to 8 minutes. Let cool completely, about 1 hour.

2 Adjust oven rack to middle position and heat oven to 325 degrees. Make foil sling for 13 by 9-inch baking pan by folding 2 long sheets of aluminum foil; first sheet should be 13 inches wide and second sheet should be 9 inches wide. Lay sheets of foil in pan perpendicular to each other, with extra foil hanging over edges of pan. Push foil into corners and up sides of pan, smoothing foil flush to pan.

3 Pulse pecans in food processor until roughly chopped, about 5 pulses. Add apple mixture and egg and whites and process until smooth paste forms, 20 to 30 seconds.

4 Set aside 2 tablespoons melted butter in small bowl. Set aside 4 teaspoons granulated sugar in second small bowl. Brush bottom of prepared pan with 1½ teaspoons melted butter. Trim phyllo dough to measure 13 by 9 inches, reserving scraps.

5 Lay 1 phyllo sheet in pan bottom, brush with 1½ teaspoons melted butter, and sprinkle evenly with 1 teaspoon granulated sugar. Repeat with 9 more phyllo sheets, smoothing each layer before brushing with 1½ teaspoons melted butter and sprinkling with 1 teaspoon sugar (you should have total of 10 layers of phyllo). Spread filling evenly over phyllo. Roll up remaining phyllo sheets into log and cut into ¼-inch-wide ribbons; repeat with scraps. Toss phyllo ribbons with your fingers in bowl to fluff up and break apart. Layer phyllo ribbons over filling.

6 Drizzle reserved melted butter evenly over top, then sprinkle reserved granulated sugar evenly over top. Bake until top is light golden brown, 35 to 40 minutes, rotating pan halfway through baking. Let bars cool completely in pan on wire rack. Using foil sling, remove bars from pan. Cut into 24 pieces before serving.

FIG BARS

Makes 16 bars

Filling

8 ounces dried Turkish or Calimyrna figs, stemmed and quartered

2 cups apple juice

Pinch salt

2 teaspoons lemon juice

Crust

¾ cup (3¾ ounces) all-purpose flour

½ cup (2¾ ounces) whole-wheat flour

½ teaspoon baking powder

¼ teaspoon salt

6 tablespoons unsalted butter, softened

¾ cup packed (5¼ ounces) light brown sugar

1 large egg

2 teaspoons vanilla extract

Why This Recipe Works Fig Newtons are one of few packaged cookies we can get behind. Even so, anything homemade is bound to be better (and include fewer ingredients). Making a bar cookie version of the classic sounded like a great way to maximize the figgy filling of these cookies. While any type of leavener is an unusual addition to bar cookies, we found that ½ teaspoon of baking powder gave the crust a bit of the soft cakeyness we love in the original cookie. For a more complex flavor, we used whole-wheat flour in addition to all-purpose flour for the dough. We needed a liquid to rehydrate the dried figs before pureeing them for the filling. Water worked, but apple juice was better; it lent a fruity sweetness. A pinch of salt and a squeeze of lemon juice enhanced the fruit's unique flavor. For the top crust, we rolled out chilled dough and laid it on top of the filling. We may still have a soft spot for the store-bought cookies, but they're no match for our rich homemade fig bars. Be sure to grease the parchment when smoothing the bottom crust and when forming the top crust; otherwise, it will stick and be difficult to work with.

1 For the filling Simmer figs, apple juice, and salt in medium saucepan over medium heat, stirring occasionally, until figs are very soft and juice is syrupy, 15 to 20 minutes; let mixture cool slightly. Puree figs in food processor with lemon juice until mixture has thick, jam-like consistency, about 8 seconds.

2 For the crust Make foil sling for 8-inch square baking pan by folding 2 long sheets of aluminum foil so each is 8 inches wide. Lay sheets of foil in pan perpendicular to each other, with extra foil hanging over edges of pan. Push foil into corners and up sides of pan, smoothing foil flush to pan. Grease foil.

3 Whisk all-purpose flour, whole-wheat flour, baking powder, and salt together in bowl. Using stand mixer fitted with paddle, beat butter and sugar on medium speed until pale and fluffy, 3 to 6 minutes. Add egg and vanilla and beat until combined. Add flour mixture and mix until just incorporated. Set aside ¾ cup of dough for topping.

4 Transfer remaining dough to prepared pan and firmly press into even layer with greased spatula. Top dough with piece of greased parchment paper and smooth into even layer. Remove parchment and bake until just beginning to turn golden, about 20 minutes.

5 Meanwhile, roll reserved dough between 2 sheets of greased parchment into 8-inch square; trim edges of dough as needed to measure exactly 8 inches. Transfer dough, still between parchment, to baking sheet and place in freezer until needed.

6 Spread fig mixture evenly over crust. Lay top crust over filling, pressing lightly to adhere. Bake until top crust is golden brown, 25 to 30 minutes, rotating pan halfway through baking.

7 Let bars cool completely in pan on wire rack, about 2 hours. Using foil overhang, remove bars from pan. Cut into 16 pieces before serving.

ALL ABOUT BAR COOKIES

If you're looking for bells and whistles, bars might just be the ultimate cookies as they often include multiple components like a crisp base, creamy or fruity filling, and/or a topping, whether it be melted chocolate, streusel, or a sprinkling of nuts. So here are the ultimate tips for the ultimate bars.

For bar cookies, simply greasing a baking pan isn't enough. Sticky fillings can glue bars to the pans. It would be hard to cut neat bars while they're still in the pan and inverting them would ruin their tops. A foil sling is a no-fuss way to extract bar cookies from the pan.

1 Line the pan with 2 sheets of aluminum foil placed perpendicular to each other, with the extra foil hanging over the edges of the pan. Push the foil into the corners, smoothing the foil flush with the pan.

2 Use the foil handles to lift the baked bars from the pan.

For the perfect ratio of base to filling in each bite of a bar cookie, you'll want to be sure to build an even, level bottom crust, whether it's a graham cracker crust like for Cheesecake Bars (page 302) or a shortbread crust like for Peach Squares (page 285). Sprinkle the crumb or flour mixture evenly over the pan bottom and press down firmly, using the flat bottom of a dry measuring cup.

Many bar cookies—such as Cheesecake Bars (page 302) and Lemon Bars (page 280)—feature delicious creamy fillings. To cut clean squares without making a mess, heat your knife by running it under hot water and then quickly dry the blade with a dish towel and slice. Repeat heating and drying the knife as needed.

There are two tricks for cutting perfect square or rectangular bars. The first is using the foil sling to lift the bars from the pan before cutting. Haphazardly scoring bars while in the pan makes for uneven edges that can crumble. Cutting outside of the pan makes even lines from edge to edge. And if you want your bars to be precise, don't just eyeball them before cutting; use a ruler to cut rows and columns at even intervals.

GRAHAM CRACKERS

Graham crackers are a bar cookie work-horse; pulverizing them into crumbs, mixing them with butter, and baking couldn't be an easier way to make a tasty base for your bars. You could make your own (see page 110), but we wanted to know which boxed grahams would fare best in bars and other desserts. We tasted three top-selling graham crackers, sampling them plain, in a chocolate éclair cake, and in the crust of Key lime pie. Our favorite brand for baking was **Keebler Grahams Crackers Original**, which

held up well in pie and bar cookie crusts and in cake, and exhibited good graham flavor. That said, we found they tasted a bit artificial when eaten plain, and we preferred other brands for snacking.

JAMS, JELLIES, AND PRESERVES

Fruity bar cookies such as Peach Squares (page 285) and Raspberry Streusel Bars (page 287) often include a layer of jam. We also use it to fill thumbprints and sandwich cookies. Is jam interchangeable with other fruit spreads? Jam is made from crushed or finely chopped fruit, which is cooked with pectin and sugar until the pieces of fruit are almost formless and the mixture is thickened. Preserves are similar, but they contain whole pieces or large chunks of fruit. Jam's good fruit flavor and relatively smooth texture make it our first choice for baking. Avoid jelly; it has a wan, overly sweet taste since it's made from just fruit juice, sugar, and pectin, so we reserve it for glazing desserts.

Jam—the Best Fruit Spread for Cookies

WORKING WITH PHYLLO DOUGH

Phyllo dough, tissue-thin layers of pastry dough, can be used in a variety of recipes both sweet and savory. On the sweet side, it's particularly well known as a primary component of Baklava (page 211), but it's also a good choice for other bar cookies, such as our Strudel Bars (page 288), when you're looking for a flaky, crisp treat. These pointers make working with delicate phyllo easier.

Phyllo is available in two sizes
Phyllo comes in full-size sheets that are 18 by 14 inches (about 20 per box) and half-size sheets that are 14 by 9 inches (about 40 per box). We use the more common smaller sheets. If you buy large sheets, cut them in half.

Thaw the phyllo dough completely
Frozen phyllo must be thawed before using, but microwaving doesn't work—the sheets of dough stick together. We prefer thawing in the refrigerator for at least 12 hours. When completely thawed, the dough unfolds easily without tearing.

Keep the phyllo covered
Paper-thin phyllo dries out very quickly. To help prevent cracking, it's important that phyllo dough be kept moist until you're ready to work with it. The usual approach is to cover the stack with a damp towel, but if the towel is too moist, the dough becomes sticky. We prefer to cover the stack of phyllo with plastic wrap and then a damp towel. The plastic prevents the phyllo from getting too wet, and the weight of the towel keeps the plastic wrap flush against the phyllo.

Throw out badly torn sheets of dough
Usually each box has one or two badly torn sheets of phyllo that can't be salvaged. If the sheets have just small cuts or tears, however, you can still work with them—put them in the middle of the pastry, where imperfections will go unnoticed. If all of the sheets have the exact same tear, alternate the orientation of each when assembling the pastry to avoid creating a weak spot.

Don't refreeze leftover dough
Leftover sheets can be rerolled, wrapped in plastic wrap, and stored in the refrigerator for up to five days. Don't refreeze phyllo; it will become too brittle to work with.

THE BEST OATS FOR COOKIES (AND BREAKFAST)

Bar cookies are often all about oats (see Crunchy Granola Bars on page 276 or Oatmeal Butterscotch Bars on page 320). Sometimes they form the base of the bar cookie; sometimes they're incorporated into a crumble topping; and sometimes they're used in every layer. While we prefer steel-cut oats for breakfast, we find that rolled oats are best for baking. Their thin, flat shape gives cookies and bars just the right amount of chew. (An exception is our Oatmeal Fudge Bars on page 317, where we use quick oats for a softer crust.) And because you can also make oatmeal with rolled oats, if you're going to choose just one oat to stock, old-fashioned rolled should be the one.

We tried several brands of oats on the market in both oatmeal and baked goods to find the ultimate multipurpose oat. We liked the substantial, chewy texture of Bob's Red Mill Organic Extra Thick Rolled Oats, with its nice plump flakes, best. Note that while the winner took time to cook—about 10 minutes for chewy oatmeal, 20 minutes for softer cereal—our second-ranked brand, Quaker Old Fashioned Rolled Oats, took only 5 minutes to prepare and tasted just as good as Bob's Red Mill in cookies. If time is of the essence in the morning, you may choose to stock Quaker.

PEAR-CHERRY STREUSEL BARS

Makes 24 bars

2¼ cups (11¼ ounces) all-purpose flour

16 tablespoons unsalted butter, cut into 16 pieces and chilled, plus 2 tablespoons unsalted butter

⅔ cup (4⅔ ounces) plus 2 tablespoons granulated sugar

½ teaspoon salt

1 cup sliced almonds

¼ cup packed (1¾ ounces) light brown sugar

4 ripe but firm Bartlett or Bosc pears, peeled, halved, cored, and sliced ¼ inch thick

2 teaspoons lemon juice

1 teaspoon vanilla extract

¾ cup cherry jam

Why This Recipe Works Apple- and berry-filled desserts abound, but pears never seem to get their due. The honey-sweet fruit is delicious in desserts and also plays well with a host of other flavors. In these bars, we match the delicate, floral notes of pear with the tart but complementary punch of cherry. However, cramming two fruits into our bars weighed down the crust and made it soggy, so instead of using whole cherries we turned to cherry jam, which we spread over the bar base. And to eliminate excess moisture from the pears, we sautéed slices in butter with a little sugar before layering them on top of the jam. Cooking the pears also intensified their flavor, which we heightened further by adding some lemon juice and vanilla extract. Parbaking the crust ensured it stayed crisp below our lively fruit filling. Almonds, which complement both cherries and pears, and the caramel notes of brown sugar enhanced the streusel topping for a perfect finish to our unique bars.

1 Adjust oven rack to middle position and heat oven to 375 degrees. Make foil sling for 13 by 9-inch baking pan by folding 2 long sheets of aluminum foil; first sheet should be 13 inches wide and second sheet should be 9 inches wide. Lay sheets of foil in pan perpendicular to each other, with extra foil hanging over edges of pan. Push foil into corners and up sides of pan, smoothing foil flush to pan. Grease foil.

2 Process flour, 16 tablespoons chilled butter, ⅔ cup granulated sugar, and salt in food processor until mixture resembles coarse meal, about 30 seconds. Set aside 1 cup flour mixture in bowl for topping. Sprinkle remaining mixture into prepared pan and press firmly into even layer. Bake until golden brown, about 20 minutes. Transfer pan to wire rack.

3 Return reserved flour mixture to now-empty food processor. Add almonds and brown sugar and pulse until just combined, 5 to 6 pulses.

4 Melt remaining 2 tablespoons butter in 12-inch skillet over medium-high heat. Add pears and remaining 2 tablespoons granulated sugar and cook until pears are light golden brown and dry, about 10 minutes. Stir in lemon juice and vanilla.

5 Spread jam evenly over warm crust, then top with even layer of pear mixture. Sprinkle with topping and bake until golden brown, 20 to 25 minutes. Let bars cool completely in pan on wire rack, about 2 hours. Using foil overhang, remove bars from pan. Cut into 24 pieces before serving.

CRANBERRY OAT BARS

Makes 24 bars

8 ounces (2 cups) fresh or frozen cranberries

½ cup (3½ ounces) granulated sugar

¼ cup water

2 cups (6 ounces) old-fashioned rolled oats

1½ cups (7½ ounces) all-purpose flour

1 teaspoon ground cinnamon

½ teaspoon salt

16 tablespoons unsalted butter, softened

1½ cups packed (10½ ounces) light brown sugar

1 large egg, room temperature

¾ cup pecans, chopped

Why This Recipe Works Dried cranberries are a go-to ingredient when we want to add tartness or chew to a cookie, but we don't use fresh cranberries often enough. That might be because fresh cranberries require a bit of work, and on their own they're a bit too sour. And like other fresh fruit, they're full of moisture. But when treated properly, they give desserts a vibrant pop of flavor. We decided to pair bright cranberries with sweet, nutty oats in a rustic, chewy bar cookie. Precooking the cranberries with a bit of sugar easily solved our fresh cranberry woes: The sugar tempered the sourness, and the cooking process thickened the cranberries' juices so they didn't leave wet pockets throughout the bars. Rich, buttery pecans contributed a crunchy element to the topping. We like using fresh cranberries, but you can use frozen. We prefer the flavor and chewiness of old-fashioned rolled oats, but quick oats can be substituted to yield softer, cakier bars. Do not use instant oats.

1 Bring cranberries, granulated sugar, and water to boil in medium saucepan over medium-high heat. Cook, stirring frequently, until cranberries have burst and juice has started to thicken, 2 to 3 minutes. Let cool for 30 minutes.

2 Adjust oven rack to lower-middle position and heat oven to 325 degrees. Make foil sling for 13 by 9-inch baking pan by folding 2 long sheets of aluminum foil; first sheet should be 13 inches wide and second sheet should be 9 inches wide. Lay sheets of foil in pan perpendicular to each other, with extra foil hanging over edges of pan. Push foil into corners and up sides of pan, smoothing foil flush to pan. Grease foil.

3 Whisk oats, flour, cinnamon, and salt together in bowl. Using stand mixer fitted with paddle, beat butter and brown sugar on medium-high speed until light and fluffy, about 3 minutes. Add egg and beat until combined, scraping down bowl as needed. Reduce speed to low, add oat mixture, and mix until just combined. Transfer two-thirds of dough to prepared pan and press firmly into even layer. Spread evenly with cranberry mixture. Mix pecans into remaining dough and sprinkle walnut-size pieces over cranberry layer.

4 Bake until top is golden brown, 40 to 45 minutes, rotating pan halfway through baking. Let bars cool in pan on wire rack, about 2 hours. Using foil overhang, lift bars from pan. Cut into 24 pieces before serving.

CRANBERRY-PISTACHIO COCONUT TRIANGLES

Makes 18 cookies

1 cup plus 2 tablespoons (5⅔ ounces) all-purpose flour

1 cup plus 2 tablespoons packed (7¾ ounces) light brown sugar

5 tablespoons unsalted butter, cut into 5 pieces and chilled

1 cup pistachios, toasted

1 cup dried cranberries

¾ cup (2¼ ounces) sweetened shredded coconut

1 large egg

2 tablespoons maple syrup

¾ teaspoon vanilla extract

½ teaspoon almond extract

½ teaspoon salt

4 ounces white chocolate, chopped

Why This Recipe Works As it turns out, you really can have it all—at least in the cookie world. This moist bar cookie features a melange of flavors and textures that complement one another, and its triangular shape makes it a looker. The base is a layer of buttery shortbread, just thick enough to support the topping. Next comes a chewy, almost candy-like layer that's chock-full of coconut, tart dried cranberries, and sweet, earthy toasted pistachios, all formed into a cohesive topping with the help of an egg and a little maple syrup. Almond extract, in addition to vanilla, gave this topping a warm, round flavor and pleasing aroma. To keep the cookies from being cloyingly sweet, we mixed ½ teaspoon of salt into the topping. And we couldn't resist a crowning touch: We dunked each cookie in complementary white chocolate, which also contributed visual appeal. We prefer white bar chocolate for the purest flavor and smoothest texture.

1 Adjust oven rack to middle position and heat oven to 375 degrees. Make foil sling for 8-inch square baking pan by folding 2 long sheets of aluminum foil so each is 8 inches wide. Lay sheets of foil in pan perpendicular to each other, with extra foil hanging over edges of pan. Push foil into corners and up sides of pan, smoothing foil flush to pan. Grease foil.

2 Pulse 1 cup flour, 2 tablespoons sugar, and butter in food processor until mixture resembles wet sand, about 10 pulses. Transfer mixture to prepared pan and press firmly into even layer. Bake until light golden, about 15 minutes. Let cool completely in pan.

3 Place pistachios in zipper-lock bag and tap them with meat pounder until crushed. Toss cranberries, coconut, and pistachios in bowl, breaking up any clumps. Whisk egg, maple syrup, vanilla, almond extract, salt, remaining 2 tablespoons flour, and remaining 1 cup sugar together in large bowl. Fold in pistachio mixture, then spread evenly over cooled crust.

4 Bake bars until deep golden brown and set, 20 to 25 minutes. Let bars cool completely in pan on wire rack. Using foil overhang, remove bars from pan. Cut into 9 squares and cut each square diagonally into 2 triangles.

5 Microwave white chocolate in small bowl at 50 percent power, stirring occasionally, until melted, 30 to 60 seconds. Dip 1 corner of each triangle in melted chocolate and place on parchment paper–lined baking sheet. Refrigerate triangles until chocolate is set, about 30 minutes, before serving.

Making the Triangles

1 Cut each square diagonally into triangles.

2 Dip 1 corner of each triangle in melted chocolate.

APPLE COBBLER BARS

Makes 24 bars

Topping

8 tablespoons unsalted butter, cut into ½-inch pieces and chilled

½ cup bread crumbs

½ cup pecans, toasted and chopped

½ cup packed (3½ ounces) light brown sugar

2 ounces extra-sharp cheddar cheese, shredded (½ cup)

¼ cup (1¼ ounces) all-purpose flour

1 teaspoon ground cinnamon

Base

3 cups (15 ounces) all-purpose flour

1 teaspoon baking powder

16 tablespoons unsalted butter, softened

⅔ cup packed (4⅔ ounces) light brown sugar

2 large eggs

½ cup apple butter

2 teaspoons vanilla extract

¾ cup pecans, toasted and chopped

1 cup dried apples, chopped

Why This Recipe Works Apple cobbler combines a homey, crowd-pleasing mixture of apples, cinnamon, and sugar with a lightly sweetened, biscuit-like topping. It's one of our favorite desserts, but it's a plated affair; we wanted to bring its flavors together in a treat we could eat anytime or anywhere. Enter: cobbler bars. Instead of using fresh apples—which would undoubtedly make for a soggy cookie no matter how much we cooked them—we turned to both apple butter and dried apples, which we added to the buttery cake-like base of our bars. The apple butter gave the bar good apple flavor without making it wet like applesauce did. And the chopped dried apples, sprinkled over the base, provided textural contrast. Next, the bars needed their cobbler topping. Adding bread crumbs to the standard mixture of flour, butter, and sugar gave it an extra-toasty flavor once baked, as well as a unique crunch. And we couldn't resist sneaking in a common New England apple cobbler accompaniment: cheddar cheese. With the contrast of salty, nutty, sharp cheese, we think these cobbler bars might be even better than their inspiration. This recipe works fine with both homemade and store-bought plain bread crumbs.

1 For the topping Adjust oven rack to middle position and heat oven to 350 degrees. Line rimmed baking sheet with parchment paper. Pulse butter, bread crumbs, pecans, sugar, cheddar, flour, and cinnamon in food processor until coarsely ground, about 12 pulses. Transfer bread-crumb mixture to prepared baking sheet and bake, stirring occasionally, until mixture is golden, 10 to 12 minutes. Let cool completely.

2 For the base Make foil sling for 13 by 9-inch baking pan by folding 2 long sheets of aluminum foil; first sheet should be 13 inches wide, and second sheet should be 9 inches wide. Lay sheets of foil in pan perpendicular to each other, with extra foil hanging over edges of pan. Push foil into corners and up sides of pan, smoothing foil flush to pan. Grease foil.

3 Whisk flour and baking powder together in bowl. Using stand mixer fitted with paddle, beat butter and sugar until pale and fluffy, about 2 minutes. Add eggs, apple butter, and vanilla and beat until incorporated. Reduce speed to low, add flour mixture, and mix until just combined. Stir in pecans.

4 Transfer dough to prepared pan and press firmly into even layer. Scatter chopped apple over dough. Top with crumb topping and bake until deep golden brown, 20 to 25 minutes. Let bars cool completely in pan on wire rack, about 1 hour. Using foil overhang, remove bars from pan. Cut into 24 pieces before serving.

CHEESECAKE BARS

Makes 16 bars

Crust

7 whole graham crackers, broken into 1-inch pieces

6 tablespoons unsalted butter, melted and cooled

3 tablespoons packed light brown sugar

2 tablespoons all-purpose flour

⅛ teaspoon salt

Filling

1 pound cream cheese, softened

⅔ cup (4⅔ ounces) granulated sugar

2 large eggs

¼ cup sour cream

2 teaspoons lemon juice

1 teaspoon vanilla extract

Why This Recipe Works Cheesecake is just as delicious in bar form as it is in cake form—there's still a substantial graham cracker crust and a tangy, cooling, custardy cake layer. But cheesecake bars are much easier to make—no water bath or leaky springform pan required. For a supercreamy cheesecake filling, we thoroughly beat softened cream cheese in a stand mixer, scraping down the bowl and paddle as needed; this ensured a light, lump-free filling and avoided overmixing later, a problem which can result in a collapsed cheesecake. We wanted more tang than cream cheese alone could provide, so we bolstered it with sour cream and a modest amount of lemon juice. We saw little need for improvement to the traditional graham cracker crust, but it did benefit from the addition of a couple tablespoons of flour, which made it sturdier. Make sure to scrape the paddle and the sides of the bowl regularly when making the filling in order to achieve a silky, smooth texture.

1 Adjust oven rack to middle position and heat oven to 325 degrees. Make foil sling for 8-inch square baking pan by folding 2 long sheets of aluminum foil so each is 8 inches wide. Lay sheets of foil in pan perpendicular to each other, with extra foil hanging over edges of pan. Push foil into corners and up sides of pan, smoothing foil flush to pan. Grease foil.

2 **For the crust** Process graham crackers in food processor to fine, even crumbs, about 30 seconds. Add melted butter, sugar, flour, and salt and pulse to combine, about 10 pulses. Sprinkle mixture into prepared pan and press firmly into even layer. Bake until crust is fragrant and beginning to brown, 12 to 15 minutes, rotating pan halfway through baking. Let crust cool completely in pan on wire rack.

3 **For the filling** Using stand mixer fitted with paddle, beat cream cheese on medium speed until smooth, 1 to 3 minutes, scraping down bowl as needed. Gradually add sugar and beat until incorporated, about 1 minute. Add eggs, one at a time, and beat until combined, about 30 seconds. Add sour cream, lemon juice, and vanilla and mix until incorporated, about 30 seconds.

4 Pour filling over crust and spread into even layer. Bake until edges are set but center still jiggles slightly, 35 to 40 minutes, rotating pan halfway through baking. Let cheesecake cool completely in pan on wire rack, about 2 hours. Refrigerate until thoroughly chilled, at least 3 hours or up to 24 hours. Using foil overhang, remove cheesecake from pan. Cut into 16 pieces before serving. (Uncut bars can be frozen for up to 1 month; let wrapped bars thaw at room temperature for 4 hours before serving.)

Chocolate Swirl Cheesecake Bars

Microwave 3 ounces semisweet chocolate and 2 tablespoons heavy cream in bowl at 50 percent power, stirring often, until melted and smooth, 1 to 3 minutes. Spoon small dollops of melted chocolate over filling and run knife through to create swirls before baking.

Strawberry Cheesecake Bars

Toss 1¼ cups coarsely chopped strawberries with 2 tablespoons warm apricot jam, 1 teaspoon lemon juice, 1 teaspoon sugar, and pinch salt in bowl. Spoon strawberry mixture over baked bars and let set for 15 minutes before cutting and serving.

PUMPKIN CHEESECAKE BARS

Makes 24 bars

1 (15-ounce) can unsweetened pumpkin puree

2 teaspoons pumpkin pie spice

½ teaspoon salt

15 whole graham crackers, broken into 1-inch pieces

¼ cup (1¾ ounces) plus 1⅓ cups (9⅓ ounces) sugar

1 teaspoon ground ginger

8 tablespoons butter, melted

1 pound cream cheese, softened

1 tablespoon lemon juice

2 teaspoons vanilla extract

4 large eggs, room temperature

Why This Recipe Works With a tangy, rich flavor and velvety consistency, cheesecake's characteristic qualities make it well-suited to variation: Lemon cheesecake, chocolate cheesecake, and berry cheesecake are all common. But our favorite variation might just be pumpkin cheesecake. We love the way the tangy cream cheese offsets the warm-spiced pumpkin, and we set out to create a streamlined version in the form of a pumpkin cheesecake bar. To avoid a soggy, heavy bar, we knew the key would be to remove excess moisture from the canned pumpkin, so we cooked the puree on the stovetop to reduce it. This step also concentrated its flavor and enhanced its sweetness so it wasn't overshadowed by the cream cheese. Adding pumpkin pie spice to the puree as it cooked allowed its flavor to bloom. We thought a gingersnap crust would be a fitting match for the pumpkin filling; but while the flavor of the crust was great, we found that the crushed gingersnaps baked up unappealingly hard. To get the flavor of gingersnaps without the tooth-breaking snap we used the traditional graham crackers and simply added ground ginger to the crackers to spice them up.

1 Cook pumpkin puree, pumpkin pie spice, and salt in small saucepan over medium heat, stirring constantly, until reduced to 1½ cups, 6 to 8 minutes. Let pumpkin mixture cool for 1 hour.

2 Adjust oven rack to middle position and heat oven to 325 degrees. Make foil sling for 13 by 9-inch baking pan by folding 2 long sheets of aluminum foil; first sheet should be 13 inches wide and second sheet should be 9 inches wide. Lay sheets of foil in pan perpendicular to each other, with extra foil hanging over edges of pan. Push foil into corners and up sides of pan, smoothing foil flush to pan. Grease foil.

3 Process graham crackers, ¼ cup sugar, and ginger in food processor to fine crumbs, about 15 seconds. Add melted butter and pulse until combined, about 5 pulses. Sprinkle mixture into prepared pan and press firmly into even layer. Bake until just starting to brown, 15 to 18 minutes. Let crust cool completely in pan on wire rack.

4 Using stand mixer fitted with paddle, beat cream cheese and remaining 1⅓ cups sugar on medium-low speed until smooth, about 2 minutes. Add lemon juice, vanilla, and pumpkin mixture and mix until combined. Increase speed to medium; add eggs, one at a time, and beat until incorporated. Pour filling over crust and spread into even layer.

5 Bake until edges are slightly puffed and center is just set, 45 to 50 minutes. Let cheesecake cool completely in pan on wire rack, about 2 hours. Refrigerate until thoroughly chilled, at least 3 hours or up to 24 hours. Using foil overhang, lift cheesecake from pan. Cut into 24 pieces before serving.

TOFFEE BARS

Makes 24 bars

1½ cups (7½ ounces) all-purpose flour

½ teaspoon salt

10 tablespoons unsalted butter, softened

⅓ cup packed (2⅓ ounces) dark brown sugar

⅓ cup (1⅓ ounces) confectioners' sugar

½ cup plain toffee bits

1 cup (6 ounces) milk chocolate chips

¾ cup whole almonds, toasted and chopped coarse

Why This Recipe Works While the buttery flavor and crunchy texture of toffee are incredibly appealing, it can be a pain to make. No shame in this game: Commercial toffee bits can be great. Even so, most toffee bar recipes lack not only toffee flavor but also a solid balance of the sweet, salty, and crunchy elements that should define them. To mimic the flavor of toffee right down to the crust, we added brown sugar to the shortbread; dark brown had the most impact. We also stirred toffee bits right into the dough to up the toffee flavor considerably. When the crust was out of the oven, we sprinkled on a generous cup of chocolate chips, which promptly melted into a smooth layer; we preferred milk chocolate for its caramel notes. Toasted and chopped almonds and, of course, toffee bits created a final layer of crunchy, chewy goodness. Note that the bars need to cool for about 3 hours in order to set the chocolate. If you're in a hurry, you can put the bars in the refrigerator for 1 hour, but don't store them in the fridge much longer than that because the crust can become too hard.

1 Adjust oven rack to middle position and heat oven to 350 degrees. Make foil sling for 13 by 9-inch baking pan by folding 2 long sheets of aluminum foil; first sheet should be 13 inches wide and second sheet should be 9 inches wide. Lay sheets of foil in pan perpendicular to each other, with extra foil hanging over edges of pan. Push foil into corners and up sides of pan, smoothing foil flush to pan. Grease foil.

2 Combine flour and salt in bowl. Using stand mixer fitted with paddle, beat butter, brown sugar, and confectioners' sugar on medium-high speed until fluffy, about 3 minutes. Reduce speed to low and add flour mixture in 3 additions, scraping down bowl as needed, until dough becomes sandy with large pea-size pieces, about 30 seconds. Add ¼ cup toffee bits and mix until combined.

3 Transfer dough to prepared pan and press into even layer. Bake until golden brown, about 20 minutes, rotating pan halfway through baking.

4 Remove crust from oven, sprinkle with chocolate chips, and let sit until softened, about 5 minutes. Using offset spatula, spread softened chocolate into even layer. Sprinkle almonds and remaining ¼ cup toffee bits evenly over chocolate, then press gently to set into chocolate. Let bars sit at room temperature until chocolate is set, about 3 hours. Using foil overhang, remove bars from pan. Cut into 24 pieces before serving.

DREAM BARS

Makes 24 bars

Crust

2 cups (10 ounces) all-purpose flour

¾ cup packed (5¼ ounces) dark brown sugar

½ cup pecans

¼ teaspoon salt

10 tablespoons unsalted butter, cut into ½-inch pieces and chilled

Topping

1½ cups (4½ ounces) sweetened shredded coconut

1 cup cream of coconut

¾ cup packed (5¼ ounces) dark brown sugar

2 large eggs

2 tablespoons all-purpose flour

1½ teaspoons baking powder

1 teaspoon vanilla extract

½ teaspoon salt

1 cup pecans, toasted and chopped coarse

Why This Recipe Works Whether you call them dream bars, magic bars, or seven-layer bars, these loaded confections should appeal to just about everyone; we certainly remember them fondly from our childhood. But our first attempt at re-creating these bars in the test kitchen led to an undeniable realization: They contain far too many ingredients, making them too sweet for modern tastes. To revamp these bars we ditched the seven-layer idea, nixing the superfluous—including chips of all kinds (from chocolate to white chocolate and butterscotch), toffee bits, and graham crackers—and choosing only the most essential and traditional ingredients: coconut and pecans. This was enough to create the chewy, toffee-flavored layer bars we desired. Making the base was easy; we mixed up a shortbread dough and deepened its toffee notes by sweetening it with dark brown sugar. After baking the base, we layered it with a pecan filling before spreading on the coconut topping. To prevent the shredded coconut from drying out, we turned to a surprising ingredient: cream of coconut. Soaking the shredded coconut in the cream resulted in a rich, moist topping that caramelized beautifully. Spread the coconut mixture as evenly as possible over the pecan layer, but don't worry if it looks patchy.

1 Adjust oven rack to middle position and heat oven to 350 degrees. Make foil sling for 13 by 9-inch baking pan by folding 2 long sheets of aluminum foil; first sheet should be 13 inches wide and second sheet should be 9 inches wide. Lay sheets of foil in pan perpendicular to each other, with extra foil hanging over edges of pan. Push foil into corners and up sides of pan, smoothing foil flush to pan. Grease foil.

2 **For the crust** Pulse flour, sugar, pecans, and salt in food processor until pecans are coarsely ground, about 10 pulses. Scatter butter over top and pulse until mixture resembles coarse meal, about 12 pulses. Transfer mixture to prepared pan and press firmly into even layer. Bake until golden brown, about 20 minutes. Let crust cool in pan on wire rack for 20 minutes.

3 **For the topping** Combine coconut and cream of coconut in bowl. Whisk sugar, eggs, flour, baking powder, vanilla, and salt in second bowl until smooth. Stir in pecans, then spread filling over cooled crust. Dollop heaping tablespoons of coconut mixture over filling, then spread into even layer.

4 Bake until topping is deep golden brown, 35 to 40 minutes, rotating pan halfway through baking. Let bars cool completely in pan on wire rack, about 2 hours. Using foil overhang, remove bars from pan. Cut into 24 pieces before serving. (Bars can be refrigerated for up to 5 days.)

WHITE CHOCOLATE RASPBERRY BARS

Makes 16 bars

1 cup (5 ounces) all-purpose flour

1 teaspoon baking powder

¼ teaspoon salt

6 ounces white chocolate

4 tablespoons unsalted butter, softened

½ cup (3½ ounces) plus 2 teaspoons sugar

1 large egg

1 teaspoon vanilla extract

5 ounces (1 cup) raspberries

Why This Recipe Works The most famous bar cookie, the brownie (for brownie recipes, see page 241), is all about deep, rich, dark chocolate flavor. But dark chocolate isn't the only confection that deserves star status in the bar world. These chewy, rich, brownie-like bars are made with white chocolate. We use just enough of the white stuff for a moist, rich-tasting bar but not so much that it's cloyingly sweet. Juicy, bright raspberries are a perfect foil to the creamy, mild sweetness of white chocolate, so we punctuated these bars with whole berries. Tossing the raspberries with a little sugar before pressing them into the batter encouraged them to caramelize and tempered their tartness a bit. Baking these bars at a slightly higher temperature than most brownie recipes call for—375 degrees instead of 350—resulted in beautifully browned edges that further enhanced the caramel notes. An elegant drizzle of white chocolate provided just the right finishing touch to these dressed up bars.

1 Adjust oven rack to middle position and heat oven to 375 degrees. Make foil sling for 8-inch square baking pan by folding 2 long sheets of aluminum foil so each is 8 inches wide. Lay sheets of foil in pan perpendicular to each other, with extra foil hanging over edges of pan. Push foil into corners and up sides of pan, smoothing foil flush to pan. Grease foil.

2 Whisk flour, baking powder, and salt together in small bowl. Roughly chop 3 ounces chocolate and microwave in bowl at 50 percent power, stirring often, until melted, about 1 minute. Chop remaining 3 ounces chocolate into ½-inch pieces.

3 Using stand mixer fitted with paddle, beat butter and ½ cup sugar on medium-high speed until pale and fluffy, about 3 minutes. Add egg and vanilla and beat until combined. Add melted chocolate and mix until incorporated, about 30 seconds. Reduce speed to low and slowly add flour mixture until combined, about 45 seconds. Stir in all but 2 tablespoons chopped chocolate.

4 Transfer batter to prepared pan and spread into even layer. Toss raspberries with remaining 2 teaspoons sugar to coat and gently press into batter, spacing evenly apart. Bake until edges are puffed and golden and toothpick inserted in center comes out with few moist crumbs attached, 25 to 35 minutes.

5 Let bars cool completely in pan on wire rack, about 2 hours. Using foil overhang, remove bars from pan. Microwave reserved 2 tablespoons chocolate in bowl at 50 percent power, stirring occasionally, until melted, about 45 seconds. Drizzle melted chocolate over entire surface of bars. Cut into 16 pieces and let chocolate set, about 30 minutes, before serving.

CHOCOLATE-HAZELNUT DIAMONDS

Makes 48 cookies

2½ cups (12½ ounces) all-purpose flour

¾ cup (5¼ ounces) superfine sugar

¼ teaspoon salt

16 tablespoons unsalted butter, cut into ½-inch pieces and softened

1 ounce cream cheese, softened

2 teaspoons vanilla extract

1½ cups (9 ounces) semisweet chocolate chips

1 cup hazelnuts, toasted, skinned, and chopped fine

1 cup plain toffee bits

Why This Recipe Works There aren't too many sweets that aren't improved with a slick of chocolate. For these elegant cookies, we spread a sheet pan–size buttery sugar cookie with a generous amount of chocolate and then sprinkled the whole thing with toasted hazelnuts and buttery toffee bits before cutting them into diamond-shaped bars. We tried cutting the cookies once everything had completely cooled and set, but this caused the thin cookie to break into uneven shards under the weight of the toppings. Slicing the cookies right out of the oven led to a chocolaty mess. We had the best luck letting the cookies cool for about 20 minutes and then slicing them when they were just warm; at this point, the base was still a bit soft and the chocolate topping was set but malleable, so it was easy to create clean lines. After cooling completely, the cut diamonds were pleasantly crisp and the chocolate topping perfectly set. Chocolate and hazelnut are a classic pairing, but you can substitute almonds here if desired.

1 Adjust oven rack to lower-middle position and heat oven to 375 degrees. Line 18 by 13-inch rimmed baking sheet with parchment paper.

2 Whisk flour, sugar, and salt in bowl of stand mixer. Fit stand mixer with paddle and beat butter into flour mixture on medium-low speed, 1 piece at a time, until dough looks crumbly and slightly wet, 1 to 2 minutes. Add cream cheese and vanilla and beat until clumps just begin to form, about 30 seconds. Transfer dough to counter; knead just until it forms cohesive mass.

3 Using your fingers, press dough into even layer in prepared sheet. Bake until light golden brown, about 20 minutes, rotating sheet halfway through baking.

4 Immediately after removing sheet from oven, sprinkle chocolate chips evenly over warm dough and let sit until melted, about 5 minutes. Using offset spatula, spread chocolate in even layer. Sprinkle evenly with hazelnuts and toffee bits. Let cool until just warm, 20 to 30 minutes.

5 Slice dough into 1½-inch diamonds with sharp knife or pizza cutter, then transfer cookies to wire rack. Let cookies cool completely before serving, about 45 minutes.

Slicing Chocolate-Hazelnut Diamonds

1 When baking sheet is just barely warm to touch, use sharp chef's knife or pizza cutter to cut diamond shapes. Make cuts 1½ inches apart at 45-degree angle along entire length of baking sheet.

2 Make cuts 1½ inches apart perpendicular to bottom of sheet, creating diamond-shaped cookies.

PB&J BARS

Makes 24 bars

2 cups (10 ounces) all-purpose flour

1 teaspoon baking powder

¾ teaspoon salt

12 tablespoons unsalted butter, softened

1½ cups (10½ ounces) sugar

2 large eggs

1 cup crunchy peanut butter,
room temperature

1 teaspoon vanilla extract

½ cup dry-roasted, salted peanuts,
chopped coarse

1½ cups raspberry jam

Why This Recipe Works Peanut butter often pairs with chocolate in desserts, but another peanut butter pairing, the classic sandwich combination of peanut butter and jelly, is also cookie-friendly. Here, a fruity jam center brightens the flavor of a sturdy but soft peanut butter shortbread base that doubles as a cobbler-style topping for this rich, satisfying bar cookie. We pat the cookie dough into a baking pan, reserving a portion for the topping. We then mixed chopped peanuts—salted for extra flavor—into the reserved dough for an extra-nutty, crunchy topping that provided a nice contrast to the softer base. Baking the crust alone for 15 minutes created a solid foundation, while waiting to spread the jam onto the base until after it parbaked prevented the jam from overcooking or making the base soggy. Feel free to use any flavor of jam here, but steer clear of jelly; it may be a childhood classic, but its weak fruit flavor doesn't stand up to the peanut butter here.

1 Adjust oven rack to middle position and heat oven to 350 degrees. Make foil sling for 13 by 9-inch baking pan by folding 2 long sheets of aluminum foil; first sheet should be 13 inches wide and second sheet should be 9 inches wide. Lay sheets of foil in pan perpendicular to each other, with extra foil hanging over edges of pan. Push foil into corners and up sides of pan, smoothing foil flush to pan. Grease foil.

2 Whisk flour, baking powder, and salt together in bowl. Using stand mixer fitted with paddle, beat butter and sugar on medium speed until pale and fluffy, 3 to 6 minutes. Add eggs, one at a time, and beat until combined. Add peanut butter and vanilla and mix until combined, scraping down bowl as needed. Reduce mixer speed to low and slowly add the flour mixture until just incorporated, about 30 seconds.

3 Reserve 1 cup of dough in bowl for topping. Transfer remaining dough to prepared pan and press into even layer. Bake until just beginning to turn golden, about 15 minutes. Meanwhile, stir peanuts into reserved dough for topping.

4 Spread jam evenly over hot crust, then drop small pieces of topping evenly over jam. Bake until jam is bubbling and topping is golden, about 45 minutes, rotating pan halfway through baking.

5 Let bars cool completely in pan on wire rack, about 2 hours. Using foil overhang, remove bars from pan. Cut into 24 pieces before serving.

OATMEAL FUDGE BARS

Makes 16 bars

Crust and Topping

1 cup (3 ounces) quick-cooking oats

1 cup packed (7 ounces) light brown sugar

¾ cup (3¾ ounces) all-purpose flour

¼ teaspoon baking powder

¼ teaspoon baking soda

⅛ teaspoon salt

8 tablespoons unsalted butter, melted and cooled

Filling

¼ cup (1¼ ounces) all-purpose flour

¼ cup packed (1¾ ounces) light brown sugar

2 teaspoons instant espresso powder or instant coffee powder

¼ teaspoon salt

1½ cups (9 ounces) semisweet chocolate chips

2 tablespoons unsalted butter

1 large egg

Why This Recipe Works Bar cookies have obvious appeal: They're convenient, easy to transport, and are a platform for displaying multiple delicious layers of flavor. These bars, featuring three distinct layers, are no different: They start with an oatmeal-laced, shortbread-like crust which is followed by a fudgy middle and then finished with a streusel crumb topping. For the shortbread base (which also doubles as the topping), we tried standard, old-fashioned rolled oats, but the resulting crust was hard and crunchy—not what we were looking for here. Replacing the old-fashioned oats with quick oats created a chewy texture, as did swapping the granulated sugar for brown sugar; plus, the brown sugar's molasses notes played well with the oats. We didn't just want to fill these bars with chocolate; we wanted a fudgy and dense yet plush, almost custardy, middle. Semisweet chocolate boosted with instant espresso provided plenty of chocolate flavor, and brown sugar again provided a subtle complexity. A scant amount of flour and an egg bound the filling and achieved the sliceable texture we were looking for. Be sure to cool the crust completely before adding the filling in step 5.

1 For the crust and topping Adjust oven rack to middle position and heat oven to 325 degrees. Make foil sling for 8-inch square baking pan by folding 2 long sheets of aluminum foil so each is 8 inches wide. Lay sheets of foil in pan perpendicular to each other, with extra foil hanging over edges of pan. Push foil into corners and up sides of pan, smoothing foil flush to pan. Grease foil.

2 Whisk oats, sugar, flour, baking powder, baking soda, and salt together in large bowl. Stir in melted butter until combined. Reserve ¾ cup oat mixture for topping.

3 Sprinkle remaining oat mixture into prepared pan and press into even layer. Bake until light golden brown, about 8 minutes. Let crust cool completely on wire rack, about 1 hour.

4 For the filling Adjust oven rack to middle position and heat oven to 325 degrees. Whisk flour, sugar, espresso powder, and salt together in bowl. Microwave chocolate chips and butter in large bowl at 50 percent power, stirring often, until melted, 1 to 3 minutes. Let cool slightly. Whisk in egg until combined. Stir in flour mixture until just incorporated.

5 Transfer filling to crust and spread into even layer. Sprinkle evenly with reserved oat topping. Bake until toothpick inserted in center comes out with few moist crumbs attached and filling begins to pull away from sides of pan, 25 to 30 minutes, rotating pan halfway through baking.

6 Let bars cool completely in pan on wire rack, about 2 hours. Using foil overhang, remove bars from pan. Cut into 16 pieces before serving.

MILLIONAIRE'S SHORTBREAD

Makes 40 bars

Crust

2½ cups (12½ ounces) all-purpose flour

½ cup (3½ ounces) granulated sugar

¾ teaspoon salt

16 tablespoons unsalted butter, melted

Filling

1 (14-ounce) can sweetened condensed milk

1 cup packed (7 ounces) brown sugar

½ cup heavy cream

½ cup corn syrup

8 tablespoons unsalted butter

½ teaspoon salt

Chocolate

8 ounces bittersweet chocolate (6 ounces chopped fine, 2 ounces grated)

Why This Recipe Works Millionaire's shortbread is a fitting name for this impressively rich British cookie/confectionery hybrid. And it has a lot going for it: a crunchy shortbread base; a chewy, caramel-like filling; and a shiny, snappy chocolate top. The only thing that could make it better would be foolproof methods for producing all three layers. We started by making a quick shortbread with melted butter rather than pulling out the mixer or food processor—after all, we had two more layers to work on. Sweetened condensed milk is important to the flavor of the caramel filling, but it also makes the filling vulnerable to breaking because the whey proteins it includes, crucial to keeping the mixture emulsified, have been damaged by heat both during processing and during the cooking of the filling. We added fresh cream to supply just enough whey to keep it together. Melting the chocolate very carefully so that it never got too hot and stirring in grated chocolate at the end created a smooth, firm top layer, which made a suitably elegant finish for this rich yet refined cookie. Grating a portion of the chocolate is important for getting the chocolate to set properly; the small holes on a box grater work well for this task. Stir often while melting the chocolate and don't overheat it.

1 For the crust Adjust oven rack to lower-middle position and heat oven to 350 degrees. Make foil sling for 13 by 9-inch baking pan by folding 2 long sheets of aluminum foil; first sheet should be 13 inches wide, and second sheet should be 9 inches wide. Lay sheets of foil in pan perpendicular to each other, with extra foil hanging over edges of pan. Push foil into corners and up sides of pan, smoothing foil flush to pan.

2 Combine flour, sugar, and salt in medium bowl. Add melted butter and stir with rubber spatula until flour is evenly moistened. Crumble dough evenly over bottom of prepared pan. Using your fingertips and palm of your hand, press and smooth dough into even thickness. Using fork, pierce dough at 1-inch intervals. Bake until light golden brown and firm to touch, 25 to 30 minutes. Transfer pan to wire rack. Using sturdy metal spatula, press on entire surface of warm crust to compress (this will make finished bars easier to cut). Let crust cool until just warm, at least 20 minutes.

3 For the filling Stir all ingredients together in large, heavy-bottomed saucepan. Cook over medium heat, stirring frequently, until mixture registers between 236 and 239 degrees (temperature will fluctuate), 16 to 20 minutes. Pour over crust and spread to even thickness (mixture will be very hot). Let cool completely, about 1½ hours.

4 For the chocolate Microwave chopped chocolate in bowl at 50 percent power, stirring every 15 seconds, until melted but not much warmer than body temperature (check by holding in palm of your hand), 1 to 2 minutes. Add grated chocolate and stir until smooth, returning to microwave for no more than 5 seconds at a time to finish melting if necessary. Spread chocolate evenly over surface of filling. Refrigerate shortbread until chocolate is just set, about 10 minutes.

5 Using foil overhang, remove shortbread from pan; discard foil. Using serrated knife and gentle sawing motion, cut shortbread in half crosswise to create two 6½ by 9-inch rectangles. Cut each rectangle in half to make four 3¼ by 9-inch strips. Cut each strip crosswise into 10 equal pieces. Serve. (Shortbread can be stored at room temperature, between layers of parchment, for up to 1 week.)

OATMEAL BUTTERSCOTCH BARS

Makes 36 bars

Bars

1¼ cups (6¼ ounces) all-purpose flour

2 cups (6 ounces) old-fashioned rolled oats

½ teaspoon baking soda

½ teaspoon salt

¾ cup (4½ ounces) butterscotch chips

16 tablespoons unsalted butter

1 cup packed (7 ounces) dark brown sugar

2 teaspoons vanilla extract

1 large egg

Glaze

¼ cup (1½ ounces) butterscotch chips

2 tablespoons packed dark brown sugar

1 tablespoon water

⅛ teaspoon salt

Why This Recipe Works "Oatmeal scotchies"—oatmeal cookies studded with butterscotch chips—appeal more to our sense of nostalgia than to our taste buds. In reality, they're usually overloaded with chips and overwhelmingly sweet. We wanted moist, chewy oatmeal bars with just enough butterscotch flavor and dialed-back sweetness. The obvious first step was to cut back on sugar. In addition, using dark brown sugar instead of granulated or even light brown was a simple way to give the bars butterscotch flavor and a more nuanced sweetness. These bars feature a generous amount of butter for richness, and we browned the butter to add a nutty depth of flavor. While we didn't like the texture of butterscotch chips in these bars, their flavor is hard to beat. Instead of stirring them in, we melted them so they blended smoothly into the batter. Quick oats will work in this recipe, but the bars will be less chewy and flavorful; do not use instant oats.

1 For the bars Adjust oven rack to middle position and heat oven to 350 degrees. Make foil sling for 13 by 9-inch baking pan by folding 2 long sheets of aluminum foil; first sheet should be 13 inches wide and second sheet should be 9 inches wide. Lay sheets of foil in pan perpendicular to each other, with extra foil hanging over edges of pan. Push foil into corners and up sides of pan, smoothing foil flush to pan. Grease foil.

2 Whisk flour, oats, baking soda, and salt together in bowl. Place butterscotch chips in large bowl. Melt butter in 12-inch skillet over medium-high heat. Continue to cook, swirling skillet constantly, until butter is dark golden brown and has nutty aroma, 1 to 5 minutes. Add browned butter to butterscotch chips and whisk until smooth. Whisk in sugar until dissolved, then whisk in vanilla and egg until combined. Stir in flour mixture in 2 additions until combined.

3 Transfer mixture to prepared pan and spread into even layer. Bake until edges are golden brown and toothpick inserted in center comes out with few crumbs attached, 17 to 19 minutes, rotating pan halfway through baking. Transfer pan to wire rack.

4 For the glaze Place butterscotch chips in small bowl. Bring sugar, water, and salt to simmer in small saucepan. Pour hot sugar mixture over butterscotch chips and whisk until smooth. Drizzle glaze over warm bars and let cool until warm to touch, about 1½ hours.

5 Using foil overhang, lift bars from pan and transfer to wire rack; let cool completely. Cut into 36 pieces before serving.

DATE-NUT BARS

Makes 12 bars

1 cup packed (7 ounces) brown sugar

¾ cup (3¾ ounces) all-purpose flour

½ teaspoon baking powder

½ teaspoon salt

9 ounces pitted dates, chopped (1½ cups)

1 cup pecans, toasted and chopped

2 large eggs, lightly beaten

2 tablespoons unsalted butter, melted and cooled

½ cup (2 ounces) confectioners' sugar

Why This Recipe Works Date-nut bread is a quick bread classic and a great accompaniment to a cup of warm tea. We wanted to bring its hallmarks—deep brown sugar flavor, chewy caramel-y dates, and buttery pecans—together in a convenient bar cookie that would be sweet and moist and chewy throughout. And happily we discovered that assembling these bars couldn't be easier: Simply whisk all of the dry ingredients together before mixing in the chopped dates (a generous 1½ cups for plenty of chewy date pockets), pecans, and wet ingredients. To put these bars squarely in the cookie category, we gave them an extra layer of sweetness by rolling them in confectioners' sugar; rolling them while they were still warm helped the sugar stick. The dough may look dry at first, but it will come together as it's mixed.

1 Adjust oven rack to middle position and heat oven to 350 degrees. Grease and flour 8-inch square baking pan. Combine brown sugar, flour, baking powder, and salt in large bowl. Stir in dates, pecans, eggs, and butter until combined. Transfer batter to prepared pan and spread into even layer.

2 Bake until toothpick inserted in center comes out with few crumbs attached, 25 to 30 minutes, rotating pan halfway through baking. Let bars cool in pan on wire rack for 15 minutes. Meanwhile, spread confectioners' sugar in shallow dish.

3 Remove bars from pan and let cool for 15 minutes. Cut into 12 pieces and roll in confectioners' sugar. Transfer to wire rack and let cool completely, about 1 hour, before serving.

Chopping Dried Fruit

Dried fruit, especially dates, sticks to knives. To avoid this problem, lightly coat the blade with vegetable oil spray; the fruit will slide right off. When chopping dates, watch for and remove pits and stems, which adhere persistently even to pitted dates.

BLACKBERRY BLISS BARS

Makes 24 bars

1¼ cups (6¼ ounces) all-purpose flour

12 tablespoons unsalted butter, cut into ½-inch pieces and chilled

⅔ cup packed (4⅔ ounces) dark brown sugar

¼ cup (1¾ ounces) granulated sugar

½ teaspoon salt

¼ teaspoon ground cinnamon

¾ cup (2¼ ounces) sweetened shredded coconut, toasted

½ cup (1½ ounces) old-fashioned rolled oats

1¼ cups seedless blackberry jam

1 cup walnuts, toasted and chopped

¾ cup (4½ ounces) semisweet chocolate chips

¾ cup (4½ ounces) white chocolate chips

¼ cup plain toffee bits

Why This Recipe Works These bars pack in something for everyone—and we mean everyone. With oats, coconut, walnuts, two kinds of chips, toffee bits, and a generous amount of blackberry jam to bring it all together, you're sure to find your favorite cookie ingredient in the mix. We found the key to preventing these ingredients from weighing down the bars was to use each in moderation and to incorporate them in different parts of the bar. The oats and coconut, for example, dress up a brown sugar cookie base and streusel-like top. We parbaked the crust for a sturdy base that could support the toppings and then spread on a layer of blackberry jam and sprinkled on toasted walnuts, semisweet and white chocolate chips, and toffee bits. The bright flavor of the jam was a nice contrast to the sweet toppings and helped them stay in place. Even though we tucked the coconut into the cookie base, we found that it gave the bars dimension and an even deeper flavor profile. Old-fashioned rolled oats are a must here. Do not use quick or instant oats; they will make the bars unpleasantly dense.

1 Adjust oven rack to middle position and heat oven to 350 degrees. Make foil sling for 13 by 9-inch baking pan by folding 2 long sheets of aluminum foil; first sheet should be 13 inches wide and second sheet should be 9 inches wide. Lay sheets of foil in pan perpendicular to each other, with extra foil hanging over edges of pan. Push foil into corners and up sides of pan, smoothing foil flush to pan. Grease foil.

2 Pulse flour, butter, brown sugar, granulated sugar, salt, and cinnamon in food processor until mixture resembles coarse meal, 4 to 6 pulses. Transfer flour mixture to bowl and stir in coconut and oats. Reserve ¾ cup flour-coconut mixture and set aside. Transfer remaining flour-coconut mixture to prepared pan and press into even layer. Bake until light golden, 15 to 18 minutes. Let crust cool in pan on wire rack for 10 minutes.

3 Spread jam over warm crust. Sprinkle jam with walnuts, semisweet and white chocolate chips, and toffee bits. Evenly sprinkle reserved flour-coconut mixture over top. Bake until bubbly and top is golden brown, 18 to 22 minutes, rotating pan halfway through baking. Let bars cool completely in pan on wire rack, about 1 hour. Using foil overhang, remove bars from pan. Cut into 24 pieces before serving.

NO-BAKE COOKIES & CANDIES

CRUNCHY BUTTERSCOTCH HAYSTACKS

Makes about 20 haystacks

1 cup (6 ounces) butterscotch chips

2 teaspoons vegetable oil

3 ounces (1½ cups) chow mein noodles

½ cup dry roasted, salted peanuts

Why This Recipe Works Haystacks are one of the most iconic American cookies, yet there's no dough or even oven involved. The cookies, named for their telltale shape, are simply a combination of crunchy chow mein noodles, salted dry-roasted peanuts, and melted baking chips. We added vegetable oil—just 2 teaspoons—to the mix to create a thinner coating so it was easier to cover every inch of the noodles, and so the haystacks dried with an appealing sheen. We simply melted the chips in the microwave, stirred in the oil, folded in the noodles and nuts, and then portioned it onto a baking sheet—that's it. After that, all we needed to do was let the haystacks chill in the refrigerator until the mounds of noodles were set. The result of this super-easy recipe is a salty-sweet treat with an irresistible crunchy texture. Although butterscotch haystacks are classic, we've come up with three equally delicious variations: chocolate, peanut butter, and white chocolate. They're so good and so simple, you could make them all in the same hour. Chow mein noodles can be found in most supermarkets with other Asian ingredients; La Choy is the most widely available brand.

Line baking sheet with parchment paper. Microwave butterscotch chips in bowl at 50 percent power, stirring occasionally, until melted and smooth, 2 to 4 minutes. Stir in oil until combined. Using rubber spatula, gently fold in noodles and peanuts until evenly coated. Drop heaping 1-tablespoon portions of noodle mixture onto prepared sheet in high mounds and refrigerate until set, about 15 minutes, before serving.

Crunchy Chocolate Haystacks
Substitute 1 cup bittersweet chocolate chips for butterscotch chips.

Crunchy Peanut Butter Haystacks
Substitute 1 cup peanut butter chips for butterscotch chips.

Crunchy White Chocolate Haystacks
Substitute 1 cup white chocolate chips for butterscotch chips.

Shaping Haystacks

1 Stir oil into melted chips until combined, then gently fold noodles and peanuts into melted chips until they're well coated.

2 Drop heaping 1-tablespoon mounds of noodle mixture onto prepared baking sheet. If necessary, use your fingers to gently arrange noodles into haystack shape.

BUCKEYES

Makes about 40 candies

¼ cup (1½ ounces) white chocolate chips

4 tablespoons unsalted butter, softened

2¾ cups creamy peanut butter

3 cups (12 ounces) confectioners' sugar

1 teaspoon vanilla extract

⅛ teaspoon salt

2 cups (12 ounces) semisweet chocolate chips

Why This Recipe Works What's a buckeye, you ask? You'd know if you lived in Ohio, where it's the official state tree, so named because its nuts resemble a deer's eyes. And you'd know if you went to the Ohio State University, where Brutus Buckeye is the beloved sports mascot. But in the test kitchen, the buckeye that matters is the chocolate-dipped peanut butter candy that resembles this nut. Buckeyes are made by rolling a mixture of peanut butter, confectioners' sugar, and butter into balls and dipping each ball in melted chocolate. While chocolate and peanut butter is always a winning combination, the recipes we tested were bland and too sweet. To fix these problems, we adjusted the ingredient proportions, cutting back on sugar and butter and nearly doubling the peanut butter. While the flavor of these buckeyes was improved, they were now too soft to dip. To remedy this, we mixed a small amount of melted white chocolate chips into our base; once they solidified, they added structure. For the chocolate coating, we melted semisweet chocolate chips instead of chopped bar chocolate. The chips contain emulsifiers, so they harden into a sturdy coating. Don't use natural peanut butter in this recipe.

1 Line rimmed baking sheet with parchment paper. Microwave white chocolate chips in bowl at 50 percent power, stirring occasionally, until melted, about 1 minute. Let cool for 5 minutes. Using stand mixer fitted with paddle, beat butter, peanut butter, melted white chocolate, sugar, vanilla, and salt on medium-high speed until just combined, about 1 minute. Roll peanut butter mixture into 1¼-inch balls and space them evenly on prepared sheet. Freeze until firm, about 30 minutes.

2 Microwave semisweet chocolate chips in bowl at 50 percent power, stirring occasionally, until melted and smooth, 1½ to 2 minutes. Using toothpick, dip chilled peanut butter balls one at a time into melted chocolate, leaving top quarter uncovered. Return peanut butter balls to sheet and refrigerate until chocolate is set, about 1 hour. Serve. (Buckeyes can be refrigerated for up to 1 week or frozen for up to 1 month.)

Dipping Buckeyes

Using toothpick, dip each chilled peanut butter ball into melted chocolate, leaving top quarter uncovered.

OREO MINT BALLS

Makes 15 balls

14 Oreo Mint Creme cookies

3 ounces cream cheese, softened

6 ounces semisweet chocolate, chopped

1½ tablespoons vegetable oil

1 tablespoon green sprinkles

Why This Recipe Works For these mint balls, we take one of America's favorite and most recognizable cookies and transform it into something completely different: a no-bake treat that's part cookie and part candy. Instead of beginning with the classic cream-filled chocolate sandwich cookies, we reached for Oreo Mint Creme cookies for a cookie ball that's both rich and cooling. A food processor, microwave, and freezer were all we needed to turn out these no-bake treats in less than an hour. We mixed ground Oreos with cream cheese and rolled the mixture into balls. After the balls spent 20 minutes in the freezer they were firm enough to dip in chocolate. We melted the chocolate in the microwave along with a little oil, which gave the coating a velvety consistency. After we dipped them, we quickly topped the balls with sprinkles before the chocolate had a chance to set and returned them to the freezer again until the chocolate hardened. The end result? Tasty, rich, minty treats made in just 45 minutes. For the proper texture, be sure to serve the mint balls chilled. You can substitute 1 cup semisweet chocolate chips for the semisweet chocolate.

1 Line large plate with parchment paper. Process cookies in food processor until finely ground, about 1 minute. Stir cream cheese and cookies in bowl until uniform. Roll mixture into fifteen 1-inch balls and space them evenly on prepared plate. Freeze, uncovered, until firm, about 20 minutes.

2 Microwave chocolate and oil in bowl at 50 percent power, stirring occasionally, until melted and smooth, 2 to 4 minutes. Using toothpick, dip mint ball into melted chocolate to coat, letting excess chocolate drip back into bowl. Return mint ball to plate, remove toothpick, and immediately decorate with sprinkles. Repeat with remaining mint balls and chocolate. Freeze mint balls, uncovered, until chocolate has hardened, about 10 minutes. Store in refrigerator until ready to serve.

WHITE CHOCOLATE–COCONUT CANDIES

Makes 30 balls

2 tablespoons slivered almonds, toasted

1⅓ cups (4 ounces) sweetened shredded coconut, toasted

8 ounces white chocolate, chopped

¼ cup heavy cream

1 tablespoon bourbon or dark rum

Why This Recipe Works When you hear "candy-making," you may think of an elaborate affair involving specialized equipment and lots of time. But that's not always the case. These no-cook treats require very little time—only a few minutes in the microwave and freezer. We created a no-fuss filling for our candies by microwaving white chocolate with cream, essentially making a rich, smooth white chocolate ganache. But we didn't stop there; we added ground almonds to the mixture for heft and bourbon for a welcome bite that provided a welcome contrast to the sweet white chocolate. To finish, we rolled the balls in complementary toasted coconut that we'd processed to fine crumbs. The key to these petite treats is to thoroughly chill the mixture in the freezer before rolling it into balls. Once firm, the candies don't fall apart when rolled in the coconut coating. You can use either white bar chocolate or white chocolate chips, but we found bar chocolate to melt more consistently. The balls will soften as they sit, so it's best to serve them chilled.

1 Make foil sling for 8-inch square baking pan by folding 2 long sheets of aluminum foil so each is 8 inches wide. Lay sheets of foil in pan perpendicular to each other, with extra foil hanging over edges of pan. Push foil into corners and up sides of pan, smoothing foil flush to pan.

2 Process almonds in food processor to fine crumbs, about 15 seconds; transfer to bowl. Process coconut in food processor to fine crumbs, about 15 seconds; spread in shallow dish.

3 Combine chocolate and cream in large bowl. Microwave, covered, at 50 percent power, stirring occasionally, until melted and smooth, about 2 minutes. Stir in bourbon and almonds. Transfer mixture to prepared pan and press firmly into even layer with greased spatula. Freeze, uncovered, for 15 minutes.

4 Using foil overhang, lift chilled mixture from pan and transfer to cutting board. Cut into thirty squares, then roll squares into balls. Roll balls in coconut to coat and transfer to platter. Freeze, uncovered, until firm, about 10 minutes. Store in refrigerator until ready to serve.

BOURBON BALLS

Makes about 24 balls

2½ cups (6 ounces) vanilla wafers

1 cup pecans, toasted

½ cup (2 ounces) confectioners' sugar

6 tablespoons bourbon

3 tablespoons light corn syrup

1½ tablespoons unsweetened cocoa powder

½ cup (3½ ounces) granulated sugar

Why This Recipe Works There are many things to love about these truffle-like treats, including how quick and easy they are to make (no eggs, no butter, and no baking) and the fact that almost all their ingredients are common pantry items. Oh, and the adult appeal of their unmistakable bourbon flavor doesn't hurt, either. The combination of ground vanilla wafers and toasted nuts contributes a unique crunch, which helps distinguish these confections from most candies. We chose pecans for the nuts; their sweet, buttery flavor was a perfect match for the caramel-y, slightly smoky notes of the bourbon. A small amount of cocoa powder brought bittersweet complexity (and helped bind the mixture) without making the bourbon balls taste chocolaty. Since these treats aren't baked, granulated or brown sugar wouldn't have a chance to melt, so we used confectioners' sugar to sweeten the balls without contributing grit. But we welcomed a little crunch on the exterior, so the finishing touch was a roll in sparkly granulated sugar.

Bourbon

Bourbon is the most popular form of American whiskey. True bourbon is made from a fermented grain mash of corn (it must contain at least 51 percent corn), wheat, rye, and malted barley. Bourbon can't go into the barrel for aging at higher than a 62.5-percent alcohol level. It's aged in charred new oak barrels that contribute bourbon's characteristic flavors of vanilla, caramel, and toasted nuts. These flavors make it a particularly appropriate addition to confections like White Chocolate–Coconut Candies (page 335) or these Bourbon Balls, where it plays a starring role.

1 Process vanilla wafers and pecans in food processor until finely ground, about 15 seconds; transfer to large bowl. Stir in confectioners' sugar, bourbon, corn syrup, and cocoa.

2 Spread granulated sugar in shallow dish. Working with 1 heaping tablespoon at a time, roll wafer mixture into balls, then roll in granulated sugar to coat. Transfer balls to large plate and refrigerate until firm, at least 1 hour, before serving.

BRIGADEIROS

Makes about 30 candies

1 (14-ounce) can sweetened condensed milk

½ cup (1½ ounces) Dutch-processed cocoa powder

2 tablespoons unsalted butter

Sprinkles, colored sugar, and/or nonpareils for coating

Why This Recipe Works It was a bright, glossy photo that first brought *brigadeiros*—the gooey, chocolaty, caramel-y Brazilian candy treat—to our attention. And we were happy to discover that the recipe couldn't be easier. Sweetened condensed milk, cocoa powder, and butter are cooked until thick and then poured into a dish and chilled before being rolled into truffle-size nuggets. The last step is simply to coat the brigadeiros in any number of fun toppings. We used more cocoa powder than is traditional for a candy that emphasizes the chocolate. Make sure to stir the cocoa mixture frequently or it will burn. You'll know the mixture is done cooking when it becomes so thick that a spatula dragged through it leaves a trail. Chilling the mixture is essential for easy rolling and decorating. If the dough sticks to your hands when rolling, spray your hands with a bit of vegetable oil spray. The brigadeiros are best enjoyed the day they're made, but they will keep in the refrigerator in an airtight container for up to two weeks.

1 Grease 8-inch square baking dish. Cook condensed milk, cocoa, and butter in medium saucepan over low heat, stirring frequently, until mixture is very thick and rubber spatula leaves distinct trail when dragged across bottom of saucepan, 20 to 25 minutes.

2 Pour mixture into prepared dish and refrigerate until cool, at least 30 minutes or up to 24 hours (cover with plastic wrap if chilling overnight).

3 Pinch mixture into approximately 1 tablespoon–size pieces and roll into 1-inch balls. Place desired coatings in small bowls and roll each candy in coating until covered. Serve. (Brigadeiros can be refrigerated in airtight container for up to 2 weeks.)

Making Brigadeiros

1 Cook condensed milk mixture until very thick and rubber spatula leaves distinct trail when dragged across bottom of saucepan, 20 to 25 minutes.

2 Pinch chilled chocolate mixture into approximately 1 tablespoon–size pieces.

3 Roll mixture into 1-inch balls.

SALTED NUT ROLLS

Makes 32 pieces

12 tablespoons unsalted butter

4 cups marshmallows

2 teaspoons vanilla extract

½ teaspoon salt

4 cups (16 ounces) confectioners' sugar

2 cups salted dry-roasted peanuts

1 pound soft caramels

1 (14-ounce) can sweetened
condensed milk

Why This Recipe Works These tidy rolls are fashioned after the old-timey Midwestern candy of the same name and feature a crunchy peanut crust, a smooth and creamy marshmallow filling, and a caramel "glue" that holds them together. Considering the nature of these ingredients, the situation would inevitably be sticky, but we wanted to keep things from getting too messy. We first heated butter, marshmallows, vanilla, and salt on the stove; when this mixture was combined and smooth, we added confectioners' sugar and then hand-kneaded this "dough" once it was cool enough to handle. The shiny mixture was then ready to be formed into ropes. Trying to coat the melted marshmallow ropes in caramel before the marshmallow hardened left us with a mess. Refrigerating the ropes solved that problem. For the coating, we kept things easy by simply melting store-bought soft caramels on the stove with sweetened condensed milk, whisking the mixture until it was smooth. The chilled marshmallow ropes were easy to dip in caramel and roll in nuts before we sliced them into sweet, salty, chewy, crunchy pieces.

1 Line baking sheet with parchment paper. Heat 8 tablespoons butter, marshmallows, vanilla, and salt in large saucepan over medium heat, whisking frequently until smooth, about 5 minutes. Stir in sugar and remove from heat.

2 When cool enough to handle, transfer mixture to clean counter and knead until shiny. Using bench scraper or sharp chef's knife, divide mixture into 8 pieces and roll each into 4-inch-long rope. Transfer ropes to prepared sheet and refrigerate until firm, about 15 minutes.

3 Meanwhile, pulse peanuts in food processor until finely chopped, about 10 pulses. Transfer peanuts to shallow dish. Heat caramels, condensed milk, and remaining 4 tablespoons butter in large saucepan over medium heat, whisking frequently until smooth, about 5 minutes. Dip chilled ropes, one at a time, into caramel mixture, then roll in peanuts, pressing to adhere. Return coated ropes to sheet and refrigerate until firm, about 1 hour. Cut ropes into 1-inch pieces before serving.

Sweetened Condensed Milk

Sweetened condensed milk is nothing more than a shelf-stable reduction of milk and sugar. To find the best product on the market, we tasted four products plain and in flan. Three of these condensed milks contained only whole milk and sugar; the fourth was made from nonfat milk "filled" with partially hydrogenated soybean oil. One was too thin and made a flan that didn't set up; another made a smooth flan but was sticky and with a funky flavor. We crowned **Borden Eagle Brand Sweetened Condensed Milk** and **Nestlé Carnation Sweetened Condensed Milk** our co-winners, and we recommend using one of these easy-to-find products in our recipes.

CHOCOLATE FLUFF COOKIES

Makes 12 cookies

12 Carr's Whole Wheat Crackers

1½ cups marshmallow crème

8 ounces bittersweet chocolate, chopped fine

2 tablespoons vegetable oil

Why This Recipe Works This cookie is a cross between two commercial treats—Moon Pies (marshmallows sandwiched between two graham crackers and smothered with chocolate) and Mallomars (graham crackers topped with marshmallows and covered with chocolate). Variations on this theme exist in many forms around the world, from teacakes in Britain to Dream Puffs in Canada. For our version, we ditched the graham crackers and replaced them with Carr's Whole Wheat Crackers, which provided a more substantial base for our cookie. We also liked Carr's crackers for their round shape, crisp texture, and gentle sweetness (the marshmallow and chocolate provide plenty of sweetness of their own). Instead of taking the time for homemade marshmallows, we scooped rounded portions of marshmallow crème right from the container. Briefly freezing the Fluff-topped cookies made coating them with chocolate a much neater process. We added vegetable oil to the melted chocolate to help it spread smoothly and stay shiny. You can use a spoon or a liquid measuring cup to pour the chocolate evenly over each cookie.

1 Set wire rack in rimmed baking sheet. Distribute crackers evenly on top of rack. Top each cracker with 1 heaping tablespoon marshmallow crème. Place baking sheet in freezer until marshmallow crème has firmed up, about 10 minutes.

2 Stir chocolate and oil in small saucepan over low heat until melted and smooth. Let cool completely.

3 Spoon chocolate mixture over each cookie to cover marshmallow crème completely. Return baking sheet to freezer until chocolate is set, about 10 minutes. Transfer sheet to refrigerator until cookies are completely firm, about 1 hour, before serving. (Cookies can be refrigerated for up to 2 days.)

Coating Chocolate Fluff Cookies

Pour or spoon cooled chocolate mixture over each marshmallow-topped cookie to coat completely in even layer. Briefly return cookies to freezer to set chocolate.

RICE CRISPY TREATS

Makes 16 treats

3 tablespoons unsalted butter

10 ounces marshmallows

½ teaspoon vanilla extract

¼ teaspoon salt

5 cups (5 ounces) crisped rice cereal

Why This Recipe Works While almost everyone is familiar with the classic recipe for Rice Krispies Treats, slight variations on the original abound. We think our recipe gets them just right, with the perfect ratio of marshmallow and butter to cereal for a bar with the sticky chew that kids love and that adults remember fondly. The basic procedure is the same as the back-of-the box recipe: Melt butter and marshmallows, mix in cereal, and press into a pan—it couldn't be simpler. But we like a generous portion of these cereal treats; for thick, substantial squares, we pat the mixture into an 8-inch square pan instead of the usual 13 by 9-inch pan. Adding a little salt to the mix kept sweetness in check. Greasing the knife we used to slice the bars ensured that we were able to produce neat, easy-to-cut squares. These rice crispy treats are delicious as is, but their simplicity also makes them an ideal backdrop for a whole host of flavorings and mix-ins, so we developed several variations sure to please any crowd. Any brand of toasted rice cereal will work in this recipe.

1 Make foil sling for 8-inch square baking pan by folding 2 long sheets of aluminum foil so each is 8 inches wide. Lay sheets of foil in pan perpendicular to one another, with extra foil hanging over edges of pan. Push foil into corners and up sides of pan, smoothing foil flush to pan. Spray with vegetable oil spray.

2 Melt butter in Dutch oven over low heat. Add marshmallows, vanilla, and salt and cook, stirring constantly, until melted and smooth, about 6 minutes. Off heat, stir in cereal until incorporated. Transfer mixture to prepared pan and press into even layer with greased spatula. Let treats cool for 30 minutes. Using foil overhang, remove treats from pan. Cut into 16 squares and serve.

Almond Joy Rice Crispy Treats

Stir 1 cup toasted sweetened shredded coconut; 1 cup toasted sliced almonds; and ½ cup semisweet chocolate chips into marshmallow mixture with cereal in step 2.

Chocolate-Cherry Rice Crispy Treats

Add ½ cup white chocolate chips to pot with marshmallows in step 2. Stir 1 cup dried cherries, chopped, into marshmallow mixture with cereal. Microwave ½ cup semisweet chocolate chips in bowl at 50 percent power, stirring occasionally, until melted, 30 to 60 seconds. Drizzle over cooled treats. Let set for 15 minutes before cutting treats.

Double Chocolate Caramel Turtle Rice Crispy Treats

Add ½ cup semisweet chocolate chips to pot with marshmallows in step 2. Stir 4½ ounces quartered soft caramels and 1 cup pecans, toasted and chopped, into marshmallow mixture with cereal. Microwave additional ½ cup semisweet chocolate chips in bowl at 50 percent power, stirring occasionally, until melted, 30 to 60 seconds. Drizzle chocolate over cooled treats and let set for 15 minutes before cutting treats.

Loaded Rice Crispy Treats

Stir 1 cup pretzels, broken into ½-inch pieces; ½ cup salted dry-roasted peanuts; ½ cup semisweet chocolate chips, and ½ cup toffee bits into marshmallow mixture with cereal in step 2.

Peanut Butter Rice Crispy Treats

Add ½ cup peanut butter chips to pot with marshmallows in step 2. Stir 1 cup dry-roasted peanuts into marshmallow mixture with cereal. Microwave additional ½ cup peanut butter chips in bowl at 50 percent power, stirring occasionally, until melted. Drizzle melted peanut butter chips over cooled treats and let set for 15 minutes before cutting treats.

Salty Cashew-Caramel Rice Crispy Treats

Stir 1½ cups salted roasted cashews, chopped coarse, and 4½ ounces quartered soft caramels into marshmallow mixture with cereal in step 2.

CHOCOLATE SALAMI

Makes 24 cookies

½ cup dried cherries, chopped coarse

2 tablespoons Grand Marnier

4 ounces dried ladyfingers (*savoiardi*), cut into ½-inch chunks

1 cup (6 ounces) semisweet or bittersweet chocolate chips

⅓ cup heavy cream

Pinch salt

⅔ cup pistachios, toasted

½ cup (2 ounces) confectioners' sugar

Why This Recipe Works Don't worry: No pork products were used in the making of this confection. This no-bake cookie may get its name from its resemblance to the Italian cured sausage, but any similarity is in appearance only: With a base of chocolate ganache akin to a chocolate truffle, chocolate salami is typically chock-full of dried fruit, nuts, and crushed cookies. The mixture is then formed into a log that's cut into rounds, much like slice-and-bake cookies minus the "bake." The result is something that's a little bit like a cookie, a little bit like a candy—and very delicious. To complete the salami look, we dredged the logs of dough in confectioners' sugar. For our recipe, we liked the combination of tart dried cherries, which we macerated in Grand Marnier for extra flavor, and rich pistachios. We used dried ladyfingers as the cookie component, although any dry, biscuit-like cookie will work. We found that chocolate chips worked better than bar chocolate here; they made a smooth mixture that was easy to mold. The result is an exquisite, unique cookie that's deceptively simple to make.

1 Combine cherries and Grand Marnier in small bowl and microwave until hot, about 30 seconds; let sit until cherries have softened and mixture is cool, about 15 minutes. Set aside 1 cup ladyfingers. Process remaining ladyfingers in food processor to fine crumbs, 15 to 20 seconds. (You should have about ¾ cup crumbs.)

2 Microwave chocolate chips and cream in bowl at 50 percent power, stirring frequently, until melted and smooth, 30 to 60 seconds. Add salt and ladyfinger crumbs and stir to combine. Add pistachios, reserved ladyfingers, and cherry mixture and stir until thick dough forms.

3 Transfer dough to counter. Divide dough in half and place each half on large sheet of plastic wrap. Use plastic to roll each dough half into tight 6-inch log, twisting ends well to secure. Refrigerate logs until firm, at least 3 hours or up to 3 days.

4 When ready to serve, spread confectioners' sugar in shallow dish. Unwrap logs and roll in sugar until well coated, brushing off excess. Cut each log into ½-inch-thick slices and serve.

POOR MAN'S TOFFEE

Makes about 16 pieces

24 saltines

1½ cups dry-roasted peanuts

1 cup (7 ounces) sugar

½ cup plus 1 tablespoon corn syrup

5 tablespoons unsalted butter

1 teaspoon vanilla extract

1 teaspoon baking powder

½ cup (3 ounces) semisweet chocolate chips

Why This Recipe Works Traditional toffee is delicious, but making it requires a fair amount of care: Cook the mixture too far and it will taste burnt; cook the mixture too little and it will taste bland and sweet. We're not always in the mood for such a finicky project, but we're always in the mood for this sweet treat. Enter: poor man's toffee. This recipe combines a crunchy peanut brittle–like mixture of sugar, corn syrup, butter, and peanuts that has a texture similar to toffee with a drizzle of melted semisweet chocolate. An unlikely ingredient, saltines, serves as the base for the toffee; they added the extra crunchy, crispy boost this easier toffee needed and also added an irresistible saltiness to the treats. The best part? The sugar mixture doesn't require stovetop cooking and careful monitoring with a candy thermometer; instead, we simply cooked it in the microwave. Adding baking soda to the caramel ensures that it's crisp and light, and doesn't stick to your teeth.

1 Line bottom of 13 by 9-inch baking dish with waxed paper and spray with vegetable oil spray. Arrange saltines, salt side down, in single layer on waxed paper.

2 Using rubber spatula, combine peanuts, sugar, and ½ cup corn syrup in bowl. Microwave mixture until sugar melts, about 2 minutes. Continue to microwave, stirring occasionally, until mixture begins to boil, about 2 minutes. Add 1 tablespoon butter and vanilla and stir until butter melts. Continue to microwave, stirring occasionally, until liquid begins to brown, about 2 minutes. Stir in baking powder until incorporated. Working quickly, pour sugar mixture over saltines and spread evenly (if mixture hardens too quickly, place baking dish in preheated 250-degree oven for 5 minutes). Refrigerate until firm, about 1 hour.

3 Invert toffee onto cutting board and peel off waxed paper. Break toffee into large pieces. Return pieces, peanut side up, to baking dish.

4 Melt chocolate chips and remaining 4 tablespoons butter in medium saucepan over medium-high heat until smooth. Stir in remaining 1 tablespoon corn syrup and drizzle chocolate mixture over toffee. Let chocolate set for 1 hour before breaking into pieces and serving.

ROCKY ROAD BARK

Makes 16 pieces

5–6 whole graham crackers

6 tablespoons unsalted butter

¼ cup packed (1¾ ounces) light brown sugar

½ teaspoon salt

6 ounces semisweet chocolate, chopped fine

¾ cup mini marshmallows

½ cup pecans, walnuts, or almonds, toasted and chopped

Why This Recipe Works The concept behind this Rocky Road Bark is similar to that of our Poor Man's Toffee (page 349). But this time, the cracker of choice is nutty-tasting graham crackers and the topping incorporates all the elements of rocky road candy, for a fun twist on classic toffee flavors. Once we poured an easy-to-make caramel mixture over the graham crackers, we spread the surface with chocolate and then added mini marshmallows for sticky sweetness and pecans for buttery crunch and a rocky top that reflects the candy's name. To avoid the painstaking process of carefully watching the sugar mixture turn from pale to golden to amber on the stovetop, we broke our own rule and turned on the oven. This was justified: We simply had to heat the caramel ingredients briefly and then baked the topped graham crackers until the caramel was bubbling, an indication that it would set to just the right texture. You can substitute 1 cup semisweet chocolate chips for the semisweet chocolate. Since graham cracker sizes can vary slightly from brand to brand, use the amount necessary to fit the pan.

1 Adjust oven rack to middle position and heat oven to 375 degrees. Make foil sling for 8-inch square baking pan by folding 2 long sheets of aluminum foil so each is 8 inches wide. Lay sheets of foil in pan perpendicular to each other, with extra foil hanging over edges of pan. Push foil into corners and up sides of pan, smoothing foil flush to pan.

2 Line bottom of pan with single layer of graham crackers, breaking them as needed to fit. Cook butter, sugar, and salt together in small saucepan over low heat, stirring constantly, until butter is melted and sugar has dissolved, about 2 minutes. Pour mixture over graham crackers and smooth with spatula to cover crackers completely. Bake until caramel is bubbling, about 8 minutes.

3 Transfer pan to wire rack, sprinkle chocolate over caramel, and let melt for 5 minutes. Using spatula, smooth chocolate into even layer. Sprinkle with marshmallows and nuts and press lightly to adhere. Freeze, uncovered, until chocolate has hardened, about 13 minutes.

4 Using foil overhang, remove bark from pan. Cut into 16 squares and serve, or transfer to refrigerator until serving time.

ALL ABOUT CANDY-MAKING

If you think candy-making is only for the professionals, think again; you can absolutely turn out tasty treats in your own kitchen. All you need is some essential—but multipurpose—equipment (like an accurate thermometer that will tell you when your toffee and caramel are done) and a few key techniques to help you create your favorite treats at home.

CARAMEL TIPS AND TRICKS

Caramel is simply sugar (sucrose) that's been heated until it melts, browns, and develops complex flavor. You can use it to make a fluid caramel sauce or chewy or hard candy by adding cream, butter, and other flavorings. The longer the mixture cooks, the more water will evaporate and the stiffer the caramel will become. With the right recipe, it's easy to overcome two main pitfalls: unevenly melted, burnt sugar and crystallized sugar. The latter happens when some of the sucrose molecules aren't hot enough to melt and break down into glucose and fructose. Instead, they bond, creating a grainy texture. Here's what to do.

1 Add Water Water, which makes a "wet caramel," helps the sugar melt evenly, reducing the risk that some sugar burns before the rest caramelizes.

2 Choose Corn Syrup Adding either acid or corn syrup to sugar as it caramelizes can prevent crystallization; both interfere with sucrose's ability to bond with itself. Acid speeds the breakdown of sucrose into fructose and glucose, both of which dilute the remaining sucrose molecules, decreasing the chance they can bond. But corn syrup already contains glucose molecules (and water), so it dilutes sucrose faster.

3 Use a Heavy-Bottomed Saucepan Sugar is prone to burning in lightweight cookware, which doesn't transfer heat evenly. A heavy saucepan helps the sugar cook evenly.

4 Don't Stir the Pot Stirring the sugar to help it melt isn't necessary. We simply swirl the pan occasionally as the syrup cooks to even out hot spots.

MAKING CARAMEL: A VISUAL GUIDE

Caramel isn't something you can set and forget; you need to watch it closely and take its temperature at various points along the way. But whether you're making Salted Caramels (page 361), a caramel topping for brownies like our Ultimate Turtle Brownies (page 252), or preparing caramel sauce for dipping and drizzling, these are the steps and visual cues that will ensure success.

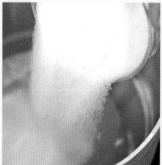  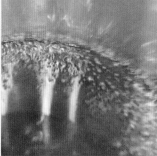 

1 Center the Sugar After combining the water and corn syrup in a saucepan, you want to pour the sugar into the center of the pan. This prevents sugar granules from getting stuck on the pan's sides.

2 Cook to Pale Golden Start by dissolving the sugar, cooking until the bubbles show a faint golden color (fully golden bubbles means you've gone too far), and then lower the heat.

3 Cook to Amber Once the caramel reaches an amber color, remove it from the heat.

4 Finish Caramel Depending on the recipe, add butter and/or cream to the caramel (it will bubble vigorously) and cook until the caramel reaches the desired final temperature. It will be a deep shade of amber.

Before inserting an instant-read thermometer into the caramel, swirl the caramel to even out any hot spots. Tilt the pot so that the caramel pools 1 to 2 inches deep and move the thermometer back and forth in the caramel for about 5 seconds before taking a reading. If using a clip-on thermometer, swirl the caramel for at least 15 seconds and tilt the caramel toward the probe.

SEA SALT

Sea salt is the product of seawater evaporation—a time-consuming, expensive process that yields irregularly shaped, mineral-rich flakes that vary in color but only slightly in flavor. While we don't bother cooking with sea salt—we've found that mixed into food, it doesn't taste any different than table salt—we love to use it as a finishing salt for cookies and candies, where its delicate crunch stands out. Texture—not exotic provenance—should be the main consideration when you're purchasing sea salt. Look for brands boasting large, flaky crystals such as Maldon Sea Salt.

CLIP-ON DIGITAL THERMOMETER

We highly recommend owning the Thermo-Works Thermapen Mk4 ($99) (see page 8). It's a great all-purpose thermometer for kitchen tasks from candy-making to testing the internal temperature of a roast chicken. But if you want to expand on this essential tool, there's another thermometer that makes candy-making particularly easy, and it's also made by ThermoWorks: the **ThermoWorks ChefAlarm** ($59). The clip-on digital thermometer allows for hands-free temperature checking, providing the temperature of the bubbling caramel or toffee every second of the way. It's also great for monitoring the temperature of oil during deep-frying (and we do deep-fry cookies; see Danish Kleiner on page 229). The super-accurate thermometer can be calibrated and features programmable high- and low-temperature alarms, adjustable brightness and volume, an on/off switch, and a small knob on the probe that stays cool for over-the-pot adjustments.

CALIBRATING A THERMOMETER

You should check your instant-read thermometer's accuracy when you first buy it and then again periodically. To do this, put a mixture of ice and cold tap water in a glass or bowl; allow this mixture to sit for several minutes to let the temperature stabilize. Put the probe in the slush, being careful not to touch the sides or bottom of the glass or bowl. On a digital thermometer, press the "calibrate" button to 32 degrees; on a dial-face thermometer, turn the dial to 32 degrees (the method differs from model to model; you may need pliers to turn a small knob on the back).

STORING CHOCOLATE TRUFFLES

Chocolate truffles are an easy make-ahead treat since they keep in the refrigerator for up to one week. The best way to store chocolate truffles is in the cocoa powder you dredged them in. This simple step keeps the chocolates from sticking and avoids the need to use more cocoa to touch them up before serving them.

BLOOMED CHOCOLATE

Storing chocolate at a temperature that is either too warm or too cool will cause a white film, or bloom, to develop on the surface. One type of bloom occurs when cocoa butter crystals melt and migrate to the surface. Another type happens in humid conditions when water condenses on bittersweet or milk chocolate, dissolving some of its sugar before evaporating and leaving behind a fine layer of sugar crystals.

In tests, we found that bloomed chocolate of either type was fine for baking. But when we dipped cookies and candies in melted chocolate with cocoa butter bloom, the chocolate took longer to set and the bloom reappeared. This is because the chocolate's fat structure had changed. Also, the sugar crystals in the melted sugar—bloomed chocolate never dissolved, resulting in a grainy coating. For the best-looking, best-tasting confections, avoid using bloomed chocolate.

Bloomed bar chocolate makes a bloomed chocolate coating.

15-MINUTE CHOCOLATE WALNUT FUDGE

Makes about 2½ pounds

16 ounces semisweet chocolate, chopped fine

2 ounces unsweetened chocolate, chopped fine

½ teaspoon baking soda

⅛ teaspoon salt

1 (14-ounce) can sweetened condensed milk

1 tablespoon vanilla extract

1 cup coarsely chopped walnuts

Why This Recipe Works Fudge isn't meant to be made just by chocolatiers; homemade fudge can be easy—if you know a few tricks. First, while many recipes call for heavy cream, we found that sweetened condensed milk worked better; it's stable and won't separate if overheated. Next, we tackled flavor: Some fudge tastes just like cubes of sugar, but we wanted ours to have intense chocolate flavor. Combining a full pound of semisweet chocolate with a small amount of unsweetened chocolate did the trick. We found that the quality of the chocolate used greatly affected the flavor and texture of the fudge. We prefer Ghirardelli semisweet and unsweetened chocolate in this recipe. Finally, we determined that the addition of walnuts was essential; the crunchy bits of chopped nuts added a crucial textural element. If you prefer, you can use toasted nuts in this recipe. Make sure to remove the fudge from the double boiler before the chocolate is fully melted. If the chocolate stays in the double boiler too long, there's the possibility of the chocolate separating and producing a greasy fudge. This fudge will become drier in texture the longer it's stored. Store the fudge, tightly wrapped in plastic, in a cool place for up to 2 weeks or in the freezer for up to 3 months. If frozen, allow ample time to let it reach room temperature before cutting. Fudge is great for gifting; to make a double batch, double the amounts of all the ingredients and make the fudge in a 13 by 9-inch baking pan. In step 2, use a large heatproof bowl and Dutch oven containing 4 cups simmering water.

1 Make foil sling for 8-inch square baking pan by folding 2 long sheets of aluminum foil so each is 8 inches wide. Lay sheets of foil in pan perpendicular to each other, with extra foil hanging over edges of pan. Push foil into corners and up sides of pan, smoothing foil flush to pan. Grease foil.

2 Toss chocolates, baking soda, and salt in heatproof bowl until baking soda is evenly distributed. Stir in sweetened condensed milk and vanilla. Set bowl over 4-quart saucepan containing 2 cups simmering water. Stir with rubber spatula until chocolate is almost fully melted and few small pieces remain, 2 to 4 minutes.

3 Remove bowl from heat and continue to stir until chocolate is fully melted and mixture is smooth, about 2 minutes. Stir in walnuts. Transfer fudge to prepared pan and spread in even layer. Refrigerate until set, about 2 hours. Using foil overhang, remove fudge from pan. Cut into squares and serve.

15-Minute Peanut Butter Fudge

Substitute 3 cups peanut butter chips for semisweet and unsweetened chocolate in step 2. Omit walnuts.

15-Minute Rocky Road Fudge

Substitute 1 cup miniature marshmallows, 1 cup coarsely chopped peanuts, and ½ cup semisweet chocolate chips for walnuts in step 3.

CHOCOLATE–PEANUT BUTTER CANDIES

Makes 36 candies

8 ounces milk chocolate, chopped

2 tablespoons refined coconut oil

1 cup salted dry-roasted peanuts

½ cup creamy peanut butter

4 tablespoons unsalted butter

1½ cups marshmallow crème

4 ounces soft caramels

1–2 tablespoons heavy cream

Why This Recipe Works These salty-sweet treats are reminiscent of Snickers bars—although we think they're even better, and prettier to boot. The base is a mixture of melted chocolate and chopped peanuts. We also added some coconut oil to this mix; we planned to freeze these treats—who doesn't love a frozen candy bar?—and coconut oil becomes solid at cold temperatures, resulting in a firm base layer with a nice snap. For the easiest-ever peanut butter–nougat filling, we melted peanut butter and butter together and then folded in marshmallow crème before mixing in more peanuts. We spread this plush confection in a thick, even layer over the chocolate base. To finish these candies, we settled on a decorative flourish of caramel and chocolate. Stirring a little heavy cream into melted store-bought soft caramels gave them just the right consistency for drizzling. Start with 1 tablespoon and add the second tablespoon if needed. With a chocolaty base; a soft, chewy, crunchy center; and a sweet topping, we may never go for a store-bought candy bar again. These bars are best served straight from the freezer.

1 Make foil sling for 8-inch square baking pan by folding 2 long sheets of aluminum foil so each is 8 inches wide. Lay sheets of foil in pan perpendicular to each other, with extra foil hanging over edges of pan. Push foil into corners and up sides of pan, smoothing foil flush to pan. Grease foil.

2 Combine 6 ounces chocolate and coconut oil in medium bowl. Microwave at 50 percent power, stirring occasionally, until melted and smooth, 2 to 3 minutes. Finely chop ½ cup peanuts; add to melted chocolate and stir to combine. Transfer to prepared pan and smooth into even layer. Refrigerate until set, about 30 minutes.

3 Combine peanut butter and butter in medium bowl and microwave until butter is melted and warm, 30 to 45 seconds. Stir until incorporated. Fold in marshmallow crème and stir until well combined (mixture should lighten in color and may look separated). Fold in remaining ½ cup peanuts. Spread evenly over chocolate layer and chill until firm, about 1 hour.

4 Heat caramels and 1 tablespoon cream in small saucepan over medium-low heat, stirring constantly, until smooth, adding additional 1 tablespoon cream if necessary; set aside. Melt remaining 2 ounces chocolate. Drizzle caramel and chocolate over peanut butter layer and freeze until set, about 30 minutes. Using foil overhang, remove candies from pan. Using greased knife, cut into 36 squares and serve immediately.

CHOCOLATE TRUFFLES

Makes 24 truffles

¼ cup (¾ ounce) unsweetened cocoa powder

1 tablespoon confectioners' sugar

8 ounces bittersweet chocolate, chopped fine

½ cup heavy cream

Pinch salt

Why This Recipe Works Making chocolate truffles usually isn't easy or fast; the process of creating a chocolate ganache base, waiting for it to firm up, shaping it into balls, waiting again, and coating the balls with cocoa or nuts can take up an entire afternoon. We wanted a quicker method that would work every time. In the past, the test kitchen has developed a ganache for truffles using chocolate, cream, butter, corn syrup (which smooths out the texture), and vanilla. Could we trim the ingredient list without sacrificing the silky texture? Several tests without corn syrup or butter revealed that, after tweaking the ratio of heavy cream to chocolate, we could indeed achieve the ganache texture that we wanted with fewer ingredients. Vanilla, too, proved optional, but salt, which amplifies chocolate's complex flavors, was essential. Careful mixing was also necessary, and the ideal utensil for mixing was a rubber spatula as it didn't incorporate a lot of air. Now we wanted to chip away at the time. Some recipes call for cooling the ganache for up to 4 hours before shaping it into balls, but we found that just 45 minutes in the refrigerator was enough time. After we portioned out the mixture using a teaspoon measure, another short chill of just 30 minutes was all the ganache needed before being rolled quickly into balls. Wear latex gloves when forming the truffles to keep your hands clean.

1 Sift cocoa and sugar through fine-mesh strainer into pie plate. Microwave chocolate, cream, and salt in bowl at 50 percent power, stirring occasionally with rubber spatula, until melted, about 1 minute. Stir truffle mixture until fully combined; transfer to 8-inch square baking dish and refrigerate until set, about 45 minutes.

2 Using heaping teaspoon measure, scoop truffle mixture into 24 portions, transfer to large plate, and refrigerate until firm, about 30 minutes. Roll each truffle between your hands to form uniform balls (balls needn't be perfect).

3 Transfer truffles to cocoa mixture and roll to evenly coat. Lightly shake truffles in your hand over pie plate to remove excess coating and transfer to platter. Refrigerate for 30 minutes. Let sit at room temperature for 10 minutes before serving. (Coated truffles can be refrigerated along with excess cocoa mixture in airtight container for up to 1 week. Shake truffles in your hand to remove excess coating and let sit at room temperature for 10 minutes before serving.)

Chocolate-Almond Truffles
Substitute 1 cup sliced almonds, toasted and chopped fine, for cocoa mixture coating. Add ½ teaspoon almond extract to chocolate mixture before microwaving in step 1.

Chocolate-Ginger Truffles
Add 2 teaspoons ground ginger to chocolate mixture before microwaving in step 1.

Chocolate-Lemon Truffles
Add 1 teaspoon grated lemon zest to chocolate mixture before microwaving in step 1.

Chocolate-Spice Truffles
Sift ¼ teaspoon ground cinnamon with cocoa powder and sugar for coating. Add 1 teaspoon ground cinnamon and ⅛ teaspoon cayenne pepper to chocolate mixture before microwaving in step 1.

SALTED CARAMELS

Makes about 50 caramels

1 vanilla bean

1 cup heavy cream

5 tablespoons unsalted butter,
cut into ¼-inch pieces

1½ teaspoons flake sea salt

¼ cup light corn syrup

¼ cup water

1⅓ cups (9⅓ ounces) sugar

Why This Recipe Works While we love chocolate, we find gourmet caramel candies sprinkled with sea salt to be the ultimate in sophistication, and knowing how to make caramels from scratch is an alluring prospect, mainly because of the challenge these tasty chews present. Sugar can be a fickle friend, taking forever to caramelize and then going from golden amber to dark mahogany to burnt-beyond-recognition in the blink of an eye. But we cracked the code and uncovered the secret to achieving chewy, delightfully sticky caramels. Caramel candies aren't just about the sugar; you need to add cream to the caramel so that it has a rich flavor and chewy—not tooth-breaking—texture. We infused the cream with a vanilla bean to give our caramels an aromatic backnote. When it came to cooking the sugar syrup, the most important lesson we learned was not to turn your back on it. When the caramel developed an amber color, we added the cream mixture, watched it bubble, and then cooked the caramel to the right temperature. We then transferred the molten mixture to a baking pan, sprinkled it with salt, and cut the caramel into candies once it was set. You will need a thermometer that registers high temperatures for this recipe.

1 Cut vanilla bean in half lengthwise. Using tip of paring knife, scrape out seeds. Combine vanilla bean seeds, cream, butter, and 1 teaspoon salt in small saucepan over medium heat. Bring to boil, cover, remove from heat, and let steep for 10 minutes.

2 Meanwhile, make parchment sling for 8-inch square baking pan by folding 2 long sheets of parchment paper so each is 8 inches wide. Lay sheets of parchment in greased pan perpendicular to each other, with extra parchment hanging over edges of pan. Push parchment into corners and up sides of pan, smoothing parchment flush to pan. Grease parchment.

3 Combine corn syrup and water in large saucepan. Pour sugar into center of saucepan, taking care not to let sugar granules touch sides of saucepan. Bring to boil over medium-high heat, and cook, without stirring, until sugar has dissolved completely and syrup has faint golden color and registers

300 degrees, 7 to 9 minutes. Reduce heat to medium-low and continue to cook, gently swirling pan, until mixture is amber-colored and registers 350 degrees, 2 to 3 minutes.

4 Off heat, carefully stir in cream mixture (mixture will foam up). Return mixture to medium-high heat, and cook, stirring frequently, until caramel reaches 248 degrees, about 5 minutes.

5 Carefully transfer caramel to prepared pan and smooth surface of caramel with greased rubber spatula. Sprinkle with remaining ½ teaspoon salt and let cool completely, about 1 hour. Transfer to refrigerator and chill until caramel is completely solid and cold to touch, about 1 hour.

6 Using parchment overhang, remove caramel from pan. Peel off parchment. Cut caramel into ¾-inch-wide strips and then crosswise into ¾-inch pieces. Individually wrap pieces in waxed-paper squares, twisting ends of paper to close. (Caramels can be refrigerated for up to 3 weeks.)

CHOCOLATE-HAZELNUT BRITTLE

Makes about 1½ pounds

1 teaspoon baking soda

Kosher salt

2 cups hazelnuts, toasted, skinned, and chopped

½ cup water

6 tablespoons unsalted butter

1½ cups (10½ ounces) sugar

1¼ cups corn syrup

2 ounces bittersweet chocolate, chopped

Why This Recipe Works While peanut brittle gets the attention, this buttery caramelized treat can be prepared with any nut. In this version, we added a touch of sophistication by using hazelnuts and then dressed it up by drizzling the finished candy with chocolate and sprinkling it with salt. Since we didn't want a chewy candy, we added fat to the mixture in the form of butter, rather than liquid cream like we use in our Salted Caramels (page 361), cooking the butter with water, corn syrup, and sugar until the amber mixture reached the right temperature. Before adding the hazelnuts to the caramel, we stirred in some baking soda; the soda neutralizes the acids and creates air bubbles in the caramel mixture so it's crunchy but not a jawbreaker. Toasting the hazelnuts added depth to the candy as did stirring some salt into the caramel mixture, which balanced the sweetness and brought out the flavor of the toasted nuts. A final sprinkling of salt over the chocolate drizzle really made all the ingredients shine. You will need a thermometer that registers high temperatures for this recipe.

1 Adjust oven rack to middle position and heat oven to 350 degrees. Grease 13 by 9-inch baking pan. Make parchment paper sling by folding 1 long sheet of parchment 13 inches wide and laying it across width of pan, with extra parchment hanging over edges of pan. Push parchment into corners and up sides of pan, smoothing parchment flush to pan. Grease parchment. Combine baking soda and ½ teaspoon salt in small bowl. Line rimmed baking sheet with parchment. Add hazelnuts in even layer and bake until lightly toasted, about 5 minutes. Keep hazelnuts warm on sheet.

2 Combine water and butter in large saucepan and cook over medium-high heat until butter is melted. Pour sugar and corn syrup into center of saucepan, taking care not to let sugar granules touch sides of saucepan. Gently stir until all sugar is moistened. Bring to boil and cook, without stirring, until syrup has faint golden color and registers 300 degrees, 6 to 7 minutes.

3 Reduce heat to medium-low and continue to cook, gently swirling pan, until syrup is amber-colored and registers 325 degrees, 1 to 2 minutes. Off heat, stir in baking soda–salt mixture and, using parchment as sling, add hazelnuts. Working quickly, transfer mixture to prepared pan and smooth into even layer with greased rubber spatula. Let cool completely, about 1 hour.

4 Microwave chocolate at 50 percent power, stirring occasionally, until melted, 1 to 2 minutes. Drizzle chocolate over brittle and sprinkle evenly with ¼ teaspoon salt. Refrigerate until set, about 15 minutes. Using parchment overhang, remove brittle from pan. Peel off parchment. Break brittle into rough squares and serve.

9

CHRISTMAS COOKIES

FOOLPROOF HOLIDAY COOKIES

Makes about 36 cookies

2½ cups (12½ ounces) all-purpose flour

¾ cup (5¼ ounces) superfine sugar

¼ teaspoon salt

16 tablespoons unsalted butter, cut into ½-inch pieces and softened

1 ounce cream cheese, softened

2 teaspoons vanilla extract

Why This Recipe Works Making holiday cookies—the rolled, cutout, and glazed butter-cookie variety—is everyone's favorite December activity. Unfortunately, these cookies either look good but taste like cardboard or have buttery, rich flavor but lack visual appeal. We wanted a simple recipe that would produce cookies sturdy enough to decorate yet tender enough to be worth eating. Superfine sugar helped to achieve a delicate texture, and using the reverse-creaming method—beating the butter into the flour-sugar mixture—prevented the formation of air pockets and produced flat cookies that were easy to decorate. (For more information on reverse creaming in holiday cookies, see page 3.) Looking to make our dough a bit more workable without adding more butter—at 16 tablespoons, we'd maxed out—we landed on the addition of a little cream cheese, which made the dough easy to roll but not too soft. Baking the butter cookies one sheet at a time ensured that they baked evenly. Do not reroll the scraps more than once; it will cause the cookies to be tough. This recipe can easily be doubled. You can decorate the cooled cookies with Easy All-Purpose Glaze (page 370) for a sweet, festive touch.

1 Using stand mixer fitted with paddle, mix flour, sugar, and salt on low speed until combined. Add butter, 1 piece at a time, and mix until dough looks crumbly and slightly wet, 1 to 2 minutes. Add cream cheese and vanilla and beat until dough just begins to form large clumps, about 30 seconds.

2 Transfer dough to counter; knead just until it forms cohesive mass and divide in half. Form each half into disk, wrap disks tightly in plastic wrap, and refrigerate for at least 30 minutes or up to 2 days. (Wrapped dough can be frozen for up to 2 weeks. Let dough thaw completely in refrigerator before rolling.)

3 Working with 1 disk of dough at a time, roll dough ⅛ inch thick between 2 large sheets of parchment paper. Slide dough, still between parchment, onto baking sheet and refrigerate until firm, about 10 minutes.

4 Adjust oven rack to middle position and heat oven to 375 degrees. Line 2 baking sheets with parchment. Working with 1 sheet of dough at a time, remove top piece of parchment and cut dough into shapes with cookie cutters. Using thin offset spatula, transfer shapes to prepared baking sheet, spacing them about 1 inch apart.

5 Bake cookies, 1 sheet at a time, until light golden brown, about 10 minutes, rotating sheet halfway through baking. Let cookies cool on sheet for 3 minutes, then transfer to wire rack. Let cookies cool completely before serving.

SOFT AND CHEWY GINGERBREAD PEOPLE

Makes about 20 cookies

3 cups (15 ounces) all-purpose flour

¾ cup packed (5¼ ounces) dark brown sugar

1 tablespoon ground cinnamon

1 tablespoon ground ginger

¾ teaspoon baking soda

½ teaspoon ground cloves

½ teaspoon salt

12 tablespoons unsalted butter, melted

¾ cup light molasses

2 tablespoons milk

Why This Recipe Works These gingerbread cookies are nothing like the stale versions you punch a hole in and trim the Christmas tree with. Our people, while still flat enough to decorate, are soft and chewy and brimming with ginger and molasses flavors, not overwhelmed by dusty spices. To put the chew in our gingerbread cookies, we needed more fat than most recipes use: 12 tablespoons of melted butter did the trick. For ease, we used a food processor to make our dough, mixing the dry ingredients first before adding the butter, molasses, and a little milk. After dozens of rolling tests, we learned that rolling the dough to a ¼-inch thickness was ideal for the soft and chewy texture we sought. We baked the cookies until they were just set around the edges and slightly puffed in the center. As they cooled, the slightly puffed cookies settled into sublime chewiness. Depending on your cookie cutter dimensions, all of the cookies may not fit on the sheets and a second round of baking may be required. We like to give our people personality by decorating them with our Decorating Icing (page 370).

1 Process flour, sugar, cinnamon, ginger, baking soda, cloves, and salt in food processor until combined, about 10 seconds. Add melted butter, molasses, and milk and process until soft dough forms and no streaks of flour remain, about 20 seconds, scraping down sides of bowl as needed.

2 Spray counter lightly with baking spray with flour, transfer dough to counter, and knead until dough forms cohesive ball, about 20 seconds. Divide dough in half. Form each half into 5-inch disk, wrap disks tightly in plastic wrap, and refrigerate for at least 1 hour or up to 24 hours.

3 Adjust oven racks to upper-middle and lower-middle positions and heat oven to 350 degrees. Line 2 rimmed baking sheets with parchment paper. Working with 1 disk of dough at a time, roll ¼ inch thick between 2 large sheets of parchment. (Keep second disk of dough refrigerated while rolling out first.) Remove top piece of parchment. Using 3½-inch cookie cutter, cut dough into shapes. Peel away scraps from around cookies and space shapes ¾ inch apart on prepared sheets. Repeat rolling and cutting steps with dough scraps.

4 Bake cookies until puffy and just set around edges, 9 to 11 minutes, switching and rotating sheets halfway through baking. Let cookies cool on sheets for 10 minutes, then transfer to wire rack. Let cookies cool completely before serving. (Cookies can be stored in wide, shallow airtight container, with sheet of parchment or waxed paper between each layer, at room temperature for up to 3 days.)

ALL ABOUT DECORATING COOKIES

The holidays are the perfect time to showcase your creativity by decorating cutout cookies using a variety of techniques and embellishments. We've outlined general tips and techniques here, but feel free to go your own way. Always let cookies cool completely before starting the decorating process.

EASY ALL-PURPOSE GLAZE
Makes about 1 cup

We decorate our Foolproof Holiday Cookies (page 367) with this easy-to-make glaze, but feel free to use it, dyed or not, on any flat cookie that could use a festive flourish. The cream cheese in the glaze gives it a slightly thicker consistency that's good for spreading, and it cuts the sweetness of the glaze with its tang.

2 cups (8 ounces) confectioners' sugar
3 tablespoons milk
1 ounce cream cheese, softened
Food coloring (optional)

Whisk all ingredients in bowl until smooth.

Citrus Glaze
Substitute lemon, lime, or orange juice for milk.

Coffee Glaze
Add 1¼ teaspoons instant espresso powder or instant coffee to glaze ingredients.

Nutty Glaze
Add ½ teaspoon almond or coconut extract to glaze ingredients.

DECORATING ICING
Makes 1⅓ cups

If you want to pipe buttons and faces with clearly defined lines on cookies such as our Soft and Chewy Gingerbread People (page 368) you'll need something thicker than a glaze, so we made a decorating icing. Whipping egg whites with sugar creates a stiffer frosting that's easy to apply and has a beautiful white gloss. This recipe makes bright white icing. For colored icing, stir 1 to 2 drops of food coloring into the icing to achieve the desired color before transferring it to a pastry bag.

2 large egg whites
2⅔ cups (10⅔ ounces) confectioners' sugar

1 Using stand mixer fitted with whisk attachment, whip egg whites and sugar on medium-low speed until combined, about 1 minute. Increase speed to medium-high and whip until glossy, soft peaks form, 2 to 3 minutes, scraping down bowl as needed.

2 Transfer icing to pastry bag fitted with small round pastry tip. Decorate cookies and let icing harden before serving.

PIPING ICING WITH CONFIDENCE

Decorating our Soft and Chewy Gingerbread People (page 368) is easy—and fun—once you know the basics. Simple designs are often the most successful; after all, this type of cookie gives you only a very small canvas to work with. And practice truly does help; if you repeat similar designs, your results will improve.

Do a Test Run
Once your icing is loaded into the pastry bag, grab the bag at the base and twist with one hand. Using your other hand as a guide, hold the tip at a 90-degree angle about ½ inch above the cookie and gently squeeze to decorate. Practice on parchment before you start decorating in earnest.

No Pastry Bag? No Problem.
A zipper-lock bag is a fine stand-in for a pastry bag. Load the bag with icing, pushing it to one corner of the bag. Make a very small snip in the corner—you can always make the cut larger if necessary.

Start with Cooled Cookies
Icing will liquefy and fail to set if it's piped onto warm cookies. Let the cookies cool completely on a wire rack.

You can do more than just spread our Easy All-Purpose Glaze (page 370) on cookies. Here are some decorating techniques for making your cookies the brightest on the holiday cookie table.

Get Organized

During the holidays you may find yourself making cookies several times over a period of several weeks. A muffin tin keeps sprinkles, colored sugars, and other decorations organized and reusable. Just cover the muffin tin with plastic wrap between uses.

Glaze From the Center Out

Spoon a small amount of glaze in the center of the cookie, then spread it into an even layer. Spreading the glaze outward from the center is the best way to ensure even coverage. Using the back of the spoon to spread the glaze will work, but you can also use a small offset spatula (see page 196), or, for the lightest touch, use a very small paintbrush. Be sure to let the glaze dry before storing or serving the cookies.

Add Embellishments

While the glaze is still soft, place decorations on the glaze and allow it to dry. Small confections, such as shiny silver or gold balls known as dragées, can be used to dress up cookies. Other small candies—gumdrops, mini chocolate morsels, jelly beans—can be used in a similar fashion. Add these candies immediately after applying the glaze. As the glaze dries, it will affix the candies in place.

Drag Two Glazes Together

Glaze the entire cookie and then pipe small drops of a second glaze in a pattern. Drag a toothpick through the glazes to create a design. As long as both glazes are still wet, you can create a range of designs, everything from hearts (shown here) to stars, wiggly lines, and swirls. This idea works best with glazes that are two very different hues.

Make Your Own Colored Sugar

Spread ½ cup granulated sugar into a pie plate. Mix 5 drops of food coloring into the sugar. Push the sugar through a fine-mesh strainer and spread the sugar back into the plate. The sugar should dry thoroughly before you use it; this might take several hours. Brush a little water on the cookies and then apply the sugar before baking.

Dip In Chocolate

Hold melted chocolate in a small bowl, which allows for a deeper pool of chocolate in which to dip the cookies. Gently dip part of the cookie in the chocolate to coat. Transfer the cookie to a wire rack set in a rimmed baking sheet and let it cool completely. Alternatively, use a brush or the back of a spoon to coat the cookie with chocolate.

LINZER SANDWICH COOKIES

Makes about 24 sandwich cookies

⅔ cup seedless raspberry jam

⅔ cup (2⅔ ounces) confectioners' sugar

½ cup hazelnuts, toasted and skinned

1 cup (5 ounces) all-purpose flour

¼ teaspoon salt

6 tablespoons unsalted butter, cut into ½-inch pieces and chilled

1 large egg yolk

1 tablespoon heavy cream

½ teaspoon vanilla extract

¼ teaspoon almond extract

Why This Recipe Works Linzer cookies are a Christmas cookie plate classic that are based on the classic Austrian torte of the same name, which consists of a buttery, nutty dough topped with jam or preserves and then covered with lattice strips of the same base dough. These cookies are very similar, yet the dough is thinner and thus more crisp. The top cookie sports a small cutout in the center, which exposes the jam filling. For a nut whose flavor would really stand out, we chose hazelnuts. We upped the nuttiness even more by also adding a hint of almond extract to the dough. While black currant jam is a traditional filling for Austrian Linzertorte, we liked the bright flavor of raspberry jam with the buttery hazelnut cookie. Chilled butter gave us dough that was easy to work with and resulted in tender yet crisp cookies that complemented the soft jam center. Using confectioners' sugar as the sole sweetener gave our cookies an extraordinarily tender texture and a fine crumb.

1 Simmer jam in small saucepan over medium heat, stirring frequently, until thickened and reduced to ½ cup, about 10 minutes; let cool completely, about 1 hour. Meanwhile, process sugar and hazelnuts in food processor until hazelnuts are finely ground, about 20 seconds. Add flour, salt, and butter and pulse until mixture resembles coarse meal, 15 to 20 pulses. Add egg yolk, cream, vanilla, and almond extract and process until dough forms ball, about 20 seconds. Transfer dough to counter. Form dough into disk, wrap disk tightly in plastic wrap, and refrigerate for 30 minutes.

2 Adjust oven racks to upper-middle and lower-middle positions and heat oven to 375 degrees. Line 2 baking sheets with parchment paper.

3 Roll dough ⅛ inch thick on counter. Using 2-inch fluted round cookie cutter, cut out rounds; space rounds ¾ inch apart on prepared sheets. Using smaller cutter, cut out centers of half of dough rounds. Gather and reroll scraps once. Bake until edges are lightly browned, 8 to 10 minutes, switching and rotating sheets halfway through baking. Let cookies cool on sheets for 5 minutes, then transfer to wire rack. Let cookies cool completely.

4 Spread bottom of each solid cookie with 1 teaspoon jam, then top with cutout cookie, pressing lightly to adhere. Let cookies set before serving, about 30 minutes.

Lemon Linzer Sandwich Cookies
Substitute ¾ cup sliced almonds, toasted, for hazelnuts. Omit raspberry jam and spread bottom of each solid cookie with ½ teaspoon lemon curd.

BLACK CHERRY AND CHOCOLATE LINZER COOKIES

Makes about 24 sandwich cookies

2⅓ cups (11⅔ ounces) all-purpose flour

1 teaspoon baking powder

½ teaspoon salt

½ teaspoon ground cinnamon

12 tablespoons unsalted butter, softened

1 cup (7 ounces) superfine sugar

2 large eggs

½ teaspoon almond extract

1 cup (6 ounces) bittersweet chocolate chips

1 cup black cherry preserves

Confectioners' sugar

Why This Recipe Works We love the simple, refined flavors of classic holiday Linzer cookies. However, we have a hard time keeping chocolate out of recipes where its flavor would be so complementary, so naturally we had to find a way to sneak it into a souped-up Linzer cookie. For this version, we were looking for a dough that was less rich than the traditional one to accommodate the extra depth from the chocolate, so we omitted the nuts for a more basic butter cookie dough. But we still wanted a subtle nutty flavor, so we kept the almond extract, which perfumed the dough with a lovely aroma. Once the bottom cookies had cooled, we spread them with melted bittersweet chocolate for a deep, dark contrast to the buttery cookie. We let the chocolate set and then topped it with the requisite jam. We replaced the raspberry jam with black cherry preserves, which have a unique, almost wine-y flavor that was a sophisticated match for the dark chocolate and a complementary pairing for the almond-scented dough. With a showering of confectioners' sugar, these small sandwich cookies are as impressive as any full-scale dessert.

1 Whisk flour, baking powder, salt, and cinnamon together in bowl. Using stand mixer fitted with paddle, beat butter and superfine sugar on medium-high speed until pale and fluffy, about 3 minutes. Add eggs, one at a time, and almond extract and beat until combined. Reduce speed to low and add flour mixture in 3 additions until just combined, scraping down bowl as needed. Transfer dough to counter and divide in half. Form each half into 5-inch disk, wrap disks tightly in plastic wrap, and refrigerate for 1 hour.

2 Adjust oven racks to upper-middle and lower-middle positions and heat oven to 375 degrees. Line 2 baking sheets with parchment paper.

3 Let chilled dough sit on counter for 10 minutes to soften. Roll 1 disk of dough into 13-inch circle, about ⅛ inch thick, on lightly floured counter. Using 2½-inch fluted round cookie cutter, cut out rounds. Gently reroll scraps once and cut into rounds. Space rounds ½ inch apart on prepared sheets. Bake until edges are lightly browned, about 7 minutes, switching and rotating sheets halfway through baking. Let cookies cool on sheets for 5 minutes, then transfer to wire rack.

4 Roll out second disk of dough. Using 1-inch cutter, cut out centers of dough circles. Space cookies ½ inch apart on prepared sheets. Bake until edges are lightly browned, about 7 minutes, switching and rotating sheets halfway through baking. Let cookies cool on sheets for 5 minutes, then transfer to wire rack. Let cookies cool completely.

5 Microwave chocolate chips in bowl at 50 percent power, stirring occasionally, until melted, 2 to 4 minutes. Spread bottom of each solid cookie with chocolate; let stand until chocolate is set, about 5 minutes. Spread 2 teaspoons preserves over chocolate on each cookie. Top with cutout cookies, pressing lightly to adhere. Dust with confectioners' sugar just before serving.

COCONUT SNOWMEN

Makes 16 cookies

⅓ cup (2⅓ ounces) granulated sugar

2 tablespoons packed light brown sugar

½ teaspoon salt

12 tablespoons unsalted butter,
cut into pieces and softened

1 large egg yolk

1½ teaspoons vanilla extract

1½ cups (7½ ounces) all-purpose flour

1 cup (3 ounces) sweetened
shredded coconut

1 cup (4 ounces) confectioners' sugar

4 teaspoons whole milk

Mini chocolate chips

Why This Recipe Works Rolling and cutting out cookies is part of the holiday routine, and while our Foolproof Holiday Cookies (page 367) are as workable as a rolled cookie can be, they still take a little time and patience. But there's no need to fuss with a fancy cookie cutter to achieve a cute, festive holiday snowman cookie. To create snowmen with ease, we formed a sturdy slice-and-bake dough into two logs (one small and one large) for the head and the body. A little brown sugar—just 2 tablespoons— gave the cookie base depth without making it taste like a brown sugar cookie. We didn't need to do much to attach the little man's head to his body; the cookies simply merge together when they spread in the oven. An easy confectioners' sugar glaze is the glue for a topping of sweetened shredded coconut that resembles snow. Mini chocolate chips are perfect for our Frostys' eyes and buttons. Be sure to sprinkle the coconut onto the glaze and adhere the chocolate chips while the glaze is still wet or they won't stick.

1 Process granulated sugar, brown sugar, and salt in food processor until no lumps remain, about 30 seconds. Add butter, egg yolk, and vanilla and process until smooth and creamy, about 20 seconds. Scrape down sides of bowl, add flour, and pulse until dough forms, 10 to 15 pulses. Transfer dough to counter and divide into 2 pieces, one twice as large as other. Roll small piece of dough into 4-inch log and wrap tightly in plastic wrap. Roll remaining dough into thicker 4-inch log and wrap tightly in plastic. Refrigerate logs until firm, at least 2 hours or up to 3 days.

2 Adjust oven racks to upper-middle and lower-middle positions and heat oven to 350 degrees. Line 2 baking sheets with parchment paper. Slice each log into ¼-inch-thick rounds. Place 1 large round and 1 small round with edges touching on prepared sheets. Repeat with remaining rounds, spacing them 1½ inches apart on sheets. Bake until edges are just golden, 17 to 20 minutes, switching and rotating sheets halfway through baking. Let cookies cool on sheets for 10 minutes, then transfer to wire rack and let cool completely.

3 Process coconut in food processor until finely chopped, about 10 seconds; transfer to bowl. Whisk confectioners' sugar and milk in separate bowl until smooth. Working with 1 cookie at a time, spread 1 teaspoon glaze evenly onto cookie, then sprinkle with coconut. Decorate with chocolate chips. Let glaze dry for at least 30 minutes before serving.

Assembling the Snowmen

1 Slice each chilled log into ¼-inch-thick rounds.

2 Arrange 1 large round and 1 small round on baking sheet so edges of both rounds are touching.

PEPPERMINT CANDY CANES

Makes about 72 cookies

2¼ cups (11¼ ounces) all-purpose flour

½ teaspoon salt

16 tablespoons unsalted butter, softened

¾ cup (5¼ ounces) granulated sugar, plus ½ cup for rolling

½ cup (2 ounces) confectioners' sugar

2 large egg yolks

2 teaspoons peppermint extract

1 teaspoon vanilla extract

12 drops red food coloring

Why This Recipe Works Red-and-white-striped candy canes are probably the most iconic sweet of the holiday season, but on their own they aren't all that interesting. We wanted to take the candy cane concept—the big peppermint flavor, the hooked shape, and the bold stripes—and reimagine it in cookie form. Two teaspoons of peppermint extract ably flavored basic butter cookies with a smooth, cool peppermint flavor. To achieve decorative stripes, we made one dough, divided it in half, and mixed red food coloring into one half. Then we rolled the portions of different colored dough into squares and stacked them before cutting them into strips. Twisting the two-toned dough strips and forming them into a cane shape gave them the classic pattern. If the dough becomes too soft to twist, simply return it to the refrigerator to firm up. You can substitute sanding sugar for the granulated sugar used to decorate the exterior of the cookies, if desired, for a super sparkly finish.

1 Whisk flour and salt together in bowl. Using stand mixer fitted with paddle, beat butter, ¾ cup granulated sugar, and confectioners' sugar on medium-high speed until pale and fluffy, 3 to 6 minutes. Add egg yolks, peppermint extract, and vanilla and beat until well incorporated. Reduce speed to low, slowly add flour mixture, and mix until combined. Set aside half of dough; add food coloring to remaining dough and mix until fully incorporated. Shape each half into 5-inch square, wrap tightly in plastic wrap, and refrigerate until firm, about 2 hours.

2 Adjust oven racks to upper-middle and lower-middle positions and heat oven to 325 degrees. Line 2 baking sheets with parchment paper. Spread remaining ½ cup granulated sugar in shallow dish.

3 Roll each dough square into 9-inch square on piece of parchment. Flip 1 dough square on top of other dough square and gently roll to adhere. Cut square in half and refrigerate until firm, about 15 minutes. Cut 1 half into 4½ by ¼-inch strips. Gently twist each strip into spiral, rolling to smooth out edges. Roll in granulated sugar, shape into candy canes, and space 1 inch apart on prepared sheets. Bake until edges are light brown, 13 to 15 minutes, switching and rotating sheets halfway through baking. Let cookies cool on sheets for 5 minutes, then transfer to wire rack. Repeat with remaining dough. Let cookies cool completely before serving.

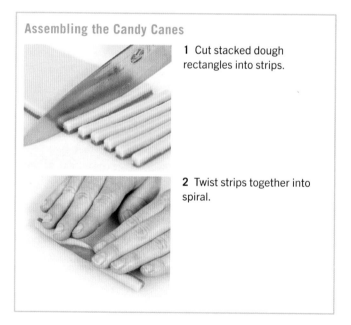

Assembling the Candy Canes

1 Cut stacked dough rectangles into strips.

2 Twist strips together into spiral.

ALMOND-SPICE CHRISTMAS WREATHS

Makes 40 cookies

Cookies

4 cups (18 ounces) almond flour

2 tablespoons grated orange zest (2 oranges)

1 tablespoon ground coffee

1 teaspoon ground cinnamon

1 teaspoon ground ginger

½ teaspoon ground cardamom

¼ teaspoon salt

3 large egg whites

1½ cups (10½ ounces) granulated sugar

2 teaspoons almond extract

1 teaspoon vanilla extract

3 tablespoons orange marmalade

Topping

2 large egg whites

2 cups sliced almonds

40 maraschino cherries (combination of red and green), quartered

Confectioners' sugar

Why This Recipe Works We love to mold butter cookie and gingerbread doughs into fun holiday shapes and decorate them at Christmastime. But we wanted a festive-looking cookie that was a little different—a different dough, a different texture, a different flavor. After some consideration, we had the idea of turning a light, flourless, nut-based cookie into a wreath-shaped Christmas treat. We made a chewy almond macaroon–like dough that, once chilled, was firm and malleable enough to form into ropes and shape into wreaths. For a unique flavor of the holidays, we added orange zest, ground coffee, and spices to the dough; we also folded in some marmalade at the end of mixing. After shaping the dough, we topped our wreaths with sliced almonds, dipping them in egg whites first so the almonds adhered. For holly-like accents, we pressed pieces of red and green maraschino cherries on top. Dusting the cookies with confectioners' sugar before serving gave them a fresh coat of winter snow. You can substitute dried cherries for the maraschino cherries.

1 For the cookies Whisk almond flour, orange zest, coffee, cinnamon, ginger, cardamom, and salt together in bowl. Using stand mixer fitted with whisk attachment, whip egg whites on medium-low speed until foamy, about 1 minute. Increase speed to medium-high and whip whites to soft, billowy mounds, about 1 minute. Gradually add sugar and whip until glossy, soft peaks form, 2 to 3 minutes. Whip in almond extract and vanilla.

2 Fold almond flour mixture into whipped whites in 2 additions until few white streaks remain. Fold in marmalade until no white streaks remain. Transfer dough to counter and divide in half. Form each half into disk, wrap disks tightly in plastic wrap, and refrigerate until firm, at least 1 hour or up to 24 hours.

3 For the topping Adjust oven racks to upper-middle and lower-middle positions and heat oven to 300 degrees. Line 2 baking sheets with parchment paper. Whisk egg whites in shallow dish until frothy. Spread almonds in second shallow dish.

4 Divide 1 disk of dough into 20 pieces. Roll each piece into 5-inch rope on lightly floured counter, shape into circle, and press ends together to seal. Dip 1 side of each wreath into egg whites, letting excess drip off, then press gently into almonds. Space, almond side up, evenly on prepared sheets. Press 4 cherry pieces into each wreath.

5 Bake cookies until firm and golden brown, 20 to 25 minutes, switching and rotating sheets halfway through baking. Let cookies cool on sheets for 5 minutes, then transfer to wire rack. Repeat with remaining dough, egg whites, almonds, and cherries. Let cookies cool completely, then dust with confectioners' sugar before serving.

STAINED GLASS COOKIES

Makes about 36 cookies

2½ cups (12½ ounces) all-purpose flour

¾ cup (5¼ ounces) superfine sugar

¼ teaspoon salt

16 tablespoons unsalted butter, cut into 16 pieces and softened

1 ounce cream cheese, softened

2 teaspoons vanilla extract

20 hard candies, assorted colors, separated by color and crushed fine

Why This Recipe Works These striking cookies are colorful and impressive, and yet they're actually quite easy to make. We started with the dough from our Foolproof Holiday Cookies (page 367), a workhorse dough that is perfect here because it bakes up with the structure we needed for the "window frames." We started by cutting out the larger shape and then using a smaller cutter in a matching shape to hollow out the cookies' interior to make way for the stained glass. The colorful glass seems to come together through magic, but all it takes is filling the empty spaces with crushed colorful hard candies, such as Jolly Ranchers. When we added the candy crumbs at the outset, they melted and bubbled up over the edges of the cookies. For a neater cookie with distinct components, we added the candy halfway through baking. Once cooled, the candy resolidified into a smooth pane of glass. The candy melts most evenly when crushed to the consistency of sand.

1 Using stand mixer fitted with paddle, mix flour, sugar, and salt on low speed until combined. Add butter, 1 piece at a time, and mix until dough looks crumbly and slightly wet, 1 to 2 minutes. Add cream cheese and vanilla and beat until dough just begins to form large clumps, about 30 seconds.

2 Transfer dough to counter; knead just until it forms cohesive mass and divide in half. Form each half into disk, wrap disks tightly in plastic wrap, and refrigerate for at least 30 minutes or up to 2 days. (Wrapped dough can be frozen for up to 2 weeks. Let dough thaw completely in refrigerator before rolling.)

3 Adjust oven rack to middle position and heat oven to 375 degrees. Line 2 baking sheets with parchment paper. Working with 1 disk of dough at a time, roll dough ⅛ inch thick between 2 large sheets of parchment paper ⅛ inch thick. Slide dough, still between parchment, onto baking sheet and refrigerate until firm, about 10 minutes.

4 Working with 1 sheet of dough at a time, remove top piece of parchment. Using 2½-inch cookie cutter, cut out shapes; space shapes 2 inches apart on prepared sheets. Using smaller cutter, cut out centers of dough shapes. Gently reroll scraps, cut into shapes, cut out centers, and transfer to prepared sheets.

5 Bake cookies, 1 sheet at a time, for 5 minutes. Fill centers with crushed candies, rotate sheet, and bake until edges are light golden brown and candies have melted, 4 to 5 minutes. Let cookies cool on sheets for 10 minutes, then transfer to wire rack and let cool completely before serving.

Crushing Hard Candies

1 Divide candies by color and place them in separate zipper-lock bags (make sure to seal bags).

2 Using rolling pin, meat mallet, or other heavy object, crush candies to consistency of sand.

EGGNOG SNICKERDOODLES

Makes about 48 cookies

2½ cups (12½ ounces) all-purpose flour

2 teaspoons cream of tartar

1 teaspoon baking soda

¼ teaspoon salt

16 tablespoons unsalted butter, softened

1½ cups (10½ ounces) granulated sugar

2 large eggs

1½ teaspoons rum extract

½ cup confectioners' sugar

½ teaspoon ground nutmeg

Why This Recipe Works Traditional snickerdoodles (for our recipe, see page 53) are delicious. The acidic cream of tartar in the dough gives the cookies a characteristic tang that offsets their cinnamon sugar sweetness; it also reacts with baking soda to make the cookies rise and then collapse during baking, giving them their crinkly appearance. We thought this classic cookie was open to reinterpretation, so we decided to make snickerdoodles infused with the flavor of everyone's favorite holiday beverage: eggnog. Simply adding eggnog to the dough threw off the ratio of wet to dry ingredients, making the cookies spread too much and become cakey; not to mention, the flavor of the 'nog was not at all detectable in the finished cookie. Instead, we took the flavors that make eggnog what it is and isolated them, adding a shot of rum extract (straight rum didn't carry a strong enough flavor) to the dough and substituting nutmeg for the customary cinnamon. We highly recommend enjoying these cookies alongside a chilled glass of eggnog. You can substitute rum for the rum extract, but the flavor won't be as pronounced.

1 Adjust oven racks to upper-middle and lower-middle positions and heat oven to 400 degrees. Line 2 baking sheets with parchment paper. Whisk flour, cream of tartar, baking soda, and salt together in bowl.

2 Using stand mixer fitted with paddle, beat butter and granulated sugar on medium-high speed until fluffy, 3 to 6 minutes. Add eggs, one at a time, and rum extract and beat until incorporated. Reduce speed to low, slowly add flour mixture, and mix until just combined.

3 Working with 1 tablespoon dough at a time, roll into balls and space them 2 inches apart on prepared sheets. Using bottom of greased dry measuring cup, press each ball to even ½-inch thickness.

4 Bake cookies until edges are lightly browned, 8 to 10 minutes, switching and rotating sheets halfway through baking. Let cookies cool on sheets for 5 minutes, then transfer to wire rack. Repeat with remaining dough. Let cookies cool completely.

5 Whisk confectioners' sugar and nutmeg together in small bowl. Dust cookies with confectioners' sugar mixture before serving.

MERINGUE CHRISTMAS TREES

Makes about 50 cookies

¾ cup (5¼ ounces) granulated sugar

2 teaspoons cornstarch

4 large egg whites

¾ teaspoon vanilla extract

8–10 drops green food coloring

⅛ teaspoon salt

Sugar stars

Multicolored nonpareils

62 Hershey's Kisses, unwrapped

Confectioners' sugar

Why This Recipe Works This standout holiday cookie pairs crisp, sweet meringue with milk chocolate kisses and an assortment of colorful, festive decorations for a showstopping treat that resembles a miniature trimmed Christmas tree. We whipped egg whites to stiff peaks, as we would for standard meringues, and then incorporated green food coloring before piping the glossy mixture onto baking sheets using a pastry bag fitted with a star tip. On top of that star we piped two smaller stars for an easy and foolproof way to shape the trees—no advanced piping degrees required. To trim the tree with colorful "lights" and "ornaments," we chose multicolor nonpareils and yellow sugar stars, but you can decorate however you like. To finish, we cut a small hole in the bottom of each tree and snuggly affixed a Hershey's Kiss (with the help of some melted chocolate) to serve as the trunk of our tree, so these cookies stand tall. You'll need a 12-ounce bag of Hershey's Kisses for this recipe (you'll have a few left over). If baking on a humid day, let the meringues cool in a turned-off oven for an additional hour without opening the door and then immediately seal them in an airtight container. We used 9 drops of food coloring; for a lighter or darker green, use 8 or 10 drops.

1 Adjust oven racks to upper-middle and lower-middle positions and heat oven to 225 degrees. Line 2 baking sheets with parchment paper. Combine granulated sugar and cornstarch in small bowl. Using stand mixer fitted with whisk attachment, whip egg whites, vanilla, food coloring, and salt on medium-low speed until foamy, about 1 minute. Increase speed to medium-high and whip whites to soft, billowy mounds, about 1 minute. Gradually add sugar mixture and whip until glossy, stiff peaks form, 2 to 3 minutes.

2 Working quickly, fill pastry bag fitted with ¼- to ⅝-inch star tip with meringue. Pipe 1-inch-wide stars, spaced 1 inch apart, on prepared sheets. Top each star with another smaller star; then pipe even smaller star on top (trees should be 1½ inches tall). Place sugar star on top of each tree and sprinkle nonpareils around sides.

3 Bake meringues for 1 hour, switching and rotating sheets halfway through baking. Turn off oven and let meringues cool in oven for at least 1 hour. Transfer sheets to wire rack and let meringues cool completely.

4 Microwave 12 candies at 50 percent power until melted, 1 to 2 minutes. Using paring knife, gently cut small hole in bottom of each tree. Press tips of remaining candies into melted chocolate and then snugly into each hole. Dust trees with confectioners' sugar before serving.

PFEFFERNÜSSE

Makes about 120 cookies

4 tablespoons unsalted butter

¾ teaspoon ground cardamom

½ teaspoon ground cinnamon

½ teaspoon ground allspice

¼ teaspoon pepper

⅓ cup molasses

¼ cup packed (1¾ ounces) light brown sugar

2 cups (10 ounces) all-purpose flour

¼ cup blanched, slivered almonds

¼ cup candied orange peel

½ teaspoon baking soda

½ teaspoon salt

1 large egg

½ cup confectioners' sugar, sifted

Why This Recipe Works Pfeffernüsse (also known as peppernuts) are a popular traditional Christmas cookie with different iterations found throughout Germany, The Netherlands, and Denmark. They're spicy, bite-size cookies that soften and develop flavor as they age. But we're no good at waiting when it comes to cookies; we wanted to tenderize this traditionally very lean dough by incorporating a little butter so that we could enjoy Pfeffernüsse when we made them. Despite their name, peppernuts don't call for nuts, but we found that adding a small amount of ground almonds helped tenderize the dough further without adding too much richness. Blooming the spices in the hot butter boosted both their flavor and their heat, making the cookies live up to their peppernut name. Candied orange peel perfumed the cookies, and its tang complemented the spices. Instead of the more traditional—and time-consuming—method of rolling each individual cookie into small balls, we rolled the dough into logs and cut them into pieces before baking and tossing in confectioners' sugar.

1 Adjust oven racks to upper-middle and lower-middle positions and heat oven to 350 degrees. Line 2 baking sheets with parchment paper. Melt butter in small skillet over medium-low heat. Add cardamom, cinnamon, allspice, and pepper and cook for 15 seconds, stirring constantly; transfer to bowl and whisk in molasses and brown sugar to combine. Let butter mixture cool completely.

2 Process flour, almonds, orange peel, baking soda, and salt in food processor until finely ground, about 1 minute. Whisk egg into cooled butter mixture to combine. Stir in flour mixture until just incorporated. Transfer dough to counter. Form dough into disk, wrap disk tightly in plastic wrap, and refrigerate until firm, about 2 hours.

3 Divide dough into 10 equal pieces. Roll each piece into ½-inch-thick rope. Using bench scraper or sharp knife, cut ropes into 1-inch lengths and space them 1 inch apart on prepared sheets. Bake until just set and edges are lightly browned, 10 minutes, switching and rotating sheets halfway through baking. Let cookies cool on sheets for 5 minutes, then slide parchment onto wire rack and let cool completely. Toss in confectioners' sugar to coat before serving.

Cutting and Coating the Cookies

1 Divide dough into 10 equal pieces and roll each piece into ½-inch-thick log. Use a knife or bench scraper to cut each log into 1-inch pieces.

2 Place confectioners' sugar in large zipper-lock bag, add the cooled cookies, and toss to coat.

PEPPERMINT MOCHA COOKIES

Makes 30 cookies

Cookies

1¾ cups (8¾ ounces) all-purpose flour

½ cup (1½ ounces) unsweetened cocoa powder

½ teaspoon baking soda

½ teaspoon salt

8 tablespoons unsalted butter, softened

¾ cup (5¼ ounces) granulated sugar

½ cup brewed espresso or strong coffee, cooled

1 teaspoon vanilla extract

Frosting

6 tablespoons unsalted butter, softened

2 cups (8 ounces) confectioners' sugar

2 tablespoons milk

½ teaspoon peppermint extract

1–2 drops red food coloring

15 peppermint candies, crushed

Why This Recipe Works In addition to holiday music in department stores and colored lights adorning houses everywhere, there's one more sign of the season that always causes a lot of excitement: The arrival of elaborate peppermint drinks at coffee shops. Peppermint mochas are popular for a reason—the minty addition of the season's iconic candy to your daily pick-me-up elevates it to full holiday status. To enjoy these flavors in another Christmastime favorite—cookies—we paired a rich mocha-flavored cookie with a peppermint frosting. But rather than adding a mere sprinkling of espresso powder to our chocolate cookies, we incorporated a whole half cup of brewed espresso. This gave the cookies a real jolt while also providing moisture to the rich, cakey cookies. We topped off these cookies in equally bold fashion, amping up a simple butter-and-sugar frosting with peppermint extract and adding a red food coloring. We could have stopped there but couldn't resist finishing these cookies with one last bit of festive flair: crushed peppermints. Once the cookies are frosted, sprinkle them immediately with the crushed peppermint candies; if you let the frosting dry, the candy won't stick. Once frosted, the cookies are best served within 1 day.

1 For the cookies Adjust oven racks to upper-middle and lower-middle positions and heat oven to 350 degrees. Line 2 baking sheets with parchment paper.

2 Sift flour, cocoa, baking soda, and salt together into bowl. Using stand mixer fitted with paddle, beat butter and sugar on medium speed until pale and fluffy, about 3 minutes. Scrape down bowl. Add cooled espresso and vanilla and beat at medium-low speed until combined. Scrape down bowl. With mixer running on low speed, gradually add dry ingredients and mix until just combined.

3 Roll dough into 1-inch balls and space them 2 inches apart on prepared sheets. Bake cookies until just set, 8 to 9 minutes, switching and rotating sheets halfway through baking. Let cookies cool on sheets for 2 minutes, then transfer to wire rack and let cool completely. (Cookies can be stored at room temperature for up to 4 days.)

4 For the frosting Using stand mixer fitted with paddle, beat butter on medium-high speed until smooth, about 20 seconds. Add sugar and beat on medium-low speed until most of sugar is moistened, about 45 seconds. Scrape down bowl and beat on medium speed until mixture is fully combined, about 15 seconds. Scrape down bowl. Add milk, peppermint extract, and food coloring and beat at medium speed until incorporated, about 10 seconds; increase speed to medium-high and beat until fluffy, about 4 minutes, scraping down bowl once or twice. Frost cookies and immediately sprinkle each with crushed peppermint candies before serving.

LEBKUCHEN BARS

Makes 24 bars

4 tablespoons unsalted butter

4 tablespoons vegetable shortening

3 cups (15 ounces) all-purpose flour

1 tablespoon ground cinnamon

1 teaspoon baking soda

1 teaspoon ground cardamom

¾ teaspoon ground ginger

½ teaspoon salt

1 cup (7 ounces) granulated sugar

1 cup molasses

2 large eggs

1 teaspoon grated lemon zest
plus 1 tablespoon juice

1½ cups (6 ounces) confectioners' sugar

3 tablespoons whole milk

Why This Recipe Works The German spice cookie *lebkuchen* is a holiday favorite that's similar to a gingerbread cookie. We wanted to take the flavor profile of traditional Lebkuchen and turn the cookie into a thick, soft bar, one that would be warmly spiced and defined by the hearty flavor and chew that molasses provides; in other words, we wanted gingerbread squared. A combination of butter and shortening gave us the right balance of rich flavor (from the butter) and cakey chew (from the shortening). Generous spice, most notably from a whopping tablespoon of cinnamon, gave the dough a serious kick while some lemon zest served to brighten the warm spice flavor. Many versions of Lebkuchen are iced, and we thought the flat bar shape of these cookies was the perfect format for showcasing a light glaze. Adding some lemon juice to the glaze gave it a pleasant tang. To test for doneness, make sure that the edges of the bars are set and the top is covered with many tiny cracks.

1 Adjust oven rack to lower-middle position and heat oven to 325 degrees. Make foil sling for 13 by 9-inch baking pan by folding 2 long sheets of aluminum foil; first sheet should be 13 inches wide and second sheet should be 9 inches wide. Lay sheets of foil in pan perpendicular to each other, with extra foil hanging over edges of pan. Push foil into corners and up sides of pan, smoothing foil flush to pan. Grease foil.

2 Microwave butter and shortening in bowl until melted, about 2 minutes; let cool slightly. Whisk flour, cinnamon, baking soda, cardamom, ginger, and salt together in second bowl. Whisk granulated sugar, molasses, eggs, and lemon zest together in large bowl, then whisk in cooled butter mixture until combined. Stir in flour mixture until just combined.

3 Transfer batter to prepared pan and spread into even layer. Bake until toothpick inserted in center comes out clean, 40 to 45 minutes, rotating pan halfway through baking. Let bars cool in pan on wire rack for 2 hours. Using foil overhang, lift bars from pan. Cut into 24 pieces and transfer to wire rack set in rimmed baking sheet.

4 Whisk confectioners' sugar, milk, and lemon juice in bowl until smooth. Spread glaze evenly over bars. Let glaze dry for at least 30 minutes before serving.

CRANBERRY SWIRL SHORTBREAD

Makes 16 wedges

4 ounces (1 cup) fresh or frozen cranberries

½ cup (3½ ounces) granulated sugar

½ teaspoon grated orange zest plus 2 tablespoons juice

¼ teaspoon ground cinnamon

2 cups (10 ounces) all-purpose flour

½ cup (2 ounces) confectioners' sugar

½ teaspoon salt

14 tablespoons unsalted butter, cut into ½-inch pieces and chilled

Why This Recipe Works While we love classic old-fashioned shortbread, its simple flavor provides the perfect base for endless variations. For a festive, colorful spin on the traditional cookie, we wanted to add a swirl of cranberries; not only pleasing to the eye, a bright red spiral of pureed cranberries added a welcome tartness to the rich, buttery shortbread. We cooked the cranberries with orange and cinnamon to create another layer of flavor and then pureed them for a smooth texture and a filling that was easy to spread and pipe. In addition to spiraling the puree on top of the dough, we sandwiched a layer in the middle of the shortbread; this allowed us to incorporate more flavorful puree without weighing down the top and making it soggy. We baked the thick shortbread sandwich in two stages to get a really crisp bottom without drying out the cranberry swirl on top.

1 Bring cranberries, ¼ cup granulated sugar, orange zest and juice, and cinnamon to boil in medium saucepan over medium-high heat. Cook, stirring frequently, until cranberries have burst and juice has just started to thicken, 2 to 4 minutes; let cool for 1 hour.

2 Adjust oven rack to middle position and heat oven to 375 degrees. Process flour, confectioners' sugar, salt, and remaining ¼ cup granulated sugar in food processor until combined, about 5 seconds. Scatter butter over top and process until dough starts to come together, about 1 minute. Gently knead dough by hand until no floury bits remain. Divide dough in half and roll each half into 9-inch circle on parchment paper; refrigerate dough for 20 minutes. Process cooled cranberry mixture in now-empty food processor until smooth, about 20 seconds.

3 Press 1 dough circle into 9-inch tart pan with removable bottom and poke all over with fork. Bake on baking sheet until edges are light golden brown, 15 to 17 minutes, rotating tart pan halfway through baking. Spread dough with ¼ cup cranberry puree, top with second dough circle, and poke all over with fork. Fill zipper-lock bag with remaining cranberry puree. Snip corner off bag and pipe remaining cranberry puree over dough in spiral shape. Score dough into 16 wedges. Between score marks, lightly run knife in opposite direction.

4 Bake shortbread until top is pale golden, 25 to 30 minutes, rotating tart pan halfway through baking. Let shortbread cool for 10 minutes, then remove outer ring of tart pan. Cut through score marks, transfer wedges to wire rack, and let cool completely before serving.

Creating Swirls

1 After filling and topping parbaked shortbread base, fill zipper-lock bag with remaining cranberry puree, snip corner off bag, and pipe puree over dough in spiral shape.

2 Using paring knife, score dough into 16 wedges. Between score marks, lightly run knife in opposite direction.

NOCHE BUENA CHOCOLATE SANDWICH COOKIES

Makes about 20 cookies

⅓ cup blanched almonds

1½ cups (7½ ounces) all-purpose flour

¼ cup (¾ ounce) Dutch-processed cocoa powder

½ teaspoon salt

¼ teaspoon cayenne pepper

4 ounces bittersweet chocolate, melted and cooled

12 tablespoons unsalted butter, softened

⅔ cup (4⅔ ounces) sugar

2 large egg yolks

2 tablespoons coffee liqueur

1 teaspoon vanilla extract

¼ cup dulce de leche

Why This Recipe Works These Christmas Eve treats are often the first to disappear from our holiday cookie tray. While we love the soft chocolate cookie component, the real star of these sandwich-style cookies is the dulce de leche filling. We wanted a sweet caramel filling that would offer up a gooey surprise when sandwiched between layers of rich, dark cookies; it should complement, not overwhelm, the chocolate. A bit of cayenne pepper contributed a spicy punch to our cookie dough, and a shot of coffee liqueur added deep, complex flavor that highlighted the chocolate, for a truly unique holiday treat. A sprinkling of ground almonds provided textural contrast and further enhanced the flavor of our cookies to complete the festive package. Use either Kahlua or Tia Maria for the coffee liqueur.

1 Adjust oven racks to upper-middle and lower-middle positions and heat oven to 350 degrees. Line 2 baking sheets with parchment paper. Process almonds in food processor until finely ground, about 30 seconds. Combine flour, cocoa, salt, and cayenne in bowl.

2 Microwave chocolate in bowl at 50 percent power, stirring occasionally, until melted, 2 to 4 minutes. Using stand mixer fitted with paddle, beat butter and sugar on medium-high speed until pale and fluffy, about 2 minutes. Add melted chocolate, egg yolks, liqueur, and vanilla and beat until incorporated. Reduce speed to low, add flour mixture in 3 additions, and mix until just combined, scraping down bowl as needed.

3 Working with 2 teaspoons dough at a time, roll into balls and space them 1 inch apart on prepared sheets. Sprinkle ground almonds on top, pressing lightly to adhere. Bake cookies until edges appear dry, 8 to 10 minutes, switching and rotating sheets halfway through baking. Let cookies cool on sheets for 5 minutes, then transfer to wire rack and let cool completely.

4 Spread ½ teaspoon dulce de leche over bottom of half of cookies, then top with remaining cookies, pressing gently to adhere. Serve.

10

YOU'LL NEVER KNOW THEY'RE

GLUTEN-FREE

GLUTEN-FREE CHOCOLATE CHIP COOKIES

Makes about 24 cookies

8 ounces (1¾ cups) ATK All-Purpose Gluten-Free Flour Blend (page 410)

1 teaspoon baking soda

¾ teaspoon xanthan gum (see page 411)

½ teaspoon salt

8 tablespoons unsalted butter, melted

5¼ ounces (¾ cup packed) light brown sugar

2⅓ ounces (⅓ cup) granulated sugar

1 large egg

2 tablespoons milk

1 tablespoon vanilla extract

7½ ounces (1¼ cups) semisweet chocolate chips

Why This Recipe Works The chocolate chip cookie is an iconic dessert, so we knew making a gluten-free version that lived up to expectations would be a challenge. We started our testing by swapping in our homemade flour blend (for more information on the ATK All-Purpose Gluten-Free Flour Blend, see page 410) for the all-purpose flour in a standard Toll House recipe. These cookies were flat, sandy, and greasy. Gluten-free flours can't absorb as much fat as all-purpose flour can, so cutting back on the butter minimized greasiness. Adding some xanthan gum, which makes the protein networks in baked goods more elastic, also helped alleviate the spread issue. (For more information on xanthan gum, see page 411.) Mitigating the sandiness required a two-step approach. The starches in our blend needed more liquid as well as more time to hydrate and soften, so we added a couple tablespoons of milk and let the dough rest for 30 minutes. Finally, we had a chocolate chip cookie that could rival the best traditional ones. Not all brands of chocolate chips are processed in a gluten-free facility, so read labels carefully. Do not shortchange the dough's 30-minute rest or the cookies will spread too much and taste gritty.

1 Whisk flour blend, baking soda, xanthan gum, and salt together in medium bowl. Whisk melted butter, brown sugar, and granulated sugar in large bowl until well combined and smooth. Whisk in egg, milk, and vanilla until smooth. Stir in flour mixture with rubber spatula until soft, homogeneous dough forms. Fold in chocolate chips. Cover bowl with plastic wrap and let dough rest for 30 minutes. (Dough will be sticky and soft.)

2 Adjust oven rack to middle position and heat oven to 350 degrees. Line 2 baking sheets with parchment paper. Working with about 1½ tablespoons dough at a time, use 2 soupspoons to portion dough and space 2 inches apart on prepared sheets.

3 Bake cookies, 1 sheet at a time, until golden brown and edges have begun to set but centers are still soft, 11 to 13 minutes, rotating sheet halfway through baking. Let cookies cool on sheet for 5 minutes, then transfer to wire rack. Serve warm or at room temperature.

If Using a Store-Bought Flour Blend

We strongly recommend you use our ATK All-Purpose Gluten-Free Flour Blend (page 410) in our recipes and that you weigh your flour. However, we've provided the weight-to-volume equivalents for brands that make acceptable substitutes.

King Arthur Gluten-Free All-Purpose Flour	8 ounces = ¾ cup plus ⅔ cup
Betty Crocker All-Purpose Gluten Free Rice Flour Blend	8 ounces = 1½ cups plus 2 tablespoons
Bob's Red Mill Gluten-Free All-Purpose Baking Flour	8 ounces = 1½ cups plus 2 tablespoons

GLUTEN-FREE OATMEAL-RAISIN COOKIES

Makes about 24 cookies

9 ounces (3 cups) gluten-free old-fashioned rolled oats (see page 410)

½ cup warm tap water

4 ounces (¾ cup plus 2 tablespoons) almond flour

3 ounces (⅔ cup) ATK All-Purpose Gluten-Free Flour Blend (page 410)

½ teaspoon salt

½ teaspoon gluten-free baking powder (see page 410)

¼ teaspoon xanthan gum (see page 411)

⅛ teaspoon ground nutmeg

8 tablespoons unsalted butter, melted and cooled

7 ounces (1 cup packed) brown sugar

3½ ounces (½ cup) granulated sugar

1 large egg, plus 1 large yolk

2 tablespoons vegetable oil

1 teaspoon vanilla extract

1 cup raisins

Why This Recipe Works You might think creating a gluten-free oatmeal-raisin cookie would be fairly easy—after all, oats are gluten-free. (For information on why some oats aren't technically gluten-free, see page 410.) But oatmeal cookies also require a good amount of flour. When we used our gluten-free flour blend, we ended up with hockey pucks; between the oats and all the starches in the flour blend, the moisture in our dough was getting completely absorbed. We tried the simplest solution first—adding water to the dough—but this resulted in cookies that were thin and tough. Thinking of ways to add moisture without encouraging too much spread, we combined a portion of the oats (toasted first to enhance their flavor) with a small amount of water. Within 10 minutes, the oats had soaked up the liquid and softened. These soaked-oat cookies set up well and were more tender, but now we had a new problem: The cookies were cakey. Substituting high-protein almond flour for a portion of our flour blend gave our cookies richness, heft, and chew without any noticeable nut flavor. After portioning the dough onto the baking sheet, be sure to flatten the dough balls to ensure the oats spread out evenly. Do not use quick oats in this recipe. Do not shortchange the dough's 30-minute rest or the cookies will spread too much and taste gritty.

1 Adjust oven rack to middle position and heat oven to 375 degrees. Spread oats evenly on rimmed baking sheet and bake until fragrant and lightly browned, about 10 minutes, stirring halfway through baking. Transfer sheet to wire rack and let oats cool completely. Transfer half of cooled oats to bowl and stir in water. Cover bowl with plastic wrap and let sit until water is absorbed, about 10 minutes.

2 Whisk almond flour, flour blend, salt, baking powder, xanthan gum, and nutmeg together in medium bowl. Whisk melted butter, brown sugar, granulated sugar, egg and yolk, oil, and vanilla in large bowl until well combined and smooth. Stir in flour mixture, oat-water mixture, and remaining toasted oats using rubber spatula until soft, homogeneous dough forms. Fold in raisins. Cover bowl with plastic and let dough rest for 30 minutes.

3 Heat oven to 325 degrees. Line 2 baking sheets with parchment paper. Working with 2 generous tablespoons dough at a time, roll into balls and space them 2 inches apart on prepared sheets. Using bottom of greased measuring cup, press dough to ½-inch thickness.

4 Bake cookies, 1 sheet at a time, until edges are set and beginning to brown but centers are still soft and puffy, 22 to 25 minutes, rotating sheet halfway through baking. Let cookies cool on sheet for 5 minutes, then transfer to wire rack. Serve warm or at room temperature.

If Using a Store-Bought Flour Blend

We strongly recommend you use our ATK All-Purpose Gluten-Free Flour Blend (page 410) in our recipes and that you weigh your flour. However, we've provided the weight-to-volume equivalents for brands that make acceptable substitutes.

King Arthur Gluten-Free All-Purpose Flour	3 ounces = ⅓ cup plus ¼ cup
Betty Crocker All-Purpose Gluten Free Rice Flour Blend	3 ounces = ½ cup plus 2 tablespoons
Bob's Red Mill Gluten-Free All-Purpose Baking Flour	3 ounces = ½ cup plus 2 tablespoons

GLUTEN-FREE CHEWY SUGAR COOKIES

Makes about 24 cookies

8 ounces (1¾ cups) ATK All-Purpose Gluten-Free Flour Blend (page 410)

4 ounces (¾ cup plus 2 tablespoons) almond flour

1 teaspoon gluten-free baking powder (see page 410)

½ teaspoon baking soda

½ teaspoon salt

½ teaspoon xanthan gum (see page 411)

8¾ ounces (1¼ cups) sugar, plus ⅓ cup for rolling

3 ounces cream cheese, softened and cut into 8 pieces

8 tablespoons unsalted butter, melted and still warm

1 large egg

1 tablespoon vanilla extract

Why This Recipe Works Sugar cookies rely on just a handful of ingredients and even minor adjustments can upset the balance. So when we plugged the test kitchen's gluten-free flour blend into a recipe, we weren't surprised that the cookies were starchy, greasy, and stale-tasting. To fix the greasiness, we cut back on the butter. But sugar cookies have such a simple flavor that eliminating any butter made the cookies too lean-tasting. We tried adding heavy cream and sour cream, but they made our dough thin, and it spread too much in the oven. Cream cheese, however, enriched the dough without making it loose. Replacing a portion of the flour blend with almond flour, as we did for our Gluten-Free Oatmeal-Raisin Cookies (page 402), remedied the starchiness and gave our sugar cookies pleasing heft and chew. Do not shortchange the dough's 30-minute rest or the cookies will spread too much and taste gritty. The final dough will be softer than most cookie doughs. For the best results, handle the dough as briefly and as gently as possible when shaping the cookies.

1 Whisk flour blend, almond flour, baking powder, baking soda, salt, and xanthan gum together in medium bowl; set aside. Place 1¼ cups sugar and cream cheese in large bowl. Place remaining ⅓ cup sugar in shallow dish and set aside. Pour warm butter over sugar and cream cheese and whisk to combine (some small lumps of cream cheese will remain but will smooth out later). Whisk in egg and vanilla and continue to whisk until smooth. Stir in flour mixture with rubber spatula and mix until soft, homogeneous dough forms. Cover bowl with plastic wrap and refrigerate until chilled, about 30 minutes. (Dough will be sticky and soft.)

2 Adjust oven rack to middle position and heat oven to 350 degrees. Line 2 baking sheets with parchment paper. Using 2 soupspoons and working with 2 tablespoons dough at a time, portion 6 cookies and place in sugar to coat. Roll each ball in sugar, then space 2 inches apart on prepared sheets. Repeat with remaining dough in batches. Using bottom of dry measuring cup, press each ball to ½-inch thickness. Sprinkle tops of cookies evenly with sugar remaining in shallow dish for rolling, using 2 teaspoons for each sheet. (Discard remaining sugar.)

3 Bake cookies, 1 sheet at a time, until edges are set and just beginning to brown, 12 to 14 minutes, rotating sheet halfway through baking. Let cookies cool on sheet for 5 minutes, then transfer to wire rack. Serve warm or at room temperature.

If Using a Store-Bought Flour Blend

We strongly recommend you use our ATK All-Purpose Gluten-Free Flour Blend (page 410) in our recipes and that you weigh your flour. However, we've provided the weight-to-volume equivalents for brands that make acceptable substitutes.

King Arthur Gluten-Free All-Purpose Flour	8 ounces = ¾ cup plus ⅔ cup
Betty Crocker All-Purpose Gluten Free Rice Flour Blend	8 ounces = 1½ cups plus 2 tablespoons
Bob's Red Mill Gluten-Free All-Purpose Baking Flour	8 ounces = 1½ cups plus 2 tablespoons

GLUTEN-FREE CHOCOLATE COOKIES

Makes about 24 cookies

12 ounces semisweet chocolate, chopped

4 ounces (¾ cup plus 2 tablespoons) ATK All-Purpose Gluten-Free Flour Blend (page 410)

¾ ounce (¼ cup) unsweetened cocoa powder

½ teaspoon baking soda

½ teaspoon salt

¼ teaspoon xanthan gum (see page 411)

5¼ ounces (¾ cup packed) light brown sugar

1¾ ounces (¼ cup) granulated sugar

2 large eggs

5 tablespoons vegetable oil

2 tablespoons unsalted butter, melted and cooled

1 teaspoon vanilla extract

½ teaspoon instant espresso powder

9 ounces (1½ cups) bittersweet chocolate chips

Why This Recipe Works There are two big issues with most gluten-free cookies: off-flavors and a dry, tough texture. But given the huge amount of flavor and moisture melted chocolate provides, you'd think that making a great gluten-free chocolate cookie would be easy. Not so fast. Even the most promising recipes we tried failed us, with subpar flavor and a pervasive dry texture. So we started by amping up the chocolate flavor; in addition to melted chocolate, we loaded our dough with chips, cocoa powder, and a little espresso powder. To address the texture, we began by tinkering with the sugar. Cookies made with all granulated sugar were too crisp, while those made with all brown sugar were flimsy and unpleasantly moist. A combination worked best: ¼ cup of granulated sugar (along with xanthan gum) provided sufficient structure, and ¾ cup of brown sugar boosted chewiness. Still, the cookies weren't chewy enough, so we turned our attention to the butter. We switched out 5 tablespoons of butter for vegetable oil to achieve the proper ratio of saturated to unsaturated fat that delivered the chewy cookies we were after. Dutch-processed or natural unsweetened cocoa powder will work in this recipe. Not all brands of chocolate chips are processed in a gluten-free facility, so read labels carefully. Do not shortchange the dough's 30-minute rest or the cookies will spread too much and taste gritty.

1 Microwave semisweet chocolate in bowl at 50 percent power, stirring occasionally, until melted, 2 to 4 minutes; let cool slightly. Whisk flour blend, cocoa, baking soda, salt, and xanthan gum together in bowl; set aside.

2 Whisk brown sugar, granulated sugar, eggs, oil, melted butter, vanilla, and espresso powder in large bowl until well combined and smooth, then whisk in cooled chocolate. Stir in flour mixture with rubber spatula until soft, homogeneous dough forms. Fold in chocolate chips. Cover bowl with plastic wrap and let dough rest for 30 minutes. (Dough will be sticky and soft.)

3 Adjust oven rack to middle position and heat oven to 350 degrees. Line 2 baking sheets with parchment paper. Working with 2 generous tablespoons dough at a time, roll into balls and space them 2 inches apart on prepared sheets.

4 Bake cookies, 1 sheet at a time, until puffed and cracked and edges have begun to set but centers are still soft (cookies will look raw between cracks and seem underdone), 12 to 14 minutes, rotating sheet halfway through baking. Let cookies cool on sheet for 5 minutes, then transfer to wire rack. Serve warm or at room temperature.

If Using a Store-Bought Flour Blend

We strongly recommend you use our ATK All-Purpose Gluten-Free Flour Blend (page 410) in our recipes and that you weigh your flour. However, we've provided the weight-to-volume equivalents for brands that make acceptable substitutes.

King Arthur Gluten-Free All-Purpose Flour	4 ounces = ¾ cup
Betty Crocker All-Purpose Gluten Free Rice Flour Blend	4 ounces = ½ cup plus ⅓ cup
Bob's Red Mill Gluten-Free All-Purpose Baking Flour	4 ounces = ½ cup plus ⅓ cup

GLUTEN-FREE PEANUT BUTTER COOKIES

Makes about 24 cookies

8 ounces (1¾ cups) ATK All-Purpose Gluten-Free Flour Blend (page 410)

1 teaspoon baking soda

½ teaspoon salt

¼ teaspoon xanthan gum (see page 411)

7 ounces (1 cup packed) light brown sugar

5¼ ounces (¾ cup) granulated sugar

1 cup creamy peanut butter

8 tablespoons unsalted butter, melted and still warm

2 large eggs

1 teaspoon vanilla extract

⅓ cup dry-roasted peanuts, chopped fine

Why This Recipe Works Gluten-free or not, most peanut butter cookies are either dry and sandy or overly cakey, and they all come up short on peanut butter flavor. We wanted a chewy, really peanut-buttery cookie that was also gluten-free. We found we could pack a full cup of peanut butter into our cookies as long as we kept the butter in check to avoid greasiness. To prevent our cookies from being cakey, we used just enough flour to provide structure and volume. Even with less flour, we found we still needed to rest the dough for 30 minutes, as with our other gluten-free cookie recipes. Granulated sugar was necessary for crisp edges and structure, while brown sugar contributed chew and a molasses flavor that complemented the peanut butter. The cookies will look underdone after 12 to 14 minutes, but they will set up as they cool. The baking time is very important; 2 minutes can be the difference between a soft, chewy cookie and a dry, crisp cookie. Do not shortchange the dough's 30-minute rest or the cookies will spread too much and taste gritty.

1 Whisk flour blend, baking soda, salt, and xanthan gum together in medium bowl; set aside. Combine brown sugar, granulated sugar, and peanut butter in large bowl. Pour warm butter over sugar mixture and whisk to combine. Whisk in eggs and vanilla and continue to whisk until smooth. Stir in flour mixture with rubber spatula and mix until soft, homogeneous dough forms. Cover bowl with plastic wrap and let dough rest for 30 minutes. (Dough will be slightly shiny and soft.)

2 Adjust oven rack to middle position and heat oven to 325 degrees. Line 2 baking sheets with parchment paper. Working with 2 generous tablespoons dough at a time, roll into balls and space 2 inches apart on prepared sheets. Using bottom of greased dry measuring cup, press each ball to ¾-inch thickness. Sprinkle tops evenly with peanuts.

3 Bake cookies, 1 sheet at a time, until puffed and edges have begun to set but centers are still soft (cookies will look underdone), 12 to 14 minutes, rotating sheet halfway through baking. Let cookies cool on sheet for 5 minutes, then transfer to wire rack. Serve warm or at room temperature.

If Using a Store-Bought Flour Blend

We strongly recommend you use our ATK All-Purpose Gluten-Free Flour Blend (page 410) in our recipes and that you weigh your flour. However, we've provided the weight-to-volume equivalents for brands that make acceptable substitutes.

King Arthur Gluten-Free All-Purpose Flour	8 ounces = ¾ cup plus ⅔ cup
Betty Crocker All-Purpose Gluten Free Rice Blend	8 ounces = 1½ cups plus 2 tablespoons
Bob's Red Mill GF All-Purpose Baking Flour	8 ounces = 1½ cups plus 2 tablespoons

ALL ABOUT GLUTEN-FREE COOKIE BAKING

Dietary restrictions shouldn't keep anyone from eating the treats they crave—especially cookies. We've developed a roster of foolproof gluten-free cookies that live up to their wheat-full counterparts. Here are some of the techniques we learned and the ingredients we turned to in perfecting gluten-free cookies.

ATK ALL-PURPOSE GLUTEN-FREE FLOUR BLEND
Makes 42 ounces (about 9⅓ cups)

When looking for a wheat-free substitute for all-purpose flour, we found that no single gluten-free flour or starch behaves like wheat flour—a blend is a must. Because store-bought blends perform inconsistently—one product might deliver great cookies but subpar cakes—we decided to create our own. We found that two flours— white rice and brown rice—provided the right baseline of protein, starch, and flavor. Since different starches absorb water, swell, and gel at different temperatures and to different

degrees, we enlisted both tapioca starch and potato starch to give our cookies the right amount of chew and structure. Milk powder was key to our blend's success, contributing proteins that help improve structure in our gluten-free cookies and, along with its sugars, undergo the Maillard browning reaction, which leads to more complex flavor.

Be sure to use potato starch, not potato flour, in this blend. Tapioca starch is also sold as tapioca flour; they are interchangeable. We vastly prefer Bob's Red Mill white and brown rice flours to other brands. You can omit the milk powder, but your cookies won't brown as well and they will taste less rich. We strongly recommend that you weigh your ingredients, as the ratios of ingredients are integral to successful gluten-free cookie baking. If you measure by volume, spoon each ingredient into the measuring cup (do not pack or tap) and scrape off the excess.

24 ounces (4½ cups plus ⅓ cup) white rice flour
7½ ounces (1⅔ cups) brown rice flour
7 ounces (1⅓ cups) potato starch
3 ounces (¾ cup) tapioca starch
¾ ounce (¼ cup) nonfat dry milk powder

Whisk all ingredients in large bowl until well combined. Transfer to airtight container and refrigerate for up to 3 months. Bring to room temperature before using.

WHAT ABOUT STORE-BOUGHT BLENDS?

Each flour blend relies on a mix of different ingredients, yielding cookies with varying textures, colors, and flavors. While we much prefer the consistent results that we achieved with our homemade blend, King Arthur Gluten-Free All-Purpose Flour and Betty Crocker All-Purpose Gluten Free Rice Flour Blend performed similarly in cookies. Bob's Red Mill Gluten Free All-Purpose Baking Flour also works, but it will add a noticeable bean flavor in most instances.

SURPRISING SOURCES OF GLUTEN

Baking Powder
Baking powder typically contains cornstarch to absorb moisture and keep the powder dry. However, wheat starch is sometimes used in place of the cornstarch, so make sure to check the ingredient list on the nutritional label when buying baking powder. Also note that some brands may be produced in a facility that also processes wheat; if this is the case, this information will be noted on the label.

Oats
Oats are gluten-free, but they're often processed in facilities that also process wheat, and cross-contamination is common. It's critical to make sure you're buying oats that are processed in a gluten-free facility; regardless of the variety of oat you're buying, check the label.

Because there is less protein in gluten-free flours than in wheat flours, gluten-free flours are not capable of forming the strong network required to stretch and surround starch granules, which result in cookies that spread too much. In our testing, we found that gluten-free flours require some help from a binder, and we use xanthan gum in our cookie recipes. Xanthan gum strengthens protein networks in baked goods and makes them more elastic. In effect, they act as the glue that gives gluten-free baked goods the proper shape. The effects of a binder are apparent in the cookies below. The cookies made without xanthan gum lose their shape and spread dramatically, while the cookies made with xanthan gum have the proper height and a distinct shape. Don't omit a binder if a recipes calls for one.

We tried two other commonly used binders, guar gum and psyllium husk. In many cases, the differences were slight, although baked goods made with guar tended to be a bit more pasty and those made with psyllium a bit drier with a coarser crumb. Also, baked goods made with xanthan had a longer shelf life. If you'd like to use guar gum or psyllium husk in place of xanthan in our baked goods, see the chart below for substitution formulas.

Substitution Formulas

SUBSTITUTIONS	
Drop Cookies	1 teaspoon xanthan gum = 1 teaspoon guar gum = 2 teaspoons psyllium powder
All Other Cookies	1 teaspoon xanthan gum = 3 teaspoons guar gum = 5 teaspoons psyllium powder

Don't let cooled gluten-free cookies sit out. The extra starch in gluten-free flour blends absorbs moisture, so gluten-free cookies become drier and more crumbly faster than cookies made with all-purpose flour—they're best eaten the day they're made. If you do store leftovers, keep them for just a day or two and don't refrigerate them—it will only make them drier. Store them in an airtight container, stacking cookies in as few layers as possible and using parchment between layers, since the cookies become delicate over time.

Cookies Made without Xanthan Gum

Cookies Made with Xanthan Gum

If you decide to use a store-bought flour blend, we strongly recommend that you weigh it. Because each blend is made of different ingredients, weight-to-volume equivalents vary from brand to brand. If you still choose to measure by volume, we've included weight-to-volume equivalents for King Arthur and Betty Crocker, as well as Bob's Red Mill Gluten Free All-Purpose Baking Flour in each recipe. Because gluten-free flours have a fine consistency, it's hard to pack the flours consistently in a measuring cup. For the most uniform results, set the measuring cup on a paper towel and spoon the flour into the cup, occasionally shaking the cup to settle the flour, until it's mounded over the rim. Don't tap the cup or pack the flour. Using the back of a knife, scrape away the excess flour to level, then funnel the excess back into the container with the paper towel.

Rice flour has a sandy texture and comes in white, brown, and sweet white varieties. Our ATK All-Purpose Gluten-Free Flour Blend calls for white and brown rice flour. White rice flour is made from rice after the bran and germ have been removed and has a neutral flavor; brown rice flour still contains the bran, so it has more fiber, fat, and protein and a nuttier flavor. White rice flour can be stored in the pantry, but brown rice flour has a shorter shelf life (because of its fat content) and should be refrigerated. We recommend Bob's Red Mill rice flours.

Made from the starchy tuberous root of the cassava plant, this white powder provides chew, elasticity, and structure to baked goods. Tapioca starch is sometimes labeled tapioca flour. Store tapioca starch in the pantry.

Many gluten-free batters and doughs benefit from a 30-minute rest before baking. This allows the starches time to properly hydrate before they go into the oven to minimize grittiness in the final product. Longer resting times are not recommended, especially as this can affect the performance of the leaveners.

GLUTEN-FREE FUDGY BROWNIES

Makes 16 brownies

4 ounces (¾ cup plus 2 tablespoons)
ATK All-Purpose Gluten-Free Flour
Blend (page 410)

½ teaspoon salt

½ teaspoon xanthan gum
(see page 411)

7 ounces semisweet chocolate,
chopped coarse

8 tablespoons unsalted butter,
cut into 8 pieces

3 tablespoons unsweetened
cocoa powder

8¾ ounces (1¼ cups) sugar

3 large eggs

2 teaspoons vanilla extract

Why This Recipe Works Fudgy brownies contain less flour than cakey ones, so it made sense to start with our favorite recipe for fudgy brownies (see page 243) and use our flour blend in place of the all-purpose. But while the original recipe delivers intense flavor and just the right rich, fudgy texture, brownies made with our flour blend were a bit dry and dense and there was a subtle graininess. Cutting back on the amount of flour helped give the brownies the right fudgy texture, and resting the batter for 30 minutes gave the starches in our flour blend time to hydrate and soften. But reducing the amount of flour had an unwanted effect: The chocolate flavor fell out of balance, and now our brownies had a bitter edge. Brownies made without cocoa lacked structure—it had to stay. Eliminating the unsweetened chocolate was a big step in the right direction, and switching the bittersweet out for semisweet chocolate eliminated the harsh flavor altogether. Not all brands of chocolate are processed in a gluten-free facility, so read labels carefully. Do not shortchange the batter's 30-minute rest or the brownies will taste gritty.

1 Make foil sling for 8-inch square baking pan by folding 2 long sheets of aluminum foil so each is 8 inches wide. Lay sheets of foil in pan perpendicular to each other, with extra foil hanging over edges of pan. Push foil into corners and up sides of pan, smoothing foil flush to pan. Spray with vegetable oil spray.

2 Whisk flour blend, salt, and xanthan gum together in bowl. Microwave chocolate, butter, and cocoa in bowl at 50 percent power, stirring often, until melted and smooth, 1 to 3 minutes; let mixture cool slightly.

3 Whisk sugar, eggs, and vanilla together in large bowl. Whisk in cooled chocolate mixture. Stir in flour mixture with rubber spatula and mix until well combined. Transfer batter to prepared pan and smooth top. Cover pan with plastic wrap and let batter rest for 30 minutes.

4 Adjust oven rack to middle position and heat oven to 350 degrees. Remove plastic and bake brownies until toothpick inserted in center comes out with few moist crumbs attached, 45 to 55 minutes, rotating pan halfway through baking.

5 Let brownies cool completely in pan on wire rack, about 2 hours. Using foil overhang, remove brownies from pan. Cut into 16 pieces and serve.

If Using a Store-Bought Flour Blend

We strongly recommend you use our ATK All-Purpose Gluten-Free Flour Blend (page 410) in our recipes and that you weigh your flour. However, we've provided the weight-to-volume equivalents for brands that make acceptable substitutes.

King Arthur Gluten-Free All-Purpose Flour	4 ounces = ¾ cup
Betty Crocker All-Purpose Gluten Free Rice Flour Blend	4 ounces = ½ cup plus ⅓ cup
Bob's Red Mill Gluten-Free All-Purpose Baking Flour	4 ounces = ½ cup plus ⅓ cup

GLUTEN-FREE BLONDIES

Makes 16 bars

8 ounces (1¾ cups) ATK All-Purpose Gluten-Free Flour Blend (page 410)

¾ teaspoon salt

½ teaspoon gluten-free baking powder (see page 410)

½ teaspoon xanthan gum (see page 411)

7 tablespoons unsalted butter, melted and cooled

7 ounces (1 cup packed) light brown sugar

3½ ounces (½ cup) granulated sugar

2 large eggs

2 tablespoons milk

4 teaspoons vanilla extract

3 ounces (½ cup) white chocolate chips

3 ounces (½ cup) semisweet chocolate chips

Why This Recipe Works Chewy but crisp around the edges, blondies are like butterscotch-flavored brownies that rely on brown sugar and butter to give them their signature flavor and texture. Right away, blondies made with our flour blend had problems: They were flat, sandy, and greasy. To fix these issues, we started by scaling way back on the butter—from 12 tablespoons to 7 tablespoons—to eliminate the greasiness. The reduced amount of butter also lightened the batter so the blondies now had a nice rise. Instead of creaming the butter with the sugar, we melted it to give our blondies the requisite chew. To eliminate the sandiness, we added a couple tablespoons of milk to hydrate and soften the flour. Chocolate chips are an essential component of blondies, and we liked a combination of semisweet and white chocolate chips. The blondies required a longer than usual baking time—almost an hour rather than 25 minutes—to properly dry them out; otherwise, they came out mushy. Not all brands of chocolate are processed in a gluten-free facility, so read labels carefully.

1 Adjust oven rack to middle position and heat oven to 325 degrees. Make foil sling for 8-inch square baking pan by folding 2 long sheets of aluminum foil so each is 8 inches wide. Lay sheets of foil in pan perpendicular to each other, with extra foil hanging over edges. Push foil into corners and up sides of pan, smoothing foil flush to pan. Spray with vegetable oil spray.

2 Whisk flour blend, salt, baking powder, and xanthan gum together in bowl. In large bowl, whisk melted butter, brown sugar, and granulated sugar together until no lumps remain. Whisk in eggs, milk, and vanilla until very smooth. Stir in flour mixture with rubber spatula until flour is completely incorporated and batter is homogeneous, about 1 minute. Fold in white chocolate and semisweet chocolate chips. Transfer batter to prepared pan and smooth top with spatula.

3 Bake blondies until deep golden brown and toothpick inserted in center comes out clean, 50 minutes to 1 hour, rotating pan halfway through baking.

4 Let blondies cool completely in pan on wire rack, about 2 hours. Using foil overhang, remove blondies from pan. Cut into 16 pieces and serve.

If Using a Store-Bought Flour Blend

We strongly recommend you use our ATK All-Purpose Gluten-Free Flour Blend (page 410) in our recipes and that you weigh your flour. However, we've provided the weight-to-volume equivalents for brands that make acceptable substitutes.

King Arthur Gluten-Free All-Purpose Flour	8 ounces = ¾ cup plus ⅔ cup
Betty Crocker All-Purpose Gluten Free Rice Blend	8 ounces = 1½ cups plus 2 tablespoons
Bob's Red Mill GF All-Purpose Baking Flour	8 ounces = 1½ cups plus 2 tablespoons

GLUTEN-FREE LEMON BARS

Makes 16 bars

Crust

6 ounces (1⅓ cups) ATK All-Purpose Gluten-Free Flour Blend (page 410)

2⅓ ounces (⅓ cup) granulated sugar

¼ teaspoon salt

¼ teaspoon xanthan gum (see page 411)

8 tablespoons unsalted butter, cut into ½-inch pieces and softened

Lemon Filling

2 large eggs, plus 7 large yolks

7 ounces (1 cup) plus 2 tablespoons granulated sugar

¼ cup grated lemon zest plus ⅔ cup juice (4 lemons)

Pinch salt

4 tablespoons unsalted butter, cut into 4 pieces

3 tablespoons heavy cream

Confectioners' sugar

Why This Recipe Works For our gluten-free version of this classic bar cookie, we started with the topping. Plenty of lemon juice plus a whopping ¼ cup of lemon zest ensured plenty of bright flavor, while butter and heavy cream added richness. This filling also needed some form of thickener so that it could set up and slice neatly. Some recipes rely on flour, but we found that eggs delivered better results. Seven yolks plus two whole eggs gave our filling a smooth, custard-like texture that set up just enough without obscuring the pure, clean lemon flavor. Next, we moved on to the base. We knew we wanted something similar to shortbread: a crisp, buttery crust that could support the topping yet slice neatly and easily. We developed a simple shortbread crust using butter, sugar, our flour blend, and xanthan gum for our Gluten-Free Ginger-Fig Streusel Bars (page 421), and it worked perfectly here as well. To ensure the base didn't become soggy, we prebaked the crust and then topped it with the custard and returned the pan to the oven. Letting the bars cool for the full 2 hours was key to ensuring the custard topping set up and was sliceable.

1 Adjust oven rack to middle position and heat oven to 350 degrees. Make foil sling for 8-inch square baking pan by folding 2 long sheets of aluminum foil so each is 8 inches wide. Lay sheets of foil in pan perpendicular to each other, with extra foil hanging over edges of pan. Push foil into corners and up sides of pan, smoothing foil flush to pan. Spray with vegetable oil spray.

2 **For the crust** Using stand mixer fitted with paddle, mix flour blend, sugar, salt, and xanthan gum on low speed until combined, about 5 seconds. Add butter, 1 piece at a time, and continue to mix until dough pulls away from sides of bowl, 2 to 3 minutes. (Add 1 to 2 tablespoons water as needed if dough appears dry.) Transfer mixture to prepared pan and press firmly into even layer using bottom of dry measuring cup. Bake until crust is fragrant and beginning to brown, 25 to 30 minutes, rotating pan halfway through baking. Transfer to wire rack and let cool for 30 minutes.

3 **For the filling** Whisk eggs and yolks together in medium saucepan. Whisk in granulated sugar until combined, then whisk in lemon zest and juice and salt. Add butter and cook over medium heat, stirring constantly, until mixture thickens

slightly and registers 170 degrees, about 5 minutes. Immediately strain mixture in fine-mesh strainer into bowl and stir in cream. Pour filling over cooled crust. Bake until filling is shiny and opaque and center jiggles slightly when shaken, 15 to 20 minutes, rotating pan halfway through baking. Let bars cool completely in pan on wire rack, about 2 hours. Using foil overhang, lift bars out of pan. Cut into 16 pieces and dust with confectioners' sugar before serving. (Bars can be refrigerated for up to 2 days; crust will soften.)

If Using a Store-Bought Flour Blend

We strongly recommend you use our ATK All-Purpose Gluten-Free Flour Blend (page 410) in our recipes and that you weigh your flour. However, we've provided the weight-to-volume equivalents for brands that make acceptable substitutes.

King Arthur Gluten-Free All-Purpose Flour	6 ounces = ¾ cup plus ⅓ cup
Betty Crocker All-Purpose Gluten Free Rice Blend	6 ounces = ⅔ cup plus ½ cup
Bob's Red Mill GF All-Purpose Baking Flour	6 ounces = ⅔ cup plus ½ cup

GLUTEN-FREE KEY LIME BARS

Makes 16 bars

Crust

6 ounces (1⅓ cups) ATK All-Purpose Gluten-Free Flour Blend (page 410)

2⅓ ounces (⅓ cup) sugar

¼ teaspoon salt

¼ teaspoon xanthan gum (see page 411)

8 tablespoons unsalted butter, cut into ½-inch pieces and softened

Filling

2 ounces cream cheese, softened

1 tablespoon grated lime zest plus ½ cup juice (4 limes)

Pinch salt

1 (14-ounce) can sweetened condensed milk

1 large egg yolk

¾ cup sweetened shredded coconut, toasted (optional)

Why This Recipe Works We wanted a gluten-free Key lime bar that balanced a tart and creamy topping with a rich, buttery base. Finding a base that would support the topping was easy; we turned once again to the buttery crust we used for our Gluten-Free Ginger-Fig Streusel Bars (page 421) and our Gluten-Free Lemon Bars (page 416). As for the filling, it needed to be sturdy and sliceable. By adding cream cheese and an egg yolk to the usual sweetened condensed milk and lime juice and zest, we created a rich and firm filling that required no precooking before baking. Letting the bars cool for a full 2 hours and then refrigerating them for an additional 2 hours were key to ensuring the custard topping set up. Key limes can be substituted for the regular limes here, although they have a more delicate flavor; you'll need about 20 to make ½ cup of juice. Do not substitute bottled Key lime juice.

1 Adjust oven rack to middle position and heat oven to 350 degrees. Make foil sling for 8-inch square baking pan by folding 2 long sheets of aluminum foil so each is 8 inches wide. Lay sheets of foil in pan perpendicular to each other, with extra foil hanging over edges. Push foil into corners and up sides of pan, smoothing foil flush to pan. Spray foil with vegetable oil spray.

2 For the crust Using stand mixer fitted with paddle, mix flour blend, sugar, salt, and xanthan gum on low speed until combined. Add butter, 1 piece at a time, and continue to mix until dough pulls away from sides of bowl, 2 to 3 minutes. (Add 1 to 2 tablespoons water as needed if dough appears dry.) Transfer mixture to prepared pan and press firmly into even layer using bottom of dry measuring cup. Bake until fragrant and beginning to brown, 25 to 30 minutes, rotating pan halfway through baking. Transfer to wire rack and let cool for 30 minutes.

3 For the filling Stir cream cheese, lime zest, and salt in bowl until no lumps remain. Whisk in condensed milk until well combined. Whisk in lime juice and egg yolk until very smooth.

Pour filling evenly over crust. Bake until bars are set and edges begin to pull away slightly from sides of pan, 15 to 20 minutes, rotating pan halfway through baking.

4 Let bars cool completely in pan, about 2 hours. Cover with foil and refrigerate bars until thoroughly chilled, about 2 hours. Using foil overhang, remove bars from pan. Sprinkle with toasted coconut, if using. Cut into 16 pieces and serve. (Bars can be refrigerated for up to 2 days; crust will soften.)

If Using a Store-Bought Flour Blend

We strongly recommend you use our ATK All-Purpose Gluten-Free Flour Blend (page 410) in our recipes and that you weigh your flour. However, we've provided the weight-to-volume equivalents for brands that make acceptable substitutes.

King Arthur Gluten-Free All-Purpose Flour	6 ounces = ¾ cup plus ⅓ cup
Betty Crocker All-Purpose Gluten Free Rice Flour Blend	6 ounces = ⅔ cup plus ½ cup
Bob's Red Mill Gluten-Free All-Purpose Baking Flour	6 ounces = ⅔ cup plus ½ cup

GLUTEN-FREE GINGER-FIG STREUSEL BARS

Makes 16 bars

6 ounces (1⅓ cups) ATK All-Purpose
Gluten-Free Flour Blend (page 410)

2⅓ ounces (⅓ cup) granulated sugar

½ teaspoon ground ginger

¼ teaspoon salt

¼ teaspoon xanthan gum (see page 411)

8 tablespoons unsalted butter,
cut into ½-inch pieces and softened

2 tablespoons packed light brown sugar

⅓ cup walnuts, toasted and chopped fine

¼ cup gluten-free old-fashioned rolled
oats (see page 410)

¾ cup fig preserves

1 tablespoon minced crystallized ginger

½ teaspoon grated lemon zest
plus 2 teaspoons juice

Why This Recipe Works For a novel approach to fig bars, we introduced the bright, slightly spicy flavor of ginger and a crisp streusel topping. A streusel bar should have a sturdy, buttery, shortbread-like base and a rich crumble topping that lends texture. For the base, we started with a straightforward combination of butter, our gluten-free flour blend, sugar, and salt. By mixing pieces of softened butter into the dry ingredients, a method called reverse creaming, we developed the ideal delicate, short crumb. But without gluten, this base couldn't support the filling and topping. Adding just ¼ teaspoon of xanthan gum gave the crust the structure it needed. For the streusel topping, we simply took a portion of our shortbread base mixture and added light brown sugar, walnuts, and oats. Fig preserves or spread provided just the right jammy consistency, and the addition of lemon juice, lemon zest, and crystallized ginger gave our bars the bright flavors we were seeking. After parbaking the base, all we had to do was spread on the filling, crumble our streusel over the top, and return the pan to the oven for a short stint.

1 Adjust oven rack to middle position and heat oven to 375 degrees. Make foil sling for 8-inch square baking pan by folding 2 long sheets of aluminum foil so each is 8 inches wide. Lay sheets of foil in pan perpendicular to each other, with extra foil hanging over edges. Push foil into corners and up sides of pan, smoothing foil flush to pan. Spray foil with vegetable oil spray.

2 Using stand mixer fitted with paddle, mix flour blend, granulated sugar, ground ginger, salt, and xanthan gum on low speed until combined, about 5 seconds. Add butter, 1 piece at a time, and beat until well combined, 2 to 3 minutes. (Add 1 to 2 tablespoons of water as needed if dough appears dry.) Set aside ½ cup mixture for topping. Press remaining mixture evenly into prepared pan using bottom of greased measuring cup. Bake until edges begin to brown, 14 to 18 minutes, rotating pan halfway through baking.

3 Meanwhile, mix brown sugar, walnuts, and oats into reserved dough. Combine preserves, crystallized ginger, and lemon zest and juice in separate bowl. Spread fig preserve mixture evenly over hot crust, then sprinkle with hazelnut-size clumps of oat topping. Bake until topping is golden brown and filling is bubbling, 22 to 25 minutes.

4 Let bars cool completely in pan on wire rack, 1 to 2 hours. Using foil overhang, remove bars from pan. Cut into 16 pieces and serve. (Bars can be refrigerated for up to 2 days; crust and streusel will soften.)

If Using a Store-Bought Flour Blend

We strongly recommend you use our ATK All-Purpose Gluten-Free Flour Blend (page 410) in our recipes and that you weigh your flour. However, we've provided the weight-to-volume equivalents for brands that make acceptable substitutes.

King Arthur Gluten-Free All-Purpose Flour	6 ounces = ¾ cup plus ⅓ cup
Betty Crocker All-Purpose Gluten Free Rice Blend	6 ounces = ⅔ cup plus ½ cup
Bob's Red Mill GF All-Purpose Baking Flour	6 ounces = ⅔ cup plus ½ cup

Conversions & Equivalents

Baking is a science and an art, but geography has a hand in it, too. Flours and sugars manufactured in the United Kingdom and elsewhere will feel and taste different from those manufactured in the United States. So we cannot promise that a cookie you bake in Canada or England will taste the same as a cookie baked in the States, but we can offer guidelines for converting weights and measures. We also recommend that you rely on your instincts when making our recipes. Refer to the visual cues provided. If the dough hasn't "come together in a ball" as described, you may need to add more flour—even if the recipe doesn't tell you to. You be the judge.

The recipes in this book were developed using standard U.S. measures following U.S. government guidelines. The charts below offer equivalents for U.S. and metric measures. All conversions are approximate and have been rounded up or down to the nearest whole number.

EXAMPLE

1 teaspoon	=	4.9292 milliliters, rounded up to 5 milliliters
1 ounce	=	28.3495 grams, rounded down to 28 grams

VOLUME CONVERSIONS

U.S.	METRIC
1 teaspoon	5 milliliters
2 teaspoons	10 milliliters
1 tablespoon	15 milliliters
2 tablespoons	30 milliliters
¼ cup	59 milliliters
⅓ cup	79 milliliters
½ cup	118 milliliters
¾ cup	177 milliliters
1 cup	237 milliliters
1¼ cups	296 milliliters
1½ cups	355 milliliters
2 cups (1 pint)	473 milliliters
2½ cups	591 milliliters
3 cups	710 milliliters
4 cups (1 quart)	0.946 liter
1.06 quarts	1 liter
4 quarts (1 gallon)	3.8 liters

WEIGHT CONVERSIONS

OUNCES	GRAMS
½	14
¾	21
1	28
1½	43
2	57
2½	71
3	85
3½	99
4	113
4½	128
5	142
6	170
7	198
8	227
9	255
10	283
12	340
16 (1 pound)	454

CONVERSIONS FOR COMMON BAKING INGREDIENTS

Because measuring by weight is far more accurate than measuring by volume, and thus more likely to produce reliable results, in our recipes we provide ounce measures in addition to cup measures for many ingredients. Refer to the chart below to convert these measures into grams.

INGREDIENT	OUNCES	GRAMS
Flour		
1 cup all-purpose flour*	5	142
1 cup cake flour	4	113
1 cup whole-wheat flour	5½	156
Sugar		
1 cup granulated (white) sugar	7	198
1 cup packed brown sugar (light or dark)	7	198
1 cup confectioners' sugar	4	113
Cocoa Powder		
1 cup cocoa powder	3	85
Butter†		
4 tablespoons (½ stick or ¼ cup)	2	57
8 tablespoons (1 stick or ½ cup)	4	113
16 tablespoons (2 sticks or 1 cup)	8	227

* U.S. all-purpose flour, the most frequently used flour in this book, does not contain leaveners, as some European flours do. These leavened flours are called self-rising or self-raising. If you are using self-rising flour, take this into consideration before adding leaveners to a recipe.

† In the United States, butter is sold both salted and unsalted. We recommend unsalted butter. If you are using salted butter, take this into consideration before adding salt to a recipe.

OVEN TEMPERATURE

FAHRENHEIT	CELSIUS	GAS MARK
225	105	¼
250	120	½
275	135	1
300	150	2
325	165	3
350	180	4
375	190	5
400	200	6
425	220	7
450	230	8
475	245	9

CONVERTING TEMPERATURES FROM AN INSTANT-READ THERMOMETER

We include doneness temperatures in many of the recipes in this book. We recommend an instant-read thermometer for the job. Refer to the table above to convert Fahrenheit degrees to Celsius. Or, for temperatures not represented in the chart, use this simple formula:

Subtract 32 degrees from the Fahrenheit reading, then divide the result by 1.8 to find the Celsius reading.

example
"Cook caramel until it registers 160 degrees."

To convert:
$160°F - 32 = 128°$
$128° ÷ 1.8 = 71.11°C$, rounded down to $71°C$

Index

Note: Page references in *italics* refer to photographs.

W

31901060816016